In below zero weather in North Korea in December, we were surrounded by battle-hardened Chinese in an isolated blocking position. In his shell-splattered aid station, Bob Jensen worked tirelessly performing major operations by the light of lanterns and was as cheerful as he was brave. Just out of medical school, he met the challenges of combat head on, and many soldiers are alive today because of the skill, dedication, determination and character of our Doc—Bob Jensen.

Maj. John Middlemas, USA Ret.

Company A/7 Korea

I have had a chance to review the manuscript of your Korean War memoirs. I found it to be a fascinating account of a battalion surgeon's experiences in that conflict. It is certainly deserving of publication.

I wish you the best of luck in pursuing the publication of your memoir.

Wayne R. Austerman, Ph, D.

Army Historian

Some members of the 7th Infantry Association have had the opportunity to review and contribute to early drafts of your book "Bloody Snow" and all have spoken highly of your memoirs. As the president of the association, I assure you that we are all looking forward to your book's publication and anticipate having book signings at our next annual meeting.

Col. Richard T. Rhoades, USA Ret.

President, 7th Infantry Regiment Association

As you are aware, on behalf of the Society of the Third Infantry Division and its Korean War veterans, I had previously granted your permission to use a few select maps, pictures and quotations from "The History of the 3rd Infantry Division in the Korean War 1950-1953" in you book, "Bloody Snow – A Doctor's Memoir of the Korean War." With the impressive Forward to your book by General Fred C. Weyand we are looking forward to the publication of your book that I expect will be of great interest to the Korean veterans of the "Rock of the Marne" Division. You may want to present yourself at a future reunion of the Society for a book signing, as some other authors have done.

Angelo "Jim" Tiezzi

National President

Society of the Third Infantry Division

BLOODY SNOW

A Doctor's Memoir of the Korean War

by
Robert Travis Jensen, MD

Cork Hill Press
Carmel

CORK HILL PRESS™

Cork Hill Press
597 Industrial Drive, Suite 110
Carmel, IN 46032-4207
1-866-688-BOOK
www.corkhillpress.com

Issued simultaneously in hardcover and trade paperback editions.
Hardcover Edition: 1-59408-540-4
Trade Paperback Edition: 1-59408-334-7

Library of Congress Card Catalog Number:2005929751

3 5 7 9 10 8 6 4 2

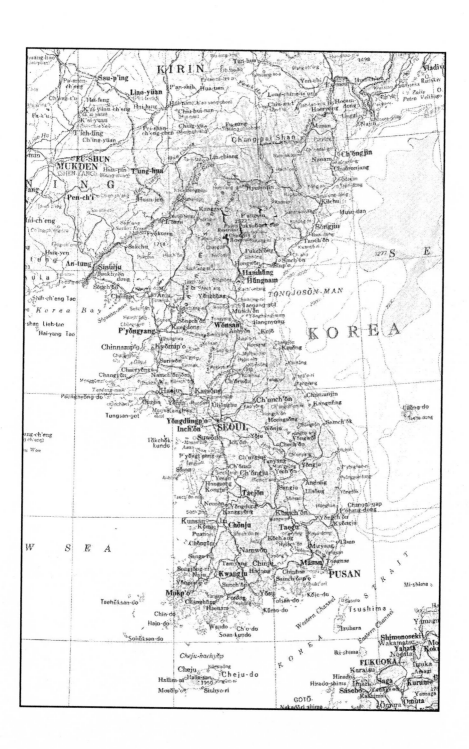

Table of Contents

Foreword
By General Fred C. Weyand, U.S. Army (retired)

During the Korean War, the author, Bob Jensen, was my battalion surgeon in the 7th Infantry Regiment of the 3rd Infantry Division. This was the brutal and so-called Forgotten War that is anything but "forgotten" in the minds of those of us who fought in it. Bob fought for the cause of freedom in that far-off land, and much of his life since then has been committed to noble and just causes through other means.

To my knowledge, this is the first book ever written by a Medical Corps officer who served in the infantry in combat in Korea. Bob Jensen, now Col. Robert T. Jensen, M.D. U.S. Army (retired), and his book give us a rare opportunity to see armed conflict through the eyes of a soldier-doctor, a battlefield surgeon.

Dr. Jensen served with me in the 1st Battalion of the 7th Infantry Regiment through the winter and spring of 1951. I commanded the battalion and he was my battalion surgeon through the most severe combat and weather conditions. We were engaged in close combat during much of that time and he was up front and directly involved. He was never far from where he needed to be to care for the wounded. His raw courage and selfless commitment to saving of the lives of my soldiers made him invaluable to the success of the 1st Battalion.

Unfortunately for me, higher authority noted Capt. Jensen's performance. He was given more far-reaching responsibilities as regimental surgeon of the 7th Infantry and promoted to major. It seems that Col. Boswell, the regimental commander, had visited the 1st Battalion, where he noted Bob busy tending to wounded soldiers, even though Bob was still wet and cold after having waded across the Han River while a battle was in progress to retrieve and resuscitate our wounded.

Jim Boswell received an earful when he asked Bob, "How is it going, Doc?"

Bob straightened up and said, "Sir, it should be the job of the battalion surgeon to lean forward with his medics in order to provide life-saving services to the rifle companies fighting across rivers and on hills in mud or snow. But it should be the regiment's job to lean forward to provide back up support for the battalion surgeons. I should not have to lean both forward for casualties and backward for evacuation support."

A week later, Capt. Jensen was called to Regiment and told by Col. Boswell, "You are now the new regimental surgeon. I want you to lean forward to serve all of the units of this regiment."

In 1950 – 1951, as a Lieutenant Colonel Battalion Commander, I had a close personal, as well as an operational, relationship with Col. Jim Boswell, the 7th Infantry Regiment Commander. He was my boss and a superb regimental commander. Thus I will add a few more comments, in the belief that they represent what the late Brig. Gen. Jim Boswell would say if he were here today.

Bob Jensen divided the resources of the Regimental Medical Company to provide one or more back-up teams of medics, litter bearers, emergency supplies, and ambulances directly to the infantry battalions that were most heavily engaged with the enemy. He always kept abreast of military planning and movements.

When there was any hesitancy in getting the support he felt he needed from the medical battalion of the 3rd Division, he called the division surgeon directly to explain the situation, and usually got immediate action. The division surgeon knew that Bob knew what he was doing.

When one or more battalions were in a serious fight, Bob often went forward by jeep to assist and encourage the battalion surgeons. Bob also maintained liaison with the S-4, who controlled the Korean labor companies. Bob had his American and Korean medics continually select and train Korean laborers as litter squad teams that would revert to the medics' control for the journey back down the hill or back from the battle.

As the little Bell-13 helicopters became increasingly used in 1951, Bob would frequently call a chopper to Regiment and then hop on the chopper and direct it forward to the battalion that needed it. This occurred even though there were often orders from higher levels that directed the helicopters to not go forward of the regimental medical station. However, by using the logic that the regimental medical station was actually wherever the regimental surgeon was flying at that moment in time, Bob would pressure helicopter pilots to fly him directly to the battalion aid stations most in need and even directly to an isolated Rifle Company with causalities.

The story told of L Company on Hill 284 and Jerry Crump, who was awarded the Congressional Medal of Honor, alive instead of posthumously, best illustrates Dr. Bob's skill and devotion to his duty. Thus Col. Boswell came not to worry about his medical support, for Dr. Bob leaned forward to keep up with the battle activity of the entire regiment, including attached units of Belgians, Turks, Filipinos and British soldiers.

But the reader will also find that Capt./Maj. Robert T. Jensen's humanitarian concerns in the Korean War extended to the plight of innocent civilians as well as to wounded prisoners of war caught up in our area of operations. I recount this because the author is uniquely qualified to "tell it like it was (and is)" on the battlefield in combat.

The letters to his family add to the authenticity and readability of this powerful insight into the character of a unique American. Bob is a man of deep faith, and he and his devoted wife, Rosemary, have spent much of their lives ministering to the physical and spiritual needs of others. Hundreds of orphans and street children in Africa now owe their lives to the work of the Rafiki Foundation, directed by Rosemary with Bob, providing medical service, personal support and loving encouragement.

If you probe further into Robert T. Jensen's life, you will also find a person who is deeply concerned with the security of our country and the preservation of the values that form the foundation of America's greatness. Beginning with the Cold War, Bob has studied source materials and carefully analyzed the insidious deeds and threats that now equate to "weapons of mass destruction." His conclusions are most sobering, particularly in light of the threat of terrorism today. I urge our national leaders to read this very special book and then also consider carefully what this wise author may have to share on issues of national concern today. Dr. Bob has done his homework.

General Fred C. Weyand, U.S. Army (retired)

Preface
March/April 2004

Friends asked why I was writing a book about the Korean War fifty years after the event. My answer has been that I haven't had time to write this story until I retired in May 1998 after working as a physician for fifty years. But the truth is that in the years immediately following the Korean War, I was too young and the events were too recent and raw for me to be objective enough. I needed time to gain perspective.

But I retained a fondness for the Korean people and an interest in Korean affairs that continued through the last half century. I have read most of the books published on the Korean War and am indebted to all of their authors for much valuable information. However, none of those writers wrote through the eyes of a battalion surgeon who was fighting to save lives.

War through the eyes of a doctor who served as a battalion surgeon and later as a regimental surgeon may provide anecdotes and insights of value to new soldiers as well as to men and women in Congress, who have had little personal combat experience—even as they now continue to send young Americans off to fight in distant lands. My hope is that our future soldiers will not be as unprepared and poorly equipped as we were in 1950.

I also realized that if I didn't write down these observed bits and pieces of Korean/American history soon, they may be lost forever. The only exception to candor in this book is the fictionalization of a few names to forestall ignoble actions from being readily traced.

During the war, I was unaware that my mother had kept all the letters I wrote from Japan and Korea in 1950 and 1951. When she died in 1971, my brother gave me a large shoebox full of letters she had kept, but I was then too busy to do anything with them other than put the shoebox in the back of a file drawer, where they rested for 25 years.

It wasn't until after my cardiac bypass surgery in December 1996 that I looked through the shoebox and discovered that it contained all of my old letters from the Korean War. As I read through the letters for the first time since I had written them, I was surprised by the amount of detail. I had been under the illusion that I had toned down the news from overseas in order to not worry my mother and dad. But the letters were far more graphic than I remembered writing. Indeed, my mother had saved a time-line of events that occurred during my 17 months overseas.

Reading through the old letters, many of which were written on the hood of a jeep, stimulated a daytime recall of events long forgotten and some unpleasant nightmares. I then began to reread and compare books on the Korean War and added new books to my collection. I have been a persistent reader all of my life.

I also thought a lot about the popular *M*A*S*H* TV series that entertained the American public for many years, but distorted the reality of the Korean War. MASH is the acronym for "Mobile Army Surgical Hospital." Although American GIs have a talent for humor, even in the midst of war, the Korean War was never a comedy. And contrary to some Hollywood worldviews expressed in the *M*A*S*H* series, there was and is no valid comparison between the behavior, politics, beliefs, and values of the North Korean and South Korean/American leadership. The Korean War was started by North Korea, a one-party state controlled by atheist Communists and supported by both China and the Soviet Union. Our military officers were simply doing their duty in a very nasty war that was not started by either South Korea or the United States of America.

Many of the doctors who served in the Korean War never had the luxury of serving in MASH units, Army evacuation hospitals, or on Navy hospital ships. The historical stories recorded in this book provide a more realistic picture of the American doctors and medics, as well as information about the many brave KATUSA (Korean Augmentation to the United States Army) soldiers who were used to fill up the empty enlisted slots in some of the American Infantry Divisions.

Most of the American doctors assigned to infantry units had just finished their internship or first year of residency training when they entered the U.S. military in July 1950—often under pressure from a unique U.S. doctors' draft, which was later struck down by the U.S. Supreme Court.

In 1950, these young non-specialized doctors were classified as general medical officers (GMO), and given the rank of Captain in the U.S. Army Medical Corps. Some were assigned to dispensary duties in the rear area, but many were separated from other physicians to serve as the only physician in an infantry battalion aid station.

Most of these doctors had no choice in the matter of where they served, and nearly all served with distinction. In 1950, most Americans were patriotic. Duty, honor, country and God meant something to most of them. Some lost their lives in the ebb and flow of battles, while others suffered great privation, beatings and death in horrific prisoner of war (POW) camps along the Yalu River, the boundary between Korea and China.

GMOs with more seniority and prior military service were assigned to positions such as regimental surgeon, medical battalion commander or division surgeon. However, at the bottom of the medical chain of command were the infantry battalion surgeons.

Also in this medical chain of command were Medical Service Corps (MSC) officers with different specialties who served side by side with the young GMOs. Dentists were also occasionally assigned to the Regimental Medical Company or to the Infantry Division Medical Battalion. Underpinning all were enlisted medics or aid-men, litter bearers, jeep and ambulance drivers, record clerks, many outstanding medical non-commissioned officers (NCOs), corporals and sergeants with varied numbers of stripes. These Medical NCOs were essential in keeping the medical platoons functioning as a military unit in combat. They also assisted their battalion surgeons in running the continual first aid training programs that were force-fed to replacements.

With the exception of the occasional medic serving in infantry rifle companies, this medical infrastructure within the infantry divisions was never explored or explained in the *M*A*S*H* series or in most Korean War books. It is a common misconception for Americans today to think that most of the doctors in the Korean War were in MASH units. The MASH units were greatly appreciated by the infantry and by the medical workers assigned to the infantry. Most of our seriously wounded soldiers could not have been properly cared for without MASH units, and they deserve the praise and recognition they have received. But the focus in this book is on the doctors and medics who were armed and embedded in the infantry. We were a part of the wartime TO&E (Table of Organization and Equipment) of an infantry battalion.

Another misperception generated by the *M*A*S*H* series was the apparent ubiquitous use of medical rescue helicopters. Even during the major Chinese offensives in April and May of 1951, when there were masses of casualties during forced retrograde movements, the bubble choppers were often not available to battalion aid stations or regimental collecting stations. Apparently this was because the helicopters were occupied with the task of moving hospitalized patients farther to the rear area or to airports for rapid evacuation to Japan.

The valuable, but vulnerable, little Bell-13 bubble chopper with two litter pods did not play a major role along the front until the second and third year of the war, when battle lines were more stabilized. Thus during the first year of the war, most of our wounded endured painful bumpy rides in jeeps, box ambulances, trucks and even on tanks. Many of our wounded did not survive the added trauma of the overland evacuation.

The current infusion in war of helicopters of all sizes and shapes has greatly changed the organization of medical support for all military services. The use of chest body armor also started during the second year of the war. This improved the survival from conventional and fragmentation weapons.

In looking back at the Korean War, I recall that our infantry leaders and battle strategists referred to the killing arenas as "the field of battle," but the grunts that experienced the field of battle called it "the meat grinder." The battalion surgeons, by the very nature of their profession and proximity to the meat grinder, tended to daily horrors. Our medical ingenuity was often overtaxed, for many could not be saved except by God. However, we continued to try and often found ourselves just looking up and asking for a miracle.

When our wounded were captured, the North Koreans and Chinese routinely shot (executed) them after questioning if they could not walk to prison camps in forced night marches. Even prisoners who could walk were often shot because the enemy did not have or did not choose to allocate the human resources needed to march the prisoners to the Yalu River prison camps. Captured medics were soon stripped of their medical supplies and were usually not given a chance to tend to the wounded. Thus we made a great effort never to leave wounded behind. It was better to drag or carry wounded soldiers even if they screamed in pain than to wait for a stretcher team. To leave a wounded man behind was tantamount to a death sentence.

The 7th Infantry Regiment of the 3rd Infantry Division was in climactic battles but was never rendered non-operational. The reason for the success of the 7th Infantry Regiment was not just the fortunes of war, but the leadership provided by brave commissioned and non-commissioned officers who had combat experience in WWII.

I never served as an infantry platoon leader in a rifle company. My task was not to kill or defeat the enemy, but rather to save as many lives as possible. But to save lives, we had to be close to those who were taking them.

I am one of the fortunate survivors still able to tell this story after a full life with a loving wife of 50 years, three wonderful daughters, three fine sons-in-law and nine treasured grandchildren. God has been good to me, not because of my merit, but because of His mercy and grace.

It is my hope that this story will please some fine old soldiers who have not yet faded away and also provide interesting reading for many young service men who have again volunteered to serve our country in a new meat grinder, this time with Islamic terrorists.

As I was making final revisions, I received a letter from Dr. Albert M. Meinke, Jr., telling me that he had written a book about his experiences as a battalion surgeon with the 10th Mountain Division in Europe in 1944 – 1945, *Mountain Troops and Medics*, published by Trafford Publishing in Canada.

It must be realized that battle experiences in different areas of the world will be unique. It is unique when soldiers are surrounded by the enemy and depending on parachuted supplies. It is unique when soldiers are facing apparent unlimited enemy manpower attacking in waves—who choose to push local civilians, men, women and children, ahead of them during attacks to absorb bullets and explode mines.

If there are other former or current battalion surgeons contemplating writing about their experiences in the infantry, I urge them to scribble on and get their stories published, for the world needs to be reminded that freedom has never been free. It has been purchased with blood. All freedoms, including our national sovereignty, freedom to vote, pay just taxes and worship God must be defended until the Lord returns.

rtj

Acknowledgements

I am especially grateful to Rosemary, my loving wife for more than fifty years, who has always kept our family focused on our savior Jesus Christ and also encouraged me in so many other ways, including my belated efforts in recording the events in this book. Our daughters, Annie, Kathy, and Tova, and their husbands, Dr. Jim Thorp, Dr. R. Duane Cook and Mr. Israel Kreps, have also encouraged me in this writing effort. Annie, of course, deserves special mention because, as a skilled editor and author, she has gone through the manuscript with a trained eye, removing needless or archaic words and paragraphs of superfluous opinions to give better focus to the unfolding story. Kathy, our compassionate, artistic daughter, has provided sketches to illustrate some events too tender for words to express. And Tova, our socially wise counselor daughter, has provided me with better reader's insight and balance.

I am also indebted to members of the 7th Infantry Regiment Association (Cottonbalers) and to members of the Society of the 3rd Infantry Division for their friendship and recall of events and names. Many of these fine old soldiers have been appropriately noted in the manuscript. Maj. Bill Herrick MSC, my battle-tested companion and best friend during the Korean War days, will always be close to my heart. Col. Fred Long has been a helpful friend throughout the writing of this book, and Gen. Fred Weyand, one of America's most outstanding infantry leaders in combat, has been both gracious and generous in his writing of the foreword to this book.

I would also like to express my appreciation to Ms. Melissa Byrd and to her younger sister, Ms. Jesse Kaminski, both of them being bright and helpful MKs (missionary kids). Melissa volunteered to read all of my old scribbled letters from Korea and type them into a computer for easy storage and retrieval. Jesse then assisted me with chores related to getting the final manuscript corrected, formatted and coupled with maps, pictures, appendices and indices and ready for the publisher. I would also like to acknowledge my grandson Joel Travis Cook who provided me with both joy and technical computer assistance during the finalization of the manuscript. And as the last galley proofs became available for review, during an unexpected illness, my very lovable, first granddaughter Tiffany Racháel C. Roach came alongside to assist with the final editing. I hope this book may be worthy of all of the good efforts made to get it finished and published.

rtj

Prologue
March 19, 2004

Today is my seventy-eighth birthday. I have been married for 50 years, and I am still in love with the same wonderful woman. I have almost finished writing this memoir of the Korean War and am thinking of other writing projects dealing with the adventures Rosemary and I have shared.

Whenever soldiers are sent into war by their country, they go equipped, for better or worse, with the baggage of their individual heritage and value system. I hope that my account of the Korean War will aid and encourage the spiritual focus of the young men and women today who are again called upon to defend the freedoms we have enjoyed in the United States of America.

Because many of the young soldiers who served in the Korean War were children of the depression years, it seems appropriate to give the reader insight into the formative background of this old soldier who came of age at the right time to enlist in the V-5 Navy program with the dream of becoming a Navy flyer in 1944. That dream was too near the end of World War II to reach fulfillment. But I was ripe for army service as a young doctor at the start of the Korean War in 1950.

Rigorous basic training and indoctrination can help to mold a unit to fight as a team and use weapons correctly. But the citizen solider needs something of value already within him to enable him to be willing to fight and die for freedom. The selection of the clay, the forming of it, the temperature and time in the kiln all determine the quality of the ceramic. The human clay that is thrust into the kiln of war is not much different.

I was born on March 19, 1926 in Minot, North Dakota, the second son of two born to John Jensen and Katherine Arnold Jensen. In late 1928, my family moved to Washington, Indiana where my father accepted a position as County

Extension (agriculture) Agent. The following year the stock market crashed and bread lines started to form.

Our home in Washington, Indiana, in the late 20s and early 30s was nice and close to my mother's family in Terra Haute, Indiana. I recall frequent pleasant visits to Grandfather and Grandmother Arnold's house, where Aunt Esther, an unmarried schoolteacher, also lived and Aunt Fay, a widow with three daughters, lived upstairs.

My grandmother's brother, Travis Trumbo, was my favorite visitor. He was the last male descendent of the three Trumbo brothers who had come over with Lafayette to fight in the American Revolution. I thought Uncle Travis was great because he took time to talk to me and encouraged me to think about things logically with him.

In 1933, we moved back north, this time to Roseau, Minnesota, where my father accepted another position as County Extension Agent. My father, originally named Johannes Jensen Kverndokka, was born in 1894 in Ulefos, Norway. He emigrated from Norway to the United States in 1910 with his 18-year-old brother, Ole Jensen Kverndokka, for economic reasons—a necessity for many of Norway's laboring class.

The Norwegian family name, Kverndokka, was abandoned at Ellis Island at the insistence of a U.S. Immigration officer, who told the brothers they would be registered as Jensen. Shortly thereafter, my father changed his first name to John. The two brothers moved west establishing contact along the way with Norwegian families that had immigrated earlier.

By 1913, John moved west to take up a 500-acre homestead in Montana. He lived alone on the prairie in a sod roof house and earned money by breaking wild horses for saddle use. Ole and John both enlisted in the U.S. Army in World War I. They were unable to enter the U.S. Navy because they were not citizens. As one recruiter told them, "one man can sink a ship, but one man can't sink an army."

Ole survived the battlefields of Europe, but John never made it there. An ammunition crate, being loaded onto a ship, fell on his leg. After his release from the hospital, still on crutches, he served as a cook in an Army mess. When the war ended, John was offered educational support by the U.S. government, which determined that his knee injury would preclude his resuming his pre-war occupation of breaking wild broncos. John used the opportunity to complete both high school and Agriculture College in four years.

My mother, Katherine Arnold, was of English and French lineage traced back to the time of the American Revolution. She met my father on a troop train during the war, and they began corresponding. She taught high school English, which I suspect made her more attractive to my father, as he was still struggling to improve his English.

An optimist might say my mother and father complimented each other. A pessimist might say they were culturally mismatched. It was, in many ways, a bicultural household, set in a Scandinavian community. My parents were very different.

Mother was strongly pro-temperance, and believed regular worship in church was essential for sustaining faith and moral perspective. She played the piano by ear, especially the old-time favorites and great church hymns. She knew the Bible had a Psalm to quote for every occasion and she often quoted them. In 1912, she participated in street marches demanding women's right to vote. She loved flowers, nature, poetry and all the great classics of English literature. At heart she was a true romantic. What little I knew of finer things and of social graces, I credit to my mother.

My father liked to argue about all the issues of the day, enjoyed hard work, and was self-reliant. He occasionally drank too much beer and could become unpleasant, but never violent. He was honest, faithful and a good person to have around in an emergency.

On one occasion in 1936, as we walked to church one evening, my father and I came across a deep sewer line trench. Planks had been placed across the narrow trench to allow people to cross over. It had been raining and the sides of the ditch had started to cave in. The planks were slick with mud from people walking across.

As we approached, we saw several men looking down into the ditch.

"What's going on there?" my father asked.

Someone replied, "It looks like someone has fallen into the trench. Someone has gone looking for a rope and a ladder."

My father slipped off his suit coat and said, "Hold my coat, and stand away from the edge before the entire trench caves in."

There was a woman lying in the bottom of the trench who was already partially covered with falling mud. My father ordered everyone away from the edge, picked up a plank and shoved one end down alongside the woman. Another upright plank was placed on her other side. As the other men held the tops of the planks upright and steady, my father slid down between the planks, taking care not to step on the woman at the bottom.

Slowly, he pulled the moaning, crying woman up out of the mud and shoved her up between the two planks. It was painful for her and exhausting for my father, but he finally pushed her up above his head. As she reached upward, other men lying on planks crossing the ditch were able to grasp her hands and pull her to safety. It took many more minutes for my father to brace himself between the planks and extract his legs from the thigh-deep mud. He slowly worked his way up between the planks. The trench continued to cave in as he was finally pulled to safety. The rope and ladder arrived as we made our way home.

I remember saying to my father, "That was really scary."

He looked at me and said, "Son, sometimes a man must do what a man must do or he isn't a man. That woman would have died under the mud while those fellows just stood on the planks above and watched it all happen."

The next day, I told my mother what he had said.

"Your father is brave," she said, "but you must also remember that a man of God must do what a man of God must do or he isn't a man of God. Sometimes what a man feels he must do and what a man of God must do are different. You must always choose wisely."

My father was my role model for courage. My mother was my role model for focusing on things of value.

That was the same year the job of County Extension Agent in Roseau was eliminated. My dad reasoned that we would never starve or freeze if we lived on a farm where we could raise a garden, keep livestock, and cut trees for firewood. For one thousand prudently saved dollars, my father was able to buy 120 wooded acres by Lake of the Woods on the Canadian border in Minnesota. He also obtained fishing rights to use pond nets. We built a 24 x 26 foot cabin, a log barn, a log icehouse, and a fish house.

The summer after I turned 11 years old, I put away my toy cars and my childhood. There was just too much work. My 12th birthday present was a new double bit ax from my dad. My brother, John, who was 15 months older, worked with my father tending the fish nets, while I cut the firewood, tended the garden, milked the cows, churned the butter, got ice from under the sawdust in the icehouse, and prepared the fish boxes for shipment.

We stored many bushels of potatoes, turnips, and carrots for winter use in a dirt cellar under the cabin. Dipping cleaned carrots and turnips in hot wax made them last longer and taste better. Every year, my mother canned nearly 1,000 quarts of food, including meat, vegetables, and berries.

Mother baked bread three times a week in the oven of our wood-burning kitchen stove. The large water tank on the side of the stove provided hot water for every purpose, including sponge baths from water ladled into a basin or bucket. The toilet was a two-hole bench seat in an outhouse, over a pit near the pile of firewood behind the house.

In the summer of 1938, Granddaddy Arnold, who had retired from the Pennsylvania Railroad, traveled by rail pass from Terra Haute, Indiana to Williams, Minnesota to visit us at Lake of the Woods. He was obviously concerned about our rather primitive living conditions, but he was careful about speaking out. This turned out to be an enjoyable summer for me, for he helped me with my chores and told me a lot of stories about his life, starting with the Civil War, when he was ten years old and Abraham Lincoln was president. Then he told me about what he was doing during the time of every president from Lincoln to Franklin D. Roosevelt. It was all very interesting, but it was a bit of an overload of history, so I finally asked him why he was telling me all of these things.

He answered by saying, "History is important, and some day you will be glad we had these discussions."

"How do you know that I will be glad to know all of these things? " I asked. His answer really opened my eyes.

"Because," Granddaddy said, "my granddaddy came to stay in my parents' home during the Civil War, and he told me everything about the times between George Washington and Abraham Lincoln."

Granddaddy Arnold, who was 84 years old, died later that year. I remember my mother crying and my father saying that G. D. Arnold was a really good man and a true Christian gentleman. I have had a fondness for history ever since Granddaddy's visit.

We had no electricity. The Rural Electrification Administration did not reach the Lake of the Woods until after World War II. We used pressure lamps with white gasoline, kerosene fueled lamps and kerosene farm lanterns. My father drilled us on what to do in case of a fire. The part I remembered was "get out of the house fast."

One winter night, my mother was reading by the light of a pressure lamp that had grown dim. She tried to pump up the lamp, but gasoline had gotten into the pump. As she pulled up on the pump piston, gasoline squirted back on her and immediately burst into flames. She screamed, my dad shouted, "Fire!" and went to help her. My brother and I slept in the same bed in a tiny room only slightly larger than the bed. I was awakened by Dad's shout. I kicked my brother to wake him, opened the window, and jumped out into a snow bank. I then ran around the house in time to see my father with one hand, throw the flaming gasoline pressure lamp out the door, where it sputtered and melted a hole in the snow. With his other hand, he threw a blanket over my mother, whose clothes were on fire, and quickly smothered the fire that had started to engulf her.

As I came into the house, my dad looked at me and said, "You should look to see who needs help before you run."

I had never before felt so ashamed of myself. Moreover, my brother hadn't even been awakened by the noise or by my kick. I apologized for my cowardly behavior and promised to do better if there was another emergency.

The winters were long and cold, but we were warm and had plenty to eat. My mother frequently gave food away to others who had not planted a large enough garden to tide them through the long winter and had exhausted their credit at the stores.

Since the depression years occurred before the invention of chainsaws, we had used axes to cut trees down and the bow saws to cut them up. We were completely dependent on wood for heating, cooking, and canning. Since we used a lot of wood and cross-cut saws took a lot of time and energy, we would often tow limbed trees to the wood pile area with the tractor and then use the tractor belt-powered circular saw bolted on the front of the tractor to cut the trees into stove-length pieces of firewood. It was a bit dangerous to work close to a whirling circular saw, but that was the way things were done in those days.

The large end of the tree would first be rested on the extended arm of the saw-stand, which was an integral part of the tractor belt pulley and drive shaft that was bolted to the front of the tractor. Then my dad would hold the big end of the tree on the left side of the whirling blade and shove it through the circular saw to cut the firewood off at the right length. My brother would hold the small end of the tree and make a measured step sideways toward my dad after each piece of firewood had been sawed off. I would catch the wood on the right side of the circular saw as it was sawed off and toss the pieces, from 12 to 18 inches in length, onto a nearby woodpile. The three of us had to work as a coordinated team. Dad usually insisted that we only cut up trees with the tractor-driven circular saw in the morning when we were most energetic and coordinated, never when we were physically fatigued, because that would be the time we would be more likely to have an accident with the whirling saw blade. There was no room for error. When done correctly, twenty or thirty de-limbed poplar, spruce, birch, or ash trees could be cut up in a half day, providing a huge pile of firewood for winter. The wood was later stacked neatly between convenient trees behind the house. No one wanted the task of digging firewood out of snow-banks in the winter. We usually selected diseased or dead trees for firewood and allowed the birch and ash trees to grow until they could be used for hardwood floors.

My dad cut pulpwood and saw logs for lumber in the winter. My brother and I did the same on Saturdays and Sundays or whenever we weren't in school. Our tools were the two-bladed axes and the bow saw, also called the Swede-saw. Steel files and a grinding stone were used to keep them sharp. We were expected to cut a double cord of eight-foot long poplar for pulpwood and stack it by a sled trail each day. The pulpwood brought around $5.00 a cord delivered at the paper mill at International Falls. It cost $1.00 a cord to get it from the woods to the train rail, about $2.00 a cord to transport it by rail, leaving a profit of $2.00 or less for a hard day's work by the time we transported the pulp sticks to the rail line and loaded it on a flat car.

As we loaded pulpwood onto the truck one day, my brother turned to me and said, "Bob, there has got to be a better way than this to make a living."

There was. We both became doctors.

It was never considered too cold to work outside. We wore felt shoes over wool socks with pullover ankle-high rubbers. Wool pants and one or more wool shirts with an outer windbreaker jacket were worn over longjohn underwear. Wool mittens with leather outers were worn on our hands and wool or pile caps with earflaps protected our ears and necks.

Even at 40 below zero we stayed warm, as long as there was food in our stomachs and we kept working. As we warmed up with exercise, we peeled off layers of upper clothes to avoid sweat buildup. As soon as we stopped work, we put on our shirts to keep from freezing.

We fished in the winter with gill nets under the ice. We used a fisherman's jigger to run a line under the ice. A jigger was a wood plank with a system of levers and steel spikes. When the rope was pulled, the spikes dug into the ice. As the rope was released, the jigger shot forward a few feet under the ice. When the correct distance was reached, we chipped out another hole in the ice, pulled out the jigger, retrieved the end of the rope, attached it to the net, and thereby were able to pull the net under the ice. At times, we went a mile or two away from the shore over the ice in search of fish.

There was always a risk of ice movement and cracking that could be heard many miles away. It was easy to miss new cracks in the thick ice if the snow had blown over them. Once, I was careless and stepped into a snow-covered crack in the ice. Fortunately, I caught the edge of the ice with my pike pole before I went completely under. My dad and brother quickly pulled me out.

My dad said, "Son, it is 20 below zero. Run for home and don't stop. If you stop to rest, you will freeze to death. We'll come as fast as we can, pulling the fish sled."

I had never been so teeth-chatteringly cold and numb in my life. As I ran, it became almost impossible to make my legs move, but somehow I finally staggered into the cabin and my mother helped strip off the frozen clothes and covered me with a stove-heated Hudson Bay wool blanket. She made me drink a lot of hot chocolate and hot soup. My dad and brother were relieved to see that I had made it all of the way to the house.

Another winter, while cutting timber, a falling tree limb broke my nose. My father cleaned the bleeding gash with snow and made sure my eyes functioned properly. He held a handful of snow over my nose to numb it, and then pushed my nose back into place with his strong fingers. I walked home and my mother cleaned the wound, closing the edges with butterfly adhesive tape. My nose was swollen and painful for several days, but it healed quickly.

John and I were always happy to get back to school on Monday so we could rest up. But we still had animal chores to do before we trudged off in the dark mornings to meet the school bus. The animal chores would be waiting for us again when we got home. I usually milked the cows while my brother distributed the hay to the cows and sheep and shoveled out the manure.

Fishing with pond nets and putting more land under cultivation kept us busy every summer. Usually my dad and John tended the nets, and I worked with the tractor, pulling stumps, burning brush, and plowing, but we all did whatever was needed.

Once, when my dad was away, my brother and I went out to lift the nets. We had a fairly heavy load of fish in the broad-beamed, 16-foot wooden boat, powered by an eight-horsepower Montgomery Ward outboard motor. As we started for home, a storm came up, and soon the only way we could avoid being swamped was to run parallel with the waves, taking the crest of each wave at a shallow angle as it rushed by. My brother was in the bow, bailing water and watching out for a dangerous reef with big granite boulders that would appear in the troughs of the waves.

Suddenly, he screamed, "Reef dead ahead! Climb the wave!"

I couldn't make out what he was saying because of the noise of the motor, pelting rain, and wind, but I knew from his lips and the terrified expression on his face exactly what he was trying to tell me. I turned the boat directly into the next wave, taking water over the bow. As we rose, I turned again, and tried to ride the crest as long as possible.

We were swept along for a few seconds and then slid down into the trough of the wave, lower and lower. Suddenly, like a monster from the deep, a huge boulder appeared just aft of the motor.

I could only cry out, "Jesus, don't let us hit that boulder!"

The water swirled around the giant rock just behind the motor and seemed to pull us backward as the boulder continued to rise up higher than our boat. Gradually, we rose up with the next wave and the huge boulder sank beneath us.

My dad's friend Barney Arneson had lost two sons by drowning. Being carried over that big boulder on a wave crest allowed me to know how close we had come to meeting God at a young age. It made me feel more dependent on Him.

When World War II began, I was in the eighth grade in a one-room country schoolhouse with 28 other children. There was one teacher, who earned $75 a month. We had a large wood stove for heat and two outdoor pit toilets—one for boys and one for girls. The county school board supplied toilet paper, but it never lasted long because students carried so much of it home in their pockets. It was much nicer than the pages from old Montgomery Ward and Sears Roebuck catalogs that most people used in their outhouses.

My brother wanted to go to college when he graduated as valedictorian from high school in 1942, but there was no money to send him. He stayed at home, helping to complete the fishing season and lay up stores for the winter. My father drove my brother, with $200 dollars in his pocket, to Baudette, where he hitched a ride on a truck going to Minneapolis. Because of mechanical trouble, the truck never made it to Minneapolis. My brother holed up in an all-night gas station during a blizzard and finally, after two days and several other hitched rides, he arrived at Uncle Ole's house in Chaska, Minnesota.

After John had spent several days trying to find work to support himself in school, he hitched on to Terra Haute, Indiana, to Grandmother Arnold's house, where he was able to find part-time work and start college. He was soon picked up by the draft and placed in the Army Air Corps, where he served almost four years before he rotated home as a master sergeant.

After seeing my brother get drafted the moment he turned 18, I decided to go to college at Concordia College in Moorhead, Minnesota during the summer session of 1943, after I completed my junior year in high school. This option was possible because during World War II many colleges accepted students, usually boys, who had not finished high school, if their grades were good.

It was also possible because my father had put up the nets and sold the livestock to go to work as a shipwright building corvettes for the Navy in a new shipyard along the lower Mississippi. He put our cultivated land out for share-cropping and my mother rented a room in a house in town and took a job teaching English at Williams High School for about $100 a month. The war split up our little family, but we all wrote letters once a week. Telephone calls were too expensive except in an emergency.

I left home for college on the bus with one suitcase and $100 in cash from my mother. That was my grubstake. The rest was up to me. I arrived in Moorhead, walked the mile to the college, and found an elderly gentleman planting flowers next to a building. He turned out to be Dr. Alfred M. Sattre, the head of the Biology department.

I told him I needed a job and a place to work for my room and board. Professor Sattre took me to Miss Amy Erickson, who was in charge of the kitchen. She gave me a job peeling potatoes and washing dishes. The professor also introduced me to Nels Mugaas, the buildings and grounds manager, who gave me a job. Every morning at five, I was to help him with whatever he needed done, including digging up old flowerbeds, taking off storm windows, or shoveling snow off sidewalks. Last, I was taken to the college dean, who told me how to register for college and assigned me a room in the men's dormitory.

I took ten credit hours that summer session and then went home to do the fall plowing. But instead of going back to finish high school, I returned to Concordia

9

and signed up for 22 credit hours during the fall semester, taking mostly pre-medical courses. I tried out for football and the college choir, but there was a time conflict, so I dropped football.

My plan was to enlist in the Navy Air Corps at the end of the fall semester, in hopes that my college credits would be accepted in place of a high school diploma. The Navy was agreeable, and I passed the written test but flunked the physical because of a mal-occlusion (overbite) of my teeth.

That was a real disappointment, but the Navy dentist said they might pass me if I had a dentist raise my bite by putting crowns on my upper molars. So after Christmas at home with Dad and Mother, I returned to Concordia and signed up for 20 more credit hours in the spring semester of 1944.

I contacted a local dentist, Dr. Runstad, who agreed to put the required gold crowns on my upper molars for $250. But that was $250 I didn't have.

I told Nels Mugaas about my troubles, as I often did, and he said, "That's not a problem. I will loan you two hundred and fifty dollars, and you can pay me back when you get in the Navy flying program. How much will you make when you go on active duty?"

I said, "I think it'll be fifty dollars a month."

"That fine," said Nels, "just send me twenty-five dollars a month for 10 months, with no interest, and we'll be square. And if you get killed learning to fly, don't worry about it. I'll consider the debt paid in full, since you died serving our country."

That was an offer I couldn't refuse, so we shook hands on this bit of high finance, and Nels gave me a check for $250.

I delivered the check the next day to Dr. Runstad and said, "Let's get started. I need to pass the Navy flight physical before I turn eighteen on March nineteenth."

In February, I passed the Navy flight physical. They didn't pay much attention to my teeth at all that time, but they also didn't put me on orders. They just said they would contact me soon. So I went back to my studies at Concordia. In May, I was ordered to report for an Army physical and induction. I took the bus back to Williams, Minnesota, and got on an Army draft charter bus for the long ride to Minneapolis, where I spent the next day without clothes, being processed into the Army.

I kept trying to get someone to look at my Navy papers, but I was continually rebuffed in the buff. At the end of the long day, as my cluster of nude men was about ready to get back into clothes, I finally got an Army official to look at my Navy papers. After some consultation and phone calls, I was given an escort to take me to the Navy induction station, with the order to bring me back so the

Army could swear me in if the Navy didn't. The Navy examined my papers and promptly swore me in as the Army escort waited.

After the Army escort left, the Navy chief said, "You are in the Navy as of today, but we have not determined your assignment as yet, so you are on active duty without pay, pending orders. Go back and finish your college semester, and we will get orders to you sometime in June. In case we miss you, here's a telephone number you can call from time to time to check on your status."

By not eating, I had just enough money for a bus ticket back to Moorhead, where I arrived late at night, tired, hungry, and broke. I ate a huge breakfast the next morning in the college cafeteria and went on with my jobs of washing dishes, shoveling snow off walks, singing in the choir, and attending classes.

Since phone calls to the Navy indicated I would not have orders until early July, I went home, did some spring plowing, and moved rocks out of the field so that additional land could be rented out.

I finally received orders to report by 2 July 1944 to the V-5 unit at Denison University in Granville, Ohio. I was surprised because I thought I would be going to pre-flight somewhere. I traveled by bus to Granville with many bus changes, but no rest stopovers. After reporting in, I soon found myself in a sailor suit and registering for more pre-med courses, only this time the Navy paid all expenses and gave me $54 a month. I had never had it so good.

But I was disappointed because no one could tell me when I would be assigned to pre-flight and flight training. I wanted to be a doctor after the war was over, but I wanted to fly in the Navy during the war.

Denison University was on the quarter system. At the end of the summer quarter, all of the V-5 students were called together and informed that none of our group was going to flight training, because the Navy had enough pilots to last out the war. We were given the option of boot camp, aircraft mechanic's school, or midshipmen training. Our academic record would determine our placement. We would not be permitted to transfer to the V-12 pre-medical or pre-dental college programs.

The next day, I gathered my college academic records and requested a meeting with the Navy commander in charge of the V-5/V-12 programs. He granted me five minutes. I told him that by the end of the fall quarter I would have completed all the pre-med requirements, even though I was in the V-5 program. I suggested it was in the Navy's best interest to transfer me to the V-12 pre-medical training program, since I would be ready for medical school in only three more months.

The commander looked surprised, amused, and sympathetic.

He studied my transcripts and said, "Young man, you certainly have been cramming in the pre-medical credit hours, and you did all of this while in V-5.

This is remarkable. Most of your V-5 classmates have been majoring in music appreciation and girl stalking. So I'll tell you what I'm going to do. I'm going to write a letter to the chief of Navy personnel and send him these transcripts. He usually gets nothing but problem sailors to deal with. I want you to go ahead with all the pre-medical courses you were planning on taking in the fall quarter So tell me, what else have you been doing that I can put in my letter to the chief of Naval personnel to give him a happy day for a change?"

"Well," I said, "I've been on the track team, running the 440, the mile relay, and the 220. I also belong to a group of Christian sailors that has formed a gospel singing and preaching team. We have been getting invitations from local churches on Sundays and invitations for Sunday dinners in the community. It's been a lot of fun."

"That's wonderful," said the commander. "I wonder why people only tell me about the sailors who screw up?"

A month later, the chief of Navy personnel approved my transfer to the V-12 pre-medical program and in January 1945 I applied for medical school at the University of Minnesota, where there was a Navy V-12 program. I thought about applying to a more prestigious school such as Harvard, but I'd been warned the Navy would drop us all as soon as the war was over, and I didn't know how I could ever pay the high fees at Harvard.

The Navy allowed me to continue at Denison University, cramming in as many courses as I could fit into my schedule. I was later awarded a bachelor's degree from Denison. I could only thank the Lord for all the educational opportunities I had received since I had left home for Concordia College two years before.

The Minnesota Medical School class starting in July 1945, in which I was accepted, was the last class in the wartime 36-month accelerated program. The program consisted of four nine-month school years in succession without a vacation. I became a doctor at age 22, in June 1948, five years after I left high school. I was sure the Lord had it all planned out, because I certainly had no clue about doing any of it when I boarded the bus to start college after my junior year in high school.

During the first six months in medical school, I wore a midshipman's uniform. The Navy paid all of my school expenses and gave me a monthly stipend of $54. But the Navy did not provide housing, so I joined the Phi Rho Sigma Medical Fraternity and shared a room with Ervin Kjenaas. Erv was in the Army Specialized Training Program at medical school.

Since I had paid Nels Mugaas the $250 I borrowed, I had $54 a month all to myself. I felt grateful to my country for all that I'd been given, but I also felt I hadn't done anything for my country during World War II, and was disappointed I had never had the opportunity to fly in the Navy.

My anatomy class partner was a Japanese-American named Joe Yamamoto. Joe was shy, but we soon became friends. When I learned his parents and other relatives were in a detention camp in the U.S., I felt anger toward President Roosevelt. Because of poor eyesight, Joe was unable to join the military, but he was allowed to apply to medical school.

He didn't have many friends and the name Yamamoto was certainly not popular because of Admiral Yamamoto's role in Pearl Harbor. I invited Joe to have lunch with me as my guest in the fraternity house. My intention was to encourage some upperclassmen in Phi Rho to invite him to become a member of the fraternity.

Boy, was I ever naive. Everyone was polite enough, but when I privately mentioned to a couple of upper classmen that I hoped they would invite Joe to join Phi Rho Sigma, I was told it wasn't possible because the fraternity constitution excluded non-Aryans. That really ticked me off. When I objected, I was told that was just the way it was.

A small group of freshmen, Jolly West (the group leader), Jim Wall, Erv Kjenaas, myself, and a few others quietly set about the task of gaining a majority among the first, second, and third year class members of Phi Rho Sigma, Theta Tau Chapter, for amending the fraternity constitution. As soon as the senior class graduated, we removed the non-Aryan exclusion clause from our constitution. Joe Yamamoto was invited to join and he did so in our second year. We all felt pretty good about ending that bit of discrimination.

My main recreation was singing with the Phi Rho Sigma men's chorus and with the choir of a little Lutheran church about a block away. And there were frequent fraternity parties, where guys and gals enjoyed beer and popcorn.

On December 24, 1945, all of the Navy V-12 medical students were released from active duty. I had already gotten a job washing dishes in the fraternity house in exchange for my meals, and the first three months, during which I was classified as V-5, made me eligible for one year of the G.I. bill, even though I was in college at the time.

But knowing leaner times were ahead, I also got a part-time job in the Bacteriology Department, feeding laboratory animals and cleaning their cages. With two part-time jobs there was less time for sleep and study, and almost no time for a social life outside of the Phi Rho Sigma Fraternity. But by selling a bottle of my type A-Rh negative blood every other month, I managed to take a girl out to a movie. I didn't try to have a steady girlfriend because I wasn't financially able to consider a committed relationship. I was fortunate to end up seventeenth in our class of 100.

I considered dropping out of medical school and working full-time for a Ph.D. in microbiology, but research scholarships in the Bacteriology Department were hard to obtain, so I didn't have time to sit around and wait.

Reluctantly, I left my work in the Bacteriology Department and took a job as an extern in Fairview Hospital during my senior year in medical school. I needed to do well during my last year. When the University of Minnesota announced a new two-year mixed internship program, I applied and was accepted

During the first year of internship, I spent four months in a pediatric rotation, four months in the emergency room, and four months in an OB-GYN rotation. The second year, I rotated through medical wards and clinics. I worked every weekday, every other night, and every other weekend.

I could seldom get my work done on Saturday before the late afternoon, and I slept hard on my Sunday off. I was provided with a room by the hospital and took my meals in the hospital dining room. I was paid $50 a month during each of the first three rotations, but during my second year, the University Hospital only paid $15 a month.

At the time, there was a selective military draft for young healthy doctors, so when the Army offered to pay interns the salary of a first lieutenant—$256 a month—if we enlisted during our civilian internships, it seemed like a good deal. I thought I probably would be drafted anyway, as soon as I finished my internship. With that kind of money, I might even buy a car and take a girl out on a date without using the streetcar or donating blood.

In 1949, I bought a used Chevy and met a nice young woman named Rachel who lived in St. Cloud, far beyond the trolley tracks. I had no idea the storm clouds of war were gathering in far away Korea.

rtj

John, age 9 (left), and Bob, age 8 (right), sitting with dog, Pal in Roseau, Minnesota; summer 1934. Pal, an American Water Spaniel, died near Lake of the Woods in 1937 from eating wolf bait laced with strychnine. In those days there was a $25 bounty on wolves. Pal was later replaced by Patsy.

Cutting out blocks of ice to slide up ramp to ice house; winter 1939. The stored ice was used for refrigeration in the summer and for fish boxes sent to the Chicago fish market.

Cabin by Lake of the Wood; 1937 – 1945

John (left) and Bob (right) with Mother (center); 1940

Dad with a large walleyed pike that he caught while fishing in
Lake of the Wood; 1950

Bob's departure by bus from Williams, Minnesota for Concordia College,
Moorhead, Minnesota; July 1943

Bob, Matthew Bescotte and Matthew's girlfriend sometime during the U.S. Navy V-5/V-12 program at Denison University; 1944 – 1945

Chapter One
Finally, after seven years' work, a time to go sailing and fishing
June 23, 1950 – June 24, 1950

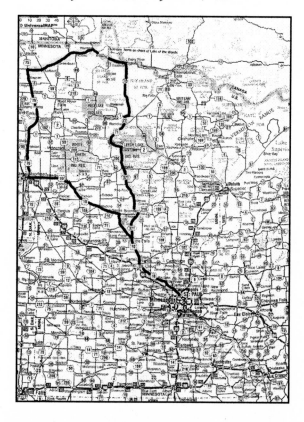

The route taken by Bob north from Minneapolis to Lake of the Woods and his
return route via Fargo/Moorhead to catch a flight from Minneapolis to San
Francisco to report to Camp Stoneman; June 1950

On Friday morning, June 23, 1950, I packed all of my earthly belongings in the back seat and trunk of my 1948 Chevrolet and drove slowly past the University of Minnesota Medical School and Hospital. I was not sure why I wanted this last look.

I had been fortunate to have been able to obtain my bachelor's degree in two years, complete medical school in three years, followed by a two-year rotating internship—all in seven years. In later years, I gave God the credit, but at the time I graduated from medical school, I was not particularly pious. As I passed by the familiar red brick buildings, I realized that I had never properly thanked the many teachers who had befriended me and helped me along the way. I had been completely self-absorbed in my studies and work. As I drove away, I felt guilty of ingratitude. I also felt lonely and more insecure than liberated from the daily grind, without a full schedule to occupy my time.

But I'd had no vacation and very little rest during the last two years. As an intern, I had been working six days a week, as well as every other night and every other Sunday for two years, except for a three-month pediatric rotation, when I was only on call every third night and every third Sunday. The pediatric rotation had seemed like heaven.

In addition to my regular schedule, the recent polio epidemic in Minnesota had caused an extra workload, especially when I was interning on a medical ward with 12 Drinker respirators with bulbar polio patients. On the rare occasions of an electric power failure, we all had to scramble to our assigned respirator tank to pump them by hand until power was restored. But my two-year rotating internship was over. I had finally crossed some type of finish line and a new phase of my life was about to begin. At the age of 24, I suddenly felt free—a feeling tempered by uncertainty about the future.

When I joined the Army Medical Corps in November 1948, during the first year of my internship, I asked to be sent to Europe, but in June 1950 I received orders to go to Japan after a 30-day home leave instead. Whether or not I would also receive orders to attend an orientation program at the Army Medical Field Service School in San Antonio, Texas had not been determined. I looked forward to Army service in Japan. I felt ready and willing to give something back for all I had received during the last seven years. But at that moment, I had 30 days of free time and I planned to make the most of it. My mind was focused on a long-planned vacation that would involve sailing around Lake of the Woods with my father. Japan and the Army could come later.

I also had been permitted to finish up a week early because of not having had a vacation. I intended to start for home on June 22, 1950. However, the transfer of patient responsibilities and packing up my few belongings had taken longer than I anticipated. I also spent a pleasant evening out with my brother, John Arnold Jensen.

Because of the four years John had spent in the Army Air Corps during World War II, he was only in his first year of medical school. My brother and I were very close. We had no other siblings and shared our meager resources as needed. Neither of us had married, but we each hoped to be happily married some day—when we could afford it. Now that I had finished my internship I was interested in trying to find the right Christian girl. However, my recent telephone efforts to try to arrange a date with Rachel, a special young lady in St. Cloud, Minnesota, had not been successful.

None of the suggested timings for my visit seemed convenient. I reluctantly came to the conclusion that I seemed to care more for Rachel than she did for me. In spite of that fact, I stopped at St. Cloud for an unscheduled visit with Rachel. I had hoped to encourage some correspondence from her while I was overseas in Japan.

While driving on north, I reflected on the fact that the narrow focus of my accelerated training had not left much time for other subjects, such as the pursuit of a romantic interest. I also realized that I knew a whole lot more about medicine than I did about how to woo a young lady.

Outside of medicine, I knew more about farming, fishing, and timber cutting than anything else—not very romantic subjects with which to impress a young lady. As I drove to Lake of the Woods from St. Cloud, I felt lonely. I had hoped that Rachel would become more than a friend. Now that I was scheduled for two years overseas Army duty, it seemed that my romantic options were being put on hold.

While driving by Bemidji toward Baudette, my thoughts turned to the task of getting the old sailboat repaired and building a bracket for an auxiliary outboard motor. I was determined to enjoy a long-delayed and much-anticipated sailing, fishing, and camping trip out among the islands on the Canadian side of Lake of the Woods. A friend from the intern program had said that he would like to go along, but he developed other plans—involving romance. However, my father had indicated that he would like to go on a sailing vacation with me, and I was now very glad that Dad and I would have this special time alone together. My brother would join us later, after he finished his exams. John and I planned to drive west to California, if the Army didn't send me to San Antonio first to attend the Army Medical Field Service School.

The farther north I drove, the more I realized how much I longed to get out in the open for a while to enjoy the pristine beauty of the north country. I didn't then realize that I would soon be spending a lot of time out in the open, but it would be in frigid North Korea and not on Lake of the Woods. Going to war had not been something I had thought about since I had been in the Navy V-5 and V-12 programs during World War II.

After a gasoline and hamburger stop at Bemidji, I headed northeast on Highway 71 and then switched to Highway 72 at Blackduck for the road straight north to Baudette, on the Canadian border. As I was leaving Baudette, I noted that the engine was missing a little and I thought I would drive by Johnny Gilley's house in Williams to see if he could check the car on Monday.

Johnny was good-natured, as usual, and agreed to check the car out at his Chevrolet garage if I drove back in from the lake on Monday. After a mutual exchange of news about family and friends, I headed north from Williams for the 15-mile trip to the home place by the shore of Lake of the Woods.

Both Dad and Mother were there to greet me when I drove in. After hugs, we asked about each other's well-being and work as we walked along the lakeshore. Ducks swam about fifty yards out from the shore, ignoring our presence on the beach. A little farther out, two loons dove for fish. Mother's old dog, Patsy, an American water spaniel, went along, but she was no longer lively.

The lake was calm and the wooded shoreline shimmered in many shades of green. The air was refreshing and free of city smog. Be it ever so humble, and it certainly was humble, there was no place like home. It was a good place to rest, reflect, and acknowledge the Lord's sovereignty over His creation, even if I didn't pray regularly.

Dad took pride in the two acres of lush green grass that stretched from footpaths leading into the woods behind their new little house down to the lakeshore. He had purchased a new riding lawn mower and enjoyed having people come over to look at the lawn and to go fishing. In the early morning, deer would enjoy the lawn, as well as Mother's garden and flowers. The woodchucks and gophers also found it tempting to build their homes in burrows under the thick sod.

Dad mentioned that if he could live there all the time, he would borrow some sheep from a nearby farmer for summer grazing on his lawn—to reduce his need for mowing so often.

His comment reminded me of the pleasure I'd had with the bottle-raised pet lambs that we'd had running around outside and sometimes inside, the old cabin.

Dad had always liked sheep because they were friendly, fun to watch, and easy to keep in the summer. But they had to be fed hay in a shelter in winter, cared for in lambing season, and sheared for their wool in the spring. He would also need another dog or two living outside to sound the alarm and protect the sheep shed from wolves that might come over the ice from Canada. Dad was not much interested in getting back into livestock care without any children at home. Raising livestock was a daily commitment, especially in the northland during the long winters.

There had been a lot of changes in the last seven years. Dad pointed out all the pine trees he had planted in 1937. They were now 15 to 20 feet tall, providing green coloring and wind protection in the winter. He had also pulled down the old log barn and the sheep shed with the tractor to allow more room to build their new well-insulated little house, which seemed quite modern, with electricity and indoor plumbing. Uncle Ole had come up from Chaska, Minnesota to help Dad build the house. My brother, John, had done the wiring and also put electric lights in the old cabin where we used to live during the depression years.

Because oil prices were low, Dad had decided on fuel oil for heat rather than on a woodstove. Mother had wanted a stove that burned wood to be set in or next to a fireplace as an alternate heating source and to keep the coffee pot warm. But Dad knew it would cost an extra two thousand dollars to install the stove, fireplace and chimney. The real reason my mother wanted the alternative wood burner in a fireplace was because she thought it would be cozier and look more rustic. The real reason my dad didn't want it was because he felt they might not be staying there all winter anyway, and if they did, he would be stuck with the job of chopping wood. It was easier to use a wood-burning stove when there were two boys at home to cut and stack the wood needed to keep the house warm in the winter.

The old log icehouse and fish-house were gone—they had fallen into the lake as the waves continued to erode the shoreline. I noticed that the old cabin had been moved back from near the lake to a new foundation that was off to the north side of the new house so as to not block the east view of the lake. The two-seat outhouse had also been moved with the cabin to a spot over a new pit. It was set back and off to the north side of the old cabin, and had a nice view of the lake if the occupant left the outhouse door open. I looked inside and found toilet paper instead of the old Montgomery Ward catalog we used to use. I accepted that improvement gladly as a sign of increased prosperity. The outhouse still had the signature of my grandfather, G. D. Arnold, on the wall, a memento of his visit in August 1938. The outhouse was seldom used in 1950 except by visiting fishermen or hunters who had rented the old cabin, but seeing Granddaddy's signature brought back fond memories.

Dad had recently taken a new job in Grygla, Minnesota, which was about 40 miles south of Roseau, near upper Red Lake, close to the Red Lake (Chippewa) Indian Reservation. His new job was teaching agriculture and farm management under the GI Agriculture Education Program. This special veterans' program had been set up to help farmers or sons of farmers who had been in the military during World War II. It was a good program that helped many veterans to become more successful farmers. I suspected that Dad studied harder than his students, for he took pride in his teaching and truly wanted his students to learn good farming methods and bookkeeping, as well. Many of these men had never finished high school, but they loved the planting and harvesting cycle of farm life and the four seasons in the northland.

The majority of his students were of Norwegian descent. But there were also a number of Swedes, Finns, and Germans, with an occasional farmer of French or Scottish descent who had drifted south from Canada before people near the border thought or cared much about exactly where it was located.

Dad's students spoke highly of his teaching ability and valued his helpful farm inspection visits. He often used his Norwegian with the older members of the farm families and usually emerged from a farm visit with a full stomach, new jokes about Ole and Sven, and when in season, a lot of garden produce.

Dad had wanted to teach the veteran agriculture class for farmers at Williams, Warroad, or Baudette, towns closer to home, but other younger World War II veterans had become the instructors for these classes. Dad, a World War I veteran, was forced to look elsewhere. Since no one wanted to teach the veterans' agriculture class at Grygla, Dad took the job to have some steady cash income, even though he and Mother would have preferred to live in their new home by Lake of the Woods.

Mother had stopped teaching school and was content to raise flowers, read good books, play hymns on the old piano, and to exchange letters with her sons and other relatives. She had a problem with carotid artery narrowing, causing some confusion in her thinking. Her mental functioning improved after carotid artery surgery at the University Hospital in Minneapolis.

As they reached their late fifties, both Dad and Mother seemed older than their years. The Depression and World War II years had not been easy on them, but they had each saved a few thousand dollars and were debt-free. They seemed to find a sense of fulfillment for their own unfulfilled dreams through John and me. World War II had interrupted the development of the farm by the lake. There had been a family plan to buy additional land and expand the farm to 1000 acres. But these plans faded when it became clear that my brother and I were going into medicine and would not return to farming again after World War II.

Dad expressed concern that John seemed to have a problem keeping his grades up in medical school, which was puzzling to my parents, since he had been the valedictorian of his high school class. Of course, the Williams High School class of 1942 only had about 30 students. But because I had gone through college and medical school with good grades, it was expected that John would also do well.

I noticed John had a harder time focusing on his studies after having spent so long in the service. John had very mixed feelings about the Army Air Corps. He had told me there were many young draftees in his B-29 Bomber Group who had college degrees, even some with advanced degrees, who refused to go to Officers

Candidate School, refused to take pilot training, were drunk on duty much of the time, and did whatever they had to do to avoid flight duty, combat, or responsibility of any kind. They slid through the war as educated smart-alecky privates. Not only did they do as little as possible, but they made fun of those with less education who earned their non-commissioned officer (NCO) stripes trying to keep the planes flying.

If they had been in the Army instead of the Army Air Corps, they might have been booted into the Infantry. But they felt relatively safe as non-contributors in the non-flying part of the Army Air Force. John was proud of his master sergeant stripes at the end of the war and disgusted with the complaining educated goof-offs he'd had to put up with in his unit. It seems obvious that these non-contributing college graduates didn't represent well the "Greatest Generation" spoken of by Tom Brokaw.

But it was also clear to me that John had lost some of his scholastic sharpness and had acquired a residue of bitterness during his World War II service in the Army Air Corps. College was easier for me because I had fewer distractions. In fact, I had just stepped onto an education and work treadmill and didn't get off for seven years.

John's only goal now was to get through medical school and a rotating internship in order to become a family practitioner somewhere in northern Minnesota. He was not interested in the research emphasis at the medical school, and that was one of his problems. Most of the medical school instructors were interested in having their students learn about their special research projects. John just wanted to learn about how to care for patients. I had cautioned John that he had to prepare for examinations based on what the instructors thought was important— not on what he thought was important.

But John was a bit stubborn. Having earned six stripes as an enlisted man trying to make the Army Air Corps administration run smoothly, he had a low level of tolerance for what he considered to be non-essentials. Thus, while he read broadly about medical practice, he missed points on his exams that pertained to the personal research interests of his instructors during the first two years of medical school. He did better in the following two clinical years of medical school.

Dad and Mother talked about my future assignment in Japan and about the possibility of the cold war getting hot; I knew that Dad was disappointed that I was not going to Europe. But our immediate task was to fix up the sailboat. Dad and I discussed cutting a trail through the woods to reach the old sailboat. We planned to put it on skids and use the tractor to tow it over to the house.

The old sailboat had been a source of pleasure for us. Dad had found the hull abandoned in Warroad, Minnesota. It was 21 feet long and had a round bottom, with a nicely tapered bow and stern. It had solid cypress planking over oak ribs. At one time in the past, the boat had had an inboard diesel engine and had been used as a mail delivery boat on the lake. Dad had restored the boat hull in 1935 when we lived in Roseau. He'd added a shallow draft, weighted keel and a removable mast, equipped with a gaff-rig sail and jib. It reminded him of the type of seaworthy boats common along the coast of Norway that went out from the safety of the fjords into the stormy North Sea.

Our immediate task was to repair a hole in the boat's side created by a rock as it came ashore during a storm several years before. Our plan was to repair the sailboat, add a bracket for an auxiliary outboard motor and to take a fishing trip around the Islands on the Canadian side, perhaps going as far as Kenora. We would put two bunks in the boat under the covered bow and cook on a little portable stove.

As our plans developed, Dad really got his heart set on fixing up the old boat and sailing around the lake. We had never had a chance to do a fun project together before. We happily spent all day Saturday afternoon and evening working out the details.

I hoped that Dad and I would have the opportunity to talk about the Lord—about what faith in Christ really meant. It was a subject that Dad didn't find easy to discuss.

One could never have a serious conversation in a boat with an outboard motor because of the noise. But it was different in a sailboat. With just two of us, we could talk as much as we wanted. We looked at Dad's maps of the lake and wished for a better compass. Compared to today, our preparations were primitive, at best. In fact, they were little better than the Vikings had a thousand years earlier. In 1950, satellites, global positioning equipment, depth sonar, transistor radios, and cell phones had not yet been invented. It didn't take long to prepare a list of needed supplies and equipment.

Mother preferred the lakeshore to being on the lake. She didn't swim well and could become seasick. But as was her nature, she took great pleasure in our happiness. She kept busy planning the meals for us and enjoyed having a family project again. She was content to "keep the home ready for the sailors' return."

The only sad note was that John would not be home until after his exams in mid-July. Since the bus no longer came through Williams, John planned to catch the bus to Bemidji, where I would go to pick him up. I looked forward to spending a few days with all of us sailing together in home waters and trolling for fish.

Since my last Army orders indicated that I should report to Camp Stoneman in California after my 30-day leave, John and I planned to drive through Yellowstone Park on the way to California. John also had some former Army Air Corps friends in California that he wanted to visit before driving back to Minneapolis.

My parents and I talked on into the night and never turned on the radio before going to bed. I remember laughing about the convenience of electricity and radio access all year. When I was a boy during the Depression in a home without electricity, we would buy a new radio battery pack each year at Thanksgiving to listen to the Christmas music and programs such as *Amos and Andy*, *Fibber Magee and Molly*, *The Lone Ranger*, *Jack Benny* with Mary and Rochester, *George Burns and Gracie Allen*, and *The Lutheran Hour* broadcast. They brought much happiness and laughter into our home on the long winter nights. But we were careful how we used the radio, for the battery pack would usually only last until March. Then we waited until the following Thanksgiving to order a new battery from Montgomery Ward. The radio was more essential during the long winter hours of darkness. During the Depression, years before rural electrification, a radio was too expensive to use year round. Transistors, which made it possible to run a radio on ordinary flashlight batteries, had not yet been invented.

In general, my folks were happier than I had seen them for years. We went to bed eager to begin work on the sailboat first thing in the morning.

Medical Interns during their final month of training at the University of
Minnesota Hospital in Minneapolis (Bob: 4th from left); mid-June 1950

Chapter Two
North Korea invades South Korea—U.S. Army leave canceled
June 25, 1950 – July 11, 1950

I woke refreshed on the morning of June 25, 1950 and sat down with my parents to a large country breakfast of bacon and eggs with fried potatoes, toast and jam. After we finished, we turned on the radio for the morning news. It was bad. North Korea had invaded South Korea in the early morning hours on the opposite side of the world.

Somehow we all knew that this new war would impact our summer vacation plans. I thought the Army would probably cancel my 30-day leave. Dad was fearful that I would be sent to the war in Korea. In my heart, I felt that Dad's fears were probably prophetic. We put off repairing the old sailboat for a day and just went fishing. Mother stayed home to wait for more news on the radio and for the telephone to ring.

On the third day home, the party line crank phone finally rang with a call from Washington, D.C. Dad and I were out fishing at the time. The caller identified himself as an Army officer. He asked my mother to have me call back ASAP. When I did, the officer identified himself and said that my 30-day leave had been canceled and that I should proceed to the nearest airport, fly to San Francisco and proceed to Camp Stoneman, California for orientation and out-processing to Japan.

The officer was irate that I was not at my assigned duty station at the University of Minnesota Hospital and wanted to know who had authorized my absence. I told him that I had not had a vacation day off in the last two years and that the hospital had allowed me to leave a week early because they had someone else to cover for that time. I was told that I should have had that approved by Washington.

I responded that I already had my orders to go to Japan after my 30-day leave. The opportunity to leave early came up at the last minute, so I used the time to move my personal effects home to Lake of the Woods and do some fishing. I had anticipated driving to California in the latter part of July.

The voice from Washington grew more irritated. He reiterated that I should go immediately to the nearest airport and then proceed to California. I asked who would make the reservation for the flight, who would pay for the ticket, and how I was supposed to get to Grand Forks or Fargo, North Dakota, the nearest airports, since there was no local bus transportation available and my car was in need of some minor repairs. I suggested getting my car repaired the following day and driving to Minneapolis, where I would turn my car over to my brother and catch the first flight available from Minneapolis to San Francisco.

The voice from Washington grew ever more agitated. He refused to believe there was no commercial transportation available. He informed me that he could send a U.S. Marshal to arrest me and take me to the nearest airport. I told him I would be pleased to have a free ride from anyone who would provide it, but there was no need to arrest me for not having a local bus service.

"Besides," I said, "I doubt there is a U.S. Marshal anywhere in northern Minnesota, and I can probably get my car repaired and drive all the way to Minneapolis before a U.S. Marshal can find me at Lake of the Woods, way up here on the Canadian border."

The officer in Washington simmered down a bit and commented that my home must really be out in the boondocks if there was no public transport. I agreed that we did live out in the boondocks and assured him there was no public transportation and that the quickest thing to do was for me to get my car repaired the next day and then I would be on my way the following day.

He told me to just make my own plane reservations and pay for my own ticket. When I got to Camp Stoneman, California, I could expect to be reimbursed. I asked him to send a wire to my Minneapolis address verifying the change in my orders so I could justify my reporting at Camp Stoneman, California, and my request for reimbursement of the plane ticket.

By this time, there were a lot of on and off clicking interruptions on the party-line phone and it was becoming difficult to hear anything, so I just hung up and proceeded as I had last stated without getting a response or return phone call. No doubt all of the clickers on the party line heard that my orders had been changed and I would soon be going to the Far East. News travels fast on a party line telephone. It also wasn't often that people got to listen in on a call from Washington, D.C.. I found the phone call rather irritating myself, because the officer suggested that he was ready to send a U.S. Marshal to arrest me. That really ticked me off.

When I tried to call for flight reservations to San Francisco, I was told that all flights to California were booked from Minneapolis, Grand Forks, and Fargo for a week. However, at the moment, my main concern was the worry on my parents' faces, for they believed I was destined to end up in the Korean War. My mother was tearful, but she was sure that God would bring me home alive if I went to Korea.

Early the next morning, I drove to Williams, Minnesota to have the car serviced. It only needed new points and plugs. Dad used the occasion to drive back to Grygla to tend to some matters related to his class. He didn't return before I left—too torn up inside by the prospect of my going to war. He didn't know how to cry.

Many Norwegian immigrant men who struggled in this new land had only learned to grieve with beers instead of tears. Many clenched their fists and ground their teeth, rather than folding their hands and praying. Dad would gladly have gone in my place if he could have done so, but there was nothing he could do about this situation.

To top it all off, after seven long years apart, our plans for time together had been cruelly snatched away by a war in faraway Korea. It was more than Dad could bear. He coped with his pain by going back to work and downing a few beers. Mother found her comfort in the Psalms.

When I returned home with the repaired car, I walked down along the beach to the place where two huge granite boulders had been pushed up by the ice onto the sandy shore sometime in the distant past. The sailboat was still upside down in the woods nearby—right where we had pulled it ashore with a block and tackle eight years earlier. That old sailboat never sailed again.

As a boy, I used to climb up on top of those boulders to daydream. It was a good spot to think and pray—especially in emergency situations. When I was younger and sat on those big boulders, I wished I could see an angel or have some personal revelation from God to really know that He was there and concerned with my welfare.

But in June 1950, as I sat down and thought back over the last seven years, I realized that God had been there helping me all along, enabling me to accomplish what I did. He had placed great opportunities before me, and given me a faith and a love for Jesus Christ, even if I didn't think about Him every day. I had committed my life to Jesus during my confirmation training in the Lutheran Church. Later, when I was at Concordia College in Moorhead, Minnesota, I was encouraged by some young Christians to ask Jesus into my heart as Lord and Savior. Thus, while I felt I had been saved, knowing Jesus didn't keep me from sin. However, He gnawed at my gut until I repented, so I knew He was there.

As a boy, I used to sing when I brought the cows home from the pasture for milking. The cows never complained and there was nobody else around to listen. But as I sat on the big boulders by the lake, I didn't feel like singing "Onward Christian Soldiers," one of my favorite hymns. I didn't feel like marching off to war, and I didn't feel triumphant or brave. Instead, I felt very small and frightened. Reality was starting to set in.

Another old hymn came to mind: "Jesus Lover Of My Soul." I sang the first two verses, which were all I could remember:

"Jesus lover of my soul, let me to Thy bosom fly.
While the nearer waters roll, while the tempest still is high.
Hide me, O my Savior hide, till the storm of life is past.
Safe into the haven guide, O receive my soul at last!

"Other refuge have I none. Hang my helpless soul on Thee.
Leave, ah leave me not alone, still support and comfort me.
All my trust on Thee is stayed, all my help from Thee I bring.
Cover my defenseless head, with the shadow of Thy wing."

It made me feel better to sing those words and they became my prayer to the Lord. I then whispered Psalm 23, which I'd memorized long ago from the King James Version in catechism class. It had always been one of my mother's favorites, and had special meaning for me that day.

"The Lord is my shepherd; I shall not want. He maketh me to lie down in green pastures; He leadeth me beside the still waters. He restoreth my soul; He leadeth me in the paths of righteousness for His name's sake.

"Yea, though I walk through the valley of the shadow of death, I will fear no evil; for Thou art with me; Thy rod and Thy staff they comfort me. Thou preparest a table before me in the presence of mine enemies; Thou anointest my head with oil; my cup runneth over.

"Surely goodness and mercy shall follow me all the days of my life; and I will dwell in the house of the Lord forever."

I prayed for God to protect me and not let my blood be shed on foreign soil. But I felt no peace—only a sense of gnawing in my guts. I felt that God was not pleased with me. What had I done wrong? What had I said that was wrong?

After some thought, I realized my prayer was very selfish. I was no more worthy of a long life than the other soldiers and sailors that had died in our nation's wars. God would not have me value my life as more worthy to be spared in war than any other mother's son.

I acknowledged that my life was in His hands, and if I should suffer injury or loss of my life in war, I prayed that God would find a means to comfort my parents and my brother. But I still didn't have a sense of peace. I didn't feel that God was pleased with me or with my prayers. Was I just frightened by the future? Was something missing?

My thoughts turned to King Solomon and his prayer for wisdom. I thought about how God had been pleased to answer that prayer. But I didn't need wisdom. I needed courage. So I prayed God would give me the courage to do my duty, no matter what happened to me. I asked for nothing more than that and left the matter in God's hands.

I sat there for some time. I didn't hear a voice from heaven or see any angels, but the gnawing in my gut was gone. I felt at peace. I felt in my heart that God had heard me and that He was at last pleased that I had just left matters in His hands. I also felt assured that Jesus would give me courage and be with me—no matter what happened to me.

I then promised God that, if by His mercy I came out of the war alive, I would return to give thanks on this same rock by the shore on Lake of the Woods.

While I felt at peace with God, I still was sorry that Dad and I never had the time to fix up the old sailboat and explore the Canadian side of Lake of the Woods. Even today, as I pen these words, I still feel that loss.

I called Dad at Grygla to say good-bye, and hugged my mother as we both fought to avoid tears. I decided to drive the long route to Minneapolis by way of Grand Forks and Fargo, North Dakota, where I again tried to make plane reservations to San Francisco. All flights were booked, so I asked to be put on the waiting list in Minneapolis.

I used the extra time to drive by Concordia College in Moorhead, Minnesota. I thought about Professor Carl Ylvisaker and how I had enjoyed his Bible teaching. Back in 1943, all of the theology teachers and most of the academic teachers at Concordia believed that the Bible was the inerrant word of God. How things have changed in these post-modern times.

I drove by the Ylvisaker house, but there was no one there, so I continued on to Minneapolis to the Phi Rho Sigma Fraternity house, where my brother John was waiting up for me. We talked until late into the night. John expressed the hope that we might go into practice together some day. That option seemed as distant as my future in the Far East.

As a student at Concordia College, I had listened to Cora Martinson and other China missionaries talk of their adventures in China, and I had felt drawn to the idea of being a missionary some day. I was not ready to make any commitments, except to the Lord.

The next few days were full of confusion. I received no new orders from the Army and continued to have difficulty getting a flight reservation. To this day, I am only sure of my departure date from Minneapolis because of John's letter, sent to Williams, Minnesota. John's letter, copied below, was among more than 100 letters that my mother had saved.

Dear Mother and Dad,   *July 5, 1950*

Well, the news of the day is one sentence. Bob left on the 5:30 plane for California this evening. He had a time getting reservations but finally got them at the last minute and packed and took off in a big hurry. His plans for music, car, etc. just didn't pan out as he wanted. Also the trip to California for both of us just wasn't to be I guess. At any rate, the car is here and will sell if the car prices go as they well might if the present situation cuts down production.

Bob was in a rather good mood, seemed like it is just another fast starting chapter in many that have been open to him since he started into college from high school. Never a wasted moment. One of these days when we both get off at the same time we'll take a good vacation. Might even be fishing. Bob mentioned all the changes up at home. Now that the trip out west looks temporarily or more like permanently out of the way for this summer—will probably get that time up at the lake.

He also said you folks were coming down this forthcoming week. We start our finals on your second day here so may not see much of you. Better get back to the studies. It looks like some rough sailing ahead.

Love, son John

After all the Army's rush to have me leave Lake of the Woods on June 27th, I was not able to get on a flight from Minneapolis to San Francisco until July 5th, and that flight was a red-eye special. I landed after midnight. Not being a sophisticated traveler, I asked in the airport if there was local transportation to Camp Stoneman. Not finding any military transport available, I tried to sleep in the airport without much success.

I wandered around outside the airport and foolishly ended up negotiating with a cab driver who said he would take me to Camp Stoneman. After driving for an hour, the cab driver pulled up in front of a little hotel, said we were near Camp Stoneman, but the base was closed at this hour, and that was as far as he was going that night.

Having no other option, I got out of the cab with my suitcase. Since I was not at my destination, we had an unpleasant argument about the cab fare. I finally paid the cab driver more than I wanted to pay, but much less than he wanted to receive. The cab driver threatened to call the police and I said that was fine with me because perhaps the police could help me get to Camp Stoneman. He finally left in a big huff.

I managed to get a cheap room in the little hotel. The hotel clerk told me he had never heard of Camp Stoneman. With that discouraging admission, I decided I was too tired to think anymore about finding the elusive Camp Stoneman until I'd had some rest.

After six hours sleep, a bacon and egg breakfast, and some telephone calls to Camp Stoneman, I found that I still had a long way to go. In fact, the hour-long cab trip in the night had not been of help at all, since I had been driven in the wrong direction. I wondered if the cab driver had just taken me to a location near his home. I also thought I might enjoy taking that cab driver hunting in northern Minnesota and lose him in the woods for a night or two. Fortunately, the next cab driver knew right where to go.

The next few days consisted of long periods of waiting and brief periods of orientation lectures in military field medicine for new medical and dental officers, all of whom enduring an involuntary trip to the Far East. Under normal conditions, the orientation program for new Army Medical Corps Officers would have been a four-week training program at the Army Medical Field Service School at Fort Sam Houston, Texas. But July 1950 was not a normal time. There was a war going on that we were fast losing, and there was an immediate need for more doctors in Japan and Korea.

Many of the doctors in transit at Camp Stoneman in July 1950 had been under Army sponsorship in civilian or military internships or residencies. Some of them had been pulled out of their residencies to be sent to war. I found a medical school classmate, Ervin Kjenaas, in my group. It was good to see a friend in the small crowd of unhappy doctors. Kjenaas had been in an internal medicine residency at Letterman Army Hospital and had just gotten married. His honeymoon trip had been suddenly abbreviated and intensified by the unexpected quick goodbye. Kjenaas claimed to be sexually exhausted from his shortened honeymoon. I told him that I didn't feel sorry for him since he'd at least had a honeymoon.

At the same time, I was relieved that I wouldn't be separated from a wife. For most of us, our worst nightmares had come true. Some crazy Communists in North Korea had started a war, and that war had not only interrupted our family lives and post-graduate training plans, but it had also placed our own lives in real jeopardy. Our busy medical training world had been turned upside down.

We were informed that only doctors that had completed their residencies would be assigned to hospitals. A number of doctors there, including Kjenaas and me, had not completed a residency. Those doctors who had completed two years or less of post-graduate medical training were to be assigned to outpatient dispensaries or to field military units. That news resulted in groans rather than applause.

The medical service corps captain giving the briefing seemed to relish giving bad news to our little group of unhappy doctors, who had no desire to be traveling in the direction of a war, much less to be assigned to field military units. Most of us didn't know one military unit from another, since such things were not taught in medical school.

Our instructor increased the discomfort level by giving an oral quiz.

"Who can tell me the composition of an infantry battalion?" he asked.

No one wanted to answer that question, even if they knew, for fear it might increase their chances of being sent to an infantry battalion. The instructor asked to see the hands of those with prior military service. A few hands went up, but no one had been in an infantry battalion. The instructor saw my hand raised, and asked me if I knew what an infantry battalion was. I had to say that I didn't, because my prior military experience had been in Navy V-5 and V-12 units during World War II.

I might have been able to tell him the difference between a destroyer, a cruiser, a battleship, and an aircraft carrier, but he didn't ask that question. I was also able to identify most World War II military aircraft. But he didn't ask that question, either, and I didn't volunteer to tell him anything he didn't ask. Proverb 17:28 seemed appropriate advice for the occasion: "Even a fool is thought wise if he keeps silent."

The instructor explained that the infantry battalion was composed of about 1000 fighting men, commanded by an infantry lieutenant colonel. Each infantry battalion had a medical platoon of about 35 men. There was one medical service corps (MSC) officer and one medical corps (MC) officer in each battalion medical platoon. He went on to explain that Army doctors who had not completed their specialty training would be classified as general medical officers (GMO) and may be assigned to the military units actually fighting the war. This clarification caused even more groans.

The instructor opened two field medical chests and spread the contents out on the floor, with the cheery suggestion that we should all familiarize ourselves with what was inside, since we would find similar medical chests in the Army's battalion aid stations in Korea. At that moment, I decided I didn't much care for the MSC officer giving the briefing. I also regretted that I was not preparing to sail across Lake of the Woods instead of preparing to fly across the Pacific Ocean. But I was glad that my parents and brother were not listening to the orientation.

I then realized that I wasn't listening to the instructor, either. I looked around and saw that most of us had tuned the instructor out. I began to wonder what Rachel was doing in St. Cloud, Minnesota. I resolved to write to her when I got to

Japan. Would I ever see her again? How long would I be away from home? How many in this room would not return home at all? There were a great many unanswerable questions. Truly, only the Lord knew the answers. But I continued to fret, even though I knew there was no use in fretting about things I couldn't control. So I tried to think of the words to "Trust and Obey," and hummed the old hymn to myself, but I could only recall the first verse and chorus:

"When we walk with the Lord, in the light of his word.
What a glory he sheds on the way! While we do His good will,
He abides with us still, and with all who will trust and obey.

"Trust and obey, for there is no other way,
to be happy with Jesus, but to trust and obey."

After the orientation lecture, I went up to sort through the contents of the field medical chests. There was an assortment of bandages, splints, hemostats, Vaseline gauze, slings, tourniquets, a sphygmomanometer (blood pressure apparatus), a stethoscope, roller bandages, roller tape, assorted pills and injections, a box of half-grain morphine tartrate Syrettes, and many other items.

A doctor from New York remarked that if he could get his hands on a few footlockers full of morphine tartrate Syrettes, he could make a fortune in New York. Another said he preferred Scotch whiskey. All I could think about was how much things had changed since I left the comforts of the University of Minnesota.

With the demonstration of two field medical chests, the medical officer's orientation to the Army was completed. Since our orientation session to the Army had taken only three hours, I couldn't help but wonder why they usually took four weeks to cover the same material at the Medical Field Service School in Fort Sam Houston, Texas.

Most of the new Army doctors retired quickly to the Officers' Club for alcohol therapy. Some tried to call home while others sat down to write the first of many letters home. I wished that I had a girlfriend with whom to share personal thoughts. It would be nice to love someone and be loved in return.

That line of thinking caused me to remember the children's hymn, "Jesus Loves Me." I was back to basics! Somebody did love me and I found that comforting during that transition into the unknown. I also felt sorry for those who were really making the transition all alone, with no one who really cared about them. It was comforting to realize that God was still there—although I wondered why God allowed wars to happen. Perhaps we will know some day.

Mother standing on the large boulder while Patsy, the dog,
tries to join her (this photo was taken from a boat during a period
of low water); summer 1939

Bob's favorite place to sit and daydream, meditate, and pray;
the large boulder by Lake of the Wood (this photo was taken during
a period of high water); summer 1998

Chapter Three
An unexpected nice hospital assignment in Japan
July 12, 1950 – October 24, 1950

The next morning, we were all bussed to Fairfield Army Airport, north of San Francisco, to board flights to Japan. The propeller-powered transport planes were flying the great circle route to Japan with fueling stops either in Alaska or in the Aleutian Islands, depending on weather conditions. I became separated from Ervin Kjenaas on the way to Japan because the plane I was loaded onto was delayed. Someone said we were overloaded. The following series of letters were written home during the next three months.

Dear Dad and Mother, *14 July 1950 11 P.M.*

Well, I am still in the States because of a transportation bottleneck. I have been at Fairfield Army airport for two days now (40 miles north of San Francisco). There was a group of about 150 medical officers and administrators who came out here. They filled three chartered planes to excess so about nine of us had to stay to wait for later shipment. They simply withdrew nine names from the list and I happened to be among them. I hope to get a plane tomorrow.

I still don't know my ultimate destination. We will be reassigned in Japan or probably have already been assigned.

The weather here is very hot during the day but nice and cool at night. Everything is burned dry (sun) here except where it is irrigated. Lawn and everything needs to be irrigated or it would be a desert. The next time you hear from me I will probably be in Japan.

Love, Bob

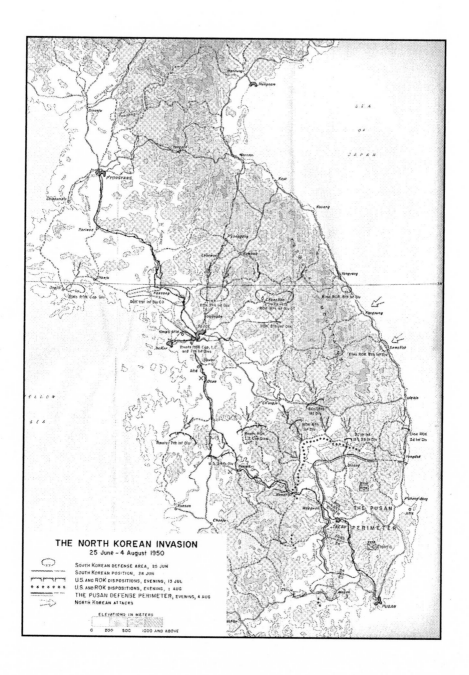

THE NORTH KOREAN INVASION
25 June – 4 August 1950

SOUTH KOREAN DEFENSE AREA, 25 JUN
SOUTH KOREAN POSITION, 28 JUN
U.S. AND ROK DISPOSITIONS, EVENING, 13 JUL
U.S. AND ROK DISPOSITIONS, EVENING, 1 AUG
THE PUSAN DEFENSE PERIMETER, EVENING, 4 AUG
NORTH KOREAN ATTACKS

ELEVATIONS IN METERS
0   200   500   1000 AND ABOVE

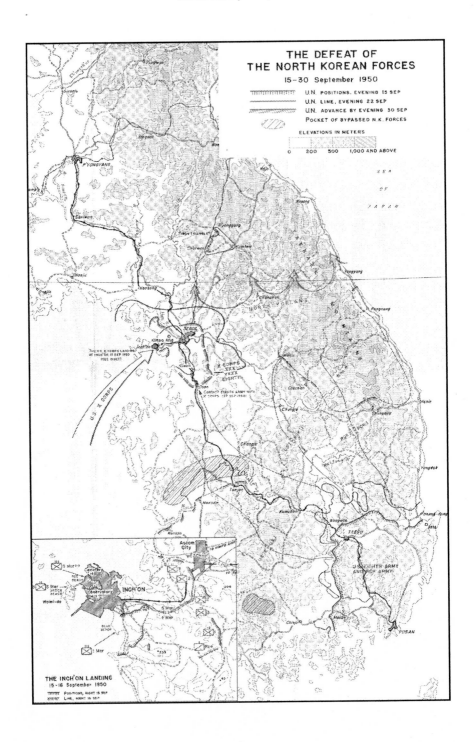

Dear Dad and Mother,   *19 July 1950*

Well, I arrived safely in Japan after a long tiring plane ride along the great circle route. That is by Alaska. I took a lot of pictures while in the air. I hope they turn out well.

At present I am in Yokohama at 115th Station hospital but have not had a definite assignment as yet. A good number of the medics are being formed in surgical combat groups and leaving for Korea. My old roommate, Kjenaas, is in the bunk next to me. He leaves for Korea tomorrow. The spirit and morale here seems to be high. I have not seen much of the Japanese as yet except on a distant impersonal basis. They are an extremely hard-working people. It is quite hot here this time of year.

I will know where I will be assigned in a day or two. I have received no mail as yet and it probably would be best to withhold writing until I can send a more permanent address.

Continued on 20 July 1950

I didn't get this letter mailed and it's just as well. I have been assigned to the 128th Station Hospital, which is about twenty miles from Tokyo. This is a beautiful camp and used mainly for convalescent cases, venereal cases, and serves as dispensary for the three Army camps near here. At present it is rather light. There are five medical officers, two dentists, two administrators, nurses and large group of enlisted personnel running the place. Commanding officer is a major and extremely well liked.

There is so much I could write even after having been here only two days. I have learned a few Japanese words already. Most of the personnel who have been here one to two years speak fluent Japanese.

MacArthur is worshipped by the Japanese. Every day when he goes and comes from work 20 to 30,000 people try to stand near by just to see him. Although the Army personnel rather hate his guts, I have not found one to admit they didn't think he was doing a wonderful job in Japan. He is an extremely brilliant man and a capable administrator. It is true he rules with an iron hand and is arrogant and conceited but I guess that's what it takes. He gets his own way. Apparently, Washington doesn't dare interfere with any of his policies because he has such prestige and he is usually always right. No one wants to tangle with him.

This station is well equipped. I neglected to say it also is a physical reconditioning center for fracture cases, etc. We have horses for riding, gymnasium, golf courses, swimming pool, tennis court, etc. All maintenance work is done by Japanese who are very competent and trustworthy. One of the fellows left his wallet in the shower, a maid ran to him with it and insisted he count all the money in front of her. No one wants to be suspected of dishonesty. It is a disgrace here.

Love, Bob

128ᵗʰ St. Hospital, APO 201 Unit 2, C/0 P.M. S.F.
Dear Folks,   *Aug. 1, 1950*

I received the first letters yesterday and today. Enclosed are some pictures taken of the trip over. I would appreciate it if you could get a large photograph album and put them in. I will be sending pictures home and it should be quite interesting to keep it up to date. It would serve as a picture diary.

We are getting in more casualties. The losses on both sides are very heavy and the fighting fierce. One patient had personally shot over 900 North Koreans with his light machine gun. The only reason they retreat is because of lack of ammunition or else the gun gets so hot he has to retreat to give it time to cool off. You probably get more war news than we do. The only direct news we get is from casualties. Stars and Stripes gives the overall picture, but little detailed information.

The general opinion over here is that we should have complete mobilization again—also re-arm to limited extent Japan and Germany and get the war over with. If MacArthur asked for Japanese volunteers he would have three million soldiers overnight.

Most of the Japanese Communists are Koreans. Since MacArthur passed the word that he didn't like the Communists the Japanese people here have automatically and obediently been persecuting Communists. MacArthur is so worshipped that most Japanese would go to great lengths to please him.

Love, Bob

It should be noted that before the Korean War started, a big part of the medical workload at the 128ᵗʰ Army Hospital was treating venereal diseases. It was common to have soldiers with three venereal diseases—syphilis, gonorrhea, and chancroid—at the same time. This triple infection was called a full house—as if they were playing poker—which, in a sense, was what they had been doing. It was a nasty combination with destructive ulcerations that required immediate treatment with multiple drugs.

One of the doctors had been taking graphic color slides of diseased genitalia to terrorize the soldiers during lectures on VD control. The unofficial recommendation to avoid VD was to get a little hooch (a place to live) and a steady live-in girlfriend, called a moose—short for *musume*, or girl, in Japanese. Sleeping with a dictionary in a little hooch just off the base also helped the GIs to learn more Japanese. Many of these relationships ended up with Amer-Asian children and in marriage. But for many American soldiers, it was a just a very pleasant Madame Butterfly-type interlude in Japan. But now it was a very pleasant interlude suddenly interrupted by the Korean War for most of the occupation GIs.

When I first arrived and heard so many GIs speaking Japanese, I thought they spoke fluently. I soon learned their Japanese was simple ungrammatical household chatter and romantic talk. I also learned from a Japanese doctor that there were many Koreans living in Japan, but they were considered to be lower class citizens by the Japanese. Some of the Koreans were reported to be sympathetic to the small Communist party in Japan. But in general, the Communist party in Japan seemed to have little influence.

Dear Dad and Mother,   *14 Aug 1950*

The last two weeks have been rather busy. We have about two hundred Korean War casualties to care for now as well as our usual load. We get a new batch of casualties in whenever we can discharge enough back to duty to make room for them. At present we are getting caught up and a few more doctors have been assigned to lighten the load. Our patients are a mixture of shrapnel, gunshot, dysentery, and malaria.

The stories they tell about the North Koreans is that they are plenty tough, good soldiers and it's only the civilian conscripts from South Korea drafted in the North Korean army that are poor soldiers. The newspapers make the picture look better than it is by emphasizing the good and playing down the bad. It is just as well they did because all too often the real truth would hurt our morale and tell the enemy where and when to strike. At least the picture is getting better every day.

What I miss most is the Minneapolis Star *paper. If I just could get one of those a week, maybe the Sunday paper, it would help to keep up on what's going on at home as well as over here.*

I mailed a present home for you, Mother. I wonder if you have received it yet. I have another couple of things to send home which will have to be as Christmas presents since I don't know just when they will arrive or whether I will be able to go shopping a month or so from now. I am going to send home a 35mm slide projector for my color pictures. I will mail home the pictures as I get them for safekeeping. Did you get the pictures of Alaska, etc. that I took?

Actually, I am extremely fortunate to be stationed where I am. It's very pleasant working conditions and country atmosphere. There still is a good possibility of going to Korea but at least it would be a lot safer over there now than three weeks ago when I came over.

I have taken a couple of short trips into neighboring Japanese villages and find them very interesting. I have a lot of fun with the children. They all know the words "Hello," "GI," "thank you" and "good-bye." They love to pose for pictures.

I have been into Tokyo and toured around the town one Sunday but there is much to see. If it were not for the war I am sure I would have had a wonderful time over here.

I was amused at my painting of yesteryear. I am returning it to you for safe keeping so I can show it to your grandchildren.

I often wonder how long it will be before I get home again. It may be a year or ten years depending on fate and Russia I guess.

I have Rachel's picture with me as a reminder of what I would like to have in my home but I suppose when the time comes I will have new interests and she, probably a family.

Hope all goes well at home. I have had but one letter from John so far. He is busy in Minneapolis now I guess. Time for sleep.

Love, Bob

We were quite busy with both outpatient and inpatient duties from an increasing number of American casualties from the Korean War. In the outpatient clinics, we saw the dependents of soldiers who had been in occupation duty and were now in the middle of a very messy war in Korea. Most of these dependents worried about their husbands or fathers fighting in Korea. But a few female dependents became flirtatious with their husbands gone. I decided to be professional and kind, but avoid getting involved with flirtatious wives left behind in Japan. Other new stateside arrivals seemed to take advantage of any sexual opportunity that presented itself overseas.

It was nice to start getting letters from home to answer.

Dear Dad,   *Aug. 28, 1950*

I received your letter of the 21ˢᵗ today. Seven days is pretty quick service. I have written three or four times so before you get this letter you should have some others. I am surprised however that mail gets through as well as it does.

I am still at the 128ᵗʰ Hospital. At present we have nine doctors assigned here including the commanding officer, Major Buerig, who by the way is one of the finest officers and persons I have ever met. He is universally well-liked and gets good work done by his staff simply because nobody would want to do anything to displease him.

We average between 250 to 300 patients as well as run two dispensaries for sick call, so the eight medics who care for patients are kept rather busy. The Major doesn't have time away from his administration to actually care for patients. I am in charge of all medical cases and average 50 to 100 patients. I have another medic, a fellow from Texas, name of Cpt. Leinhard, who is assigned under me. We split the patient load and once a month we have joint rounds to see each other's cases. It is interesting work. Some diseases I have never seen before, such as malaria, Schistosomiasis (a parasitic worm infection of intestines). We all have our share of bullet wounds and shrapnel cases to care for. The fighting in Korea is rugged. I have one patient with severe burns on his hand from touching the barrel of his automatic rifle. Another patient was shot behind the right ear and the bullet came out his left cheekbone. Believe it or not he wasn't even knocked unconscious and has no permanent damage. Strange things can happen with war wounds.

Last night we were listening to Seoul City Sue on the radio. She is the English-speaking North Korean radio propagandist. To hear her talk, the Americans are merciless fiends and the South Koreans are puppets and traitors.

We have managed to go to some Japanese hotels for parties, trying out the Japanese food and drink. Their idea of taking the shoes off on entering the house is a good one. Their houses are clean as can be.

I have not heard from John since school ended. I hope he didn't do poorly in his finals and is taking make-ups if needed.

Another fellow and I bought a jeep together for $300 each. We have a legal agreement on it. So far we have taken a few trips on Sunday afternoon and evening. There are many spots of interest within a short radius of here and also it is good to get away from the hospital even if it is for a few hours.

I have bought you a birthday present, which I hope to mail as soon as I get to Yokohama again. I hope you will find time to use it in the future. I bought John an ivory chess set but don't tell him. I am mailing it to him as a surprise.

Just how long I will be here I don't know. I could go to Korea tomorrow or stay for two years at the 128th.

Sorry to hear about Granny but we all know it was for the best and everyone including Granny would have been better off if it had happened several years ago.

It looks like we will be involved in war for the next ten years. The next move is up to Russia. I personally expect Communist China to attack us and thus leave Russia free for further preparing. The Korean War was a sad mistake for them because it is giving us a chance to prepare. It is inevitable that the standard of living in the U.S. will fall but that would be better than being collectivized or sent to labor camps if you don't agree with the government. Bad as our government is, they still can't shoot you for criticizing it.

The people here feel that if they had a man like MacArthur in Europe they would be a lot better off there. He just doesn't tolerate any foolishness from Communists and politicians. When the Russians objected to his policies here, he told his interpreters to give them the word for bologna and show them the door.

Love, Bob

Dear Mother and Dad,   *10 Sept. 1950 Sunday night*
A short note before bed: First of all there is no change in my status. I could be called for Korean duty tomorrow or stay for ten years for all I know. Two of the medics from this hospital were called yesterday which leaves the remaining MDs with more work.

I received the paper and clippings. They are interesting to read. I spent the afternoon at a Japanese doctor's home and had supper there. It was a very enjoyable and interesting experience. He and his wife were very gracious and courteous hosts as only the Japanese can be. I think Dad that you would like their food. Meat, fat, and various vegetables, fried over charcoal fire. Highly seasoned. Rice, fish, and soups that I never tasted before.

I bought a 35mm slide projector, which I shall mail home after I have used it awhile. I will send home my color pictures as I take them. The projector over here is much cheaper than stateside. I am also going to send home a few records of Japanese songs and a photograph album. Enclosed are a few more pictures.

P.S. Had an earthquake today. It shook the BOQ for about a full minute. I guess Tokyo was rattled good. No one worries about the quakes here. Minor ones are frequent. It probably cracked the cement in the swimming pool again.

Love, Bob

Dear Mother,   15 Sept. 1950

Enclosed are some more snaps of Japan. I have some good color shots also. I was in Tokyo and visited a little Lutheran mission, which has just started up. It's headed by a young former China missionary, Olaf Hansen. He is from the Evangelical Lutheran Church of New York State. They just started but are growing rapidly. MacArthur is very encouraging for the Protestant missionary groups.

If you could get some of the corner tabs to paste in the photo album it would make it easy to take pictures out and read the writing on the back. I will mail a photo album home soon. The pictures tell more of Japan than I can say in words. I guess Confucius was right.

Love, Bob

When I wrote the letter on 15 September, I was not aware of the two-phase (between tides) amphibious assault on Inchon that was underway by the 1st Marine Division and the 7th Infantry Divisions. The successful amphibious landing at Inchon by the 1st Marine Division composed of the 1st, 7th, and 5th Marine Regiments, led to the recapture of Seoul that General MacArthur announced on 26 September. It took three more days for the Marines and the U.S. Army 7th Infantry Division to mop up the remaining North Korean People's Army (NKPA) defenders. The successful Inchon Invasion effectively broke the back of the NKPA and brought an end to the blood shedding in the Pusan Perimeter.

The Marine Corps literally had to scrape the bottom of their manpower barrel to bring the 1st Marine Division to full fighting strength for the Inchon Invasion. Moreover, the U.S. Army 7th Infantry Division, which landed after the 1st Marine Division cleared the way for them at Inchon, was in far worse shape than the 1st Marines in both manpower and equipment. The Army's 7th Infantry Division, stationed in Japan on peaceful occupation duty, had been stripped of many of its officers and key cadre to supplement the thinning ranks of the 1st Cavalry Divisions and the 2nd, 24th, and 25th Infantry Divisions that were struggling to hang on in the Pusan Perimeter in Korea. Many of the units in these divisions had suffered 50 to 70 percent casualties. Their replacements were cooks, clerks, band members, and new raw recruits of both American and Korean vintage. They went into battle with orders to hold or retake strategic hills or die.

In the Pusan Perimeter battles, they were fortunate that the NKPA continually made the mistake of attacking everywhere at once so that they had few fresh troops available to exploit their breakthrough opportunities. But Gen. Walker had his hands full shifting his forces around to plug the holes being punched in the main line of resistance (MLR). To his great credit, Gen. Walker fought on against very formidable odds. But in the midst of these crucial battles, much to the consternation of Gen. Walker and the beleaguered defenders of the Pusan Perimeter, MacArthur suddenly switched the replacement pipeline from the 8th Army in South Korea to the 7th Division in Japan just before the Inchon Invasion. Still lacking essential manpower in the 7th Division, MacArthur ordered 5000 Koreans drafted from the streets, refugee camps, and out of the rice paddies within the Pusan Perimeter to be sent to Japan, clothed, and instantly trained, as if that were possible, in order to fill the empty manpower slots in the rifle companies of the 7th Division, as they prepared for the imminent amphibious assault. These Korean, involuntary draftees from the Pusan Perimeter were called KATUSA, which was an acronym for Korean Augmentation to the United States Army. Never in the history of the American Army have we asked so much of so few experienced junior officers and NCOs, who did their best with faulty equipment and without interpreters or dictionaries to turn the tide in a vicious war that had been using up raw American and Korean recruits by the hundreds, if not thousands, in the war's daily battles. If this was a police action, as President Truman claimed, I would truly feel sorry for the police.

The one bright spot for the 7th Infantry Division was that the U.S. Army, in their desperate search for skilled military manpower, had stripped the Artillery School at Fort Sill, Oklahoma and the Infantry School at Fort Benning, Georgia of their most capable training NCOs, to enable the artillery men and weapon crews of the 7th Infantry Division to shoot straight and also to give on-the-job training in the middle of battles to the many new GIs and KATUSA draftees that had somehow managed to stay alive.

The recapture of Seoul by the 1st Marine and 7th Infantry Divisions stopped the blood-letting in the U.S. 8th Army defending the Pusan area in South Korea. Gen. Walker's 8th Army was able to take a deep breath and attack the NKPA. With dwindling supplies, the NKPA was soon forced to retreat in disorder.

In the meantime, back in Japan, we had a great surge in our casualty load during and after the Inchon Invasion with no time for letter writing until October. But then, to our great joy, the casualty loads slacked off. It was time to share the good news.

Dear Dad and Mother,　　　　*2 Oct. 1950*

The war is looking good now and should soon be over unless Russia decides to start something somewhere else. I missed out on the shooting end of the war and in a way I feel bad about that although admittedly I am better off. I guess it's just a craving for excitement in me that hasn't yet burned out with age. The stream of casualties has now fallen off greatly—probably because the North Koreans are disorganized and often out of ammunition. I hope I don't get stuck in the occupation force of Korea but there is a good chance that may happen. As it is, they have more doctors over here than they need but I see by the paper that they are drafting more.

Two weekends ago (just before the Inchon Invasion) I went to a seashore mountainside resort called Atami. It's about 40 miles down the coast from Yokohama. Fred Snyder, my partner in the jeep, and I stayed at a Japanese hotel and tried the oriental way of life, including food, clothing, steaming bath in large pool, and sleeping on a mat on the floor. They have many customs which I think are good, such as removing your shoes at the door and wearing sandals in the house. Clothes are removed in the room and the maid presses them and from then on in the hotel you just wear a Kimono. I took some pictures, which I mailed to John and he should be sending on to you. As a matter of fact, the Kimonos are worn in the streets at the resort towns as often as ordinary clothes.

John is probably hard at work now and the crops are probably in. It is getting chilly now and the rice crop is being harvested all around. We go into our winter uniforms soon.

I hope to be able to get down to southern Japan because that is where the real resort centers are. I am sending a couple of photo albums home. I bought one but later found a much better one in a Japanese store and couldn't resist buying it. My color pictures are very interesting. I will try and mail some to you by Christmas along with my projector.

Love, Bob

On October 1, 1950, Mao Tse-tung announced to the people of China that the Chinese people would not tolerate foreign aggression and would not stand aside if the imperialists wantonly invaded the territory of their neighbor. This was noted in the local press on October 3, 1950, but was considered to just be more Communist propaganda. In truth, it was a declaration to the Chinese people that the Communist government would no longer be subservient to the West, and indicated that the grandeur and hegemony of China would again be sought with force by the Chinese Communist leadership.

The intervention by China greatly inflated the pride of the Chinese people. I recall some old China hands remarking that the Chinese would rather be number one in the world under Communism than number ten in the world under a democratic government. Time will reveal if this is an accurate assessment.

To make the matter clear to Western governments, the Chinese foreign minister, Chou En-Lai, called the Indian Ambassador, Sardar K. M. Panikkar to his office on 3 October, 1950, where he was given a clear message to relay: If the United States' or the United Nations' forces crossed the 38th Parallel, the Chinese People's Republic would send troops to aid the People's Republic of Korea. They wouldn't take that action, however, if only South Korean troops crossed the border.

This message was sent to the United Nations in New York, to Washington, D.C., and to European capitals, with the added advice from India that the U.N. forces must not cross the 38th Parallel into North Korea.

Washington relayed the message about the Chinese intentions to MacArthur as information, but without comment or fresh instructions. In effect, Washington responded with silence, which assured the entrance of the Chinese Communist Forces (CCF) into North Korea.

There was something the Americans didn't know at that time that gave China much greater freedom to be belligerent in 1950. The Russians, through master spy Kim Philby, had an open line into the most private discussions between Harry Truman and Clement Attlee, who was Prime Minister of Britain from 1945-1951. Because of concern over Hong Kong, Clement Attlee had insisted that under no circumstances would U.N. forces ever be used against Chinese territory. That was the price Harry Truman paid to get the Brits to enter the Korean War. Unfortunately for America, Kim Philby was stationed in Washington, D.C. between 1949 and 1951. Philby was one of the "magnificent five" British traitors from Cambridge who had been spying for Russia since Arnold Deutsch, an Austrian Communist working for the KGB, had recruited them in the mid-1930s. Philby knew most of Britain's secret deals and probably more, because while in Washington, Philby became a family friend of James Angleton, the CIA Chief of Counterintelligence. It is worth noting that few, if any, of the books on the Korean War have mentioned the Philby factor behind China's belligerence in 1950.

Angleton apparently burned the top-secret memo file on all of the discussions between Angleton and Philby in his embarrassment after Philby defected to Moscow in 1963—ten years after the Korean War cease-fire. If Russia and China were informed by a reliable spy informant, such as Philby, that the U.N. forces in Korea would be self-prohibited from attacking Chinese territory, then the intervention of the CCF into the Korean conflict was assured, because war damage would be limited to Korea. China couldn't hope for a better deal than that.[1]

It is unlikely that Truman told MacArthur about his binding deal with Attlee concerning never attacking China, no matter what China did—a deal that meant MacArthur would be forced to fight the Chinese only in Korea with one hand tied behind his back. The subsequent disagreements between Truman and MacArthur that led to MacArthur's dismissal were primarily about striking back at China directly.

The Truman/Attlee prohibition against attacking Chinese territory also had a disastrous impact on the protracted and bloody cease-fire talks that were to go on later in Korea. The Chinese and North Koreans were able to rub America's nose again and again in the fact that they were far less concerned about excessive and needless loss of lives than we were. We made their day by cringing over the continuing, losses along the cease-fire line. Had we blockaded and blasted some of the Chinese coastal cities in response to their continuing violation of cease-fire talks by bringing in new supplies of weapons to sustain nightly bloody assaults over the many cease-fire hills, they may have agreed to terms two years earlier.

Before Mao and Chou ever spoke to the Chinese people, they had started moving great armies north to the Korean border. They knew what they were going to do, because they already knew what we were *not* going to do—strike back at China.

In addition, there is another factor that may have been in play. The Chinese mainland had been conquered by the CCF, who had been supplied with weapons both directly from Russia and indirectly from the United States via the failures of Chiang Kai-shek's armies.

In spite of the brutality of the Communist regime, nearly all Chinese longed for the day when China would again be the number one power in the world. A Chinese Communist humiliation or defeat of Western nations, especially Britain and the United States, nations that had humiliated China with gunboat diplomacy and invasions during the last century, would win the hearts and loyalty of the Chinese masses. Neither Truman nor MacArthur seemed to recognize that China desired to be a world-respected power more than our partner for world peace.

At the time of the Chinese announcements, I was too caught up in my hospital duties to pay much attention. I had made a sincere effort to be nice to the

---

[1] Wright, Peter. *Spy Catcher*. Viking Press. 1987; page 41, Philby was appointed M16 Head of Station in Washington, D.C. in 1944. It should be assumed that master spy Philby relayed all inside information to Russia.

Japanese workers at the 128th Station Hospital. Japanese culture and value system intrigued me, and I wished to understand it better. One day in early August, as I came on duty, I noticed one of the Japanese nurses had been crying. I asked her what was wrong, but she wouldn't tell me.

A little later, a Japanese male orderly came up to me when no one was watching and said in his limited English, "Captain, you want know why Miss Zige cry?"

"Yes," I replied. "Why Miss Zige cry?"

The orderly said, "You no get me trouble if I tell you why Miss Zige cry?"

"No," I replied. "I no get you trouble if you tell me why Miss Zige cry,"

"Okay," he said. "You meet me Sagamiona Bar after work. I tell you why Miss Zige cry."

So we agreed to meet about 5:30 PM at the bar.

I was more than a little curious about what the young orderly might tell me about Miss Zige, and I wondered what he was afraid of. When we met in the bar, he again wanted assurance that I would not get him into trouble.

Finally he said, "Captain Laymore is very bad man."

"Why is Captain Laymore very bad man?"

"Captain Laymore in charge of Japanese workers. He makes Japanese girls in hospital go pom-pom with him or lose jobs. He say they Communist. Miss Zige no want pom-pom with Captain Laymore and he say he fire Miss Zige as Communist. That why Miss Zige cry today."

I talked to the orderly some more and came to feel he was probably telling the truth. "Cpt. Laymore" had shown pornographic movies at stag parties and bragged about not having any lace on his shorts—whatever that meant. He was, by reputation, what the GIs called a coxman. He was part of the U.S. occupation forces in Japan—even though his wife and children were with him. I was angry that Laymore had such power over people's lives.

The next morning, I asked for permission to see the commanding officer (CO). Alone with Maj. Buerig, I related the story, noting that I had told no one else, and was leaving the matter up to him.

The CO thought for a moment and then said, "I have been wondering about that S.O.B. for some time. The last thing I want in the middle of this war is a messy investigation. Fortunately, during a war, there are more convenient ways to handle these matters."

I said nothing as he continued.

"I have on my desk this morning a request for a MSC captain to report to an infantry division in Korea. That bastard will be gone from this hospital tomorrow morning. You can get back to your work, but say nothing about this matter to anyone. You're dismissed."

The following morning, Cpt. Laymore was indeed gone, and to my surprise, I found the Japanese staff greeting me with smiles, lower than usual bows, and special deference. Overnight, I had become a celebrity among the Japanese workers. I was apparently being credited with the sudden departure of the much-disliked Cpt. Laymore. The Japanese staff always seemed to understand what was happening. It seemed Americans, as with all sojourners overseas, were continually being weighed by the native population, and in the case of Cpt. Laymore, he was simply found to be in want of acceptable standards of behavior.

The following morning, I was awakened at 5:00 AM by "Baby-san." Baby-san was the nickname given to a very pretty young Japanese maid who cleaned the officers' quarters.

She was sitting rather intimately on the edge of my bed and smiled as she said, "Captain Jensen good man and you help Japanese people. You like Japanese people. Miss Zige not like Americans. Miss Zige not good for you. But I love Captain Jensen. I want have baby for you. I have key and come see you early every day. Some day you marry me?"

She smiled and silently slipped out to attend to her duties in the bachelor officers' quarters (BOQ). I was left a bit confused, and, of course, tempted by this sudden overture for sensual bliss. But it was obvious that my life could become rather complicated very quickly. That very morning after hospital rounds, I went to see the CO again, and asked about the current need for doctors in Korea.

Maj. Buerig told me that he expected to be levied for doctors for field duty soon. I reminded him that I was single and all the other doctors were married, so I figured I would be the first to go, anyway. He might as well put my name on the top of his list. He didn't tell me whether or not my name was already on the top of the list but I suspected that it might have been. I didn't tell him about the deference of the Japanese workers or about Miss Baby-san, but I felt that it was time for me to move on.

The following day, I was invited by Miss Zige to meet her family. She made it clear that this was to be a Japanese family ceremony of thanks for helping her. No personal relationship was implied and it was not to be assumed. It was over an hour ride on trains, with many changes. Since Miss Zige was from an upper-class family, she didn't wish to sit beside me as we traveled because it would cause gossip to the effect that she had become a GI's girlfriend. Therefore, I was to enter the back door of the train-car and she would enter the front door. I was to watch her carefully and get off and on whenever she got off and on.

I almost missed one train change because I became so interested in watching some children. Zige had to pound on the train door to attract my attention. I barely got off before the train door slammed shut. That was fortunate, because I had no idea where we were or how to get home again.

Zige's parents' home was only a short walk from the final station. There were seven or eight adult members of her family waiting. We stood in a circle without our shoes as I was introduced to her uncle, who was in charge, since Zige's father was recently deceased. I was introduced next to her mother, other uncles and aunts, and a couple of senior family friends, who seemed to be highly respected by all the rest. Zige tried to translate all that was being said, but she had great difficulty finding English words for the very formal Japanese language being used. I am not sure of what all was said, but I gathered that they were thanking me for protecting their daughter's honor.

I was presented with a gift of silk tapestry. I was also presented with Zige's deceased father's gold watch, since I had acted as her father to protect her in her time of need. After a sumptuous meal and many bows and expressions of thanks, I was ushered out by Miss Zige to return on the train—again getting in separate train-car doors and sitting apart.

I watched Zige carefully on the return trip so I would not get lost. When I reached my home station, Miss Zige returned on the train to her home. It was all very formal and proper. I had been thanked and honored, but not really accepted. I was a foreigner who had respected their honor and thereby earned their thanks. They, in their own way, had sought to honor me to repay their debt. They were not soliciting my friendship—they were fulfilling a family obligation.

As I walked back to the Army hospital officers' quarters that night, I thought about Miss Zige and agreed with what Baby-san had said. Miss Teruko Zige was not right for me, but then, neither was Baby-san, although she was much better-looking and certainly far less complicated, as she really did like Americans in general and, of late, me in particular.

Baby-san soon realized that my affections were elsewhere when she saw I had Rachel's picture on my desk in the BOQ. I had put Rachel's picture up as a deterrent to any future amorous invasions in the early hours of the morning, when I would be most vulnerable. As I wondered about what Rachel was doing, I realized that I longed for some encouragement from the other side of the ocean. I wrote to Rachel again to let her know I would be reassigned soon—probably to Korea.

A few days later, I received orders to join the 7th Infantry Regiment. I sold my share in the jeep and reduced the volume of my worldly possessions to duffel bag size. That night, I enjoyed a farewell party with close friends Cpt. Wendell Leinhard (internist) and Cpt. Darrel Vanderploeg (dermatologist). I arranged for several boxes of personal belongings to be sent home and sent Rachel a portrait that a Japanese artist had painted from her snapshot. The painting would not fit in my duffle bag. I later lost Rachel's photo somewhere in Korea.

It had been a very pleasant tour of duty at the 128th. I went around to say *sayonara* to the Japanese staff in the hospital and BOQ. Baby-san bowed with a forced smile and teary eyes as we said good-bye. I gave her an American-style hug, which might have caused her to feel slightly embarrassed. It was difficult to be kind to Baby-san without encouraging the desires she had for a committed relationship.

When I made rounds for the last time, Miss Zige gave me a letter as she bowed to say sayonara. This was an easier, more formal farewell. Ours had been a philosophical relationship. I didn't try to give her a hug because she had made it quite clear that she was not interested in a physical relationship. I sent her letter with the silk tapestry along with my letter home.

Dear Dad and Mother,   *24 Oct. 1950*
Enclosed is a letter, which was given by a Japanese nurse who works here in the hospital. It was intended as a farewell note. This nurse is an extremely bright girl, reads widely and thinks a great deal. Like so many thinkers she has toyed with the idea of Christianity versus Communism, etc. We spent a great deal of time talking about a great many subjects including Christianity and democracy. The Captain Laymore she refers to is a rather shady U.S. Army officer who was connected with black markets, etc., and also was in charge of the Japanese laborers. He had forced some of the girls to do things they didn't want to do. Because of this she had a great deal of hatred for him and for Americans in general. This is the background for the letter, which is self-explanatory in its own self-taught style of English.

Tomorrow I leave by train for Southern Japan to join the 3rd Infantry Division. I have no idea where we are going but we have full field equipment. New Address: 3rd Repel. C., 3rd Inf. Div., APO 468, c/o P.M.S.F.

Also enclosed are a few slides I forgot to mail with my projector and other slides. Hope all goes well at home. Sounds as if this is a good year to have a salary job and not depend on crops.

Love, Bob

(Miss Zige's letter)
Dear Dr. R. T. Jensen,   *Friday, 20 Oct. 1950*
Thank you very, very much for you from the bottom of my heart. You have given tons of Spiritual gifts, which are too precious to appraise, to the people. Sincerity shown by you, with my bad feeling against Captain Laymore will not disappear physically and metaphysically as long as the time lasts. Your warm and kind attitude full of humility in spite of your brilliance must be what we call humanism and true Christianity that was and is the unique motivation for the establishment of peace and philanthropy beyond racial prejudice and it will be the spear head to bring out happiness

and improvement of all the man in the world. Please allow me to appraise your great mental influences and to tell of them as many people as I can contact, parents who brought me up, teachers and friends and not only while you are in the universe but perpetually you'll be made to live within the heart of the people.

Dr. Jensen this means very deep, but I can't explain English very well, if you can understand what means, I'm glad very much. Be good and take care of yourself always.

Truly yours, Miss Zige

The gold watch given to Cpt. Jensen by the family of Miss Teruko Zige; on the inside of the back cover is engraved "COMRAD 85026"

Flying over Alaska; July 1950

Flying over Anchorage, Alaska on the way to the Shimia Island
in the Aleutians; July 1950

U.S. Army 128th Hospital in Japan

Cpt. Jensen in front of the Bachelor Officers' Quarters (BOQ)

Maj. Buerig and wife at an officers' party

Cpt. Jensen (left) and Lt. Fred Snyder (right) dressed in Japanese robes standing in front of their jointly-owned jeep at the hotel Atami; September 1950

Cpt. Wendell Leinhard (left) and Cpt. Darrel Vanderploeg (right)
in front of BOQ

Dr. Nadamoto (left), a Japanese-American, with his Chinese-American wife
(center) and a newly arrived American doctor (right)—welcomed additions to
the staff of the 128th Station Hospital

A post-card of Mt. Fuji as seen from Lake Kawaguchi, Japan

A post-card of Gen. MacArthur's Headquarters in Tokyo; the Japanese people would gather there daily to see Gen. MacArthur arrive and depart.

Miss Watanabi, a Japanese nurse,
who worked in Cpt. Jensen's ward at the 128th Station Hospital

A group of children from the village of Sagamiona, Japan
near the 128th Station Hospital

The local girls' softball team, Japan

The softball team in action near the 128th Station Hospital

Cpt. Jensen (left) and the Japanese youth (right) who ran the officers' club and aided Cpt. Jensen in learning about the Japanese people

A rice field in Japan

Chapter Four
A sake-wacky train ride to join the 7th Infantry Regiment, 3rd Division
October 25, 1950 – October 26, 1950

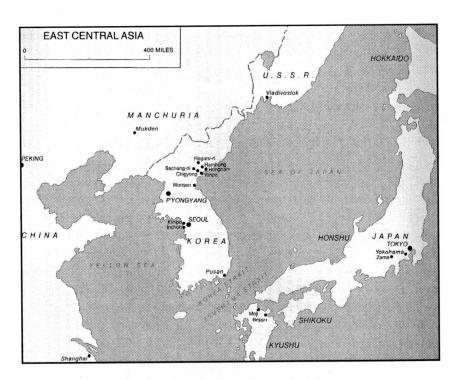

At 6 AM on the morning of 25 October 1950, I reported as instructed to Maj. Buerig in my winter uniform with all of my belongings in a backpack and duffel bag. After saluting Maj. Buerig, I received my military service record to carry and a very warm farewell handshake. I learned that the major would soon be a lieuten-

ant colonel. That didn't surprise me, because he was a top commander and a good doctor. He had seen a lot of service in North Africa and Italy in World War II.

There were 12 enlisted men, including one staff sergeant, waiting for the Army bus to take us to a train bound for Beppu in southern Japan. The sergeant had the service records of the enlisted men. Some had been at the 128th Hospital, but most were from nearby military units. None were happy to leave the occupation duty comforts of Japan for the war in Korea, but most were resigned to their fate. Some even joked about the fact that their turn for rough duty was long overdue. One corporal commented that they had joined the Army and should expect to do their share of the fighting. I noted the corporal had an expert rifleman badge. I thought to myself, some infantry platoon leader will welcome him to Korea.

Since it was going to be an all-day train trip, the hospital kitchen had prepared a big box of sandwiches for us with soft drinks. As we settled into the seats in the railway car, I noted a Caucasian male dressed in a Japanese-type business suit. He was conversing pleasantly in Japanese with some Japanese passengers. As I watched with interest, he looked at me, a captain in the U.S. Army Medical Corps. He nodded with a smile and came over to introduce himself. He said he was a U.S. Army major who worked in civil affairs. "Maj. Dutch" was a linguist who was able to speak Japanese, Mandarin, German, Dutch, and English. He had been educated in both Europe and Asia.

His Army civil affairs job after World War II had been to maintain good relations with mayors and senior officials in the cities along the main rail line from Tokyo to Beppu. He was expected to keep up on who was who and what was happening. He was one of those unusual international personalities who had a flare for languages, great social sensitivity, and the gift of gab attributed to a skilled raconteur.

Maj. Dutch had been given orders to join the 3rd Division as an interpreter and intelligence officer, but had not had time to properly say *sayonara* to all the mayors and other senior officials along the rail line to Beppu. These people had been his special friends and useful contacts for the last few years, and he was reluctant to leave without a proper Japanese-style farewell ceremony. He was trying to come up with a way to compensate for the Army's usual lack of social sensitivity when it came to issuing orders.

While the Army may not have considered Maj. Dutch very important in the big scheme of things, the mayors along the rail line from Tokyo to Beppu apparently thought of him as second only to Gen. MacArthur. Maj. Dutch was by nature a kind person, who had gained Japanese respect by getting to know their families and by helping them in many little ways. Whenever there were problems to be solved, Maj. Dutch knew how to blend in and work both the U.S. Military system and the Japanese social system so that everyone's ego was appropriately stroked and mollified. He had apparently been successful in his job—a job not without a few special perks.

Maj. Dutch felt it was not correct for him to simply disappear, so he had arranged to have the train stop at significant cities, where city officials would be waiting to greet him on the train platform for a grand farewell. He had a big box of gifts that he had purchased himself, all properly wrapped and addressed for each of the mayors' families. His only problem was lack of balance in the farewell ceremonies.

I failed to appreciate the scope of the major's problem, but the fact that he perceived he had a problem tweaked my compassion and interest. I asked how I could help. It was just the opening Maj. Dutch had been waiting for. Before I had time to think about it, he suggested that perhaps my 12 enlisted men and I could provide a retinue behind him at each stop, which would provide some balance to each side in the platform ceremonies as we provided a few respectful salutes and bows with the gift exchanges and farewells.

While this country boy from Minnesota was not up to speed on the retinue business, I felt I might learn something about the local culture, and it also seemed as if it might be a fun thing to do. I couldn't help wondering how late our train would be arriving at Beppu if we had a dozen or more ceremonial stops on the way, but Maj. Dutch didn't seem to think that would be a problem.

I talked to the sergeant, who called the men together to practice a military formation with a saluting and bowing routine, as suggested by Maj. Dutch.

One of the soldiers, who apparently had not learned manners as a child, asked, "What's in it for us?"

"I will receive two-liter gift bottles of the finest sake at each stop, which you can share among yourselves between stops," Maj. Dutch answered.

The sake news made the entire retinue business far more interesting for the soldiers, who had nothing more to look forward to than hospital sandwiches on the way to Beppu. Thus, for the sake of sake and America's proper oriental protocol honor, the GIs quickly got into the spirit of the ceremonial occasion as they practiced their upcoming routines. Indeed, the GIs began to look like sharp soldiers for the occasion, rather than sad sack GIs on their way to join the infantry.

Maj. Dutch went into some detail, explaining their "very significant role" in maintaining good relations with leading Japanese citizens. I thought the men might as well cherish a few ceremonial highlights, for there might be more than a few terrifying firefights ahead of them in Korea.

The first ceremonial stop soon arrived and, sure enough, there was a Japanese formation from the local city hall awaiting us on the platform. The train engineer skillfully brought the train to a stop at the most appropriate spot. We all filed out by rank. I stood to the left of Maj. Dutch; the sergeant on my left gave the commands to the 11 other soldiers, who lined up smartly with six soldiers on each side.

As Maj. Dutch introduced each dignitary, we all saluted and then bowed after each exchange of gifts. Dutch explained in Japanese and then translated into English the sorrow of parting, the solemnity of the occasion, and his deep appreciation for their friendship over the last few years. They, in turn, expressed their appreciation for his kind assistance and sincere friendship that had earned their great affection. It really seemed to be a mutual admiration event. The local celebrities seemed quite impressed with the importance of Maj. Dutch and the honor guard provided him for this special occasion.

The ceremonious event took less than 15 minutes, but I soon discovered some problems. There were so many mayors' receptions before we finally reached Beppu that I lost count of the exact number. This caused our train not to arrive until the early hours of the following day.

When we were asked why the train was late, Maj. Dutch suggested that the train seemed to have brake problems. I elected to remain silent and let him do the talking, since he was extremely proficient at it. After a while, it occurred to me that our late arrival might be construed to be a brake problem, because the engineer did actually use the brakes to stop in the designated cities, using a list supplied by Maj. Dutch at the exact spot where the engineer saw the mayor's reception on the platform. Certainly it was the brakes that caused us to stop.

Another problem was that after the 12 soldiers had shared the third or fourth round of ceremonial sake, they were not particularly functional, to the point where some of them could hardly stand up to salute, let alone bow without being unseemly. Some of us recognized our limitations before we became sake-wacky. But by the time we reached Beppu, there were only four of us still doing our ceremonial duty. The soldier who had asked, "What's in it for us?" was busy throwing up. Apparently, he also had never learned that sake was meant to be sipped and savored, not chug-a-lugged.

To make matters worse, the soldiers used up all the train's hot water to warm up the sake, causing some grumbling from other passengers in our car. Maj. Dutch managed to solve this problem with the aid of his silver tongue and by including the Japanese passengers in our sake libations. After our Japanese fellow passengers were also somewhat sake-wacky, they lost some of their reserve and toasted everyone at every ceremonial stop with more sake.

The wide sharing of sake had the beneficial effect of limiting the total amount of sake our soldiers drank. All 12 soldiers were still able to walk, or at least stagger, off at the end of the line accompanied by a nice memory, however vague, of a very festive train ride, in which they did their very best for their country to maintain excellent Japanese/American relations.

Maj. Dutch appeared quite pleased with his mayoral farewells. He was met at the station by a black sedan, and that was the last we saw of him. From our conversations, I assume he ended up in a warm bath in a nice hotel, with Geisha girls giving him a gentle scrubbing and then helping him into bed for a nap before he changed into a cleaned and pressed uniform and reported for duty with the 3rd Infantry Division.

After Maj. Dutch departed, the rest of us had to wait for a long time for our Army bus to re-arrive at the train station. The bus had come earlier, but had left when our train didn't arrive on time. Thus, it was early on the morning of 26 October, after a bumpy ride, we finally arrived at a place called Jumonji, somewhere on the island of Kyushu. We were directed to a squad tent that functioned as the administrative headquarters of the 7th Infantry Regiment, where we all turned in our service records and reported for duty.

I was instructed to report to the adjutant, a young captain by the name of Olin E. Smith, who is now a retired brigadier general. Cpt. Smith was polite and had a pleasant voice that made me feel welcome as he told me I was to be the battalion surgeon in the 1st Battalion of the 7th Infantry Regiment of the 3rd Infantry Division of the United States Army. He asked if I had any questions. I took a deep breath, because I had so many questions that I hardly knew where to start.

"Yes, I do have some questions. For a starter, would you explain the organization and the relationships of divisions, regiments, and battalions? The reason I ask this very basic question about the Army is because I know next to nothing about the Army. I enlisted in the Navy V-5 program in 1944, hoping to become a Navy flyer on an aircraft carrier, but I was so late getting into the service in World War II, that the Navy still had many future pilots in their training pipeline. So my V-5 group was sent to a Navy V-12 college program to wait for an opening in the Navy pre-flight program that never came. I was eventually transferred to the V-12 premedical program because I already had completed most of the college courses for pre-med. I had just gotten into medical school when World War II was over. I finished medical school in 1948. During a two-year civilian internship, I joined the Army, at the end of which, some idiots in North Korea invaded South Korea and I received orders to go to Japan ASAP. I didn't go to the Army Medical Field Service School—therefore, I would appreciate anything you might care to tell me about the Army."

For a moment, Cpt. Smith rested with his elbows on his desk and his head in his hands. Then he looked up with a benevolent smile and explained that there were three corps in an Army, three divisions in a corps, three regiments in a division, and three battalions in a regiment. Each of those elements named had supporting elements of artillery, tanks, supply, and medical units. The basic fighting unit was the infantry battalion, which had three rifle companies, a heavy weapons company, and a headquarters company, which included the medical platoon to which I was being assigned. Each rifle company should have 160 to 200 men in it, subdivided into platoons and squads. Usually, medics from the medical platoon were assigned to each infantry platoon and sometimes to squads.

After that helpful overview, I was assured by Cpt. Smith that the MSC officer and the medical platoon sergeant would be able to answer any more questions I might have. I could also have questions answered by the regimental surgeon, Maj. Bennett, and his assistant, Cpt. Jennings.

I was ushered out and taken to the Regimental Collecting Company (RCC) tent, where I had a pleasant get-acquainted cup of coffee with Maj. Bennett and Cpt. Jennings, both medical corps officers. Maj. Bennett seemed to be more of a gung-ho/macho type of man than Cpt. Jennings, who gave the impression of being more spiritual. By his speech and demeanor, I guessed that Cpt. Jennings was a Christian—a hunch that turned out to be true.

I was also introduced to two key men in the Medical Company—Master Sgt. Andrew Koschak and Sgt. 1st Class Clifford May. Koschak was an older man, perhaps in his mid-forties. He kept the Medical Company running smoothly, with or without the assistance and direction of the MC or MSC Officers. Koschak had a very capable deputy in Sgt. 1st Class May, who was an intelligent, observant, and very efficient NCO.

Both men were career NCOs (non-commissioned officers) with World War II combat experience, and both could provide detailed explanations and suggestions on the daily operations of the Medical Company and Regimental Headquarters if a new officer had enough sense to ask questions rather than just stumble along in ignorance.

After the coffee interlude with Maj. Bennett and Cpt. Jennings, the captain took me to the 1st Battalion aid station, which was located in a small (9 x 14 foot) tent with a black-out entryway. There, I was introduced to 1st Lt. Rudolf A. Sarka, MSC, and Sgt. 1st Class Bill Herrick.

As I gazed at my new universe, I thought: *this small aid station tent is certainly not a hospital, and it's not an outpatient clinic, but it seems to be my workplace for the unforeseeable future.* It would be my job to provide primary medical care to the officers and enlisted men in the 1st Battalion from that little tent. I realized I had a lot to learn about the Army in a short period of time and 1st Lt. Sarka and Sgt. 1st Class Herrick could each teach me a few things. I prayed that I would succeed as the leader of the medical platoon.

I couldn't help but remember that only four months earlier, as I drove home to Lake of the Woods, I had longed to spend a little time out in the open. I had certainly gotten my wish, minus the sailing and fishing. As I contemplated my new status, I realized that growing up knowing how to use a rifle and how to survive outside in cold weather might prove useful.

After a brief time of getting to know one another, I told Sarka and Herrick that I was tired and hungry, having been up for the last 24 hours. Herrick volunteered to take my gear and get me set up with a cot in a squad tent while Sarka took me on a little tour of the area and found me something to eat.

By mid-afternoon, I had completed a tour around the battalion, downed a couple of C-rations, and was finally able to stretch out on a cot with my boots off. The sake-wacky train trip was fast becoming a surreal memory, pushed aside by the reality of the infantry that seemed to envelop me. Having missed a night's rest, I fell asleep almost immediately and awoke early the next morning, ready to learn more about the 1st Battalion of the 7th Infantry Regiment of the 3rd Infantry Division of the U.S. Army.

Chapter Five
GIs and KATUSA soldiers train together on the muddy hills of Kyushu, Japan
October 27, 1950 – November 15, 1950

After I became better acquainted with 1st Lt. Sarka and Sgt. 1st Class Herrick, I realized how different their skills and aptitudes were. Sarka didn't have the practical leadership skills of Herrick, but did know all that an MSC officer was supposed to know about field sanitation, mess inspection, field water purification, basic first aid, medical supply, and who to see about whatever the question was.

He was a big, strong redhead, of Hungarian descent. Neither gregarious nor pushy, he showed a lot of deference to doctors, which bothered me a little. I wondered if he thought there were limits to his social acceptance. I suspected some pompous M.D. had dumped on him in the past. As I got to know Rudy Sarka better, I asked him to keep me informed about everything going on in the battalion. Also, since I didn't know much about the Army, I asked him to let me know if he saw me doing or saying something that wasn't right from the Army's point of view. I, in turn, would teach him about medicine.

After that exchange, I discovered that Sarka was truly a vacuum cleaner for all of the scuttlebutt and happenings in the battalion. Because of his sanitary inspection routines, he got to know all of the company grade officers and most of the NCOs throughout the battalion on a personal basis. Sarka had a habit of listening more than he talked. In fact, he had a raspy, irritating voice that encouraged others to continue talking. Sarka aided friendly informative conversation by inserting comments such as, "You don't say? What happened next? Is that so?" and "What do you think about that?" So if someone had something on their mind and no one was listening, Sarka provided a public service and encouragement by his friendly listening.

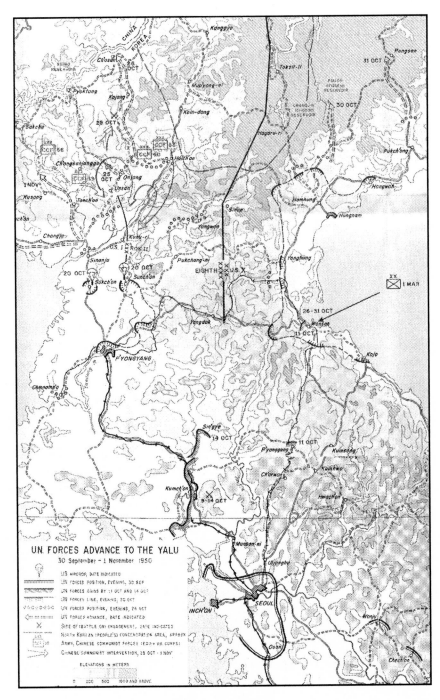

Wonsan, North Korea

Sarka quickly became my eyes, ears, and loyal informant on what was happening where and when in the battalion. Since I was often busy with patients, this was a valuable personal service to me. I remember thinking that he would make a good supply officer, because he had a good nose for supplies, and if he talked long enough, people would eventually give him anything to get rid of him. Later, that proved to be true.

The medical platoon sergeant, Bill Herrick, was a good old boy from Arkansas and a colorful character. He had an insightful, humorous way of using picturesque or base anatomical words to get a point across to reluctant or bungling soldiers. Herrick was one of the survivors who crossed the beach at Normandy on D-Day. He lasted out the war in Europe until Germany surrendered, and then married a German girl. Herrick knew how field medics were supposed to function.

Before World War II, Herrick had worked briefly as a carnival wrestler—volunteering to take all comers. He was still willing to take on all enlisted men who didn't agree with his ideas about how to run the medical platoon. He also had worked as a surgical technician in the operating room and understood operating room procedures. Herrick had a keen understanding of the post-slavery problems of the blacks, and he knew how to talk like a regular home boy without a hint of prejudice or condescension. I instinctively liked that country boy from Arkansas, who claimed he had come from "about three wagon greasings out of Little Rock."

I enjoyed working with Bill Herrick, as most others did, too, because he was evenhanded, even as he insisted on performance. He also was known to give every man an equal break, whether white, black, or Oriental. Even the 20 or more KATUSA soldiers in our platoon soon came to view Sgt. Bill Herrick as their mentor and father figure.

The KATUSAs were Korean civilians who had recently been unwillingly plucked out of the Pusan Perimeter, given haircuts, deloused, scrubbed, x-rayed, shoved into American Army uniforms, and dropped on us via planes to make up for our lack of American GIs. I soon learned that we only had about 40 percent of our authorized number of American enlisted men. Many of the rifle companies in the 7th Regiment could count only 40 American enlisted men in their morning reports, although they had their full compliment of officers and NCOs. As with the 7th Infantry Division before the Inchon Invasion, MacArthur, with President Syngman Rhee's approval, solved our low enlisted count by depositing 8,500 bewildered KATUSAs onto the 3rd Infantry Division.

I felt good about both Herrick and Sarka, because their talents complimented each other well and they were mutually respectful.

When I first shook hands with Herrick, I could tell he was sizing me up, even as I was trying to take his measure. I presume he was pondering three questions:

What is this young doctor from Minnesota made of? Does he have common sense? Will he stand up under fire? Those were the same questions I was asking myself.

As we trained together, I felt I could depend on Herrick to help me learn more about the infantry and combat medics. Like a good sergeant, he did that without giving the impression that he was instructing an officer. Herrick took pleasure in introducing me to the other NCOs in the platoon. Sgt. 1st Class Charles Ogden was Herrick's deputy. Ogden, like Herrick, had a similar country boy understanding of how to lead men, but Ogden was a bit more of a straight arrow and less colorful than Herrick. Ogden functioned as Herrick's backup NCO and was second in line.

The other five sergeants in the platoon, Sgt. Bull Adams, Sgt. Bill Bowie, Sgt. 1st Class Guy Byland, Sgt. Wilfred Fournier, and Sgt. Nicholas Prystas, had worked together in Fort Devens, Massachusetts. They knew how to function in their medic support roles, and by their war record in difficult circumstances.

All of the platoons' sergeants were southerners and career soldiers. They all had mechanical and carpentry skills, as well as medical aid skills. Because of their intelligence and grit, it was expected that Fournier and Prystas would become top sergeants some day, when there were opportunities for advancement—provided they survived the war. Adams was a skilled mechanic. Bowie was a general handyman and gofer. They both had a history of whiskey problems and had been busted, but they were the kind of men who would do anything they were told to do or die trying. As Herrick noted, that last talent was most useful in combat. Herrick, Ogden, and Byland were old friends, and they talked about opening a construction business named "HOB" after they retired from the Army.

In addition to the seven sergeants, there were about ten American enlisted draftees of recent vintage. The rest of our oversized platoon was made up of the KATUSA. It was obvious that the seven sergeants had their work cut out for them training new medical aid men and litter bearers, including the newly-integrated KATUSA, with whom we had no common language, dictionaries, or interpreters.

Much later, someone told me that the Korean word for American was *migukin*, the Korean word for English was *migugo*, and the Korean word for the American Embassy was *miguk*. When an American pointed to himself and said "American," the Korean responded by telling the American the corresponding Korean word for American—migukin or miguk—which the Americans heard as "me gook." Thus the Americans, in their linguistic ignorance, began calling the Koreans *gooks*, a term the Koreans detested and considered insulting. I wondered if anyone in MacArthur's headquarters was aware of the origin of the word *gook*.

Since we were supposed to train with live ammunition for an amphibious invasion in less than one month's time, military instructions were given in English, but supplemented by demonstrating, pointing, and many repetitions. In moments of frustration, shouting, cussing, pushing, and occasional butt-kicking augmented the KATUSAs' instruction. In my observation, some of the company grade infantry officers in other platoons couldn't curtail this frustration-born training behavior. But our focus was to save lives, not to kill the enemy. That made a lot of difference in how a sergeant dealt with frustration—especially when handling live ammunition in field training.

I made the time to patiently examine our KATUSA soldiers on sick call. I wanted my show of compassion for our Korean brothers to be emulated by our sergeants and on down the line. Sgt. 1st Class Herrick had a knack for patiently demonstrating and encouraging our Korean soldiers. As a result, our American NCOs and enlisted men tended to follow Herrick's leadership example in their one-on-one dealing with our Korean buddies.

MacArthur's declaration that language would not be a problem in integrating young Korean men into American Army units was arrogant stupidity, at best. The subsequent failure of the MacArthur high command to publish convenient pocket-size English/Korean/Japanese dictionaries and a useful English/Korean/Japanese military glossary and phrase book resulted in perhaps thousands of extra lives being lost due to miscommunication.

In my first full day with the medical platoon, I enjoyed inspecting all of the weapons and visiting with the infantry sergeants of the 1st Battalion, who knew how to use all of the weapons of war. I later obtained a Table of Organization and Equipment (TO&E) list of all of the weapons that were allocated to a fully equipped infantry battalion in 1950. This list included the following weapons:

534 Rifles, caliber .30 M1
253 Carbines, caliber .30
130 Pistols, automatic caliber .45
45 Automatic rifles, caliber .30
13 Machine guns, caliber .30 (air cooled)
4 Machine guns, caliber .30 (water cooled)
8 Machine guns, caliber .30 (vehicle mount)
9 Mortars, 60 mm
4 Mortars, 81 mm
9 Recoilless rifles, 57 mm
4 Recoilless rifles, 75 mm
9 Rocket launchers, 2.36"
11 Rocket launchers, 3.5"

After several hours of inspecting weapons, including test firing some of the rifles and machine guns, I went back to the aid station to hold sick call, and ate another C-ration can of something unworthy of recall. When I crawled into my sleeping bag, I was dead tired, but I managed to write a letter home to tell my parents about my new home in the infantry.

Dear Dad and Mother,   27 Oct. 1950

So much has happened during the last few days that I hardly know where to start. I have been transferred from the 128th Station Hospital to a field unit. It was part of the Army plan to try to rotate medics from field duty to hospital duty when feasible. I am glad since I think I am going to enjoy this more rugged life. My address is: Cpt. R. T. Jensen, M.C. 060761, Med Co. 7th Infantry R.C.T, 3rd Inf. Div, APO 468 c/o P.M.S.F

I am writing this letter by candlelight in my tent. Tomorrow we get stoves in the tent. To keep warm we have sleeping bags and all the blankets we can carry.

I don't think we will be here very long. This regiment was supposed to have gone in at Inchon but it was not needed. Again it was scheduled to go in above Pyongyang— the North Korean capital, but the resistance was so little it was not needed. Now we are scheduled to go in along the Manchurian border and help mop up and occupy North Korea until elections are held. After that we may be pulled out and sent to Europe.

Two days from now we go on maneuvers. It will be a little rough hiking up and down these mountains but I should get into shape in not too long a time.

Well I have to dash off a letter to John now and then to bed. I go to sleep about 8 PM and awaken at 6 AM.

Love, Bob

The next day, the medical platoon was involved in full-time training. We pulled the medics (aid-men) assigned to the rifle companies back to the battalion aid station for a refresher course. We held first aid classes with bandages, splints, tourniquets, morphine shots, and started I.V. solutions. The medics practiced carrying each other on their backs, over their shoulders, in blankets, on stretchers, in a two-man carry, and in a one-man backward crawl-and-drag with a piece of canvas under the "wounded" soldier to preserve his clothing. On the real battle-field, the backward crawl-and-drag, using a pistol belt or ammo belt around the chest of the casualty, would be used with no consideration of damage to clothing if standing up was hazardous or suicidal.

Field sanitation included instruction in cat holes, slit trenches, and water purification in canteens and Lister bags. Either chlorine powder or iodine tablets could be used, with specific instructions for soldiers not to swallow the water purification tablets and then chase the pill with unclean water from a stream. It would seem that no one would be as stupid as to swallow an iodine water purification tablet and chase it with dirty water from a stream, but according to Army lore, it had happened before.

The Koreans continued to require special consideration because of communication problems. Some of them had never been to school and couldn't read or write either Japanese or Korean, let alone English. Attempts to make written lists of useful words were frustrated by not having paper thick enough to be used as flash cards. A lot of verbal repetition was necessary. Fortunately, the Koreans appeared to have good memories, and considering what they had been through, good manners. Those who were especially intelligent were given crash courses in English vocabulary, and the larger and smarter Koreans were given leadership training. Those who proved themselves were made honorary corporals or sergeants.

There was no set pattern laid out from the top brass about how to communicate with or train our Koreans, so it was left up to the sergeants to figure out how to get the job done in the little time allotted. There was also no organized system of integrating the Koreans into the American Army. We medics simply pinned their unofficial stripes on upside down to distinguish them from American corporals and sergeants. Our Koreans were quite happy with this arrangement and, after a time, I noted that some of the infantry platoons were doing the same thing with their Koreans.

The point was that the people in the Far East command, as well as the leaders at Army and division levels had no plans or ideas about how to integrate the KATUSA into the American divisions. They insisted it would not be a problem and looked the other way, letting the troop leaders figure it out as best they could. Because we had so many Koreans named Kim, we ended up putting numbers on their shirts and helmets following the letter K (for Korean) and calling them by their "K number."

I did make it clear in our platoon that no Korean was to be called a gook, and anyone that called them gooks could kiss their stripes good-bye. The Koreans seemed to appreciate my defense of their personhood. As could be expected, the amount of integration success varied widely, with some American Army platoons and companies failing miserably because of inept or prejudiced company level leadership. In retrospect, I believe that some infantry NCOs and company grade officers were so exasperated that they became depressed at the thought of going into combat with soldiers with whom they could neither understand nor communicate.

Weapon training was the most worrisome problem, because the M-1 rifle was not properly sized for many of the smaller Koreans. We tried to swap some

M-1s for the smaller carbines, with occasional success. Collection of unused ammunition after target practice was essential to prevent accidents.

We were told to paint over all of the Red Cross signs on our medic jeeps and ambulances. The North Koreans carried both soldiers and ammo in their ambulances. Ostensibly, they assumed we did likewise, making the Red Cross signs on our medical vehicles tempting targets. All of our medics carried weapons, usually a pistol or carbine with a sling, in addition to their medical kits.

The daily sick call presented a challenge because of the language barrier. The Korean word for pain or hurt, *apuda*, combined with pointing, was used to locate what was wrong. The KATUSA could only gesture to indicate where and in what way they hurt. A physical examination with finger palpation was essential. As time went on, we developed a pigeon-type English-Korean-Japanese medical and military vocabulary that elicited some laughter but decreased some of the confusion.

Problems such as gonorrhea, dysentery, cuts, and bruises were, of course, rather obvious. Sore throats, ear infections, eye infections, and lung infections could be confirmed with appropriate battery-powered medical tools and a stethoscope.

Field sanitation was another matter. It took a lot of effort to get the Koreans to cover cat-holes or use slit trenches. It also took extra work to get the Koreans to urinate on the ground some distance from the tent, rather than just outside the tent or, worse yet, by just aiming the urine stream out through the tent flap.

During sick call, we usually took the temperature of the soldiers waiting in line to ascertain who had a fever. Herrick noticed that some of the Koreans simply got up and wandered off after the thermometer was pulled from their mouths, apparently thinking the medical treatment was over when the thermometer was removed.

After a few days of local training, we went on maneuvers in the mountains, and I moved my few belongings into a pup tent that was to become the home I would carry with me to Korea. If the weather was nice, I could sleep under the stars, with the pup-tent canvas spread out flat under the sleeping bag. If it was raining, I tried to find a little mound or elevation of ground for the floor of the tent and then would dig a little furrow to guide any rain runoff around the tent to prevent the water running through the tent as a surprise in the middle of the night. I was usually successful in selecting and preparing the spot for my tent, but some poor souls just didn't seem to remember that water always runs downhill, becoming a river of mud in the process.

Our battalion went on mock offensive and retreat maneuvers in the muddy mountains. It didn't take long to become camouflaged with mud. It also became clear why infantry troops are called foot soldiers. We went many places on maneuvers in the mountains where jeeps, trucks, and tanks couldn't go. As a result, in moving mock casualties, we had to use manpower, and it became obvious that the three four-man litter squads listed in the medical platoon's TO&E would not be adequate for anything more than a picnic in the hills. I began to realize that we didn't have adequate manpower or means to evacuate a large number of battle casualties from steep hills or valleys. In any real shooting-shelling-wounding-killing war in muddy hill country, we were going to have problems getting the wounded out of harm's way.

During our field training, it also became apparent that our Korean brothers were a godsend to the problem of moving ammunition up hills and casualties down. They were surefooted and, with a little practice, they could easily coordinate with each other in handling stretcher patients. As a result, we took all of the Koreans we could get into our medical platoon.

There was some talk about helicopter evacuation, but our few bubble Bell H-13 helicopters with two litter pods were usually so occupied with moving generals and colonels around to keep them aware of troop location during maneuvers, that they were not available for routine medical evacuations during our training exercises.

Muddy mountainsides with trees are not ideal spots for either helicopter landings or for locating battalion aid stations. Moreover, if two rifle companies were attacking, with each company going up a separate ridgeline with a deep ravine between them, there was no way the aid station could support both companies. In such an event, we would need to divide up our medical support resources and place a small medical team behind each company. That couldn't be easily done without prior team selection and training. Fortunately, we got several days of sunny weather to dry out and to test our new strategy.

During maneuvers, I decided that it would be best to have Lt. Sarka be our eyes and ears as he tended to the sanitation issues and coordinated medical evacuation at a base near the battalion headquarters. Sgt. 1st Class Herrick would develop the mobile support teams to follow the rifle companies into combat. I would move to the area with the most casualties and direct my efforts at resuscitations and stabilization of the most severely wounded. We tried to think through many circumstances while on maneuvers in the hills of Kyushu, but it was obvious we would need to be flexible in developing plans for evacuating combat casualties in Korea.

So many of the things I had learned in medical school had little application. But the skills in cold weather survival I had learned while working outside cutting timber at 20-40 degrees below zero in northern Minnesota were of great value. I again prayed for the courage to do my duty.

That night, I settled into my little one-man tent, snug from the rain, and stretched out to write another letter home. I didn't write about our Korean soldiers because we were instructed not to mention them in letters. I tried to get a letter off to my parents at least once a week—more, if something unusual was happening. Some days it was difficult to express my feelings because I didn't want to cause undue anxiety at home.

Dear Dad and Mother,   *4 Nov. 1950*

As yet I am still situated in Japan. I expect to go to Korea with the 7th Regimental combat team in a week or two at most. Just where we will go in Korea I don't know. We may go to the southern part or up to North Korea where we will be fighting the North Korean and Chinese Communists. I think the Chinese Communists are just trying to drain our strength to the Pacific so the Russians can sweep across Europe. Only time will tell.

We have been having beautiful Indian summer-like weather in the mountains the last few days. Yesterday we were out on all-night maneuvers again. It is all good preparation for whatever lies ahead. Time to crash into the sleeping bag.

Love, Bob

When we finished our allotted training time in the hills, we were told to put our duffel bags on a truck, roll up our sleeping bags in something waterproof, tie them on top of our backpacks, and march the ten to fifteen miles down, out of the hills, to a hotel, where our battalion would stay until we boarded a ship for Korea. Since it was a cold, rainy day, it wasn't easy walking down from the hills. I remember being so tired after a few hours of walking and sliding with a pack on my back that I thought we would never reach our destination. We finally arrived at an old hotel, where I washed the mud off of my clothes and found some dry clothes in my pack to sleep in. Most of us slept on our sleeping bags on the floor.

The next day, the sun came out and we were able to dry out and rearrange our gear. As we prepared to embark for Korea, the regimental surgeon told me to make sure our aid station had plenty of supplies, because the three battalions might be forced to operate in Korea away from the regimental headquarters, as separate battalion combat teams, which meant we would need to function on our own in the field for extended periods of time. I wondered why the regimental Medical Company was not doing more planning for us in that matter.

I loaded up on bandages, splints, aspirin, I.V. fluids, and morphine tartrate, but there was not much in the way of antibiotics, surgical clamps, or tracheotomy sets available. I worried that if we became separated from other units, and if medical evacuation was hindered, I might be forced to do more procedures than I was expected to do in a battalion aid station. I was also concerned that we might run into louse or tick-born diseases, as well as typhoid, dysentery, pneumonia, vene-real diseases, and wound infections not only in our own soldiers, but also among refugees.

As I thought about those needs, I remembered an Army medical supply center near the old Army 128th Station Hospital. Since I had gotten to know the officer in charge, I found a military phone and called him. We had become friends as I listened to his stories from World War II.

Once I asked if he ever lifted weights, since he was powerfully built. He answered my question by putting the back of his legs next to a jeep rear bumper, bending his knees, gripping the inside of the bumper, and straightening his legs, lifting the back end of the jeep off of the ground. He casually noted that it saved time when changing a tire. He said he could lift the front end, as well, but it caused stars in his eyes, so he just did one front wheel at a time. I didn't try to imitate his performance in jeep lifting. I didn't offer to arm wrestle him, either.

When I finally got "Cpt. Supply Source" on the other end of the line, I explained my problem and was told he couldn't send anything to me. However, if I could get a three-day pass and fly up, he would let me fill a couple of big foot-lockers with whatever I needed for Korea. Inventory was coming up, and he could write stuff off as out-of-date or damaged. It was an offer I couldn't refuse.

I was able to wrangle a three-day pass, but was warned to get back on time or I would miss shipping out and would be considered absent without leave (AWOL). I managed to get a flight north and booked standby on a return evening flight. Cpt. Supply Source sent "Sgt. Finagler," a man I knew from the 128th Station Hospital, to pick me up at the airport, take me to the BOQ in the Hospital, and then to the medical supply center the next day. At the medical supply center, I was given two oversized footlockers, which I filled with antibiotics of all types for oral, I.M., and I.V. use. I also obtained some minor surgery sets, as well as boxes of clamps, boxes of hemostats of different sizes, surgical blades, sterile sutures with needles, and I.V. fluids. They were out of tracheotomy sets. Many of the medi-cines had recently-expired dates, but that was not of concern to me in comparison to the danger of a patient expiring without the needed drug or antibiotic.

When the two footlockers could hold no more, I returned to the hospital with Sgt. Finagler who had a list of flights going back to Beppu. Every flight was booked. He had already talked to a sergeant friend of his at the Air Force flight desk about the schedule. Sgt. Finagler told me this was an emergency situation that required his special expertise.

He explained, "There is not a snowball's chance in hell you are going to get on a plane with your two heavy footlockers and no authorization other than an expiring three-day pass." He went on, "You must present yourself at the air base with 'priority orders' to personally deliver 'emergency medical supplies' to a troop ship leaving soon. The name and destination of that ship will, of course, be kept secret."

A bit naively, I asked, "Where can I find someone to issue such orders?"

"Don't worry, Doc," he said. "I know a brigadier general who will give just such an order. Leave your footlockers with me for some 'official' labels, and you just go in the Officers' Club and enjoy a beer and a hamburger and say nothing, and I mean nothing, to anyone about this, while I type up some official-looking orders."

I did as instructed, but with a distinct feeling of unease. After about two hours, Sgt. Finagler came by to tell me to come immediately so he could take me to the airport. As we got in the jeep, he handed me four copies of official-looking orders to take "emergency medical supplies" to Beppu. They were signed by a fictitious brigadier general at a known headquarter, but with an incorrect phone number.

When we arrived at the departure desk, my two footlockers and I were given priority, while two other poor souls, both full colonels, were removed from the plane's manifest. I was asked for three copies of my orders, one of which would be retained at the airport flight desk and would eventually be destroyed, while the other two copies would be processed back through channels. There were some loud complaints from the two colonels who had been bumped off of the flight. During the confusion, I stayed in the background and looked the other way while Sgt. Finagler "retrieved" the two extra copies of my orders that had been set on the out-box pile of orders to be retro-processed. As I went through the door to the plane, I turned to wave to the sergeant who saluted and waved with a big smile. He had finagled the system again.

When I arrived, Sgt. Herrick met me at the airport and made sure the two footlockers were taken immediately to our battalion aid station container.

He turned to me and said, "Sir! I have been sweating you out. I was afraid you wouldn't be able to get back because all of the flights were overbooked. How did you ever manage to get on that plane?"

"Bill," I said, "I don't think it would be very smart for me to say anything about that now. Maybe, 50 years from now, I'll tell the story, but for now, if anyone asks, just say that I was fortunate to be able to get on a flight."

I wondered how often Sgt. Finagler had pulled that stunt and what the punishment was for traveling on fictitious orders. I had a lot to learn about the American Army and about the finagling of clever old Army sergeants, who thought nothing of using fake orders in an emergency to make the Army run more efficiently. Sgt. Finagler probably thought it was just another way to help the war effort.

The previous ten days had been very busy. Our battalion was given four days to rest up before being trucked to the ship in the port, the majority of which I had spent on a three-day pass scrounging medical supplies, returning just in the nick of time to board our troop ship. As the ship headed out of the harbor, bound for Korea, I was finally able to relax my sore muscles in a bunk and quit worrying about the fake orders. In any event, it seemed highly unlikely that someone caught using fake orders to get extra medical supplies for the war in Korea would be removed from a ship en route to Korea. I snuggled down in my bunk and wrote a letter home.

Dear Mother and Dad,   *14 Nov. 1950*

For the first time in the last few weeks, I have some time to sit and write without being tired. Right now I am on the Navy troop transport, General Black, *steaming at 15 knots through heavy seas northwest from the port of Maji in southern Japan. Destination is Wonsan, Korea, and after that nobody knows what, but it will undoubtedly be combat.*

I am now in the 1ˢᵗ Battalion of the 7ᵗʰ Infantry Regiment where about 50% of the troops in the regiment are Koreans who have been integrated into our outfit. In my medical platoon I have one lieutenant, 35 enlisted men, including 17 Koreans. I have been trying to give the new men some instructions in 1ˢᵗ aid and emergency work in general. The Koreans are quick to learn and for the most part are able to put on better bandages than the average GI. I have several old sergeants who are very excellent and keep things running smoothly.

Continued on 15 Nov. 1950

We have been given winter equipment but for the most part I don't think it will be entirely adequate. I would like for you—or probably John would have to get it—to airmail me an air mattress to put under a sleeping bag. That is the only way to keep the cold from the ground from seeping into a sleeping bag. Just what we will need exactly will depend on where we are going. The climate at Wonsan is not too bad.

The old 128ᵗʰ Station Hospital has been disbanded and the personnel scattered to other areas. This is because the 141 Army General Hospital came over complete with personnel from the States and took over the hospital to turn it from a 300-bed hospital to a 1500-bed outfit. Oh well, I was lucky to have been there as long as I was. I don't know when I will get this letter mailed. We dock tonight at Wonsan but may not unload until morning.

Love, Bob

As it turned out, we didn't dock at Wonsan; rather, we anchored somewhere out in the harbor. I had been under the false impression that we would be landing at a dock in Wonsan harbor, since we had been informed before we arrived that the South Korean military had already taken the harbor from the North Koreans. But it wasn't long before dozens of little wave-tossed landing craft were circling our ship, even as landing nets were released over the side from the lower decks. I then realized that we were supposed to go over the side and climb down the rope nets with our packs on our back. It would be a new experience for most of us, who were slowly being herded toward an assigned position by the rail.

Some soldier joked that he always wanted to take a cruise, but next time, he hoped he wouldn't be going "U.S. Army economy class" with rope ladders and all of the other military frills, like full field packs. I thought it would have been helpful to practice climbing down a 30-foot rope ladder with a full pack. But on second thought, I decided it was not unlike jumping out of a plane in a para-chute—one just had to do it right the first time. On land, we had functioned as a medical platoon, but now, as I waited my turn over the rail, I felt rather alone. It was a good time to check in with the Lord. My future was in His hands.

Chapter Six
Wonsan to Sachang-ni via rope nets, landing craft, train, and truck
November 16, 1950 – November 25, 1950

The deck bosses called out each platoon's designation. When our platoon was called, we moved to an assigned position by the rail. There was some joking going on, but apprehension reflected on the faces of the soldiers around me. I presume I reflected the same apprehension, because I was afraid my arms might not carry my full weight, with pack, if my feet slipped off the rope ladder.

As I climbed over the rail, one of the deck bosses shouted, "Get your feet firmly on a horizontal rope! Don't let your legs go through the net! Lower yourself with your hands holding a vertical rope! Don't put your hands on a horizontal rope or the man above may crush your fingers with his boots! Move steadily down and watch out for men above and below!"

I tried to follow the instructions, but it wasn't easy. I had a heavy backpack and had never before climbed over the side of a ship and down a rope net to a target craft that was continually moving up and down and to and fro from the ship's side. The movement of the landing craft caused the rope ladder to sway as the men below me struggled to set their feet firmly on the bouncing deck. Provided I got down safely, I expected to see some of our troops on sick call with bruises and scrapes. I hoped there would be no broken bones. I was thankful to be carrying a pistol and not an M-1 rifle.

About halfway down, I felt my foot and lower leg slip through the net. It was difficult to pull up high enough to extract my leg. If both of my feet had slipped through the rope net, I would have ended upside down, hanging by my knees. As I pulled up, it was tempting to grab the horizontal rope with my hands, but boots were coming at me from above. I finally managed to extract the leg that had slipped through the rope net and kept moving down until I saw the landing craft thrusting up and down below me.

I touched the deck momentarily, but the craft moved down and away. I thought another step down on the horizontal rope should do it—but my feet couldn't find the rope. As the craft shoved up again, I placed both feet on the deck and released my hands, just as the landing craft was tossed back against the side of the ship. I fell, landing on my backpack in the bottom of the landing craft.

Someone hauled me to my feet and shoved me out of the way of down-coming traffic. I watched as some managed to land and stay upright while others fell over, but no one seemed to land as clumsily as I had. My clumsy landing caused a few laughs among the soldiers about the doc's "crash backpack landing."

After our landing craft was filled with soldiers, it moved away, to be replaced at the ship's side by an empty craft. In short order, we were deposited at the edge of a beach and marched to a waiting truck that took us to a bivouac area north of Wonsan. Once there, we had a roll call of our medical platoon, assembled our equipment, set up our aid-station tent, and identified the location of the other units in our battalion. I reported to the battalion headquarter tent to find out what we should expect next and let them know we were ready to hold sick call. I was grateful we hadn't had to shoot our way onto the beach.

Our battalion water trailers showed up, seemingly out of nowhere, to fill canteens and kitchen cans. Garbage pits were dug, as well as narrow slit trenches in designated areas for straddle defecation and standing urination. Bare butts in action were a common sight. Fortunately, there were no female soldiers around competing for space over a slit trench or trying to find a spot to dig a cat hole. Those who want women in combat infantry units need to realize that there are no privacy screens or portable toilets available. Portable toilets on the front line would soon become laugh-of-the-day targets for enemy rifles, mortars, machine guns, or grenades.

Toilet paper was a luxury found in C-ration boxes and treasured as much as chocolate bars. Later, the most treasured item was extra ammunition.

In Korea, our steel helmets became our personal washbasin. With a little washcloth and a bit of soap and water, one could take a semblance of a sponge bath, provided the weather was not freezing. But as the weather became colder, our sweaty, dirty clothes became 24-hour apparel, although we ceased to notice each other's body odor. It is a merciful provision of our Creator that when un-washed people start to stink at the same time, it doesn't take many days before noses cease to detect the bad odor until after a good bath. It is no wonder that unwashed infantrymen, who live, sleep, eat, excrete, fight, and die on hills, fields, rice paddies, foxholes, and trenches are often referred to as "grunts."

Most of our rifle companies hung up 30-gallon Lister bags to prepare chlori-nated water for drinking. Later, in freezing weather, it became necessary to heat the water before putting it in a Lister bag exposed to the elements. For the first night ashore, the Headquarter (HQ) Company cooks heated large containers of water filled with rations cans. The cans were ladled out either slightly warm or too hot to handle, depending upon how long the frozen cans had been in the water. Not caring for frozen ration cans, some of us rigged up wire holders and draped a row of cans over a jeep's motor. Occasionally, a can would get too hot and explode, leaving a mess under the hood.

But the C-rations filled the stomach and the cold ground was always available for a soldier to lay out his poncho or pup tent and fold it over his sleeping bag for a bit of rain or snow protection. The smart soldier soon learned to put some insulation such as leaves, straw, or wood between the sleeping bag and the ground, especially when the ground was frozen. I personally found it comfortable to sleep wearing my helmet liner on my head as a pillow, and it was warmer to sleep on a couple of boards than on the frozen ground.

The next day, we loaded up all of our gear on trucks and headed north to a place called Kowon. From there, patrols were sent out to the west. After we set up our camp and aid station and had established perimeter defenses, we waited for the return of the infantry patrols. There were not many soldiers coming for sick call. The 1st Battalion chaplain, Cpt. (Father) Joseph Carroll came by to say hello. We quickly became good friends. Later, I wrote the following letter to my brother.

Dear John,   *18 Nov. 1950*

Well, here I am in Kowon, Korea (30 miles northwest of Wonsan) sitting in my aid station which we just finished setting up in the back room of an abandoned schoolhouse. The 7th Regimental combat team is getting plenty to do clearing out guerilla sporadic attacks on supply lines. As yet I have not seen any Chinese Communists.

After traveling in this God-forsaken country, I can find little reason for fighting for it except for the principle of saving face for democracy. Everything over here smells. Brown fields, brown hills, brown people, and brown feces being used for fertilizer daily. There has been GI talk that the Korean combat ribbon will be five shades of brown.

I have written Mother for a few things I would like you to send to me by airmail as soon as possible.

1. Air mattress to put under sleeping bag to keep the cold of the ground out. Send two of them. They should have them in sporting stores or war surplus.

2. One canvas sleeping bag—cover with or without a down liner. I think they'll have this in war surplus store. Our sleeping bags are not adequate for this cold, although I have all the blankets I want.

3. One pair of leather finger gloves with wool finger inserts from war surplus store.

Other than that, I am pretty well situated with winter clothes.

At the present time, we are operating as a battalion combat team so I am the only doctor for 2500 men. In our combat team we have a company of tanks, antiaircraft artillery, etc. attached.

I don't know how long I will be situated here or how much action I will see. We are lobbing heavy mortar shells at the Koreans in the hills from in front of the schoolhouse (aid station).

Fortunately, they don't have any heavy stuff to throw back.

Time to hit the sack.

Love, Bob

Note: Change address to: Cpt. R. T. Jensen M.C 060761, HQ. Co. 1ˢᵗ Battalion Med. Platoon 7ᵗʰ Infantry, 3ʳᵈ Div. 6 PO 468

We had a continuing problem with accidental injuries from misuse of weapons and equipment. The battalion commander, Lt. Col. Timothy "Toddy," clamped down on weapon discipline and insisted on proper clearing and cleaning of weapons, as well as proper use of passwords for identification at night. A couple of our soldiers had been shot by our own people at night, resulting in an increased stress on training and more careful integration of our Korean soldiers with American buddies. We still had no bilingual or trilingual dictionaries. We never did get any.

A few days later, I sent the following letter to my parents.

Dear Dad and Mother,   22 Nov. 1950

The aid station is not so busy now so I will try and scratch out a note. This warfare is quite like the old days of the Wild West where there was an Army outpost, which sends patrols out in the hills to chase the Indians. At the same time, one wonders whether the Indians will get enough strength to attack the supply line or outpost.

Tonight the North Koreans are lighting signal fires in the hills for some kind of code messages. A patrol is going out in the moonlight tonight to try to ambush a group of North Koreans that a scout spotted so I expect a few casualties tonight.

I haven't heard any war news since I got to Korea so I don't know just what is happening, but I guess everything is good. We will leave for the North tomorrow or the next day. I think we will be situated around one of the big reservoirs where the marines are fighting now. I haven't received any mail for some time with all the moving around. I hope it comes through soon.

Love, Bob

We hadn't had many casualties, but there were bumps and bruises and cases of diarrhea without fever, for which bismuth and paregoric were useful. Our Korean troops complained about not having any rice or kimchi.

Kimchi is a type of cooked cabbage, fermented with garlic and pepper. We could always tell if the Koreans had been eating kimchi because of the strong odor of garlic. Some of our Koreans were gaining weight because they would eat three or four cans of C-rations if they could get them. Accustomed to eating a lot of rice, one can of C-rations didn't seem like enough bulk in their stomachs.

There were many Korean refugees, including women and children, along the roads. When I had time, I would walk among the refugees with Imm Yung Hee, a Korean medic I had selected as my personal assistant. I also worked with Bak Su Han, nicknamed "Big Bak," to look for disease or injury among the civilian population. We found ear and eye infections, as well as dirty wounds, untreated fractures, diarrhea, and a lot of just plain hunger.

I was surprised that so many of our Korean soldiers and American GIs could ignore the suffering around us. The unfortunate masses of displaced humanity became a part of our daily reality. I was pleased when our medics, Korean and American, began to notice individuals with needs and either tried to help them or brought them to me. As they grew more experienced, they treated civilians themselves, as best they could, when I was not available.

At battalion headquarters, when I expressed my concern that the world should know about the thousands of miserable refugees, one crusty old soldier remarked, "Hell, Doc, the world doesn't want to know about all of the miserable refugees. There is an old saying that the first casualty in any war is truth."

I mulled that over for a moment before responding, "If the first casualty in every war is truth, then the second casualty in a war must be compassion."

But I refused to have my compassion erased by the war.

My response didn't stimulate further discussion, so I continued doing what I could to help the refugees. It is a sad fact of war that a soldier may become so inured to suffering and death, and so bitter over his buddies being killed, that his spirit of compassion withers and dies. When that happens, a soldier is in danger of becoming no better than his enemy.

I believed that medics and chaplains had a unique opportunity and a moral obligation to nourish the spirit of compassion, in spite of the killing going on. As a Christian, it was also my moral obligation to hold onto my sense of compassion and exercise it whenever possible, lest I win the war yet lose the peace in my own soul. I came to see, as the war progressed, that by God's grace, compassion could be awakened by example, even in the midst of continuing carnage.

The footlockers filled with antibiotics and other materials were being put to very good use. I stopped feeling guilty about bumping two colonels off of the flight from Tokyo to Beppu. In view of the suffering around me, I felt that the two footlockers with medical supplies were worthy of priority consideration—even if it required a finagling sergeant and fake "top priority" orders.

One day, in going through our aid station supplies, I noticed two five-gallon cans of 200 proof ethyl alcohol.

I asked Sgt. Herrick, "Why do we have these five-gallon cans of alcohol taking up space among our supplies?"

"Sir," he said, "that is 200 proof ethyl alcohol. It is just a part of our TO&E supplies. Medical alcohol cans were a part of routine field medical supplies during World War II and, as far as I know, ever since the Civil War, when doctors mixed up some of their own elixirs."

I was familiar with tinctures or elixirs of quinine, digitalis, belladonna, opium (paregoric), ephedrine, emetics, cough mixtures, iron, vitamins, and tonics. But I didn't think doctors had been mixing those medicines with alcohol since before World War I.

"What do we use it for now?"

"Sir, a shot of that in a can of fruit juice will sure warm you up on a cold day. It's useful as barter for supplies. Medics often need favors. We just keep it hidden for use on special occasions, sir."

And that was how I learned about our most important five-gallon cans of 200 proof ethyl alcohol. It was one of the best-kept secrets of the U.S. Army Medical Corps. When I tried a shot of alcohol in a canteen cup of fruit juice, I found out it tasted awful. Those who liked it were obviously drinking for effect, not flavor. We continued to carry the alcohol with us as part of our medical supplies for the special emergency occasions that came up.

On 24 November 1950, we were ordered to move north again. We loaded onto open freight cars for a rickety, 40-mile train ride from Kowon to Chigyong, which was about eight miles south of the city of Hamhung. Early the following morning, we were loaded onto trucks for a slow, 65-mile trip on a winding mountain road west over the Nangnim Mountain range to Sachang-ni, a small village located on the upper reaches of the Taedong River, which ran through Pyongyang[2] to empty into the Yellow Sea. The Taedong River flowed west, so we knew that we had crossed over the mountains that separated rivers flowing east from the rivers flowing west in North Korea.

We couldn't find Sachang-ni on most of our maps. However, I noted on a map in battalion headquarters that Sachang-ni was almost half way across Korea, a few miles north of a line drawn between Yonpo—which is just south of Hungnam on the east coast, and the cities of Sinanju and Anju—located by the Chongchun River, which empties into the Korean Bay of the Yellow Sea on the west coast of Korea.[3]

---

[2] 'Pyongyang' can also be spelled 'Pyungyang.'

[3] See maps.

The following letter was written on our arrival at Sachang-ni:

Dear Mother and Dad,   *25 Nov. 1950*

The last four days have been very fatiguing. We left our station at Kowon by rail and what a train. We were loaded into open cattle cars with our packs and jolted along a rickety railroad to Chigyong, near Hamhung, where we pitched our tents for the night.

Early this AM (three o'clock) we had breakfast (pancakes and scrambled eggs) and loaded ourselves into trucks, jeeps, etc., and the entire 1st Battalion with artillery, mortar and other supporting units. It made a long line of about 100 vehicles. We traveled west by northwest through high mountain passes, forded streams because of blown-up bridges and after traveling about 65 miles over treacherous roads, arrived at a small valley village called Sachang-ni. It probably isn't on the map. Militarily speaking, we are about three miles from the front lines but in these mountains the front lines mean nothing.

It is bitterly cold in the mountains with chill winds and light snow. It is the dry time of the year here or we would have much more snow.

The 8th Army on the west side of Korea is making a concerted drive north to trap the Korean and Chinese between themselves and the 7th Infantry Division and South Korea (ROK Divisions) and 1st Marines, which are on the northeast front. We are located in one of the main mountain passes to prevent them from slipping out of the trap. So far it has been quiet today with only patrol skirmishes. However, it may liven up soon.

I am very tired and want to get some sleep while I can. I am the only doctor here in this mountain pass with about 2000 men. Fortunately, I have a good bunch of aid men.

Love, Bob

When we arrived at Sachang-ni, the 26th Republic of Korea (ROK) Infantry Regiment had been occupying the town and nearby hills. There were no North Korean civilians to be seen. Shortly after we arrived, Lt. Col. Toddy received a radio message from regiment to prepare defensive positions around Sachang-ni and await further orders.

He assigned defensive positions immediately. Able Company took over the hill north of the town, Baker Company covered the south and east extending across the Taedong River and Charlie Company covered the road west and a prominent trail to the northwest. Dog Company and HQ Company were spread out over the center section of the town covering the flat area along the north side of the Taedong River. Our tanks and trucks were located near a two-story building.

Sarka, Herrick, and I went on a quick tour of the town, in search of convenient houses for an aid station. We rejected the idea of using the large two-story wooden school and community center because of its obvious vulnerability to enemy fire. We scouted further among the buildings and picked out two small contiguous houses near the road to serve as an aid station and an overflow building that could also be used for sleeping. Most of the houses had straw thatch roofs or a combination of black tarpaper, thatch, and thin corrugated metal roofing for drainage.

Sgt. Herrick said, "These grass roofs sure as hell will not stop a mortar, and a big mortar will blow this house apart."

The other medic sergeants agreed with Herrick's assessment.

Sgt. Byland commented dryly, "Anyone interested in protecting his fanny from shrapnel had better start digging a personal foxhole."

Sgt. Ogden added, "Make them two-man foxholes with one GI and one Korean for each hole and ask your sergeants where to dig so that we have clear walking paths in our area."

I was pleased the way our GI sergeants were automatically doing what needed to be done. As it turned colder that evening and started to snow, we knew in our bones that trouble was coming.

The cooking areas of our little houses were in lean-to shelters with a large clay or iron water pot built in above an outside firebox. We discovered that the chimneys ran under the cement floor to the opposite end of the houses. It only took a little fire to heat water and warm the house floor. We learned the hard way that a large fire would make the floors too hot to sleep on and also cause fleas, bed bugs, and crab lice to hop or crawl all over the place, including on us.

We used the house next door to our aid station house primarily for sleeping, although some slept in the aid station building. Our American and Korean soldiers were put to work digging underground bunkers on both sides of the aid station house. I wanted our shelters to be at least five or six feet deep, but we couldn't get more than four feet deep because of rocks. We scraped the bottom, built up the sides to keep water out, and scrounged up boards, timbers and sheet metal for a roof. We installed cross-timbers over vertical pillars to support a load of dirt on top of it all.

As the 26th ROK Regiment soldiers left later that afternoon, our Koreans became very concerned about rumors of the Chinese approaching and wanted to get out of this cold spot before it became a hot spot. The 26th ROK Regiment loaded onto the trucks as quickly as we released them.

The most disturbing information was that some of the Korean soldiers in the 26th ROK Regiment told some of our KATUSA that they had heard Chinese voices nearby for the previous few nights. This information was enough for me to have the medical platoon start digging foxholes and two big bunkers for holding casualties, and also to start sandbagging and blacking out the two houses we were using as our aid station.

Having studied the map at battalion headquarters before starting our journey to Sachang-ni, I knew the town occupied a strategic position astride the upper reaches of the Taedong River. There was a fork in the road at Sachang-ni. One road went northwest, over a mountain pass and down to the valley carved by the Chongchun River on its journey to the Yellow Sea near Anju. The second road continued southwest to Pyongyang. That main road forked again a few miles west of Sachang-ni, with one branch going north to Huichon and then northeast to Kanggye near the Yalu River. That would be the most likely route used by the Chinese if they wanted to attack Hamhung and Hungnam from the west. But there was one obstacle facing the Chinese armies marching along the only road going east direct to Hungnam. That obstacle was the 1st Battalion of the 7th Infantry Regiment of the 3rd Infantry Division now in Sachang-ni.

We continued digging in at Sachang-ni, even as we discarded any notion about going farther west to join up with Gen. Walker's 8th Army. The fragmentary reports about fighting Chinese to the west and north and our common sense, told us we would not be mopping up North Korea, and we would not be home for Christmas. The Chinese had come into North Korea by the hundreds of thousands. As we studied the map and looked at the terrain, we wondered if we would still be alive by Christmas.

After Sgt. Herrick posted a rotation of paired GI and Korean guards all around our platoon area for the night, the rest of us had a peaceful night—sleeping side-by-side on the floor of our two commandeered aid station buildings. It seemed that those who did the most digging, also did the most snoring.

Landing craft leaving the troop transport in Wanson, Korea

U.S. troopship

KATUSA soldiers in the Medical Platoon of the 1st Battalion, 7th Infantry Regiment. (1st Lt. Sarka: back row, 2nd from left; Imm Yung Hee: back row, 5th from left; Sgt. 1st Class Herrick: back row, 2nd from right)

Left to right: 1st Lt. Sarka, Sgt. Byland, Father Carroll, Sgt. 1st Class Herrick, Sgt. Ogden, and Cpt. Jensen outside a temporary aid station

Hungry children with empty tins begging for food in North Korea

Chapter Seven
The six-day battle with the Chinese from Sachang-ni to Huksu-ri
November 26, 1950 – December 2, 1950

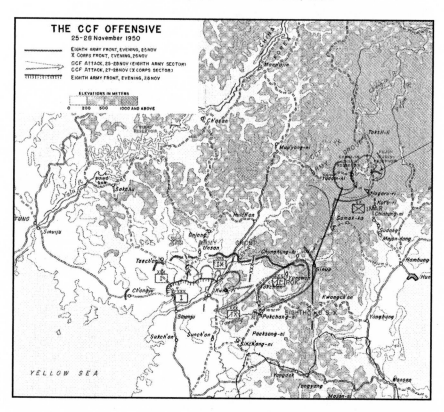

When I left for Korea in 1950, I was an admirer of Gen. MacArthur and disliked Truman because he had gutted the American military and then sent us off to fight in Korea as a so-called "police action" without asking Congress for a declaration of war. I also disliked Truman because of his decision to drop atom bombs on two cities in Japan, rather than dropping one bomb as a demonstration in a more remote area, such as near Mount Fuji, where the Japanese could observe it without great loss of life. He could then have threatened to drop the second atomic bomb on the Emperor's Palace if they didn't surrender after the demonstration bomb.

As a medical student at that time, I felt ashamed that our president didn't have greater wisdom in how he should have used our two atom bombs to end the war. Truman, who loved to read history, didn't seem to grasp the future historical significance of his own decisions. I felt that any person with average intelligence should have realized that, in world history, what goes around comes around. If, in the future, someone drops atom bombs on American cities, we'll find that people around the world will say it was our turn and we brought it on ourselves by atom bombing two cities in Japan first. We forever stigmatized America by being the first to use nuclear weapons on civilians. That is what happens when we elect limited people to high office.

On 25 November 1950, we were out on a limb in Sachang-ni. The water in the nearby river was now running southwest instead of east. We were at least one-third of the way across North Korea on the mission to join up with the 8th Army. But at that time, in late November 1950, the foot soldiers in the X Corps on the east side of Korea weren't aware that the 8th Army had already had pitched battles in the west with significant Chinese armies during the first week of November 1950. The 1st Cavalry Division had suffered major losses, with some of their battalions rendered non-functional. The 24th U.S. Infantry Divisions, the 2nd Infantry Division, and several ROK Divisions had also been heavily engaged.

After that first Chinese offensive, the Chinese army simply faded away into the hills and valleys away from the roads. If they waited for more cold weather, they wouldn't need any of the bridges across the Yalu River. Their needed food, guns, and ammunition would soon be carried by several hundred thousand foot soldiers and thousands of mules across the frozen Yalu.

Thus, while the Chinese moved silently through the hills and valleys, unbeknownst to us, they knew exactly when we were on the main roads, which could be attacked from all sides, especially at night, when our airplanes were less effective.

Our front line battalions learned about that new type of warfare the hard way. The Chinese tactics may not have been taught in West Point. However, Sun-tzu, in 1070 AD, and George Washington, in 1776 AD, both understood the value of doing the unexpected at night. If it was impertinent for Washington to cross the Delaware, in spite of some ice on Christmas Eve, it was no less impertinent for the Chinese to hide until after the Yalu was frozen over before launching a sustained major offensive southward.

The mountains and valleys in North Korea may not have seemed significant on the war maps in Tokyo, but on the ground in North Korea, with 15 to 20 miles or more between our infantry battalions, there was no possibility of coordination with friendly infantry units on our flanks, leaving abundant opportunity for enemy forces to surround us, which they did.

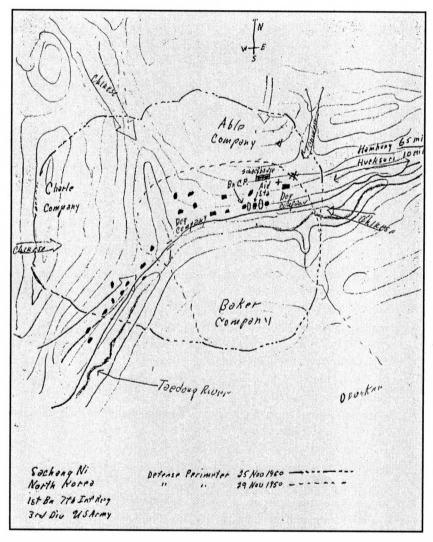

There were supposed to be several South Korean divisions west of Sachang-ni, under the control of the 8th Army. We had no physical or radio contact with them, but we were supposed to pass through those ROK units west of us to link up with the 8th Army to participate in the mopping up of the North Korean army and any Chinese volunteers that had come across the Yalu River. At least, that was the plan we were given, but it was a plan that few of us believed in.

However, the Division, Regiment, and Battalion commanders in the 8th Army on the western side of Korea weren't fools. They knew that there were a lot of Chinese soldiers out in front of them somewhere, because they'd already had significant battle contact. But where were they on 10 November 1950? That was a worrisome, unanswered question. So the field commanders did the logical thing and sent out patrols to locate the enemy. Of the many patrols sent out, only one patrol accomplished the mission of locating the enemy. That one successful probe was commanded by 1st Lt. George C. Viney.

Col. Viney, after 33 years of military service, retired on 31 January 1976 and is now living quietly in San Antonio, Texas, with Margaret (Peg) his wife of over 60 years. He had been awarded The Distinguished-Service Medal, Silver Star with Oak Leaf Cluster, Legion of Merit with Five Oak Leaf Clusters, Bronze Star Medal, Meritorious Service Medal, Air Medal with Seven Oak Leaf Clusters, Army Commendation Medal, Purple Heart with Cluster and a Combat Infantryman Badge—Second Award. He had commanded every infantry unit in combat from platoon to brigade. He was truly a professional Infantry Officer.

He had served in the 101st Airborne (Screaming Eagles) and the 2nd Airborne Division, as well as with Green Beret units in Vietnam and in several senior staff positions. His military career started in World War II as an enlisted volunteer. He became a 2nd lieutenant from an Officers Candidate School before joining the 6th Army in the Pacific. In Korea, he was assigned to the 5th Infantry Regiment and served consecutively as platoon leader, company commander, and battalion and regimental S-3 (plans and operations). It is probable that if he had been a graduate of West Point instead of an OCS graduate, he would have become a general officer. Military historians might find it of interest to spend some time with this outstanding professional soldier.

I asked Col. Viney to write a piece for this book about his unheralded but singularly successful combat patrol in North Korea on 10 November 1950, in which he came upon an assembly area of the Chinese armies as they were preparing for the battles that battered so many of the UN forces two weeks later. It was an important piece of military history, because if 1st Lt. Viney's observations had been properly evaluated and sent to higher headquarters, the history of the Korean War might have been different. Below is his summary:

"To: Dr. Robert T. Jensen, Subject: Combat Patrol in North Korea.

"The 8th U.S. Army had been attacking north toward the Yalu River since October 1950 and encountered some Chinese personnel that had pulled back for some reason not known to the frontline troops. Thereafter, during November

1950, our army continued the attack north of the Chongchon River and was slowly proceeding toward the Yalu River. The only problem was that 8th U.S. Army had lost contact with the enemy.

"On or about 10 November 1950, the 5th RCT (Regimental Combat Team), 24th Infantry Division, a part of I Corps of the 8th U.S. Army, was given the mission of making contact with the enemy. It is very bad to lose contact with the enemy when you are in combat. The second platoon, Company B, 1st Battalion, 5th RCT was given the mission of sending a patrol to the front of the army to make contact with the enemy. I was blessed with this mission.

"The patrol consisted of two M4A3E8 Sherman tanks from the Tank Company, two squads from my platoon, a jeep, a radioman with a portable radio, a medic, and an air OP, to be provided by division when we moved out. We moved out at approximately 1000 hours, speeding at 35 miles per hour toward the north on what would be a major gravel road. There were no hardtop roads in our area.

"About 20 miles in front of the friendly lines, we ran into two Russian T-34 tanks. One was in the ditch on the right side of the road and the other one was in the ditch on the left side. They didn't fire, so we drove straight into both tanks. We found them without crews; ammo was loaded, the tanks were completely operational, but there was no one around. This was a little unusual, but we didn't have any thermite grenades to ruin the engines and guns. Moreover, I didn't want to waste any 76 mm ammo on them because I might need everything I had to get back to the friendly lines. One had the feeling that we were being watched, but my mission was to contact the enemy. Since I was a gung-ho type, we took off to the north.

"The air OP checked in and stayed on line for a short time, but said they were running out of gas and would have to go all the way back to Pyongyang to refuel. We never heard from them again. That is when you say thanks for nothing. Since we were young soldiers, we shrugged this failure off and continued the attack to the north.

"With our tanks still roaring along at 35 miles per hour, we came upon a village, and the village chief had all the people out to welcome the victorious American Army, which had come to liberate them. They were shouting "banzai, banzai, banzai" and raising their hands in unison over their heads. The Japanese hadn't been gone too long from their country. We nodded and roared onward to the north.

"We went over a pass and down a road with rice paddies on both sides that were frozen, but there was no snow. As we were all looking to the front and to the sides, we didn't notice that one of our tank tracks had caught the telephone lines and was pulling telephone poles out of the ground and throwing them in the road behind us. About that time, one of the poles with cross bars crashed down upon us, it smashed my radioman, crushed his radio, broke his weapon, and cut up his head. We bandaged his head, put him in the jeep and continued the attack. By now, we had lost our OP and our radios, except for the local radios on the tanks. We still hadn't accomplished our mission, so we attacked ever onward into the fog.

"It was now about 1700, and we were 30 miles in front of the friendly lines, and as we went over a pass and down a road at our 35 mile an hour pace, we drove right through a small village loaded with Chinese. They were cooking their evening meal and they were as surprised to see us as we were to see them. Of course, the fight began, but the Chinese didn't want to fight then, because what we had done was to burst right into a large Chinese assembly area where they'd been hiding, in preparation for a big Chinese offensive, which started on 27 November 1950 in our area of operation. They left their food and ran in a column up a draw toward the mountains. Our tanks and all the infantrymen blistered their bottoms as they ran up the hill. The 76 mm shells tumbled them as they ran and, of course, we infantrymen put our sights on their backs and let the bullets fly. The Chinese fired Japanese .50 caliber elephant guns at our tanks and many of those rounds hit in the rice paddies around us. We didn't know how many we had killed or wounded, nor did we stay there to find out. Another fact that convinced us that these men were Chinese soldiers was that they wore packs, while the North Koreans didn't wear them. We didn't probe into the large valley before us to see what all was there. We'd made contact with the enemy. We were probably surrounded, but didn't know it.

"As I prepared to break contact, since we had accomplished our mission, I noticed a dead American by the roadside. His pile cap and boots were gone and his pile jacket had been pulled over his head. His extremities were frozen, but when I rolled him over, blood and water came out of burp gun holes in his stomach, which meant he hadn't been dead too long. I noticed a letter on him, indicating that he was an engineer sergeant from Tennessee. We put him in the back of the jeep. I also found an army captain's helmet nearby. I later learned that this engineer captain had a reputation for wild reconnaissance patrols to find tank trails. I didn't find his body, and it may be he was captured. We didn't find his jeep. It may have been there, but we could spend no more time looking around. It was time to go.

"My radioman, who was wounded and had his head bandaged, didn't have a weapon, and could have stayed out of the fight, but he noticed the driver had joined the fight and had left the jeep in the road. The radioman left his place of cover and rescued the jeep by driving it around a nose of the mountain behind us. It took me nine months to get him a Bronze Star for his actions.

"I went to the back of the tank commander's tank and got him on the phone. Our plan to break contact was for the tanks to continue to fire and cover us till we were behind the nose of the hill where the jeep had been moved. I threw a smoke grenade to signal the tanks to pull back, and we jumped on their backs as they came by with one gun pointed forward and the other to the rear. We left at the same speed with which we had come!

"The villagers cheered as we went by. I later learned that the guerillas had been watching from the hillside and came down that night and beat the living daylights out of them. We later attacked through their village and they did not cheer.

"We went by the T-34 tanks and they were still there ready for their crews, if and when they got some gas. It was getting dark and we had a long way to go, so we didn't tarry there to try to shoot them up.

"We returned after dark to the 1st Battalion CP of the 5th RCT for the customary debriefing. The body of the sergeant was turned in to the morgue. My radioman was treated. The tankers and the infantrymen returned to their bivouac areas, quite happy to still be alive.

"This action occurred 30 miles out in the front of the 8th Army lines. It was reported to be the only action that day where contact was made across the entire 8th U.S. Army front. The frontline soldier doesn't know what action is taken on the information he passes to higher headquarters, but there was ample warning that the Chinese were massing for a major attack.

"Unfortunately, there is a great tendency in the intelligence community to not want to be confused by the facts when their minds are made up."

George C. Viney, Colonel, Infantry (Ret)

Of course, it wasn't known to us when we entered Sachang-ni on 26 November that the Reconnaissance Team of the 5th RTC of the 24th Infantry Division on 10 November had actually pushed north beyond the Chongchon River toward the Yalu River, to establish contact with the assembling Chinese armies that had been attacking the 8th Army forces in late October and early November. It was patently obvious to Lt. Viney that these were real Chinese soldiers and not a gathering of Chinese volunteers coming to help out the North Koreans. But a young lieutenant can only be debriefed by his superior officer, and his superior officer determines what is reported. If all the other patrols found nothing, what weight should the superior officer give to Lt. Viney's report? That was where our army may have had a flaw in their thinking processes.

From the standpoint of a physician, ten negative biopsies would never outweigh one clearly positive biopsy for cancer. It would be considered gross malpractice to do so. One reason the other U.S. Army patrols may not have found any Chinese was because they hadn't gone far enough. But it also may have been that most of the Chinese had gone to that one assembly area for supplies and for their future marching orders.

It's too bad that our military intelligence people didn't fly Lt. Viney to Gen. Walker, the Commander of the 8th Army, or even to Tokyo, to inform MacArthur. It was a golden opportunity to order a massive air strike to carpet bomb the Chinese army assembly area south of the Yalu River. But on that occasion, our chain of command procedure was our worst enemy.

After Lt. Viney returned to his unit, he found that his promotion to captain had come through. Before he returned to the United States a year later, he would be promoted to major. Two promotions in combat was a testimony to his leadership ability.

Maj. Gen. Charles Willoughby, MacArthur's Intelligence Chief (G-2) probably didn't even receive the information provided by Lt. Viney's patrol. In any event, his mind was probably made up and we were urged to complete the conquest of North Korea quickly, in order to be home for Christmas. But the radios of our communication people warned us that the Chinese were already in Korea in big numbers. We wondered why we weren't being kept better informed through Army channels.

Clay Blair describes the reason for this lack of proper intelligence in his 1988 book, *The Forgotten War*, starting at chapter 14 (page 375), "The Chinese Strike." I refer the interested reader to *The Forgotten War* text if they would like more information. Suffice to say here it wasn't because our troops hadn't taken enough Chinese prisoners. Rather, MacArthur's G-2 chose to not believe the evidence. Gen. Willoughby had his own pet theories about what the Chinese might do and would not do. But Gen. Willoughby was wrong in his suppositions.

MacArthur's pool of good luck was drained by men such as Maj. Gen. Willoughby, who continued to tell MacArthur what he wanted to hear, even if what Willoughby said was foolish and sometimes concocted. There were good strategic reasons for the Chinese to wait until the U.S. forces were over-extended and near the Yalu River. The supply lines were much shorter for China in the far north of Korea. There were also many mountain valleys with few roads for our trucks and tanks. In these valleys, it would be possible to hide entire armies of foot soldiers, especially with overcast winter skies making aerial observation difficult. The Chinese had the best chance of isolating, surrounding, and destroying significant portions of the U.N. troops in the far north.[4]

---

[4] Written by Sun-tzu in 1070, *The Art of War*, deals explicitly with disinformation, deception, and destruction of the invader's armies. Sun-tzu's text is still used today in Chinese military schools.

The Inchon Invasion was successful because it was a surprise attack on the North Korean's over-extended supply lines. But MacArthur then made the same mistake as the North Koreans. When he headed north for the Yalu, he reached too far, and played into Chinese hands. Perhaps he had hoped to occupy all of Korea before the Chinese could respond, but his forces were too few to "police" all of the frigid mountains of North Korea and then defend the territory from hundreds of thousands of Chinese troops who could simply walk across the frozen Yalu River. Between Willoughby's denial of intelligence, and MacArthur's risky roll of the dice of war, the U.N. Army received a very bloody nose.

In hindsight, it's likely that if MacArthur hadn't tried to swallow all of North Korea in one gulp, the dividing line between North and South Korea might extend from Hungnam to Anju, in which case there wouldn't be enough of North Korea left to again threaten South Korea, as it's doing today.

But let us get back to the story of what happened in Sachang-ni. While our medical platoon was preparing two little houses to become our aid station and also digging bunkers for protection and patient storage, I received a runner from the Battalion Commander telling me to report in to the Battalion Headquarters. I arrived at the two-story wooden community building and found Lt. Col. "Toddy," the battalion commander, there with his staff.

Maj. Lawson Magruder (battalion executive), Cpt. Walter Turner S-1 (administration), Cpt. John McAuliffe S-2 (intelligence), Maj. Ronald Kapp S-3 (plans and operations), Cpt. Letcher Crawford S-4 (supply and support services), Cpt. Howard Giebel (D Company commander), and Cpt. James Baker (HQ Company commander) were all sitting in a staff meeting with Lt. Col. Toddy. As I walked in to report, I looked around at the many glass windows with no blackout screening. The place was a firetrap. A carbine could shoot through the thin wooden walls with ease. Needless to say, I was surprised the building had been selected for use as battalion headquarters during a war.

I reported directly to Lt. Col. Toddy.

After I saluted, he said, "Doc, the second floor of this building might be a nice place to put the aid station. What do you think?"

"Yes sir, I'll look it over."

I didn't want to immediately reveal my reluctance to putting an aid station on the second floor until I'd had a chance to look around and figure out the best way to refuse. I climbed the stairs to the second floor. There was a nice view of the village and surrounding hills from windows located on every side of the second floor—no doubt pleasant in peacetime.

Although the rifle companies on the perimeters were digging in and preparing firing lanes for machine guns, I didn't observe anyone from headquarters digging foxholes or preparing underground shelters. I wondered about that, because our Korean soldiers had told us that the ROK 26th Regiment had been hearing Chinese voices during the night. I'd wrongly assumed that our Battalion Command Center had received the same information from the departing ROK Commander.

As I returned downstairs to face Lt. Col. Toddy, I was unable to think of a tactful way to decline his suggestion for using the second floor for an aid station.

So I just said, in front of everybody sitting there, "Sir, I don't think it's wise to carry litter patients up stairs. Moreover, we can't black out the windows, and if we come under attack, this place would be an indefensible firetrap."

As I now look back on that exchange 50 years later, I realize that I should have said, "Sir, may I speak to you privately for a moment?"

But I didn't have the maturity or wisdom to think of that then and apparently Lt. Col. Toddy didn't think of it, either, because he conducted most of his business in front of his staff, thereby forfeiting his opportunity to give and receive private counsel. Speaking up as I did precipitated an awkward silence.

Finally, Lt. Col. Toddy spoke, saying, "Do you have a better idea, Doc?"

"Yes, sir," I answered. "We've picked out two little houses, fifty yards from here, near the road, and have already started to sandbag and black out the windows and to dig foxholes and underground bunkers nearby for patients and men."

This caused another moment of silence, until Toddy broke the silence, "Captain Baker will go with you to check out what your men are doing, and if it looks okay to Captain Baker, it's okay with me."

I wondered why he hadn't suggested Cpt. Turner do that, since the medical platoon was the responsibility of the S-1. But not wanting to prolong the discussion, I said no more.

Cpt. Baker was a good old soldier who had come up through the ranks in World War II and was experienced in combat.

He looked over our work in progress and then said, "It looks fine to me, Doc. I'll tell the colonel it's okay."

I noticed the surprise on Cpt. Baker's face as he looked at our bunkers. It caused me to wonder if the battalion headquarters staff had been properly briefed.

I then informed Cpt. Baker about the soldiers of the 26th ROK regiment telling our KATUSA Soldiers that they'd been hearing Chinese voices at night.

Cpt. Baker was startled with that news, but simply said, "We'll soon be busy digging holes, too."

While all that was going on, the cooks had opened large cans of rations and made coffee. We soon had a hot meal in our cold metal mess kits. The food was eaten quickly, before it could freeze, because the air temperature had fallen below zero and it had started to snow.

Earlier that morning, Lt. Col. Toddy had sent out patrols to see what was out there. The company commanders continued to dig in their defensive perimeters and cleared overlapping firing lanes for the machine guns. Likely trails and probable assembly points for an enemy attack were identified. The freshly-fallen snow made tracking easier. Small and large mortars were zeroed in. Lt Col Toddy had assigned defensive positions.

Able Company took over the hill north of the town, Baker Company covered the south and east extending across the Taedong River, and Charlie Company covered the road west and a prominent trail to the northwest. Dog Company and Headquarters Company were spread out over the center section of the town, covering the flat area along the north side of the Taedong River. Our tanks and trucks were located near the two-story building.

The 105 howitzers, as well as tank cannons and ring-mounted .50 caliber machine guns on trucks, were lined up on paths likely to be taken by attackers. We knew we were now potential targets. It was a good thing we had started digging the day we arrived.

The battalion headquarters wasn't as well prepared. When the mortar shells started dropping on and around the two-story wooden building, the headquarters staff quickly moved to our backup aid station house. After that building was also hit, they moved into the bunker we'd prepared between our two houses.

The official record of the events of the next four days, copied below, is taken from pages 86-87 of *A History of the 3rd Infantry Division in the Korean War Compiled in 1953*. It doesn't provide all of the details, but it's a useful overview of the action.

"At 1900 hours on the 26th, the 1st BCT 7th RCT was in a blocking position near Sachang-ni. Twenty Chinese attacked an outpost using grenades and small arms as they closed in shouting "GI, GI," in an attempt to confuse the defenders and cause them to hold their fire. The defenders didn't. They killed four of the Chinese without loss to themselves. The attack was renewed at 0230 hours (27 Nov.) and was driven off, but around 1930 hours the enemy began shelling the battalion positions. Two hours later 500 Chinese Reds attacked the perimeter. The battalion CP and fire direction center were knocked out by mortar fire. Communications to companies were disrupted until 0530 the next morning. C Company positions were penetrated, but the attackers were driven off by daybreak.

"On the 28th, [Lt. Col. Toddy's] men at Sachang-ni captured prisoners who were identified as being from the 89th Div, CCF. Throughout the day the BCT was subjected to harassing small arms fire. In the early hours of the next morning (29th Nov.) the Chinese launched a heavy assault from northeast, north and northwest. The attack was beaten off by 0730 and the battalion S-2 estimated the attacking force to be 2000.

"The assault on the 1st Battalion was only a minor incident in the overall pattern of the day's events in Korea. For on that date, the CCF armies unleashed a gigantic counter-assault across the breadth of the Korean peninsula. In the west, the Eighth Army was stopped cold. Korean (ROK) divisions in central Korea simply vanished before the onslaught. Near Kunu-ri, the gallant Turkish brigade fought with cold steel and superb courage to hold the avalanche of Chinese and protect the exposed flank of Lt. Gen. Walton H. Walker's hard beset troops.

"Only the day before, the 1st Mar Div. had occupied the town of Yudam on the western side of the Changjin Reservoir. In a dangerously exposed position at the end of extended lines of communications, the Marines were a fat objective for the Chinese attack. Far to the north, many mountainous miles from the coast, elements of the 7th U.S. Division were on the banks of the Yalu River where they enjoyed a Thanksgiving Day dinner in a festive mood. ROK troops pushing northward in their sector along the Sea of Japan toward the Korean Russian frontier were in a potentially critical position."

My own recall of those events is given below, but was supported by a paper I wrote in early 1952 while attending the Advanced Officers Course at the U.S. Army Medical Field Service School in San Antonio, Texas. In it, I discussed the medical support provided during three battles in Korea. The first battle was our struggle while surrounded in Sachang-ni.

The intensive infantry preparation of defensive positions by our battalion on 25 and 26 November was time well spent. While the two bunkers on either side of the aid station house were neither deep enough nor big enough to use as an aid station, they served as a place to store the wounded until they could be evacuated. The aid station house was protected by a sturdy shelf of logs under the windows, covered by sandbags. As we had time, we filled more sandbags and placed them under the logs to provide more support.

Inside of the house, army blankets were nailed over the windows and blackout blankets were nailed inside the doors, allowing the doors to be opened without exposing much light. We had two gasoline pressure lamps for light, and large buckets to place over the lamps for temporary blackouts.

Patient stretchers were placed on tables or chairs, and a small worktable was found for surgical instruments. Hand washbasins, with iodine-based disinfectant, as well as sterile towels and sterile rubber gloves, were available, but in limited supply. We usually worked with bare hands that had been thoroughly scrubbed and rinsed in disinfectant solution. We were vulnerable to mortar and direct small arms fire, but we had prepared a place to work as best we could in the short time available. It was up to God to keep the 120 mm and 82 mm mortars from coming through the grass roof.

I asked Lt. Sarka to maintain contact with battalion headquarters and keep me informed of what was going on there. That proved to be more important than I'd anticipated, because our HQ was hit and moved twice during the night on November 26th. Sarka also assisted the wounded in finding our aid station in the dark. He remained active above ground outside, despite scattered mortar and small arms fire. Others tried to maximize the time they spent cowering in foxholes. Sarka later received a Bronze Star with V-Device for his efficient work under fire.

In the very early morning on November 27th, there was a lot of small arms fire and grenade explosions from the direction of Charley Company. Repeated explosions of incoming large and small mortar shells occurred throughout the battalion area prior to the Chinese infantry attacks. I soon learned that the brief incoming whine of a mortar shell meant feeling the following explosion. Thanks to the coordinated activities of Lt. Sarka, Sgt. 1st Class Byland, and Sgt. Prystas throughout the HQ and Dog Company areas, many of those wounded during mortar barrages were quickly moved to our aid station. Some were transported by GI and Korean litter squads, but most arrived under their own power, leaving bloody trails in the newly-fallen snow. Lt. Sarka and our sergeants controlled the entrance to the aid station and guided those who had been bandaged and stabilized to our underground bunker.

Early in the evening of the first night's battle, I asked for Sgt. Herrick and the battalion chaplain, Father Carroll. I expected their help throughout the night. Since they didn't respond, I assumed they'd gone to visit a rifle company and had been caught there during the firefight.

I shouted loudly, "Sergeant First Class Charles Ogden –wherever you are— get your *** into the aid station now!"

That command received an immediate, "Yes, sir!" from Ogden, who crawled out of the relative safety of the east bunker.

One of our medics, resting in the relative safety of the bunker remarked, "I sure am glad I'm not a sergeant."

Someone else added, "I would rather be a live PFC than a dead sergeant."

A major problem for our medics working above ground in the infantry platoons was avoiding being confused with the enemy and receiving friendly fire, or stumbling into one of our many machine gun firing lanes. One of the infantry NCOs, who'd been wounded by mortar fire, was killed by our own machine guns as he crossed the Taedong River en route to the aid station.

As Chinese mortar shells continued to land, our mortars, tanks, and 105 howitzers opened up on the previously sighted-in trails and likely enemy attack staging areas. Many of our support guns concentrated on the area in front of Charley Company, which had been enveloped by attacking Chinese. The noise was deafening and the carnage terrible.

We often couldn't tell which explosions were incoming shells and which were outgoing cannon fire. There was a strong temptation to hide in a foxhole until morning, especially when shells exploded near the aid station house. That night seemed very long. I quickly resolved to keep with me in the aid station only the number of medics needed for the workload at hand. If we took a direct hit with a 120 mm mortar, I wanted as few killed as possible. Sgt. Ogden became my chief assistant and coordinating nurse during the first busy night.

I vividly recall how our house shook when a 120 mm mortar shell landed nearby as I was trying to start an I.V. on a wounded GI and clamp bleeders to keep him from bleeding to death. After the explosion, I glanced around at the medic's faces in the white light of the pressure lantern. Every face reflected wide-eyed terror. We all wanted to dive into a foxhole, fearing the next mortar round really would land on our heads. But we couldn't hide in a hole, because we still had several wounded soldiers to treat.

Afraid that panic might break out, I spoke loudly and firmly, "We will not leave patients that haven't yet been treated to take cover in a foxhole or bunker. We can't examine or stabilize patients in the dark in a hole in the ground. We are Army medics and we will stand our ground and do our duty, no matter what happens to us. Our men are fighting outside. We will do our duty here and now, and for as long as is required. We'll save lives as long as we're alive. Is that clear?"

Apparently, it was very clear, because no one spoke and we all resumed working. I was having trouble getting a needle into the patient's vein, my hands were shaking, so I prayed, "Lord Jesus, help me, How can I do my duty, if I can't keep my hands from shaking? I not only need courage, but I also need help getting this I.V. started."

Even while praying, I experienced His presence. My hands stopped shaking, I was able to start the I.V. of saline and albumen, and also to find and clamp the bleeders. I looked up half expecting to see Jesus standing across from me, but I only saw the faces of the medics around me. The men looked different now. Their wide-eyed panic was gone. They were working quietly and without apparent fear.

"I'm pleased with the courage you're all demonstrating," I told them. "You're behaving like soldiers."

That night, we established the standard of behavior for our medical platoon under fire. We would continue to do our duty for the wounded, no matter what happened. Our infantry brothers soon came to understand and appreciate that this was the standard expected of the medical platoon of the 1st Battalion of the 7th Infantry Regiment of the 3rd Division.

After bandages had been applied to the last of the night's casualties, they were moved to the patient bunker, with two medics in attendance to remove I.V. needles when the fluid had been received. With the coming of daylight, the shelling, shooting, and shouting died down. In the distance, I heard a Chinese bugler.

As I stepped outside in the early morning to see how the patients in the bunkers were doing, a parting mortar shell whizzed down and landed in the shallow ditch just across the narrow dirt road in front of the aid station. The shell exploded, but the side of the ditch prevented fragments from hitting me as I jumped into a foxhole. To my surprise, I landed on a bale of blankets.

In my exasperation, I kicked them and said, "I've been looking for these damn blankets all night! I wonder who dropped them into this hole."

As I was speaking, the bale of blankets groaned and said, "Who the hell kicked me in the back?"

"Is that you, Herrick?" I said. "I should give you another kick! I've been looking for you all night!"

With that remark, Herrick stood up in the foxhole, with a guilty look on his face.

"Yes, sir," he said.

I lashed out angrily as Herrick stood at attention.

"I needed you last night and I didn't know where you were. Now I want you to get out and bring in the wounded from every company. Start with Charley Company, then go to Able, Baker, and Dog. Round up the litter squads and don't stop until you've brought in every wounded GI, Korean, and the Chinese, too. If you don't know where to look, follow the damn bloody snow trails back to the infantry platoons. We have to prepare all the casualties for evacuation and get ready for another battle tonight, so move your *** or lose your stripes."

"Yes, sir!"

Herrick leaped out of the foxhole and started rousting up the men of the medical platoon, as a good sergeant knows how to do. As he left, I realized how very tired I was. The emotional impact of the night's work was wearing heavily on me. I wanted to find a safe place to sleep, but that wasn't possible. I started to climb out of the foxhole with the blankets and found Father Carroll offering me a hand up, just as another shell landed across the road.

"Just get up behind me, Doc," he said. "I don't think their mortars can go through me to you."

I looked at the padre's 250-pound girth and couldn't help but agree. We both laughed.

Then Chaplain Carroll spoke to me gently.

"What happened to Bill last night was my fault," he said. "It was quiet yesterday evening, and I had a half bottle of Jack Daniel. Bill and I killed the bottle, climbed into foxholes and slept through the night. We missed all of the fireworks. I'm sorry, Doc. You must have had a busy night."

He extended his hand and I shook it. I had no desire to do anything except forgive, forget, and go to sleep until I had to get back to work. It wasn't to be. Walking wounded arrived as the aid station was being cleaned up to receive them.

As I passed by our patient bunker on the way back to the aid station, I heard one aid man bragging to another, "I stood with the doctor all night, holding the light so he could see. Even when the mortars were landing, and my arms were tired, I still kept holding the light."

I paused to thank the Lord for the courage that had settled over my medical platoon. My prayer had been answered for all of us. I felt as if God was watching over us and I was grateful. Later, I wondered if God had allowed Herrick to get drunk that night so I'd be forced to place my trust in Him alone. With His help, my leadership under fire of the medical platoon had been affirmed.

In the meantime, Sarka had checked in with HQ. An armed convoy was prepared to escort our attached box ambulances as soon as we had them loaded. We were also expecting an airdrop of food, ammunition, and medical supplies, including a case of universal blood for transfusions. We needed that blood badly. Sergeants Herrick, Byland, Prystas, and Ogden were spread out over the area, each with a team of men to retrieve the parachutes.

Ogden made a list of the night's casualties, and Sgt. Adams and Sgt. Bowie supervised the loading of the ambulances with wounded. A truck, carrying a ring-mounted machine gun and gunner, was set aside for the bodies of our dead soldiers.

The Korean soldiers in our medical platoon couldn't have been more hardworking or faithful. But some of our infantry sergeants reported dissatisfaction with the behavior of their Koreans under fire.

Upon hearing those complaints, Sgt. Herrick responded angrily by saying, "If you treat people like ****, you should expect **** in return."

The buddy system we'd put in place in the medical platoon, one Korean with one American GI, had been working well. One of our medics said we should have a new U.S. Army song called "Me and my ROK." Too bad we had no composer or poet to prepare the tune and lyrics.

Lt. Sarka, who knew all of the company grade officers and sergeants in the battalion, continued to be a vacuum cleaner for scuttlebutt. He kept the facts straight, and generally to himself, aside from informing Herrick and me about what was happening. While Herrick was out scouring the far reaches of every infantry platoon, checking up on and encouraging the company aid men, and sending sick and wounded back to the aid station, Sarka came in to give me a rundown on who was up fighting the Chinese, and who had hidden in foxholes during the night. I learned that the headquarters building had been hit by mortar rounds and abandoned early in the shelling. Our second aid station house next door had been taken over by HQ. They had moved their communication center with them into the kitchen area of the house and were set up and functioning as the battalion command center when a 120 mortar landed on the west side of their house. Shell fragments had flattened the tires of Lt. Col. Toddy's jeep, including the spare, and damaged the roof and west wall of their new HQ, which had been our reserve aid station house.

Another 120 mortar round had come through the roof, directly into the room occupied by the HQ staff, and failed to explode. When the shell landed, the entire staff immediately bailed out of the building and dove into our second patient bunker, on the west side of the aid station. The distance between the aid station and the now-damaged HQ building was about 40 feet. The shell fragment and blast damage would have been worse if the battalion commander's jeep hadn't absorbed so much of the first 120 mortar blast. If the second 120 mortar round hadn't failed to explode, most of the HQ staff would have been killed.

The communication equipment, radios, and phone center in the adjacent kitchen area were undamaged, but also unattended for a time. The communication officer, 1st Lt. Joe Piaseczny, came over in the midst of the shooting, shouting, and shelling to find out why the HQ command center wasn't answering calls. Piaseczny found the communication equipment fully functional, but neither live nor dead soldiers were found in the house. He searched around the house until he came upon an antenna sticking out of our west bunker entrance hole.

Joe Piaseczny was a likable officer of Polish decent from Milwaukee who didn't get riled up easily. He was prematurely bald and was sometimes referred to as "Nude-knob." It didn't seem to bother Joe. What did bother him was finding one of his best battery pack radios in a hole in the ground with its antenna sticking out.

He shouted down into the bunker, "Who in hell is at the other end of this radio?"

"This is Corporal Jones, sir," came the reply.

"Why in hell is your radio turned off?" Piaseczny shouted back.

"I was told to turn it off to save battery power," the corporal said.

"Who is that S.O.B. in the hole with you?"

"This is Lieutenant Colonel Toddy," said a new voice.

"Yes, sir!" Piaseczny said. "I'm just checking out the battalion command center's communication systems to make sure everything is operational—sir."

Piaseczny returned to the kitchen area in the battalion command center of the damaged house and began answering calls, relaying information, and encouraging the rifle companies. In essence, he played the role of the battalion commander. He knew how important it was for each rifle company to know that they weren't the only company still fighting. Apparently, nobody had told Piaseczny about the 120 mm dud round that had landed in the next room, only a few feet away from him. It was still sitting there, waiting to go off.

Piaseczny, of course, expected Lt. Col. Toddy to come out of the bunker and join him at the communication center at any moment. Whether the colonel came out of the bunker before the Chinese blew their retreat bugles and the mortar fire slacked off, I don't know. Some of our brave mortar men removed the dud Chinese 120 mortar round in the morning and exploded it in a nearby foxhole, making the HQ building habitable again—an event I didn't observe because I was busy with patients in the next building.

Warrant Officer John N. Middlemas of the HQ Company also came by during the night to see how HQ and the aid station were doing. He had looked in on Lt. Piaseczny during the night. Middlemas had assumed the task of organizing an inner defensive circle using the Heavy Weapons (D) Company and the trucks with mounted machine guns belonging to HQ Company. Our mortar men, the 105 howitzer crews, and our two tanks continued to fire at previously assigned targets and at any other targets called in. I have no idea how many new targets were called in or where the rest of the HQ's staff spent the night, but they all showed up for breakfast after the shooting and shelling stopped.

We weren't able to use our west bunker for many patients because of the relay of HQ's staff checking in to rest before heading out again. Once the casualties started flowing in, I seldom got out of the aid station until long after the Chinese bugles had ordered withdrawal.

In the light of dawn, there were Chinese bodies scattered willy-nilly all around, near and far. Our companies' machine-gun lanes and indirect fire weapons, aimed at paths and trails, had exacted a high price in human life. The Chinese attackers never got our defense system figured out before their ammunition ran out. I was relieved to hear their retreat bugle sound in the early morning hours before some Chinaman poked his head in our aid station and sprayed us with a burp gun.

To my observation, it was Middlemas, Piaseczny, Turner, and Sarka who coordinated battalion activities in the heat of the first night of battle. That night formed an unspoken bond between us. Years later, John Middlemas referred to that special bond of soldiers who continued to do their duty in battle as "the clan of warriors."[5]

---

[5] Refer to Middlemas' letter at end of book.

After Herrick had finished his medical rounds to every platoon of each infantry company, he approached me when I was alone, saluted and said, "Sir, I let you down last night. Everyone knows how you stood your ground and took care of our casualties while others hid in holes. I should have been at your side, but I failed you by sleeping off too much whiskey. But, sir, if you will only forgive me this one time, I swear by all that is holy, I'll never let you down again."

I looked at him with tears in my eyes and said, "Bill, I forgive you. And if you never let me down, I'll try to never let you down, and then perhaps the Lord in His mercy will allow both of us to come out of this war alive."

Herrick never let us down again.

From that moment on, Bill Herrick became a legend on the line for rescuing wounded soldiers under fire. Some of the infantrymen he served so valiantly said that he had a charmed life, because he was never hit. Herrick received two Silver Stars, a Bronze Star, and a battlefield commission, but no Purple Hearts. How he escaped receiving any Purple Heart-worthy injuries, God alone knows. But to all appearances, it seemed that God had chosen to give Bill divine protection.

The fighting continued nightly for the next three days. I wrote the letter below on the night of November 30. I compressed and softened some facts so as to not cause my parents undue alarm.

Dear Dad and Mother,   *30 Nov. 1950*

For the first time in several days, I have a little time for sleep. First of all, I received your packages, shoes, hand gloves, etc., and also the cap from John. We have been issued winter equipment but in this climate one needs plenty.

I have had my fill of fighting in the last week. The little village where we are situated is a hot spot in the front lines, which is the area of the pinchers between the marines to the northeast and the 8th Army to the south and west.

Ever since we moved into Sachang-ni until last night, we have been attacked nightly by bands of Chinese Communists. The first night the outer patrols were attacked but for the four following nights the attacks were increasingly fierce. Night before last was the worst with heavy casualties on both sides. If a man falls, he is apt to freeze to death if not found within a few hours. The aid station is in a house during the daytime and in holes at night. The Chinese zeroed in on our area with mortars. They hit the C.P. next door and laid six shells within 60 yards of the aid station but but didn't damage it. We had to move all of our casualties out and under ground.

Thankfully the Chinese are a little short on mortar ammunition or they would have leveled the place. We had to throw everything into the line two nights ago, cooks, clerks, aid men etc., to stop them. The first about 10:30 and the second about 3:00 a.m. During the day we have nothing but sniper fire.

We sent out 40 casualties yesterday a.m. and six today so far. It is a five-hour ride via ambulance over mountain passes to Hamhung. By helicopter it's 40 minutes. I sent one severe casualty out by helicopter yesterday. He had his legs nearly blown off with a hand grenade.

The sniper opened up while we were loading a stretcher. It's an uncomfortable feeling to be standing there with bullets hissing all around. I got out of there fast after the stretcher was loaded and back to the aid station. With my field glasses, I could see a sniper on the hill so I got my rifle, raised the sight to 1000 yards and blazed away. I don't know whether I hit him or not because he was gone when I looked again with the glasses.

Today we have had terrific air support with Marine fighter-bombers raking the Chinese with jelly gasoline and machine cannons.

Last night we received reinforcements in the form of troops and an antiaircraft battery. The battery is a group of two tank-mounted twin automatic 40 mm canons and two half-tracks with quad mounted .50 cal. machine guns in a turret. They must have spotted them coming because they didn't attack last night. The ach-ach (antiaircraft) bunch is used just for antipersonnel work with the twin 40's and quad 50's. The hillsides can be completely cleaned of the enemy.

Last night was the first night's sleep I have had in five days except for a little catnap now and then. I have gotten used to our artillery, which is situated about 200 yards from us. It rattles the windows every time they blaze away. By the way, the black sweater you sent was put to good use. One of the patients yesterday forded an icy river to escape when his position was overrun. I gave him the sweater and loaded him on an ambulance.

The situation now looks a little better, but two days ago we weren't sure whether we would be able to hold out or not. Try to not worry too much. I am in about the safest spot in the battalion and we will be operating completely underground soon. It's hard digging all day and fighting all night.

I have my camera with me and have taken some interesting shots. The mail situation is pretty good now and some of the back letters are reaching me now.

I don't know how long we will be here but this war can't get over too soon to suit me. We have taken a few Chinese prisoners.

Note: Blacked out three line section of letter here.[6]

---

[6] Three lines of the letter above dealing with POW's were blacked out, apparently from a censor.

Right now the Marine planes are diving over our position and blazing away at the Chinese on the next hill. Send this letter on to John, as I am too tired to write another today.

Love, Bob

I think the lines that were blacked out in my letter may have been about a wounded Chinese officer that had been shot by one of our Korean medics. I had handed him a Syrette of morphine tartrate and told him to give the Chinese prisoner a shot of morphine for his pain. I turned away to start an I.V. of blood on another casualty and a moment later, the Korean medic shot the Chinese officer through the head with his carbine.

When I turned to see what had happened, the medic patted his carbine and said with a big grin on his face, "Carbine shot better than morphine shot for Chinese officer. Chinese officer shoot Korean prisoners in head with pistol."

Apparently, the Chinese officer had also said something very rude to the Korean medic about worthless Korean dogs helping Americans. That insulting remark fatally changed the type of shot he received from the KATUSA medic.

A big stink was created back in 3rd Division Headquarters because that Chinese officer had been wanted for questioning by our intelligence people.

I had no time or energy left for the niceties and complications of a court martial, which would have cast a cloud over our relations with all of our South Korean friends. I was also afraid that someone at Division might take all of our Koreans out of the medical platoon, so I decided to preempt the decision.

Before any higher-up officers could get involved, I again gave a talk to the medics about our duty to treat all casualties, including North Korean and Chinese prisoners, with kindness and stressed that no wounded prisoner would ever be shot when in our custody, except in self-defense. I announced that since that Korean medic seemed to like to shoot Chinese, I was having him transferred to a rifle company, where there was an ongoing need for people who were good at shooting enemy soldiers between the eyes. That got the attention of all of our aid men, especially the Koreans. Since we were still under attack, that Korean medic was immediately transferred to a rifle company. We all knew that his chance of surviving the war was slim to none.

Lt. Col. Toddy took some heat about that incident because he'd already informed higher headquarters that we'd be sending back a wounded Chinese officer for G-2 questioning. How much of the true story reached higher headquarters, I don't know. But Toddy appeared to be satisfied with my remedial action and I apologized personally to him for allowing such a thing to happen in our medical platoon. I felt personally responsible and sick over the entire incident.

We continued to work on our defensive positions, but we never were able to get our medical bunkers big enough or deep enough to use them as an aid station.

They were only used for storing patients until they could be evacuated. The sniper that I shot at wasn't 1000 yards away, as stated in my letter, but less than 200 yards away. My father, as an experienced hunter, would know that any good sniper should be able to hit someone easily at only 200 yards. It only would have caused my father to worry.

The Marine Corps helicopter that brought medical supplies and more blood was the first helicopter to reach us, but it had no litter pods. However, I was determined to use the opportunity to evacuate three badly wounded soldiers. One was a young enlisted man, Pvt. 1st Class Henry Franklin West of Kingsport, Tennessee, who could only sit up with difficulty because of his wounds. The second man was an American GI who'd had a grenade explode between his knees. He was brought before me on a stretcher with blood running in through an I.V. and out from his shredded legs. Just then I saw the helicopter land about 75 yards away. I was determined that that "gift from God helicopter" wasn't going to leave without taking three wounded soldiers, including the stretcher patient, back to a MASH unit or hospital ship.

As we rushed the stretcher out to the helicopter, the Marine pilot shouted, "I can't take a stretcher patient unless I take a window panel out of the helicopter."

As he spoke, snipers from the hillside just north of us opened up. They soon drew answering fire from ring-mounted machine guns on trucks, which raked the hillside randomly to distract snipers.

When the shooting began, the pilot insisted that he had to leave immediately. I insisted instead that he get busy with his screwdriver and take out the window panel, because he wasn't leaving without my stretcher patient. Since the pilot was on the ground, and we medics, including Big Bak, outnumbered him five to one, he started unscrewing screws as fast as he could. In a long two minutes, we had the window out. The two wounded men who could sit, Pvt. 1st Class West and another soldier who'd been shot through one arm, were buckled into the back seat. The stretcher patient was then shoved headfirst through the window opening, with the removed window on top of him. We tied the stretcher patient's ankles to the handles of the stretcher with multiple wrappings of roller gauze and wrapped surgical tape around both the patient and stretcher, to make sure his shredded legs wouldn't blow away. It would have been nice if we'd had duct tape, but it wasn't available. We hung up the stretcher patient's I.V. and added a bottle of blood inside the helicopter. Pvt. Henry West was given the task of watching the blood I.V. drip run into the arm of the stretcher patient and was instructed how to clamp the tube when the bottle was empty and to pull out the needle and put pressure on the arm where the needle came out.

As the helicopter rose, the ends of the gauze bandages blew merrily in the rotor wind. I never found out what happened to the stretcher patient, but I found out later that Pvt. West ended up on a Navy hospital ship, so I assume the other two soldiers did, as well. I'm also sure the helicopter pilot was glad to get away in one piece. I never saw that Marine pilot again.

With the sniper(s) still pinging away, the litter bearers scattered for cover and I did a 75-yard dash back to the aid station in record time. When I reached the aid station, I grabbed my binoculars and a loaded M-1 rifle. I was angry and my blood was hot. I'd been listening to machine-guns, rifles, and mortars all night while I'd worked in an exposed position and, finally, I had an opportunity to shoot back. Was I a little crazy?

I returned to the edge of an open area near to the sniper's field of fire and assumed a prone position behind some sandbags to study the hillside with binoculars. As I searched back and forth, I thought I saw a head appear between two rocks. I heard a rifle shot, and the head disappeared. There was a soldier nearby, and I asked him to take the binoculars and focus on a black spot on a large exposed rock on the hillside near the sniper's notch and tell me how close I came to the black spot. With the rifle resting on a sandbag, I squeezed off a round.

"Doc," he said, "You hit about three feet low and about a foot to the left of the black spot."

I then asked him to focus the binoculars on the notch between the two rocks to the right and tell me if a head appeared.

The soldier suddenly said, "I think I see him!"

I quickly squeezed off a round, aiming about three feet high and a foot to the right of the notch between the rocks. The head simply disappeared and the firing stopped.

I returned to the aid station to get back to work, feeling drained. Firing a couple of shots at a sniper had released some tension, but it gave me no pleasure. In fact, it made me feel a little sick. I wondered about the family he'd left behind. I enjoyed hunting for meat in northern Minnesota, but I never really enjoyed the killing part. I much preferred to save lives.

Later that day, two Marine Corsairs machine-gunned the hill and burned it with napalm. We were close enough to wave to the pilots, and to feel the heat of the napalm. After the Corsairs had dipped their wings and parted company, Able Company reoccupied the strategic hill, in preparation for our exit strategy from Sachang-ni.

As an addendum to the sniper incident, about three months later, in South Korea, I had an infantry sergeant as a patient who had a non-disabling wound that would get him home, happy and in one piece. As we chatted, he told me he had a souvenir Mouser rifle that he'd taken from a dead Chinese sniper. It was a 7.9 mm Mouser, made in 1937. He said he'd been thinking of converting it into a sporting rifle when he got home. However, he couldn't take it home with him through the medical evacuation system, so he asked if I wanted to keep it.

"Sure," I said. "Where did you pick it up?"

"It was at a place called Sachang-ni in North Korea," he answered. I wondered if the rifle had been taken from the sniper I'd shot at in Sachang-ni. I'll never know for sure. I still have the rifle, but today it has a new plastic stock and it does shoot straight.

After the sniper interlude, I returned to our aid station area and sorted through the wounded in our bunker. To my surprise, I found Lt. Arnold Galifa, sound asleep. In the early morning hours, Galifa had been lightly wounded. He'd carried another more seriously wounded soldier down off the hill and then had sat down to rest for a few minutes next to his friend. They both fell fast asleep. It had been a rough night for them.

Galifa was a big, strong man. He'd earned the reputation of being able to throw a grenade farther and more accurately than any other soldier in the battalion. He would actually rifle a grenade as if he were throwing a football. I guess that was to be expected from the quarterback of the championship 1948 West Point football team.

I woke Galifa and said, "Arnold, it's time to get back to your platoon."

He looked rather embarrassed and hurried to rejoin his unit.

The longevity of infantry platoon leaders in combat was brief. John Trent, a close friend of Galifa, had been the captain of that 1948 West Point football team. He had been assigned to the 15th Infantry Regiment, also a part of the 3rd Division. Trent had the dubious distinction of being the first member of the 15th Regiment to be killed in Korea. Later, the Army started rotating West Point infantry platoon leaders off of the line in Korea after six months. Had they not, there would be very few members of the West Point Classes of 1948, 1949, 1950, and 1951 left alive to celebrate reunions.

Galifa was pulled off the line a few months later for emergency leave, and soon after became an aide in MacArthur's Headquarters, where I visited him when I went on rest and relaxation (R&R) leave.

The next morning, we awoke early. As we passed through the mess tent, we received a stack of hot pancakes flooded by boiling-hot syrup. We wolfed it down before the pancakes could freeze in our mess kits. It didn't taste good, but it was hot and filling. When Lt. Col. Toddy came through the line, the cooks created a corner of the tent where he could eat in a more stylish manner, out of the freezing weather.

He took one mouthful of pancakes and almost gagged as he said, "What kind of syrup is this? It tastes terrible!"

As it turned out, it wasn't syrup at all. It was actually boiling-hot bacon fat. In the freezing weather, anything hot seemed good, even if the taste was peculiar. That load of pancakes and hot bacon fat stayed in our stomachs and stuck to our teeth all day.

On the evening of 30 November, George (G) Company, commanded by Cpt. Ed Bruger from the 2nd Battalion, arrived from Huksu-ri to reinforce the 1st Battalion. There was some disagreement about how to deploy G Company. Cpt. Bruger wanted to keep G Company intact and under his control, while Lt. Col. Toddy wanted to assign a platoon from G Company to support each of his three rifle companies.

That night, the Chinese attacked from the east instead of the north and west. John Middlemas and the field artillery team turned the four 105 howitzers around and sighted the barrels directly at the advancing Chinese. Cpt. Turner, who was up and fighting, said later that the tips of the 105 howitzer barrels that were being repeatedly fired horizontally glowed red during that night. The other indirect fire weapons—four 81 mm mortars, and four 4.2-inch mortars of D Company—continued to fire at pre-selected targets until new targets were called in. The small 60 mm mortars were under the control of the A, B, and C Company commanders.

Not to be outdone by our indirect fire weapons, our four attached Sherman tanks with 76 mm cannons and machine-guns, the newly arrived M-31 with twin automatic 40 mm AA cannons, and the half-track, with a quad AA .50 caliber machine-gun turret, also provided deadly fire support from directly behind our aid station. We were very glad to have the AA people with us. With all of our heavy shooting toward the Chinese trying to rush up on us from the east, we didn't know what was happening. But we were open for medical business and everyone knew where we were located.

Hundreds of Chinese were killed that night as they tried to overrun our battalion from the east, northeast, and southeast. As the Chinese bugles sounded on the early morning of the first of December, I realized that they had tried to get us from every side, but the only way they'd succeeded was when we carried their wounded survivors to our aid station in the morning after the nightly firefight.

During that time, Sgt. Terry L. Tennant, who was a squad leader in a heavy mortar (4.2-inch) platoon, had been sent forward with George Company of the 2nd Battalion on 30 November 1950 to reinforce the 1st Battalion at Sachang-ni.

Sgt. Tennant's group was at the tail end of the G Company column. Their heavily-loaded truck and trailer, containing all heavy mortar equipment, ammunition, and the soldiers' personal equipment, broke through a blown bridge that had been hastily repaired with logs. The truck rolled down the cliff side, along with the displaced logs, to the semi-frozen river below. Only the driver had remained on the truck before trying to cross the bridge, and he managed to nimbly leap clear as the truck rolled over the edge.

Sgt. Tennant's group was left behind with two 6 X 6 Jimmies, one half-track with quad .50 caliber machine guns and one M-31 full-tracked vehicle with twin 40 mm canons. There were three sergeants and 25 American and South Korean enlisted men, but no officers left behind from the tail of the G Company column. The lead part of the G Company column had fought its way on through the last mile to Sachang-ni. Sgt. Tennant became the leader of the left-behind group and he immediately turned his soldiers to the task of retrieving all the equipment and loading it onto the remaining vehicles. Lugging the 190-pound mortar base plates and ammunition up the cliff side was a daunting task that required several hours. There was no way for them to retrieve the truck and trailer. The left-behind unit managed to find a slightly wider section of road to turn their vehicles around. After posting guards, the men got into the vehicles and huddled together in sleeping bags to share body heat.

According to an article written by Sgt. Tennant for *The Cottonbaler.*[7]

"Some time after dark, all hell broke loose up the road in the 1st Battalion's area. We could hear explosions and small arms and machine gun fire. We had a view right up the valley beside us. The sky came alive with tracers flying in all directions. As I was observing the activity, for an instant I saw many dots of light that seemed to be almost hanging in space. Suddenly I realized that they were tracers heading our way as they passed over our heads.

"They were the 1st Battalion's .50-caliber machine guns shooting at the enemy on our side of the perimeter. We quickly moved down the road to a safer spot around a curve where the hill gave us some protection from the wild rounds. The 1st Battalion was really catching hell, and I am sure I wasn't the only one thinking maybe we had the best deal for the night being out there all alone."

What Sgt Terry L. Tennant described was the early morning of 1 December, when the Chinese attacked the 1st Battalion from the east and we turned our 105 howitzers around and fired on the level, accompanied by our truck ring mounted 50s, the half-track quad 50s and the 40 mm twin Bofors mounted on the M-31. That was a lot of firepower to be thrown directly into the teeth of hundreds of attacking Chinese trying to overpower us from behind. They were slaughtered for their effort.

---

[7] *Winter in North Korea 1950*, published in the fall issue of the 1997 *Cottonbaler*, a newsletter of the 7th Infantry Regiment Association.

On 1 December, after we'd beaten the Chinese off with heavy losses, they moved east toward Huksu-ri and delivered fire onto Sgt. Tennant's group from above, but were again driven off by heavy return fire. The next morning, after Tennant returned to the 2nd Battalion at Huksu-ri, an engineering team was dispatched back up the road to Sachang-ni to repair the blown bridges.

While the details on everything that happened in the 1st Battalion during 25 November to 2 December 1950 time period are no longer clear, what is clear is that our aid station remained operational 24 hours a day, and I came to feel that the Lord had his hands over us, because mortar shells fell all around us and seemed to hit every building in town except the one in which we had our aid station.

During the daytime lulls in the fighting day, I tried to review our work with our medic sergeants and Lt. Sarka. We ended up with ten observations to remember:

1) In cold weather with loss of blood, arms and legs freeze quickly. The wounded must be brought in quickly and warmed up to prevent hypothermia, frostbite, and death.

2) Cold arms and legs won't absorb morphine tartrate injections given for pain. Repeated injections given for pain on the way to a MASH don't help. When the patient is finally warmed up and hydrated in a hospital, all the morphine injections are absorbed at one time and some patients will die from morphine overdose.

3) In freezing weather, only give morphine for severe pain. Inject into the chest muscle and massage it in. Be sure to note, on the medical tag, the time, place, and dose of morphine given.

4) Sucking chest wounds are a major problem. The use of Vaseline gauze as recommended on a sucking chest wound to serve as an air valve is unsatisfactory. It tends to neither open nor close at the right time to avoid lung collapse or tension pneumothorax. A better option is to put a tube in the chest cavity, which can be clamped and released, and then closed over the tube by using a heavy suture to pull a flesh flap over both hole and tube. A medic attendant can clamp the tube, even with fingers, on inspiration and open it on expiration as needed until the patient reaches the hospital.

5) Head and neck injuries are big problems. To rig up a suction apparatus, I could connect an empty saline bottle to the suction tube on a jeep windshield wiper to aspirate secretions and blood out of throats or chests. It's necessary to place the stretcher across the hood of the jeep with the feet elevated to help clear the throat. (I had one patient with half his lower jaw torn off by a large piece of shrapnel and lots of bleeding from what remained of his tongue. Not having a tracheotomy set, I turned him over on the litter with his face down to allow the

blood to run out of his throat instead of into his lungs. I used mosquito forceps to clamp the bleeders in his tongue and jaw. The man was given blood and warm saline I.V. after being loaded into a box ambulance for the long, rough convoy ride from Sachang-ni to Hamhung. There were no helicopters available at the time. I never heard whether he survived or not.)

6) Circulatory collapse and shock are difficult to manage. If a man has both hypothermia and vascular collapse, a bottle of near-freezing blood or saline in the veins will quickly finish him off. To warm I.V. solutions, we can use a bucket of warm water on the stove or have some of our enlisted men carry I.V. solution bottles inside their shirts, next to their skin, to keep the fluid near body temperature. (The treatment of shock and the aspiration of collected secretions were major problems in the battalion aid stations of 1950. We needed a battery-powered suction apparatus.)

7) Wet, frozen, bloody, and dirty clothes are a problem because the aid station doesn't have a supply of clean, dry clothes, or oversized clothes and boots, to put over bandages. (This problem was addressed by medics sharing their own few spare clothes and by removing clothes from the dead. We tried to gather and dry out as many extra clothes as we could find.)

8) Training never stops for American and Korean medics. There is always a better way to do things. This applies to stopping hemorrhages, putting on bandages, applying splints, giving comfort to the injured and the dying, and many other things. Coordination with the chaplain is essential. Leaving a wounded man to go for help could be a death sentence, either from freezing to death or from being stripped and killed by the Chinese or North Koreans. (Sergeants Ogden, Byland, Adams, and Prystas supervised ongoing training. Medics serving with the rifle platoons frequently had to be replaced or given relief.)

9) Some soldiers will have automatic discharge of urine and feces upon being wounded. Others will be constipated and unable to void. It's a problem to get the soiled wounded cleaned up to prevent them from contaminating their wounds. The Chinese would usually pass a bulky rice stool after being wounded and I used gloved hands to remove it, because neither GIs nor Koreans would clean up after a Chinese prisoner. As one of our wounded infantrymen said, "Doc, I would rather blow a Chinaman's brains out, than wipe his ***." The bowel and bladder care of the wounded stored in bunkers continued to be a problem for which we were ill-prepared.

10) Record keeping for Purple Hearts is also a problem. In general, a Purple Heart requires an enemy bullet or piece of shrapnel that draws blood. It was usually not awarded for skinning knees while diving into a foxhole, for getting headaches, or by becoming confused from nearby shells exploding.

The 3rd Battalion of the 7th Infantry Regiment 3rd Division became a part of Task Force Dog that battled north to Chinhung to hold open the road through which the Marines would pass with attached Army units.

The Chinese lost heavily because thousands of their soldiers only had light tennis shoes on their feet and insufficient layers of clothing. As difficult as the cold was for the Americans and South Koreans, thousands of Chinese Communist soldiers were rendered helpless by the cold and many simply froze to death.

In the U.S. 8th Army to the west, every infantry unit suffered numerous casualties, most notably the 2nd Infantry Division and the 1st Cavalry Division. The cold was not as severe in the west, but the number of Chinese troops was far greater.[8]

During the second Chinese offensive, my friend, Dr. Ervin Kjenaas, achieved some notoriety. I learned about his exploits later when we met in South Korea.

The 8056 MASH, to which Cpt. Kjenaas was assigned, had been situated far north of Pyongyang. There was a report that 60 to 70 litter patients had been brought across the Chongchon River to Anju and were awaiting transport south from Sinanju. An ambulance platoon from the 8056 MASH was assigned the task of going north to load up the litter patients and then to return to join the 8056 MASH as it moved south in advance of the Chinese onslaught. Something discouraged the ambulance platoon from completing its mission—perhaps fear of being caught out in no man's land.

When the ambulance platoon returned empty, the deputy commander of the 8056 MASH fired the MSC Lieutenant who'd been commanding it and appointed Cpt. Kjenaas as the new ambulance platoon commander. Kjenaas located the platoon sergeant and ordered him to round up all the drivers and attendants for the box ambulances immediately for a return trip north to rescue the abandoned litter patients.

When the sergeant refused to obey a direct order because "it would be a suicide mission," Kjenaas cocked his .45, shoved the barrel into the belly of the man and told him he had the choice of "dying now as a coward, or dying later as a hero trying to rescue litter patients."

With .45 caliber encouragement, the sergeant rounded up the drivers and attendants, and the platoon of ambulances headed north again. By that time, there were few American Army vehicles on the road. But there were also no Chinese because they were marching over land to avoid the main road and U.S. air strikes.

---

[8] See Clay Blair's book *The Forgotten War* for a more exhaustive coverage of these events.

The ambulances reached Sinanju, 60 miles to the north, where the platoon eventually located the litter patients after spotting one of the wounded patients searching for food and water for the other. The wounded were given food and water and then stuffed into the overloaded ambulances for the ride back south to join up with the 8056 MASH.

In the meantime, the 8056 MASH was also heading south by an alternative road to the west. In doing so, the MASH commander was going against the specific orders of Maj. Gen. Kaiser, commander of the 2nd Infantry Division, to which the MASH was attached. Gen. Kaiser had ordered both his division medical battalion and the 8056 MASH to wait for the 2nd Division to accompany them as an armed escort for their trip south on the main road.

However the 2nd Division was badly clobbered by the Chinese on their journey south. Gen. Kaiser himself escaped only by walking past troops who either would not or could not move, even when ordered to do so.

The 2nd Division Medical Battalion commander obeyed Gen. Kaiser's last direct order to wait. They were captured by the Chinese the next day. At that time, all of the American wounded who couldn't march overland to prison camps far north by the Yalu River were simply executed by the Chinese and North Koreans. The stretchers were then used for the Chinese wounded.

The 8056 MASH, with all of their staff and extra patients, made it out alive. The 8056 MASH commander saved them by disobeying a direct order, illustrating the maxim espoused by Admiral Arleigh "31 knot" Burke: "Any commander who doesn't exceed his authority is of no use to his subordinates."

Clay Blair, in his book *The Forgotten War*, recounts our seven days in Sachang-ni on pages 459-460. Blair noted that the stiff resistance provided by the 1st Battalion at Sachang-ni and the 2nd Battalion at Huksu-ri diverted significant Chinese forces away from the battles going on farther north around the Chosen Reservoir. It also provided time for preparation for the defense and successful evacuation from Hungnam.

When George Company arrived in the early evening of November 30th, Lt. Col. Toddy told Cpt. Bruger, "I want you to take your company out in the morning on an extended patrol to see what's out there."

Cpt. Bruger demurred and suggested instead that a 12-man patrol be sent out, rather than risking the entire company. The discussion between Toddy and Bruger became moot after that night's battle with the Chinese. Early morning on 1 December, as the battle subsided, Regiment ordered Cpt. Bruger to bring G Company back to Huksu-ri to form a blocking position with other 2nd Battalion elements west of Huksu-ri, through which the 1st Battalion would withdraw on the following day. Cpt. Bruger left with his intact G Company on December 1st and the 1st Battalion prepared to conduct a fighting withdrawal the following day.

As a diversion, Lt. Col. Toddy ordered an attack toward what was presumed to be the enemy HQ positions northwest of us. Tank and artillery support were provided with our attacking infantry elements, even as the bulk of our forces prepared to depart to the east at the appropriate time.

I don't know who originated that plan, but I suspect that Maj. Magruder, the executive officer, Maj. Kapp, the S-3, and Cpt. McAuliffe, the S-2, all had a hand in planning the exit strategy, which worked quite well.

I heard that Lt. Col. Toddy and Maj. Magruder had a discussion about who should lead the attack, and who should be in charge of the rear elements as they left Sachang-ni.

Maj. Magruder was reported to have said in no uncertain terms, "Both tasks are the responsibility of the battalion commander, because that's where the action is going to be and if I was battalion commander, I would insist on doing both jobs myself."

Apparently, Toddy listened to Magruder, because we heard he was very active in leading the attack, and it seemed to improve his reputation in the battalion. The Chinese were forced to reorder their troops to repel the attack. That readjustment opened up our exit route and our battalion was able to surprise them again by suddenly changing directions and heading east.

The general consensus was that Toddy had confused the Chinese by attacking their HQ and supply base with his tank-led infantry charge. The Chinese had to protect their precious supply base at all cost, because their supplies had been brought in on human and mule backs.

After our diversionary attack was well underway, our retreat from Sachang-ni was successfully initiated. It seemed as if the Chinese had become confused, because they'd removed some of their forces from our exit route, and our fighting retreat was started with only light opposition. A Company took the lead on the way out and B Company brought up the rear, with Lt. Col. Toddy. Platoons of C Company were scattered through the middle of the column to support the HQ Company and heavy weapons platoons, with tanks in front and behind.

The medics were sprinkled throughout the column, with Lt. Sarka in the front and Sgt. Herrick toward the rear. My jeep was near the middle of the column. The majority of our troops walked, and the wounded were placed on every available vehicle. I could hear shooting up ahead, as well as behind us, but as we moved along, my section of the column was free of incoming fire. I almost felt apologetic.

We had to stop periodically to fill in craters in the road. The fighting at the front was cleared by our troops climbing the hills after our mounted machine-guns and small mortars had chopped up the hillsides. At the rear, B Company had a veritable swarm of Chinese attackers fighting them most of the way out from

Sachang-ni. It was often necessary to send squads of soldiers up the cliff sides to clear out pockets of newly-arriving enemy firing on the road below.

Pvt. 1st Class Albert Walton of B Company, currently retired in Carthage, Missouri, gave the following account of his efforts to eliminate the recurring road-blocks created by Chinese soldiers firing down from above the road:

"My platoon was rear guard when we were ambushed by Chinese at a road block coming out of Sachang-ni in North Korea. My squad was told to fix bayo-nets and while another squad gave covering fire we were to charge up the hill and clear the block as quick as we could because the rest of the column was still mov-ing down the road ahead of us. I was assistant squad leader and was in the back slot of a diamond formation when we jumped off up the hill. We got about up to where the Chinese were when a Chinese threw back a mat with snow on it right in front of me but behind the other people of my squad. He didn't see me but he was getting his rifle ready to shoot when I jumped him. He swung his gun around on me and I had to knock it away to one side, striking him in the throat with my bayonet. About that time I realized that he wasn't over 15 years old.

"This was the closest I had been to a Chinese that I had killed. I have had many nightmares from seeing a young Chinese face pop up out of a snow bank and even now it is quite vivid. On up the hill I had a Chinese jump from a ledge with a knife, landing on my back—which knocked me down. I was able to get his arm in my hands and hold on until the ROK that was with us came over and hit him on the head with his rifle, getting me out from under him. When we got back to the road, I could hardly talk because I was so scared."

Because of the ice, our tanks had traction problems on the road back from Sachang-ni, especially at higher altitudes. The hard rubber blocks on the tank tracks simply couldn't grip the icy road. On one hairpin turn, someone poured gasoline on the road and started a fire to melt the ice. It helped, but delayed the evacuation. In the end, we lost two tanks as they slid out of control over the edge of the road. Fortunately, the crews were not lost. They set fire to the tanks and put thermite in the breech before the tanks were allowed to roll on down into the valley.

As we passed through the defensive positions of the 2nd Battalion west of Huksu-ri, the Chinese swarm following us engaged G Company in close combat. One Chinese soldier fired a burst from a Thompson submachine gun, striking Cpt. Bruger in the legs and knocking him to the ground. While the attacker replaced his clip to fire again, Cpt. Bruger sat up in the road and killed his attacker with his .45 pistol.

Bruger continued to lead his company in repelling the attackers, assisted by artillery and air strikes. He was an upfront leader of men who should have been awarded the Distinguished-Service Cross for his continued leadership in battle, even after being painfully wounded.

As we rolled through Huksu-ri, I hoped to stop and consult with Cpt. Gerald Swab, the 2nd Battalion surgeon, about the emergency care of eye injuries, since he had been in an ophthalmology residency when he was called to join the 7th Infantry in Japan, but the Chinese soldiers that followed us out of Sachang-ni were already attacking Huksu-ri and there was no time for visiting.

The 1st Battalion's Battle of Sachang-ni ended in a vicious new battle involving the 2nd Battalion at Huksu-ri. The 1st Battalion loaded onto more trucks with supplies at Huksu-ri and moved a few miles east to set up a new line of defense, leaving the 2nd Battalion battling at Huksu-ri until they, in turn, were ordered to withdraw and regroup again farther east of us.

Through all of this, Lt. Joe Piaseczny, our efficient communications officer, and his enlisted crew had the Herculean task of running and repairing the telephone wire lines between the rifle companies and the battalion, as well as between our battalion and the regiment, more than ten miles away. The hazards of communication work before the days of transistor radios and satellites is illustrated in the following citation:

Award of the Bronze Star to Sgt. Frank D. Grothe

"During the action on 28 November 1950, when 1st Battalion 7th Infantry was attacked by two Regiments of CCF, Sergeant Grothe was on duty with the communications section. When mortar rounds fell into the battalion perimeter, the communication lines were disrupted and contact to the units under attack was lost. Sergeant Grothe, without hesitation, volunteered to replace the lines. He moved through the shell-torn area with complete and utter disregard for his life, checking the lines and splicing when necessary. During several occasions, he was forced to fight his way. Keeping a constant blaze of fire pouring from his own weapon onto the enemy, he moved steadily on to repair disrupted communications. The brave action on the part of Sergeant Grothe was the primary factor in returning the communications, enabling the battalion commander to effectively deploy his troops and keep in constant contact. Sergeant Grothe's actions were in keeping with the highest traditions of the U.S. Army"

In May 1951, several members of the medical platoon of the 1st Battalion 7th Infantry were honored for their service at Sachang-ni, including the two that follow. A list of all the awards given in the 7th Regimental Medical Company is provided at the end of this book.

Award of the Bronze Star (posthumous) with V-Device to Cpl. Willie P. Parrish

"On 29 November 1950, near Sachang-ni Korea a call was received that a soldier, located on the side of a high rocky mountain, was wounded. Corporal Parrish took a litter team up a treacherous mountain trail to evacuate the wounded man. On their return trip to the aid station with the injured man, he and his team were pinned down by intense enemy small arms fire. With complete disregard for his own safety, Corporal Parrish continuously exposed himself to this fire in order to insure that the wounded man was brought to the aid station as quickly as possible. The heroism and devotion to duty displayed by Corporal Parrish reflect great credit upon him and are in keeping with the high traditions of the military service. Entered the Military service from the State of Tennessee."

Award of the Silver Star to Cpt. Robert T. Jensen

"During the night of 28-29 November 1950, near Sachang-ni, Korea, a battalion of the 7th Infantry was under very strong attack from an estimated two enemy regiments. Captain Jensen, battalion surgeon, heedless of his own safety, continued personal emergency medical attention to wounded above ground although heavy artillery, mortar, and small arms fire caused him to place his aid station and most of its personnel underground. In the morning, he called for helicopter evacuation of a very seriously wounded man. The enemy directed a heavy concentration of fire on the helicopter, but Captain Jensen, although exposed to this fire, unhesitantly accompanied the patient across one hundred yards of open ground and supervised the loading of the wounded man into the helicopter. Captain Jensen's gallantry and selfless devotion to duty reflect great credit upon himself and the military service. Entered the military service from the State of Minnesota."

Maj. George C. Viney after promotion from captain in Korea: 1951

Col. George C. Viney, Chief of Staff, 5th Army–Fort Sam Houston 1970's

The hill described in Middlemas' letter

A KATUSA soldier bringing a prisoner of war (POW)
with a minor wound to the aid station

Inside the aid station during a night battle in Sachang-ni.
(drawing curtesy of K.A.J. Cook)

A battalion aid station with a Bell-13 helicopter in South Korea

A trailer mounted .155 cannon (background),
jeep wiper used for suction (foreground)

Following a litter jeep; notice the steel hook on Cpt. Jensen's jeep, which was used to cut wires placed by Chinese soldiers to decapitate unsuspecting jeep passengers.

Pvt. 1st Class Albert Walton,
age 18

Albert Walton, age 72

Chapter Eight
The fighting withdrawal from Pungson-ni and evacuation out of Hungnam
December 2, 1950 – December 25, 1950

On December 2, 1950, the 1st Battalion of the 7th Regiment passed through G Company of the 2nd Battalion, scraping a lot of angry, screaming, shooting Chinese off of B Company and onto G Company at Huksu-ri. Over the next three days, the 2nd Battalion 7th Regiment was in a continual firefight in the environs of Huksu-ri, in an effort to keep the Chinese from breaking out into the foothills and plains east of there.

Dr. Schwab, of the 2nd Battalion, and Dr. Campbell, of the 3rd Battalion, were each awarded Silver Stars for gallantry in action while attending to their medical duties under fire. The 7th Infantry had honored all three of their battalion surgeons. But when I stop to think about it, what else could we have done? Hide in a foxhole and let casualties bleed to death? A doctor had to respond to the needs of bleeding and dying soldiers. None of us had been trained for combat duty, but we all responded as physicians to the demands of war and tried to do whatever we could, wherever needed, to the best of our abilities with our limited resources.

The 1st Battalion moved east to set up new defensive positions in the region of Pungson-ni[9], 15 miles east of Huksu-ri. When we arrived, we set up our aid station tent again, and prepared for more wounded. We were close, perhaps a few hundred yards behind our rifle companies, only this time we were not in the middle of a circle.

Our three rifle companies were strung out in a line, with our heavy weapons company units spread out behind them. The 15th Infantry Regiment was tied in on the 1st Battalion 7th left flank. I don't recall who was tied in on our right flank;

---

[9] 'Pungson-ni' may also be spelled 'Pongson-ni.'

it may have been an ROK regiment. The 2nd Battalion 7th was still fighting at Huksu-ri and the 3rd Battalion 7th was still up north with Task Force Dog trying to help the 1st Marine Division. Since we were not engaged, I found time to scratch out another letter while sitting on a warm jeep hood.

Dear Folks,   *3 Dec. 1950*

So much has been happening it is difficult to know where to start. The Chinese Communists are pouring in all over North Korea. You undoubtedly know more about it than we do here. We conducted a somewhat bloody retreat yesterday; burning everything we couldn't carry and firing all the extra ammunition at the Chinese positions. Most of our battalion got out O.K. but the tail end company was shot up a little.

We are now setting up a new line about 80 miles west of Hamhung. Everyone wonders if and when an atom bomb will be dropped. It's a cinch; we don't have enough men in the entire U.S. Army to stop all the Chinese that are apparently coming across the Yalu now. Actually, we are not situated too badly and we have a good escape route to the sea if need be while the enemy must come through a couple of Korean valleys and our troops are there as well as on the surrounding hills.

I am wearing the pilot boots now but still want a pair of felt shoes size 7 EE with rubbers. Food such as cold cuts, etc. are reaching some of the fellows and provide a tasty moment or two. Food here is poor. Usually only two meals a day. Yesterday only one. Today we have more food again, however. We have medicines, food and ammunition dropped by airplane every so often.

Right now everything goes to the Marines and 7th Division. They are catching hell now.

Love, Bob

The returning ambulances brought back rumors that the 8th Army, on the west side of Korea, had suffered a great many causalities. It was also reported that the 2nd Infantry Division had suffered major losses, including the loss of their division medical battalion. The 8th Army, on the west side of Korea, had learned the hard way that it served no purpose for American Army doctors to stay behind with the wounded. Those who did were stripped of their medical supplies and treated like any other prisoner of war (POW) in the hands of their oriental captors. At the time, we didn't know the Chinese and North Koreans routinely executed all of the wounded POWs who couldn't walk to prison camps after capture. It was simple expediency on their part. They had little in the way of transport. They moved prisoners by forced marches at night and shot all stragglers, believing that the more Americans they killed, the sooner we would leave and allow the war to end on their terms.

I wondered how some of my medical school classmates were doing during that difficult time. We were more fortunate than some battalion surgeons who had been killed or wounded in action, or suffered great privation and ignominious deaths in atrocious POW camps.

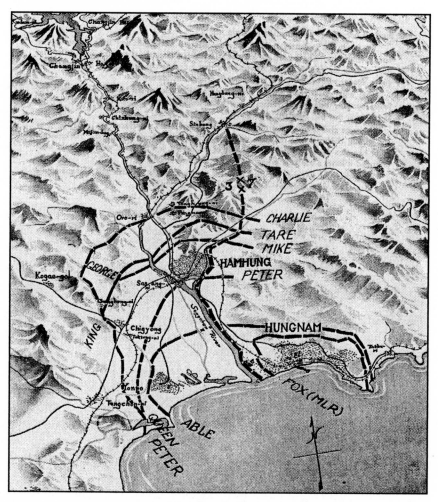

Successive defense lines leading to Hungnam

To the north, the 5th and 7th Regiments of the 1st Marine Division had extended around the south and west side of the Chosen Reservoir before being hit with repeated night attacks by the Chinese. Units of the 31st Regiment of the 7th Infantry Division had deployed northeast of the Chosen Reservoir, where they suffered horrific losses from overwhelming Chinese attacks. Some members of the 31st regiment escaped by crossing over the ice of the reservoir. At Hagaru, a provisional Army battalion of less than 500 men was formed from the survivors of the 31st Regiment of the 7th Infantry Division[10]. Some units of the 7th Infantry Division reached the Yalu River in the northwest region of Korea, where they found themselves surrounded by Chinese and North Korean forces. The 7th Infantry Division had a fighting withdrawal toward Hungnam, but perhaps not quite as excruciating as the withdrawal experienced by the 1st Marine Division and its supporting Army units from Hagaru.

The Marines, with some Army help, had built a runway, 2,900 feet long and 50 feet wide, for C47 aircraft. At the elevation of Hagaru, the runway should have been 7,600 feet long. This rough runway was completed on December 1, 1950. During the next week, the Far East Air Force (FEAF) evacuated 4,312 wounded from the primitive, but lifesaving, airstrip at Hagaru, including 3,150 U.S. Marines, 1,137 Army soldiers, and 25 British Marines. The C47s also brought in 537 Marine replacements (recovered from previous wounds) and many tons of ammunition and supplies. The Hagaru airstrip was a blessing, because maintaining wounded in fighting units without definitive surgical hospital facilities was an intolerable burden for commanders and for the doctors assigned to the infantry units. At the time, helicopter evacuation of casualties was a rare event and the evacuation of 4,300 casualties from the altitude of the Chosen Reservoir would have been impossible for little Bell-13 bubble helicopters with twin patient pods of *M*A*S*H* TV fame, even if they had been available.

When Ray Murray's 5th and Homer Litzenberg's 7th Marine Regiments reached Hagaru from Yudam, they were relieved of the burden of tending casualties, and received needed replacements as they took positions within the 1st Marine Division to face the Chinese Armies encircling Hagaru. The Chinese were stopped at Hagaru with great loss to themselves. The subzero weather caused many frostbite casualties. The Marines were forced to strip clothes and boots from their own dead to obtain additional layers of protection from the bitter cold. Frozen feet and fingers and amputations were common along the road out. Many Chinese soldiers in snow bank foxhole positions froze to death or became too numb to function as ordered.

In that subzero weather, there was a need for very thin lubricating oil to keep weapons from jamming. From my experience growing up on the Canadian border of Minnesota, I knew that kerosene was a useful subzero lubricant, but it was

---

[10] Please distinguish between the 7th Infantry *Division* and our 7th Infantry *Regiment*, which is a part of the 3rd Infantry Division.

not available to us. Instead, warm urine, applied directly by the nearest soldier, helped get weapons working, although it did freeze and tended to be corrosive.

On December 7, 1950, the 1st Marine Division, commanded by the unflappable Maj. Gen. Oliver P. Smith, fought their way out through legions of attacking Chinese by systematically attacking and taking every strategic hilltop along the main supply route (MSR) using rifles, bayonets, machine guns, tank guns, mortars, and artillery. Close air support during daylight, when not obscured by blizzard conditions, greatly assisted the fight to pass through Koto and the Funchilin Pass to Chinhung, where Task Force Dog was in control. In a few sad instances, bullets and napalm from our own aircraft hit our own people. Task Force Dog provided cover in and around Sudong, along with two battalions of the 65th Regiment of the 3rd Division that moved north to protect the road to Hamhung.

Lt. Gen. Ned Almond, the X Corps Commander, flew in and out of Hagaru frequently before the breakout. According to rumors, the Marines generally held Almond and his ideas in contempt. I never heard anyone in the Army say complimentary things about Lt. Gen. Almond, either. Almond was brave and aggressive, but also arrogant, glory-seeking, bullying, impulsive, and at times, foolish.

One idea of the FEAF, supported by Almond, involved having the Marines destroy their equipment and evacuate by air from Hagaru. Maj. Gen. Smith rejected the plan as unrealistic. As a battalion surgeon, I had never observed a corps commander exerting his command prerogatives, but I came to believe that generals should not expect to be admired by subordinate commanders in the field if they come forward to micromanage, propose unwise ideas, and waste the precious time of unit commanders charged with directing their troops during fighting. Should there be a failure by a subordinate commander to produce, a replacement must be made, but in Korea, unit commanders were usually replaced only when they had been killed, wounded, or exhausted—not because of incompetence or cowardice.

While the 7th Infantry Regiment had many killed in action (KIA) and wounded in action (WIA), no entire platoon or company of ours was ever exterminated in battles, as occurred in many ROK units and in some units of American divisions of the 8th Army in West Korea. Some of the units within the 2nd Division, 1st Cavalry and 24th Division had to be reformed from scratch. Our 7th Infantry Regiment always had survivors in every platoon and every company after a battle. These units were filled up with replacements without needing to start over. This was important in maintaining fighting skills and *esprit de corps*.

We were experiencing what can only be called war in Korea. The media in America failed to describe this truth accurately, perhaps, in part, because there were no reporters embedded in Army units at the battalion or regimental levels in Korea.

Because the 7th Infantry Regiment always had survivors in every platoon and in every company after every battle, the 7th Infantry Regiment experienced more days in actual combat than any other unit in Korea, in spite of our late entry into the war.

My year with the 7th Regiment amounted to a near full-time deployment. When we received a group of replacements, each company or platoon sergeant, in his own home-spun way, tried to instill a lot of "how to do your job and stay alive" advice in a short period of time. Our medical platoon was no different from the rifle companies, except that we kept the new replacements around the aid station for orientation before sending them out to serve as medics with infantry platoons. Sgt. Herrick took a special interest in orienting our replacements, both individually and as a group. When Herrick gave an orientation, he expected total attention. On one occasion, a clueless replacement was giggling and not paying attention.

Sgt. Bill Herrick responded by shouting, "Attention!"

He then pulled out his shiny sharp bayonet and slowly, with stern deliberation, walked up to the replacement, who stopped whispering and giggling and stood at attention. Herrick aimed a verbal blast directly at the hapless replacement.

"We are in a messy war. Not all of us standing here today will be going home alive. Some of us will be wounded and some of us will be dead. I have been giving you a few suggestions today about how to do your duty as medical aid men and also how to go home alive. Now, private first class laughing boy, do you really think this is a laughing matter?"

"No, sir," the giggler said, along with most of the other replacements, who were also standing at attention.

"It's a good thing you don't think this is a laughing matter, because I'm ready to cut a hole in your ball bag, shove your head between your legs, and let you die laughing at your butt. Because it would be better for you to die now, laughing at your butt, than for you to get yourself and others killed doing the wrong thing on the battlefield because you were too stupid to listen to a bit of advice. Now do I now have your undivided attention?"

"Yes, sir!"

From that point on, Herrick had their solemn attention, even as some of them may have been considering the physical contortions implied by his suggestion.

Most of the issues discussed by Herrick in his standing orientation seminars had been informally discussed by Herrick, Ogden, Byland, Prystas, Sarka, and me. There was a continuing effort to learn from our mistakes. Every medic loss was painful to us. The following are some of the points that were repeatedly stressed:

1) The person that stands up to look around on the battlefield is the most likely to get killed. Always keep a low profile and learn to crawl—low and fast.

2) When you hear the call for a medic, check with your infantry squad leader or platoon leader to verify the wounded man's location, and ask for covering fire. There is no point in running out to be a hero and getting shot by our own people, the enemy, or both. A smoke grenade to one side or the other can be helpful, but it can also provide cover for the enemy to run up on you. Your infantry buddies must know where you are at all times, and you must keep your weapons with you at all times and use them as needed. Grenades also help to create a diversion, but not if you don't know where to throw them without hitting our own people.

3) There are no Red Cross medic armbands in this war because they draw fire. The aim of this war is to kill or capture the enemy. Any American wounded who is captured on the battlefield will be tortured for intelligence information and if he cannot walk to a prison camp in forced night marches, he will receive a bullet in his head and be stripped of his clothes, personal possessions, and weapons. Our objective is to leave no wounded behind. We also try to retrieve the bodies if it can be done without further loss of life.

4) First, stop the bleeding. Use pressure bandages, tourniquets, or a surgical clamp on the bleeding artery if you can locate it, even though the clamping process may hurt. It is no use dragging or carrying a wounded man to safety if you arrive with a corpse and a blood-red trail along your path.

5) It is better to drag a wounded man out of a foxhole to safety by grabbing his belt, or using his ammo belt around his chest and under his arms. It is often possible to crawl backward, dragging a wounded man for twenty or thirty yards to a safer position. To stand up in a field of small arms or machine gun fire with a wounded man over your shoulder is a good way to get two people killed. It is better for a wounded man to have some skin scraped off his backside by being dragged a few feet, than to send out a litter squad to be slaughtered. Gloves and extra padding on the knees is helpful in crawling. Extra clothing tied around the wounded man's backside saves wear and tear. It is easier to drag a man over snow and through mud than over rocks and gravel, so think first if you start to drag a wounded man.

6) Never leave a wounded man behind with the promise that you are going to get help. Drag him, carry him, or hobble along with him, supporting each other if you are both wounded, but get the man back to where there are other GIs to help you. The chances of your going back with help before the enemy sneaks in to strip our wounded of valuables and finish them off are practically nil. If you volunteer to stay with the wounded, you will become a POW, and our wounded will be stripped and exterminated by the enemy. The people we are fighting don't have

enough medical supplies for their own wounded, so we must never leave our wounded behind or wait as sitting ducks with them in no man's land.

7) If you are cut off with wounded and our planes come over to strafe, get up and carry the wounded with you, walking toward the friendly side. Wave at the planes and point at the enemy. Our pilots will not expect to see the enemy carrying people toward the friendly side, and will come have a closer look, and may give you some close air support. If you try to hide or shoot at the planes, you will be considered enemies. It is likely that your best chance of escape will be during an air attack, when all enemy guns will be directed at our attacking airplanes. Our planes may also call for a rescue attempt, so don't hide during an air strike, but move out quickly toward the friendly side and carry the wounded and your weapons with you.

Being spread out made it more difficult to maintain close support for all rifle companies, especially when all three were on the line and the 1st Battalion HQ and D Company support weapons continually changed their positions.

Finding the regimental HQ units and 3rd Division Medical Battalion involved using many different trails and roads. Depending on the distance and road conditions, some casualties were taken directly to hospitals in the rear without being filtered through the regimental collecting stations or division medical battalion. This was more the exception than the rule. It was also a matter of the severity of the injury and the need to save time.

The change to less mountainous terrain was good news for our tanks, providing them with greater freedom of movement. They covered a wide area, supporting our infantry and plugging holes in the line wherever there were infiltrations by clusters of burp-gun shooting and grenade-throwing Chinese trying to create confusion behind the line. We never knew when they might turn up, so we stayed on continual alert. As we slowly moved from Pungson-ni toward Chigyong, the 1st Battalion spread out even farther, to intercept any Chinese going around our line with the intention of creating havoc in the Hamhung/Hungnam area.

Sometimes I almost felt sorry for the Chinese. As we withdrew, our signal crews left voice sensors wired in with the coordinates recorded for our artillery. The Chinese would settle into areas we had previously occupied and suddenly be hit with multiple artillery shells landing on the sensor targets. This ploy was used over and over again, resulting in a great many Chinese casualties. The Chinese had no hospitals nearby and carried most of their supplies on their backs or on A-frames on the backs of forcefully indentured Koreans.

I believed the wounded Chinese and North Koreans considered themselves lucky if they fell into our hands, because they received medical care from our side. For our wounded, it was a death sentence to be left behind. If the Chinese had left more of their wounded behind, we would have cared for them but, in general, the Chinese leaders preferred to remove their injured from the battlefield, even if they died due to lack of definitive surgical treatment.

While the Chinese continued to probe every night, they limited their movements during the daylight, especially on clear days, to avoid our air strikes, artillery, and naval gunfire. But if they were in a position to overwhelm a relatively isolated ROK or U.S. unit, they would launch an all-out attack to destroy it. There were many such bloody affairs all along the line that kept the flow of casualties coming. As we slowly withdrew toward Hamhung, Tempo Airbase, and Hungnam, the Chinese continually probed for soft points where they could break through to attack headquarter units or any other soft target from the rear at night.

I picked up an American-made Thompson submachine gun from a wounded Chinese soldier and kept it handy with three extra clips filled with .45 ammo in addition to the revolver on my belt. I practiced with the Tommy gun, to be sure I could handle it for both single shots and short bursts of three or four rounds.

The GIs needed to test fire every weapon left by the Chinese, because abandoned weapons could have defective firing pins, or barrels plugged with lodged bullets from defective ammunition. One American officer carried a liberated Thompson submachine gun on several missions only to discover it wouldn't fire because of a defective firing pin. It was fortunate he hadn't had to use it.

All of the companies of the 7th had challenging firefights, resulting in KIA and WIA on both sides. But C Company had another problem that began at Sachang-ni. The commander of C Company had demonstrated hesitant leadership. I presume that was the reason he was relieved of his command. One thing soldiers cannot abide is a cowardly commander. Military units cannot expect more from the troops than is demonstrated by their leaders, and cowardice is a contagious disease that may result in "bug out fever."

Despite the change of commanders after the fighting ended at Sachang-ni, the C Company soldiers were still not fighting well. They lacked confidence in themselves and their leaders.

The first sign of trouble was the arrival over a 10-day period of five soldiers from C Company with gunshot or other injuries to hand or foot that could have been self-inflicted. While it was difficult to prove that a self-inflicted wound (SIW) was intentional, a cluster of suspicious injuries suggested a mini-epidemic.

The new C Company Commander, Lt. Art Gregory, had his hands full trying to change the mind-set and stiffen the spine of the despondent rifle company in bitter cold weather while facing repeated Chinese night attacks on positions they had been ordered to hold at all costs.

As I pondered the SIW problem, Pvt. George "Nibbet" was brought in from C Company. He had discharged his M-1 Rifle through the top of his left foot. He claimed he had rested the barrel on the top of his boot to keep snow out of it and the rifle went off by accident. I began to cut his boot from his mangled foot when the field phone rang. Lt. Gregory was on the line asking about Pvt. Nibbet. It had been reported that Nibbet had told one of the other soldiers that he was going to get himself evacuated, one way or another.

I could hear the anger and fatigue in Gregory's voice as he said, "Doc, I can't tell you what to do, but if Private Nibbet gets medically evacuated, you may have another half dozen like him down there before morning—followed by the Chinese. I have been going all along the line, from one platoon to the next, keeping our men fighting. Charlie Company must learn to stand and fight."

"What would you like me to do?" I asked.

There was no immediate answer.

Finally, he said, "Doc, I need every man on the line."

It was a statement, not a request.

I asked, "If I send Private Nibbet back to you—dosed up with morphine, with his foot bandaged and covered with a cut-out oversize shoepack, would you put him back in his foxhole, give him back his rifle, and tell him which direction to shoot to stop the Chinese? And would you make sure word of his return is passed up and down the line to every platoon and squad to confirm the fact that a soldier no longer gets a medical evacuation by shooting himself in a hand or foot? After the point is made clear to everyone, and after Nibbet has cried all night, we will pick him up in the morning."

"Thanks, Doc, that will help us out a lot," Gregory said.

As I looked at the poor kid who had blasted a hole through his foot, writhing in pain, I felt great sorrow and personal agony. For the first time, I had crossed the line between personal health care of a patient and the public health need to preserve the fighting strength of a unit in wartime. I knew that the SIW epidemic had to be stopped, and that was the only way I could think of doing it. But as a doctor, I felt I was betraying my profession by not evacuating the soldier.

Harry Truman said, "The buck stops here."

In the war in Korea, the buck stopped not with the President of the United States, but with the soldier trying to do his duty in combat and with the soldier trying to avoid the enemy in a fight. I didn't like the buck that Pvt. Nibbet had dropped into my lap, but no American infantry officer was in a position to make this career-ending decision. Only their Doc could make this call, and I hated doing it.

In Communist armies, company commanders were authorized to execute reluctant soldiers with a bullet to the head. The problem of SIWs didn't come up in the Chinese or North Korean armies. In the American Army, we were supposed to use JAG officers, witnesses, and court martial procedures. But how were we to tell the Chinese to hold up the war for a few days because we needed to take time out for a legal procedure? There was also nothing Lt. Col. Toddy could do that wouldn't cause a bigger mess. So without equivocation, without evacuation, and without consultation, I made the decision at the aid station level.

I gave Pvt. Nibbet 15 milligrams of morphine tartrate and an atropine tablet to reduce nausea. I cleaned up his wound, cut the top out of a big shoepack, and wrapped his foot in it with 4-inch elastic wrapping. We gave him some warm cocoa and then I told him that he was still able to function and his platoon needed him to fight off the Chinese.

He was sobbing as Sgt. Herrick and an infantry sergeant carried him between them, hobbling on one leg, back up to his foxhole to face the next wave of Chinese. His platoon sergeant gave him back his rifle and he was told to shoot at any Chinese coming his way because he wasn't going to be able to run very fast or very far. Charlie Company held their position during that night and on subsequent nights.

I don't know if Pvt. Nibbet fired his weapon again—but he was there, filling his foxhole until he was evacuated the next morning. The news was spread up and down the line and apparently throughout the battalion. The epidemic of self-inflicted wounds stopped and Charlie Company fought and continued to hold their position.

The next day, when I visited Battalion Headquarters, Lt. Col. Toddy, in front of others, which both embarrassed and frustrated me, asked why I had refused to evacuate a wounded soldier. Bad news without explanation travels fast.

I said, "I did not refuse to evacuate the soldier who had shot himself in the foot. I only delayed his evacuation about eight hours in order to stop an epidemic of self-inflicted wounds. Furthermore, this action may have prevented the Chinese from joining the battalion commander for breakfast here this morning."

I immediately regretted making the last smart-aleck remark. There was total silence from the HQ staff. No one wanted to touch that hot potato. I wondered if they were thinking my action carried the implication that had the battalion commander gone along the line encouraging his rifle companies instead of enjoying his breakfast several hundred yards to the rear, this entire SIW mess might not have occurred.

After an awkward pause, I tried to explain further.

"I did what I felt I had to do under the circumstances. It is a very difficult thing for a doctor to be forced to choose between the best health care of an individual soldier and the welfare of a fighting unit, and I would prefer to not discuss this painful matter anymore."

It was never again discussed in my presence.

After being dismissed by Lt. Col. Toddy to return to my work, I had mixed emotions. I did not like myself, and I didn't like what I had done to Pvt. Nibbet. I could just visualize the press getting into the story.

I resented the apparent lack of battalion leadership support for a rifle company struggling to repel repeated Chinese assaults. Above all, I detested the fact that people were being chewed up in the meat grinder of war. But I resolved, with God's help, to keep doing what seemed essential until someone else had a better idea of how to solve these daily bloody problems. I was open to guidance, but resistant to stupid nonsense.

After I returned to the aid station, I was still ticked off. It was the second occasion on which the battalion commander had questioned me in front of his staff on a subject which I felt, for his sake as well as mine, would have been better discussed in private. I wondered if our battalion commander was handicapped by a lack of common sense. If Toddy had been a doctor, I would have felt he didn't have a good bedside manner.

The more I thought about my response to the battalion commander, the more convinced I became that I had not handled things properly. Lt. Col. Toddy was a gentleman who never used alcohol. He seemed out of place in an Army in which the use of alcohol was endemic. I probably came across to him as a prickly pear of a young doctor. As I look back at these issues with a half-century of hindsight, I realize I was in error. After all, Lt. Col. Toddy was also new to combat, and as the 1st Battalion commander, he was within his rights to suggest or challenge, openly or privately, as he saw fit. My sharp response had not helped him do his job better, which should have been my primary goal, rather than personal defense. However, as a 24-year-old doctor, new to the Army, I was not mature enough to consider my responsibility to help my commander become better. Again, I should have said, "Sir, may I speak to you privately about this matter?" but it didn't occur to me back then.

I would have been pleased if Lt. Col. Toddy, or anyone else in the battalion headquarters, had asked me to sit down and have a cup of coffee or take a little walk together to find out what I was doing, and to share ideas on how I might do things better. It never happened. Instead, I felt I was on my own as the only doctor in the battalion. I had no idea if HQ approved of what I was trying to do for them, or if they just thought I was a pain in the butt.

I had not seen our regimental surgeon since we landed at Wonsan, forcing me to learn about the Army from Sergeants Herrick and Ogden, Lt. Sarka, and by osmosis from the infantry ambience that enveloped us in a shooting war. I realized there was a real possibility that I just didn't understand enough about the infantry commander's ways of doing things.

However, after the SIW incident, I was more fully accepted by the infantry officers and sergeants. When I visited the companies on the line with Herrick or Sarka, I was always warmly received.

I especially appreciated a remark made by one infantry platoon sergeant.

He said, "Doc, the men know you are there for them, but they also want to know their doctor personally, because they never know when they will be looking up at you from a litter, and praying you can keep them alive."

Thereafter, I tried to get to know more of the men personally, but it made it hurt more when they were lost. While writing this book, I spoke with an old infantry officer, asking if he could recall a particular person. Finally, he confessed that he tried to not get to know people during the Korean War because it hurt too much to lose them. I understood what he was saying, but I couldn't function that way. I was glad the Lord knew each one of our names and I wished I could have done the same, even if they were dying.

The good news out of the whole SIW business was that Charley Company continued to improve as they gained pride in their fighting ability and leaders.

A week after the incident, an American reporter visited our aid station. According to Lt. Sarka, the reporter had been hanging around the evacuation hospital near our beachhead at Hungnam. I wondered what he knew and why he wanted to see me privately. When we were finally alone, he asked if I could help him with a personal problem. It turned out he had gonorrhea and was looking for a doctor to treat him away from an Army hospital, hoping to not leave a record. I laughed with relief as I treated him—and did not record his name.

As I sat down to write another letter, I realized that I couldn't remember what I had written last. I knew that at times I must be repeating myself. But letters were usually written quickly to maintain communication and to let the family know I was still alive. From time to time, I would stop, tear up a letter, and start over, because I remembered I had written the same thing before or because I had written something too descriptive or with such poor handwriting while on the hood of a jeep that I couldn't read it myself.

This next letter reveals my tendency to speculate, ramble, re-hash old material, and stress the safety of current positions to decrease the worry back home.

Dear Dad and Mother,   6 Dec. 1950

All is quiet where I am at present. We are now located just outside Hamhung in preparation for the defense of the city. The fleet is nearby in case we have to evacuate. Actually, since the night of the 4th we have not been under attack except for patrol skirmishes.

We have not heard much news here but it is obvious that there are at least six million or so Chinese Communist troops coming down on us. We all wonder just what the U.N. is going to do. It is the opinion of most of the troops that I have talked to, that the U.N. will lose everything it has gained and more if they back out now. I think the CCF is just using this as a wedge to get into the U.N.

There is developing a great mass of troops, tanks and artillery around Hamhung, which will slaughter a good many CCF if they attack. With air and naval support, it will be rough. So far their tactics have been sheer numbers. When we had the heavy attack on our Battalion on the 29ᵗʰ we counted 400 dead Chinese in the morning and estimated 1200 wounded. We found out later that we had been attacked by two Regiments but they withdrew and went around us because losses were too high.

I hope all goes well at home.

Love, Bob

We soon realized that our medical platoon needed to look after ourselves. I gave Sgt. Herrick the task of coordinating with the rifle companies, Sgt. Ogden was to set up and maintain the functional integrity of the battalion aid station, and Lt. Sarka had the task of facilitating evacuation. In addition to supervising the care of the sick and wounded, I also took upon myself the task of maintaining contact with 1ˢᵗ Battalion Headquarters. While Lt. Sarka had been doing that before, he had little clout with the battalion HQ brass and was not always able to effectively comment on actions or decisions that might complicate the mission of the medical platoon. So unless I was needed by patients, I tried to attend the battalion commander's staff meetings, where I found my suggestions on medical support and evacuation planning were as welcome as support planning for food and ammunition.

It was easy for an infantry battalion to become so involved in fighting the war that they forgot about their medics—until the sick or wounded were in danger of being left behind. I had to become more involved in battle planning to anticipate where future casualties would likely occur, before the infantry began screaming for medics.

While our aid station was usually close to the battalion headquarters and never far from the rifle companies, we were certainly much safer than we had been when we were all bunched up in a defensive circle at Sachang-ni. While the rifle companies had intermittent firefights out in front, I found moments of relative tranquility, except when the shells from the battleship Missouri were going over our heads, which sounded like a freight train going through a squad tent.

I was irritated by radio commentator Walter Winchell, who predicted that the "U.S. forces will be slaughtered on the beach by the Chinese." My brother wrote to me concerning some of the statements made by Winchell, which made me fantasize about unloading a clip of .45 slugs from my Tommy gun into his office when I got home because his comments must have upset mothers and fathers on the home front. Not a good idea, but odd thoughts occurred to many of us amid the chaos of war.

During one tranquil period, the following series of letters were written home, stressing mundane personal items, the overriding goal of which was to prevent my parents from worrying.

Dear Dad and Mother,   *Dec. 7, 1950*

Today has been a quiet day. It is all probably a lull before the storm. I haven't heard any news for some time—so don't know what is going on.

There is one thing you could airmail to me and that is a half dozen or so jockey short underwear (size 32 waist or medium). Laundry is a problem here and with an occasional soiling of a pair from diarrhea I am running short of shorts. Diarrhea comes and goes in all armies with changes in diet, uncleanness and general tension. So far it has not been a major problem with diarrhea. Clears up with a little bit of paregoric and bismuth.

There have been quite a few tattered North Korean peasants passing by. They are searched and allowed to pass. Time to curl up in my sleeping bag.

Love, Bob

Dear Folks,   *8 Dec. 1950*

Just received your letter of 23 Nov. concerning Thanksgiving. The situation at present has not changed any. We have withdrawn as I mentioned in the last two or three letters and are no longer in combat with the Chinese Communists, only North Korean guerilla activity, which doesn't bother us much.

Everyone here is hungry for news concerning the U.N., atom bomb etc. There will probably be a hell of a big battle around Hamhung soon but we don't worry because the fleet is standing by to evacuate us if the going gets rough. I was back to Hamhung today and saw dozens of heavy tanks and other equipment along the way. Yes, the Chinese will face a wall of artillery and tank fire if they hit the flat land around Hamhung.

I was glad to get the pictures; I can bet that Phi Rho Sigma didn't win the purse on the homecoming decoration.

I am going to send this letter stamped airmail and another letter free to see which gets there the quickest.[11] *I don't know where I would get stamps over here anyway.*

The winter here has not been too bad for us now since we are down out of the mountains, but while in the mountains it was miserable. The Chinese wear quilted

---

[11] Although this letter was sent stamped and the following not, both were delivered on the same day.

cotton uniforms, which are quite warm when dry. This is the dry season in Korea and although the weather is below freezing all the time there has been little snow. Today we had about three inches of snow and we are all hoping the Chinese get wet because those cotton uniforms are cold when wet.

One sergeant sardonically said the only good thing about Korea was that we didn't have to pay income tax but he would gladly change places with any taxpaying U.S. citizen.

There is the lighter side of life, even here with so few comforts. The GI is able to make light of anything to bring out a little humor. My 1ˢᵗ Sgt. Herrick is a grouchy old soul but has a heart of gold and a sense of humor. He uses analogies in his speech that would grace any joke book. He just was talking about two Army nurses he knew, one was so fat she reached two ax handles and cud of tobacco across the fanny, and the other was so skinny that if she drank a bottle of red strawberry pop she would show up like a thermometer.

Speaking of Thanksgiving—we also had turkey but it probably wasn't as good as the way it's fixed at home.

Love, Bob

Dear Folks,   8 Dec. 1950

Enclosed is an example of the 3ʳᵈ Infantry Division newsletter. As is usual, they talk about everything but the 3ʳᵈ Division. These papers usually get to us about three days late.

The aid station at present is in the teacher's apartment along the side of an old Korean schoolhouse so we are snug as can be. I have a winter sleeping bag, which is very warm, even when I have slept in a foxhole. I am situated all right for warm clothes but as I mentioned before, clean underwear shorts and a pair of felt shoes are about the only things I need.

I am sending this letter the same day as another one with stamps to see which gets to you first.

Love Bob

Because of the number of unmarked roads to the rear, it was sometimes difficult to decide which road from a battalion aid station would be the most direct route back to the regimental medical collecting station. To prevent people from going off in the wrong direction, the Medical Company would occasionally station a squad at a crucial junction to steer vehicles in the right direction and defend the road junction from mischief by Chinese infiltrators. At other times, two soldiers were left without a vehicle in order to hide nearby, observe traffic, and walk back to the Medical Company later in the night. The following excerpt was written by one of those soldiers, Sgt. Kenneth Bonner:

"It was the night of December eighth, 1950, somewhere above Hamhung, North Korea. I was out in the middle of nowhere in a mud hut with one of my ROKs—the one I called 'Squint,' as he always had one eye half-closed. I was to direct any wounded coming down the crossroad back to the Collecting Company. Suddenly I heard a jeep coming and noted it was pulling a trailer. As I was about to direct him to the Collecting Company, the driver said he had to get back right away and he had nine KIAs to leave with me. It didn't seem to matter to him that I had no vehicle and no radio. When Squint came to help me unload, he pulled the tarp back and seeing all the bodies at night like that, he was so scared that he ran into the hut and wouldn't come out. When I got a good look at the bodies, I noted that Captain Concannon was right on top and they were all frozen stiff. I had known Captain Concannon as a fine officer and I felt bad about unloading them all there beside the hut and then just leaving them there. I reported the location of the bodies, but the Medical Company was pulling out and I never knew if the nine bodies were retrieved or not. About 35 years later, I had a call from a retired colonel who said he was trying to find out any information available for Concannon's son, who was only three years old when Cpt. Concannon was killed. So I told the colonel what little I knew, and stressed how sorry I was to not have been able to bring the bodies out. At this point, the colonel said, 'Sergeant, I can put your mind at ease for Captain Concannon is now buried in Arlington Cemetery.'"

A truck from the 1st Battalion 7th came through before morning and picked up the bodies. The regimental Medical Company along with Sgt. Bonner had moved out before the truck arrived.

The next day, December 9, 1950, the last of the Marines and survivors of the 31st Regiment of the 7th Infantry Regiment arrived from the frozen Chosen Reservoir and passed through our area on the way to Hungnam. The 3rd Battalion of the 7th Infantry Regiment was defending the regiment's tail from a bunch of determined Chinese soldiers. In anticipation that the 3rd Battalion of the 7th Regiment may have some casualties, someone in the regimental Medical Company sent Cpt. Donald Wilson MSC with several litter jeeps forward to await them by an old school house near a frozen river.

Sgt. Bonner wrote about it as follows:

"I was volunteered to also go with the team. The plan was to stay until the 3rd Battalion 7th came past the schoolhouse that we were using as an advanced collecting point. The 3rd Battalion was expected around five or 6 PM. That time came and went with no sign of the 3rd Battalion. Around 8 PM, I told Captain Wilson we should pull out because the 3rd Battalion might have crossed the river on the ice anywhere up the road. Moreover, the bridge about a half-mile down the road was supposed to be blown up at six in the morning and we should get across before then. His answer was the 3rd Battalion hadn't come down the road yet. Then, in the middle of the night, there was a lot of activity, with bugles and green flares just north of us. Someone had dug foxholes all around the school, so we occupied the holes and set up a defensive perimeter. We didn't have much ammo, so we just kept quiet. Gradually, we realized that the Chinese could be heard on all sides of us, but they didn't seem to know we were there.

"About an hour later, I heard someone trying to start a jeep. I crawled over to the building where the jeeps were located and found Captain Wilson there. I whispered to the captain, asking him what the hell he thought he was doing, making all that noise. He said he was just making sure the jeeps would start and he was thinking of trying to contact the 10th Engineers to see if they were still going to blow the bridge. I told the captain that if we got out from the middle of all of the Chinese it would be by walking out while the Chinese were asleep. Then, about 5:45 am, a reinforced platoon from A company came barreling down the road to get us out of there before the Chinese could figure out what was happening. We all skinned out of there without firing a shot.

"The 3rd Battalion had crossed over the ice farther up to tie into a new defense line next to the 1st Battalion, which had pulled back to form a new defensive line. Somehow the 1st Battalion got the word that fourteen medics with jeeps from the Medical Company of regiment were still unaccounted for out in the middle of newly acquired Chinese territory. We didn't need to worry about cranking up our cold jeeps because the A Company Platoon's jeeps just pushed them back up the road until they started. The A Company platoon had the task of getting us out fast, and they did.

"The 3rd Battalion commander wanted to give all of us Bronze Stars for coming forward to help them with their wounded. But Captain Wilson declined, saying we didn't need any medals for what we did. I thought that was a bunch of crap—throwing away ten points for rotation out of Korea. How could an officer be so unhelpful to his men? I was really pissed off."

Bonner's story illustrates the need to continually follow up on details and not assume that someone else has taken care of the matter. If the 7th Regimental Medical Company leadership had maintained contact with the 1st Battalion aid station as they should have been doing, rather than stick a few men out on a crossroad, they would have known that a retrograde adjustment of our line was about to occur. This was one sign of the systemic problem in which the regimental Medical

Company and the regimental surgeon were not leaning far enough forward to properly support the three or more battalion aid stations.

Someone from 7th Regiment HQ must have inquired about the whereabouts of Cpt. Wilson's litter jeeps and men. If those 14 men had been lost because of such casual negligence, someone's head should have rolled. But as so often happens with lackadaisical leadership, nothing was done when things turned out all right. This error in judgment by the Medical Company for not maintaining liaison with the battalion aid stations was soon forgotten. I wonder how many other lives were lost in similar circumstances.

While Task Force Dog under Brig. Gen. A. D. Meade helped extricate the Marines in the north, another Task Force under Lt. Col. Fred C. Weyand worked in the Wonsan area to move out all supplies and equipment before relinquishing it to Communist control again. It was a major accomplishment, including not only the out-loading of all supplies and ammunition brought into Wonsan Harbor, but also the screening and evacuation of many North Koreans who had joyfully welcomed the American and ROK military forces when they advanced northward.

Many North Korean Christians had gleefully opened their boarded-up churches, and dug out their Bibles and hymnbooks to preach and sing praise to the Lord for freedom. They were terrified at the thought of what would happen to them after we left for the south again.

While en route north through Wonsan, I had treated a number of civilians, and had chanced to meet some of the North Korean Christians who had been hiding their faith for five years under Communism. Now that we were retreating, these people and their children would be marked for death. There were many spies among the refugees who would point fingers at any Christian or other North Korean who had welcomed Americans. We were all pleased to hear that Task Force Weyand was able to save 7,000 North Korean friends of freedom in the Wonsan area along with the removal of all supplies and equipment on December 9, 1950.

Farther north, there was a rapid gathering of almost 100,000 Korean refugees in the Hamhung/Hungnam area, pleading to be evacuated to safety in South Korea. They had welcomed the U.S. and U.N. forces as liberators, and now faced a difficult situation as we withdrew. I learned that from the continuing stream of sick or injured refugees we tended every day. In the midst of it all one night, I got off a letter to my brother John.

Dear John,   *12 Dec. 1950*
I have been writing home to the folks a little oftener than to you I am afraid. I hope they send the letters on to you.

I am still situated in a little house next to a schoolhouse just outside of Hamhung. The comforts of life, i.e., food, shelter and clothing, are adequate. We have a stove rigged up, which keeps the aid station warm. Food is as good as field rations usually are and come two times a day. Clothing—we live out of our packs, which we carry on our back. I have worn the same pants for a month but have two sets of long john under-wear, which I rotate. My extra clothing has been dissipated on patients who didn't have any. I actually have no need for more clothing now because I don't want to bother carrying it. I have finally rigged up a canvas cover for my sleeping bag—using an old half pup tent. I recently acquired a feather down sleeping bag, which is warm as toast. Up until now, I have just rolled up in about ten Army blankets. If you haven't sent the sleeping bag, don't bother. The air mattress, however, would still come in handy.

I had a pheasant dinner the other day, which although not as good as Mother could make, was tasty considering what we had been having. One of the tankers shot it with a carbine. I tried to get a second one with an M-1 rifle but missed. We had one of the cooks fry it and make about a gallon of gravy to which we added a loaf of bread and rice and stirred it up into a pile of sludge so that everyone in the tank crew and aid station could have a taste.

The last few days there has been no activity and everyone is wondering what happened to the big Chinese push. We have no official word, but rumor has it that we are going to evacuate North Korea. I imagine MacArthur's plan is to draw the Chinese out where we could plaster their supply lines. Anyhow, in the next few weeks you may hear from me down around Pusan. The way things change every day, it's hard to say what will happen.

The opinion of many GI's is that they need a housecleaning in Washington, D.C. to include H.S.T. and Atchison.

It looks like a rather bleak Christmas here this year, but it seems good to be where we aren't being shot at. They are setting up a rotation plan for doctors so that everyone gets a crack at front line duty, they say, anyway. They are starting to send some Navy doctors into the lines with the Army—boy, do they bitch, and I don't blame them.

I hope all goes well with your schoolwork, girlfriend, etc. Write when you can. I know you are busy now cramming for exams. Don't worry about me too much since I am sitting in a good spot and there is a fleet, flocks of tanks, and all the artillery from three divisions to protect us around Hamhung if the Chinese should be foolish enough to come out of the mountains and cross the flat land to Hamhung.

Love, Bob

The commander of the 10th Corps determined that the 3rd Infantry Division would be the unit responsible for defending the evacuation of the Hungnam beachhead. In order to accomplish that, the 7th, 15th, and 65th Infantry Regiments, together with all of the 3rd Infantry Division's support units, including tanks, artillery, engineers, medical, and other support detachments, came together as a unified and coherent fighting force under its capable commander, Maj. Gen. Robert H. Soule. "Shorty" Soule was fluent in both Chinese and Russian from his long experience in the Far East. Someone told me that Gen. Soule had been stuck at the rank of captain for more than 20 years before being promoted. I guess that gave him the opportunity to learn both Russian and Chinese.

When Maj. Gen. Soule finally got the pieces of his division together for the defense of Hungnam, instead of having battalion combat teams spread out all over half of North Korea, he proved his worth as a good division commander. Shorty Soule visited every front line unit of the 3rd Division, including the 1st Battalion 7th Infantry Regiment—with the simple order to keep shooting, because it was hard for them to shoot at us while we were shooting at them. Traveling by jeep or helicopter, he assessed the position of every line commander—ever encouraging and tactically adjusting as needed. I saw the diminutive, courageous old soldier come and go, but never got to shake his hand. The fighting infantrymen had first priority in that pleasure, as it was the infantry work that was his primary concern at that moment.

With naval gunfire from destroyers, cruisers, and the battleship Missouri, as well as multiple batteries of artillery from the beach, we had so many high explosives going over our heads that I wondered if there were any intact Chinese left where all of the shells were landing.

To read a more complete account of the evacuation from the port of Hungnam, see *Miracle in Korea – The Evacuation of X Corps from the Hungnam Beachhead* by Glenn C. Cowart. That book has a complete listing of the American, U.N., North and South Korean, and Chinese units involved.

The following citations for Distinguish-Service Crosses to 1st Lt. James Kidd and 1st Lt. Charles Butler, both in the 2nd Battalion, and Cpt. John Powers of the 1st Battalion of the 7th Infantry Regiment, are only three of many deserving recognition during that encounter, and suggest the nature of the fighting going on along the shifting front line.

Award of the Distinguished-Service Cross to 1st Lt. James K. Kidd

"First Lieutenant James K. Kidd displayed extraordinary heroism against an armed enemy during an enemy attack upon Company E, 7th Infantry, in the vicinity of Yongan-ni North Korea, on 13 December 1950. When the 3rd Platoon, Company E, was attacked by a numerically superior Chinese Communist Force, causing the platoon to withdraw due to heavy casualties, Lieutenant Kidd proceeded immediately to the disorganized platoon. Finding the platoon leader severely wounded and all non-commissioned officers wounded or killed, he quickly reorganized the platoon, reinforced it with men from the adjacent platoon, and arranged for the evacuation of the wounded. Repeatedly exposing himself to heavy enemy fire at short range and with utter disregard for his personal safety, Lieutenant Kidd then led the counterattack of the platoon against well dug-in enemy across open terrain and through hostile cross fire. The men, inspired by this remarkable display of courage on the part of Lieutenant Kidd, charged the hill with minimum casualties. Lieutenant Kidd personally led the assault against two enemy machine guns and three mortar positions. As a result of Lieutenant Kidd's courageous action, the numerically superior enemy force was forced to retreat in disorder and confusion."

Award of the Distinguished-Service Cross to 1st Lt. Charles L. Butler

"First Lieutenant Charles L. Butler (then Second Lieutenant), a member of Company F, 7th Infantry Regiment, 3rd Infantry Division, distinguished himself by extraordinary heroism in action against the enemy near Singyang-ni, Korea on 15 December 1950. On this date, Lieutenant Butler commanded 'Task Force Fox' which had been organized in an attempt to relieve a platoon of Company G when that platoon was enveloped by a numerically superior enemy force. While en route to the objective area, 'Task Force Fox' was ambushed. With no thought to his personal safety, Lieutenant Butler was continuously in the forefront of the battle rallying his men on to their objective. In the ensuing fierce encounter, he was wounded in the left arm. Despite his painful wound, he continued to press his men forward, reassuring them with words of encouragement as they advanced. It was then he received a second wound, in the abdomen. Even though seriously wounded, Lieutenant Butler refused medical attention and continued the attack with the assistance of his platoon sergeant. When the order was received to withdraw, he was unable to walk but requested he be lifted onto the tank so that he could fire the machine gun mounted on the turret to support his platoon in the withdrawal from its encircled position."

Award of the Distinguished-Service Cross to Cpt. John J. Powers

"Captain John J. Powers, Company B, 7th Infantry Regiment, distinguished himself by extraordinary heroism in action against armed enemy of the United Nations near Chung-jung-ni, Korea on 15 December 1950. At approximately 0930 hours, Captain Powers, upon being notified that the enemy surrounded the 3rd Platoon of his company, immediately formed a task force consisting of a reinforced platoon and three medium tanks. After advancing about half way to the beleaguered platoon, Captain Powers' unit came under withering automatic weapons and small arms fire from the front right flank. Exposing himself to the enemy observation and fire, Captain Powers deployed his men and directed such destructive retaliation that the enemy was soon pushed back from the right flank.

Fighting with great skill and courage, Captain Powers and his troops charged into the frontal area, blasting their way through a veritable wall of fire, when suddenly the enemy delivered a murderous volume of automatic weapons, mortar, and small arms fire from the left flank. Captain Powers was hit during this encounter, but selflessly continued to deploy his unit, assign firing missions to tank commanders and direct the fire of the riflemen. The enemy inflicted many casualties in this action, but Captain Powers, with unwavering resolution to reach the besieged platoon, regrouped his troops and forged on. Again the unit received a heavy barrage of mortar fire, seriously wounding Captain Powers, who refused evacuation and ordered the unit forward. The determined foe then launched another vicious assault and Captain Powers received a third and more grievous wound. Realizing the impossibility of reaching the isolated platoon, Captain Powers, constantly suffering agonizing pain and weakening from loss of blood, reorganized the task force, supervised the loading of the wounded on the tanks and ordered a withdrawal. Only after movement of the unit to the rear had begun would he consent to ride on the tank with the disabled. Upon returning to the company perimeter, Captain Powers refused aid until he had reorganized the company and the other wounded had been treated."

As a result of Cpt. Powers' action, the beleaguered, surrounded platoon did not give up, but organized an attack of its own, and succeeded in fighting its way through the weakened Chinese forces to return to the main B Company position. Cpt. Ray Blanding followed Cpt. Powers in command and proved to be an equally courageous leader of Baker Company. Our medical platoon was honored to provide medical support for brave soldiers such as those.

The story of Cpt. John Powers would be incomplete without again mentioning Pvt. Albert Walton. Walton ran through enemy fire to rescue Cpt. Powers when he was struck down and unable to get up again without help. The following is Albert Walton's written account:

"On the morning of December 15, 1950, our 3rd Platoon of Company B 7th Inf. 3rd Div. was cut off during the night and my 2nd Platoon with two M-4 tanks was given the job of breaking through to them. It was 20-25 below zero. We struck out about 8:00 to do our job. The first sign of trouble was a bazooka shell flying just over the tank closest to me and enemy mortar shells starting hitting all around us.

"My company commander, Cpt. John J. Powers, was ahead of me. I got the BAR team behind a terrace and cranked up when I saw the CO go down. He was trying to get up when he was hit again and was floundering around trying to get up without using his hands. He had been hit in his left elbow and down around his right shoulder and both arms were causing him trouble getting up. I saw he couldn't make it by himself, so I ran to him, helping him to his feet. He was probably 100 feet ahead of me.

"Once he was on his feet, he could run, with me holding his arm. We started back to the medic who was treating my squad leader, when I saw bullets hitting the snow in a wide arc heading right for the two of us. Sure enough, I was hit in the left heel and knocked flat on my back. The captain asked how bad I was hit and I told him not too bad, for him to go on to the medic, and I would be back as soon as I could. I was told later that I was put in for a Bronze Star for exposing myself to help the CO, but never heard anything more about it.

"When I got to the medic, I laid down between the CO and the medic to see how bad I was hit. Just then, a mortar shell hit right behind me and shook me like a dog would [shake] a bone. I was hit approximately 20 times with large pieces and many more small pieces of shrapnel. I had a broken left arm, lost the vision in my left eye, shattered the tailbone in my back and chipped my left leg in four places. The medic was hit, my squad leader was hit again, but the CO didn't pick up any shrapnel because I must have stopped what was coming his way. The CO said for us to stay where we were and he would get the tanks turned around and load up the wounded as soon as possible.

"I must have passed out for a few minutes, because when I came to, the medic, whose name was Elmer Foster, my squad leader, and I were all that was left on the battlefield that I could see. The squad leader was hit real bad and was bleeding to death. The medic and I couldn't stop the flow from his neck. We put compresses on each side of his neck but couldn't stop the bleeding and he died lying across my legs. After a while, the medic and I decided we would crawl to a dike so we would have some protection from the cold wind, but when we started crawling, there were shots fired from the hill.

"The bullets hit just ahead of us and we got the message real quick that the Chinese didn't want us to move. We lay there until 11:00 or 12:00. The medic said he thought he could walk and he was going to go back to get some help for me. He lit a cigarette for me and started back to our lines. I was laying on my right side with my broken arm lying on top of my body and I couldn't see him leave.

"All of a sudden a Chinese grabbed my shoulder and pulled me over on my back. I was looking up the barrel of a .45 caliber Thompson machine gun. All I could do was watch his finger on the trigger, but he never pulled it. This was a little traumatic for an 18-year-old and is still traumatic for me today. I saw our medic, being marched away. Elmer Foster never made it out of their prison camp, if he ever got that far, because his name never appeared and he was declared dead years later. The Chinese picked up our rifles, ammo, and our cartridge belts from my squad leader and me. My feeling at that time was that I was going to get out of this mess, even if I was alone. The cold weather had frozen the blood from most of my wounds and that saved my life, I'm sure. But my eye continued to drip blood.

"In about an hour, another Chinese came down the hill, bayoneted me in my left leg, and turned me over on my stomach. He went through my pockets, taking what he wanted and then fastened some of my buttons back on my jacket, sweater, and shirt. About that time, I heard a small plane, as did the Chinese, who froze in place until the spotter plane went by. There was then a shout or two from the hill, and he left me on the run. I was sure the tanks would come back to get me, and I guess the Chinese were waiting to try and knock one of them out.

"As it was getting late in the afternoon, I realized that I needed to start back or I would freeze to death. The sun was not far from the mountain peaks, when four Navy Corsairs came in on a rocket run, right over where I lay, and plastered the hill. They made three more passes with machine guns. After that, I could hear lots of commotion and talking on the hill from the Chinese. The shell cases from the Corsair machine guns had fallen all around me and made the snow sizzle. I decided that I had to get moving. I crawled to a dike ledge and was able to get on my feet. It was slow going, but I started limbering up the farther I walked. I found a stick that one of the tanks had run over, breaking it just the right length to fit up my coat sleeve and stabilize my broken arm. I followed the tank tracks back and found a package of C-ration jelly that had fallen from someone on the tank. So I had a feast right then, because it was the first food I'd had so far that day. I still like jelly and think about that experience every time I eat some.

"But my next experience on the way back made me think 'The Man Upstairs' was stuttering on my name. There were still the problems of the Chinese, the weather, and the possibility of getting shot by my own people if I ever got back to our lines. I followed the tank tracks back to where we had left early that morning. It was beginning to get dark and very cold. Next I came to a group of North Korean civilians around a fire using sticks to get stuff out of a fire [that was] burning some Army packs. I knew that one of the packs was probably mine. I just looked at them as they looked at me. There were no words or gestures. I walked on by them, which scared the hell out of me because some of the civilians didn't care for American troops being in their country—looking back, I didn't want to be in their country, either.

"Right after I passed them, I found out why they didn't bother me, because a tank started up on the next hill, 500 yards away from me. I was surprised and elated. I started hurrying down into the small valley and tripped over a wire I hadn't seen—falling flat on my face. I hurt my arm and back very much and when I tried to get up, I just floundered. I realized the tank was turning around. So I decided to crawl over to a small tree about 25 feet away. By using the tree, I was finally able to get to my feet, but the tank was now out of sight. Gradually, the sound of the tank also disappeared and it was a still cold night. I was just stunned that the tankers hadn't seen me. I felt desperate. I knew I had better get moving again, because I was stiffening up. I got to the tank tracks and kept plodding along. I knew if I stopped, I would soon freeze to death.

"I lost track of time as I moved slowly along in the tank tracks, but I guessed it must have been about midnight. Suddenly a mortar shell exploded nearby between the trail and nearby creek. I guessed the mortar was one of ours and they were just zeroing in for the night and I would need to be real careful. Then I heard some American voices up ahead and spotted a little bridge. So I decided to move to the middle of the trail in sight of the bridge and just holler as loud as I could. I said I was a wounded GI and needed help and was going to stand still in the middle of the trail where they could see me.

"There was suddenly a mass movement of troops and I bet I heard 30 safeties coming off. A voice answered and told me not to move because a medic and some cover soldiers were coming to get me. When the medic and three soldiers reached me, the medic looked me over and hollered for someone to get a jeep up there quick because I needed help bad. I was in the 15th Infantry. A lieutenant told me my 7th Infantry unit had passed through about five hours ago and by looking at their map, I had walked about 11 miles from where I had been shot up.

"I have had a lot of resentment about being sent to Korea in severe winter conditions with only a field jacket and a blanket to keep me warm. During the month I was in Korea, I never stayed in a building of any kind. I slept in a foxhole or out in the snow with temperatures as low as 30 degrees below zero. The politicians that let the Army decrease in men and equipment to its 1950 level should see the dead and wounded Americans they were responsible for. We still haven't learned that strength is the best defense."

Albert W. Walton, B Company, 7th Regiment 3rd Division

Pvt. Walton soon found himself on the *Ainsworth*, a troop ship with a fully-equipped hospital unit in Hungnam harbor, where initial repair surgeries were done. He was evacuated to the States, where several more months were spent recuperating in hospitals before he finished his tour of duty as a mechanic in an armored unit.

The good and faithful medic, Elmer Foster, was a member of the 1st Battalion medical platoon assigned to B Company. Foster, himself wounded, stayed with Walton when he passed out, and then went for help, but was captured by the enemy just before the Corsairs struck. If Elmer was not killed in the Navy Corsair strike, he probably was executed by the Chinese after they interrogated him because he would have been unable to walk the long distance to one of their POW camps.

The American tank driver carrying Cpt. Powers and the other wounded on top of the tank probably thought the three left behind were dead. To go forward to retrieve the bodies would have exposed those riding on top of the tank to machine gun fire from the hill. The Navy Corsair strike provided Walton an opportunity to walk away, in spite of his injuries. Perhaps if Elmer Foster had stayed with Albert Walton for another 15 minutes, until the Corsairs struck, he could have walked out with Walton. The fact that Walton walked eleven miles in freezing weather with his severe injuries was a major feat of endurance, if not a miracle.

Pvt. Walton deserves a Bronze Star with V-Device for his actions in climbing the hills and clearing the road blocks of Chinese on December 2, 1950, a Silver Star for coming to the aid of his fallen Company Commander, John Powers, on December 15, 1950, as well as clusters on his Purple Heart for his multiple wounds.

As for Cpt. Powers, the following article appeared in the Fall 2002 issue of *The Cottonbaler*, a publication of the 7th Infantry Regiment Association:

"The Last Christmas Card," courtesy of James V. Tully, Sr.

"In December of 1950 in North Korea, the Chinese were overrunning Company B and other units. Captain John J. Powers Jr. was our commander and was badly wounded—the third time he had been wounded. Even though wounded, he was more concerned about the welfare of his soldiers than he was about himself. He was a great commander! Over his objections, we carried him to a tank and put him inside the escape hatch and he survived. He was awarded the DSC [Distinguished-Service Cross] for his gallantry and was awarded three Purple Hearts. He was a graduate of West Point, Class of 1945, and he went on to serve a full military career in a variety of demanding assignments.

"Each of his company soldiers [including Pvt. Walton] sent him a Christmas card every year to show their respect and admiration for him and to tell him how much we thought of him. Since he has now left us, on 3 May 2002, there will be no more Christmas cards. We will keep him in our thoughts and prayers, for he was a 'Damn Fine Soldier, Cottonbaler by God.'"

As we drew into a half-circle around both Hamhung and Hungnam, the Chinese attacks slacked off. I suspect they couldn't get enough supplies and replacements through the mountains to sustain their attacks in more open country. Certainly our artillery, naval guns, and air power made their lives short, or at least miserable.

During the two weeks before Christmas 1950, the 10th U.S. Army Corps continued to shrink as the 1st Marine Division, the 7th Infantry Division, U.S. and ROK forces left Hungnam. The 3rd Infantry Division, under Maj. Gen. Robert H.

Soule, provided cover for all other units to evacuate and we continually occupied new areas as troops and equipment evacuated behind us, causing the front line to contract toward Hungnam. During the withdrawal, the engineers drove trains and trucks off broken bridges, causing them to become burning wrecks.

It was often difficult to know just where to position our aid station for maximum efficiency in meeting the needs of widely spread rifle companies.

As I considered the problem of medical support, it occurred to me that my primary job was to *lean forward*, operationally speaking, to support the rifle companies and battalion headquarters elements. But I also found I was having to *lean backward* to keep track of the box ambulance platoons and the medical collecting unit under the command of the regimental surgeon. I had no social or operational contact with our regimental surgeon until we reached the beach of Hungnam. He never came to the battalion aid stations to see how we were doing. I wondered why our regimental surgeon didn't lean forward to encourage the battalion surgeons as the regimental commander, Col. John S. Guthrie, leaned forward to support the three infantry battalions in combat. As our three-battalion combat teams drew close together, Col. Guthrie made his presence known. It was my first opportunity to meet that capable gentleman soldier, and I felt more a part of the 7th Infantry Regiment.

When the 2nd and 3rd Battalions of the 7th Infantry HQ were not far away, Chaplain Carroll would travel to other units to hold mass and hear confessions while the two Protestant chaplains, Cpt. Brown and Maj. Lewis, from the 2nd and 3rd Battalions, would rotate over to the 1st Battalion to hold a Protestant service. The 3rd Division chaplain was a Lutheran, who held either a general Protestant service or a liturgical service for Lutherans or Episcopalians when requested.

I tried to write letters to the families of the soldiers in our platoon who had been killed, but it was an impossible task, not just because I had neither a typewriter nor a dictionary, but also because I didn't have any uninterrupted periods of time. The chaplains in the regiment were equipped and trained for that task better than I, and had the right connections with the personnel office and with the grave registration office (GRO).

Lt. Sarka, Sgt. Herrick, Father Carroll, and I often slept in the same room, tent, or battalion aid station. Father Carroll wanted to be near the wounded and dying, and we often functioned as a team. During lulls, Father Carroll and I had philosophical and theological discussions. As we became better acquainted, he asked me for suggestions about what he might include in his Sunday sermons and in his counseling for Protestants, since we were at times separated from the battalions with Protestant chaplains. I suggested a few Bible passages as listed below.

John 3:3-18

Romans 4:3-24, 5:1-10
Ephesians 2:1-20
I Corinthians 13:1-13

Father Carroll marked some of them in his Bible to use in his counseling and preaching. I hoped they would bring as much comfort to wounded and dying soldiers as they had to me.

We moved our aid station location at least a half dozen times between Pungson-ni and Hungnam beach. Sometimes we slept in the open or in a tent, but most of the time we occupied a local house. Often there would be twenty or more of us side-by-side in one room in an effort to escape the cold.

One evening, Father Carroll came in late, having spent a very sorrowful day giving last-rights to some of our dying or recently KIA soldiers. He was obviously tired and distraught over the horror of it all. He looked in his bedroll, and turned to me.

"Doc," he said, "would you, by chance, have a bit of whiskey in your bedroll?"

"No, Father," I said. "I was hoping you might have a bottle of communion wine that you hadn't blessed yet that you could give me."

He replied, "No, Doc, I don't, but I am expecting a case of wine tomorrow and I would be happy to share a bottle or two with a Lutheran, before it's been consecrated, provided you don't tell the Army or the Pope."

"Oh, I won't tell," I said, "but I bet the Pope would grant us an indulgence for our indulgence if he were with us now."

Father Carroll tried to hide an impish smile behind a fierce scowl. Then he brightened up a bit.

"Isn't that Herrick's bedroll over there in the corner?" he asked.

Before I could answer, he headed for Bill's bedroll, reached in, and pulled out a half-full bottle of whiskey. He plopped down on his own bedroll near the little stove and with a look of joyful anticipation, he took a long swig of whisky. I watched a large number of bubbles enter the bottle. In only a few minutes, Carroll was relaxed, face flushed red, and no longer cold. His sadness was erased as the whiskey tranquilizer dulled his anguish over ministering to so many dead and dying soldiers.

A minute or two later, the door burst open and Herrick entered with a blast of freezing air, heading straight for his bedroll. Reaching inside, he found nothing but his spare pair of socks.

He tossed the bedroll aside and bellowed, "Who the hell has been in my bedroll?"

Bill looked at me but I just shrugged – trying not to appear knowledgeable. Looking around, Bill soon spotted Carroll sitting red-faced by the stove, his arm extended, holding the bottle.

"Is this what you're looking for, Bill?" Carroll asked, with a benevolent smile.

"Yes, it is, Chappy," said Bill, somewhat crestfallen, as he stretched out his hand for the bottle, the contents of which had been greatly diminished.

As Bill reached out, Carroll pulled the bottle back, leaning away from Bill, and clutching the whisky bottle to his chest.

"Bill," he said, "I'll split it with you."

He swung the bottle to his lips and took a parting swig before handing it over to Bill.

Bill snorted and said, "Chappy, I bet your mother never had to spank you for holding your breath. You not only drank half of my whiskey, but then you volunteered to split the remainder of my whiskey with me, and then you drank first!"

Carroll tried to look penitent as Bill downed the remaining whiskey in long bubbly gulps. He wiped his mouth.

"I thought I should just go ahead and drain the bottle," Bill explained, "because I was afraid if I stopped before the bottle was empty that someone, who has already had too much to drink, might want to split the remainder with me again."

He sighed comfortably. The firewater was warming him up.

After another deep breath, he tossed the bottle aside, saying, "There goes a dead soldier. I had hoped that soldier might have lasted a bit longer."

Father Carroll replied, "I know what you mean, Bill. I spent the whole day giving last rights and helping the GRO load a truck with dead soldiers. I too hoped and prayed those soldiers might have lasted longer, but they didn't."

His last statement stopped all banter and we all curled up on the hard floor in our sleeping bags, each with our own thoughts. I kept picturing the truckload of bloody, frozen GI and South Korean bodies outside in the cold. I heard some nose blowing from the other sleeping bags. I felt sad, too, but also lucky and blessed to still be alive.

The shells from the naval cannons and artillery continued to scream or roar overhead, depending on their size, and explode west of us, hopefully beyond our troops. The noise made sleeping difficult. Most of us wanted to stop thinking for a while. Whiskey helped. War and killing was a miserable business. I don't mean to belittle the power of prayer, but sometimes prayer and whiskey together worked better to lessen the emotional pain of those caught up in the messy miseries common to the clan of warriors engaged in the business of war.

In late December 1950, we received word that some of the units within the 1st Battalion could divide themselves into shifts to rotate through a shower not far from the beach and receive an issue of clean clothes. Up until that time, I had occasionally bathed out of my steel helmet—the so-called "whore's bath." I also washed my socks and undershorts in my helmet—after I had finished shaving and scrubbing down with a soapy dirty undershirt.

Washing clothes was not easy, because of the extreme cold and because there was no place to hang clothes to dry. When we acquired body and/or crab lice from heating and sleeping in abandoned local houses, we had to use louse powder. It killed the lice and nits (after they had hatched), but caused a lot of itching. It was with joyful anticipation that I went to the shower tents in the rear area.

During the previous five weeks, I had allowed my mustache to grow, but shaved off my beard every two or three days. I didn't particularly like the mustache, especially when it had frozen icicles in it, but I thought it made me look older. I debated shaving it off, but decided to keep it as an emblem of maturity.

After showering, I went to the clothing issue tent, where clean clothes had been set out according to size. We could take two sets—one set to wear and one set for our backpacks. As I gathered my rank insignias and personnel items from my dirty clothes, I was amazed at how bad my old, dirty clothes smelled. Less than an hour before, I had been wearing those stinking clothes, and I hadn't noticed the smell. I hadn't noticed how bad everyone else smelled, either. It took just one delightful, hot, soapy shower for my sense of smell to return. What a blessing it had been, before I joined the field infantry, to be able to start each day with a nice hot shower and shave.

Being insensitive to our stinking clothes, I thought, was like being insensitive to our own sins—until the Bible makes them apparent, and faith in Jesus was like a hot shower, covering us with His righteousness. In the last few weeks, I had learned that it was possible to become inured to anything—from the killing of thousands of soldiers, to the pitiful plight of thousands of refugees struggling to get out of the line of fire while clutching children to their sides and babies to their breasts. I had hardened, but I had not lost my sense of compassion. I continued to grieve for the miserable refugees.

I found that I had to purposefully resist becoming inured to the suffering around me. I found strength in the book of Psalms, chapter 28, verses 1 to 7.

The words of Jesus in Matthew 19:14 kept running through my head: "Suffer the little children and forbid them not to come unto me; for such is the kingdom of heaven."

I assumed other battalion surgeons also struggled to help the masses of refugees as their time allowed. Many were brought to our aid station for care; the extra supplies from our two special trunks were being used up.

As we continued to close in on the beach, I wrote a few letters home.

Dear Folks,   *14 Dec. 1950 (AM)*

The sleeping bag and air mattress arrived in good shape and I tried it out last night. I was nice and warm in my foxhole. We are slowly evacuating Hamhung. There is not much pressure from the Chinese in our area. We have had no official word yet but I think we will all be boarding ships and heading for South Korea, probably Pusan.

The Marines are leaving by boat now. They were severely battered up north around the reservoir. That was where we were supposed to have gone except for a last minute change in plans.

Love, Bob

An interesting Marine sideline was their propensity to steal Army vehicles and give them a quick paint job with Marine vehicle numbers. I was told an Army team in Hamhung was busy identifying stolen Army vehicles and re-designating them as Army vehicles, as the Marines and vehicles were loaded onto ships. There were some traditions the Marines liked to perpetuate, and stealing from the Army was one of them.

Should the Army accuse the Marines of stealing, the Marines could claim the Army was stealing the Marine close air support to help the infantry, because the newly emancipated U.S. Air Force didn't know how to provide close air support for the Army and didn't seem interested in learning that dangerous business.

The old Air Force P51s were notorious in Korea for shooting wildly at the wrong targets. There was limited radio contact from ground forces to close support aircraft in the Korean War. Serving with front line infantry as close air support coordinators was not a favored assignment for either United States Air Force (USAF) or Marine pilots, according to some of the more distinguished pilots I have talked with over the years. The flyers chosen for ground observer assignments were usually men the better pilots would not want as wingmen. The Army was not much different in their selection of personnel for outpost duty or "bringing up the rear" duty. A good sergeant or company commander would tend to select his least able soldiers for such duties, and to preserve his best fighters in his unit.

On occasion, an Army Ranger leader would come by, asking for volunteers. There were usually a few volunteers from Army infantry units, but the Army company commanders tried to squash the recruitment of soldiers for special missions, because the recruiters often stole the guts out of a company, leaving too few real warrior-soldiers in each squad to lead others in combat.

Dear Folks,   *14 Dec. 1950 (PM)*

Nothing new to report. I am at Yonpo and should be on board a ship soon. The big question is about the international situation.

At present I am in a warm house with my aid station. The sleeping bag is swell. I gave the old one I had to my assistant Lt. Sarka.
Love, Bob

Dear Folks,   *17 Dec. 1950*
Still sitting at Yonpo but will withdraw to Hungnam and board ship probably tomorrow. There has been very little pressure from the CCF in our sector. The mail situation has been erratic because the APO has moved out to ships.
My sleeping bag is nice and warm. The weather today is quite cold especially since there is a stiff wind blowing.
The aid station is in an old Russian type building and has a furnace built of brick between two walls, which heats up the place nicely.
Love, Bob

While poking around in our area, Sgt. Herrick made a delightful discovery. Among the items set aside for destruction were many boxes of special foods from Lt. Gen. Almond's private kitchen. There were cans of ham and yams, special cheeses, nuts of all kinds, and other tasty items. We took all we could carry back to our units and gave many items to the refugees. Plenty of unflattering remarks were made about Almond's attempt to live high during the war. We wondered what had happened to Almond's table wine. Army scavengers assumed the Marine scavengers had gotten to it first. But it's more likely that the X Corps HQ staff used up the wine before we had gotten our chance to pig out. The opportunity to stuff ourselves on delicacies raised our spirits and provided a few moments of humor in the midst of our evacuation.

Between the fifteenth and twenty-second of December 1950, the defense line around Hungnam shrank as the military units were systematically out-loaded, leaving the 7th, 15th, and 65th Regiments and supporting units in the 3rd Infantry Division as the lone fighting units at the beach.

On the afternoon of December 23, Gen. Almond presented the Distinguished-Service Cross to Gen. Soule on the crowded beach of Hungnam.

Award of the Distinguished-Service Cross to Maj. Gen. Robert H. Soule

"Major Gen. Robert H. Soule, as Commanding General, 3rd Infantry Division, displayed extraordinary heroism against an armed enemy in Korea during the period 1 December to 24 December 1950. Assigned the mission of covering the withdrawal of those elements of X Corps in the Chosin Reservoir and Hagaru-ri areas, Gen. Soule displayed sound judgment, high professional skill, and untiring energy in directing the operations of his Division. Although faced with a numerically superior force, freezing temperatures and an aggressive foe, Gen. Soule's action enabled the successful withdrawal of the entire 1st Marine Division and elements of the 7th Infantry Division. Subsequently, Gen. Soule continued his covering mission so successfully that the enemy was continuously beaten back from the beachhead, allowing a complete and orderly withdrawal of all units of X Corps from the Hungnam area with a minimum loss of personnel and equipment. His continued presence at the front under bitter winter conditions and with total disregard for his personal safety and under small arms and automatic weapons fire was an inspiration to the men during this historic operation. His aggressive leadership, courage under fire, and personal heroism are in keeping with the highest traditions of the military service."

The U.S. and South Korean troops got out, but there were still thousands of North Korean refugees who had not yet escaped. Then a miracle happened. Four U.S. Army colonels boarded the *Meredith Victory*, an unarmed merchant ship with aviation fuel on board. The colonels persuaded the ship's captain to enter Hungnam harbor and take on the remaining 14,000 refugees. It was a crowded and difficult journey, with scant food and water and no facilities. The November/December 2002 issue of *The USAA Magazine* published an article entitled "Voyage of Mercy," by Rosanne Fohn, giving the details of this merchant ship's rescue of these North Korean refugees on the *SS Meredith Victory*, with pictures and the names of the senior members of the crew. I refer the reader to this source if they desire more information. That *Meredith Victory* journey is a poignant story and an important historical document of the Korean War that merits wider distribution.

In all, nearly 100,000 refugees were taken out of Hungnam on 150 ships or watercraft of every description, from LSTs to merchant ships.

The next day, December 24, 1950, as we awaited our turn to board a landing craft to ferry us out to a troopship, I noticed a lot of black powder mixed in with the sand on the beach. One of the artillery men said there had been hundreds of cannons placed for miles along the beach over the previous few weeks, and the black powder was exactly what it looked like—gun powder. The weather was cold and damp, but I hoped nobody would toss a lit cigarette into the blackened sand.

According to our sergeants, who had past experience with troopships, we should not leave anything of value stored in the hold of our vehicles to avoid Navy pilfering. Lt Sarka and I, along with our NCOs, divided up the drugs, especially morphine tartrate Syrettes, barbiturates, and antibiotics, and carried them in our backpacks.

The only question that remained was how to get our remaining five-gallon can of pure ethyl alcohol on board. We decided to put a "Poison: For External Use Only" label on the can and have Chaplain Carroll carry it on board. When we arrived at the ship, a long stairway was lowered from topside down to our landing craft. The good chaplain was unable to carry his pack, his considerable corpulence, his duffel bag, and the five-gallon can all of the way up the stairway. Less than halfway up, he called to a sailor at the rail to lower a rope for his overload—the five-gallon can of alcohol.

This caused a minor panic as we watched our precious can of alcohol hoisted skyward by the Navy. Sgt. Herrick grabbed Sgt. Ogden's duffel bag and pack and sent Ogden scurrying double time up the stairs past the chaplain and everyone else. He arrived just in time to retrieve the can of "poison" before the sailors figured out what was in it.

When I reached the deck of the troop ship *General Randall,* I paused to catch my breath and look back at the Hungnam beach we had just left. I was far enough away so that the few people still on shore looked very small. Suddenly there was a chain of explosions that spread south along the beach ending in a gigantic mushroom cloud over the harbor. I whipped out my camera and took pictures of the rising cloud. A moment later, a blast wave hit our ship, causing no damage, but raising concern for the men still on the beach.

The exploding trail of black powder had found its way to an ammunition dump, causing the large explosion and subsequent mushroom cloud. Our regimental surgeon, Maj. Ray Bennett, was among the last group preparing to leave when the explosions occurred. He was standing behind a sandbag wall at the last medical collecting station on the beach. The powder blast knocked over the sand bag wall, covering him with sand and sandbags. He had to dig himself out. Others were not as fortunate. The explosion caused a number of deaths on the beach. Several landing crafts near the beach were capsized, causing some soldiers to drown from the weight of their packs. It had been only twenty minutes since we had crossed the beach.

As we moved to our assigned quarters, I found that officers had a bunk of their own, while enlisted men were two to a bunk. Lt. Sarka ended up with the five-gallon alcohol can in his bunk. In addition to American soldiers on board, there were hundreds of KATUSA soldiers with no bunks at all, who slept on decks, stairs, and along every passageway on the ship.

I wondered why they didn't assign three enlisted men to a bunk in eight-hour shifts for both Korean and American soldiers with two company grade officers to a bunk, and allow only the field grade officers (major and above) to have a bunk to themselves. That certainly would have been more respectful of our Korean soldiers. But none of us had slept in a bunk or bed of any description since we landed in Korea, and everyone was happy to be on board, especially our KATUSA soldiers. Fortunately, our troop ship, *General Randall,* was not torpedoed, because (I was told by a sailor) there were more souls aboard than there were life preservers or lifeboats. Although we were crowded, the food was great.

The ship heads (toilets) had waiting lines. Some men tried to urinate over the sides of the ship. But the wind at shipside could be very tricky, causing urine to spray back on the person emptying his bladder as well as on his close associates and those on lower decks. It was preferable to urinate in a can, which could be emptied over the side of the ship or in a shower stall—which became backup urinals.

There are some things that officers and gentlemen should not become involved in. For instance, how many cases of grapefruit and orange juice should be traded by two Navy chief petty officers in exchange for one quart of pure 200 proof ethyl alcohol offered by two Army sergeants? The exchange rate (I heard) varied from 10 to 15 cases of juice per quart of alcohol.

By the time Father Carroll conducted Christmas Eve Mass, there had been a lot of loud Christmas carol singing before and after the Protestant chaplains read the Christmas story recorded in the Gospel of Luke. The chaplains had an extremely joyful and thankful congregation that night. But many of the soldiers, after the first spiked cup of juice, preferred the second cup as straight juice.

Father Carroll managed to slip me a bottle of his unconsecrated communion wine to take to my bunk, where I sipped it as I wrote a Christmas Eve letter.

Dear Dad and Mother,   24 Dec. 1950, 8 PM

Here it is Christmas Eve and I am safe aboard the U.S.S. troop ship General Randall. *I only wish I could get this letter to you today so you would not spend Christmas Eve worrying. For the last week I have not written since I knew no mail was either going out or coming in since the A.P.O had moved out to the ships.*

We in the 3rd Division are pretty disgusted with the news broadcasts concerning our withdrawal and amphibian landing in reverse at Hungnam. Walter Winchell said we were almost annihilated. That is a complete lie. Actually since we got out of the mountains we have had very little pressure. The coverage from our artillery and heavy mortar, navy guns, and aircraft was such that the entire evacuation was carried out with very few casualties.

This morning, about 10:00 AM, we loaded our packs on our backs and trudged down to the beach where we loaded into amphibian tractors, trucks and other landing craft, which shuttled us out to the ships off shore a mile or so. The big Missouri *battleship was there with her 16-inch guns to protect us. By 1300, the last of the 3rd division was loaded. What would have been a flawless operation was marred somewhat by the premature explosion of an ammunition dump on the beach, which killed several men.*

The biggest pleasure was to take a shower on the boat.

Just where we are going I don't know but it will probably be Pusan. No one thinks we will stay in Korea very long because we will probably be needed else where in the world more in the near future.

I have taken quite a few pictures. I am going to mail a couple of rolls home to John. He can get it developed. There is nowhere I can develop the pictures and I may lose them in travel. When I get home I will have to explain where and when and what they are all about. As you will note in some of them, I have grown a mustache, which is quite a hideous affair, but they are in style over here.

I hope John got through the finals O.K. I hadn't had any letters for some time. We were told that all mail was sent to where we are going so I should get a sack in a day or so.

My sleeping bag and air mattress are wonderful. I sleep nice and warm, no matter how cold. The air mattress makes the big difference since it keeps you off the ground and still doesn't allow a draft under you. My number one Korean has it all blown up for me every night.

I hope you don't worry too much about me. Remember, I am situated behind the lines so have a much better than average chance. The newspapers distort the news a good deal and report heavy fighting where there has been only a skirmish between patrols. Time for a nice soft Navy bunk.

Love, Bob

After a short, but good, night's sleep, I awoke on Christmas morning and went out on deck to offer a prayer of thanks and to inhale some fresh air. The *General Randall* was churning along peacefully, heading south. I checked in sick bay and found a few soldiers with headaches, but nothing more serious. I had to step carefully. There were Koreans sleeping in every corner, in every possible position. Later, I wrote another letter home.

Dear Folks,   25 Dec. 1950

Christmas day aboard the Randall. *Food like one seldom sees in the Army. Anything we wanted for breakfast. Filet mignon steak for dinner and delicious ham for supper.*

There was a large attendance at church service and they had several services to accommodate all the men. The enlisted men had the same food we did, only in a different mess hall. They are extremely crowded in the hold with two men per bunk so they sleep in relays. The morale and spirits are very good. The men are just happy to be on board a ship. At present, we are anchored off Pusan and will probably disembark tomorrow some time.

I am sending a couple of papers home, which will give you an idea of how we get the news, if and when we get it.

We had a western show tonight. Ironically, the best laugh of the show came when a tired cowboy in the movie said he hadn't had a shower in three days. That really brought down the house, since most of the men had their first shower in six weeks yesterday.

Love, Bob

Jensen (left) and Sarka (right) in North Korea after pulling through Pyongsong-ni; notice sandbags around the aid station; December 1950

Who's who on the 1st Battalion toilet?
A luxury four-hole pit-latrine with box cover near Hamhung

Frozen ground near Hamhung; December 1950

Abandoned building in Hamhung; December 1950

Marine helicopters near Yonpo

Back row, left to right: Byland, Herrick, and Flint; front row, left to right:
Imm Yung Hee, Ogden; Hungnam

Sgt. Herrick with one of the many orphans in Hungnam

Left to right: Jensen, Herrick, Imm Yung Hee; Hungnam

Left to right: Flint, Piaseczny, Herrick; Hungnam

Supplies stacked in Hungnam; December 1950

Supplies in Hungnam; some were burned to make room
for the thousands of refugees going to South Korea.

Displaced Korean civilians in Hungnam

Ships in Hungnam harbor, awaiting troops and
North Korean Refugees; December 1950

Troops loading to leave Hungnam; December 24, 1950

Landing ship tanks (LST) starting south out of Hungnam

Cpt. Jensen took these photos of the progression of the beach explosion just after boarding the deck of a troopship in the Hungnam harbor.

The gigantic mushroom cloud caused by the beach explosion

Moments after this last photo was taken,
the blast wave of the explosion hit Jensen's troopship.

Chapter Nine
Respite in Pusan—Medical Platoon supports KATUSA home visits
December 26, 1950 – January 10, 1951

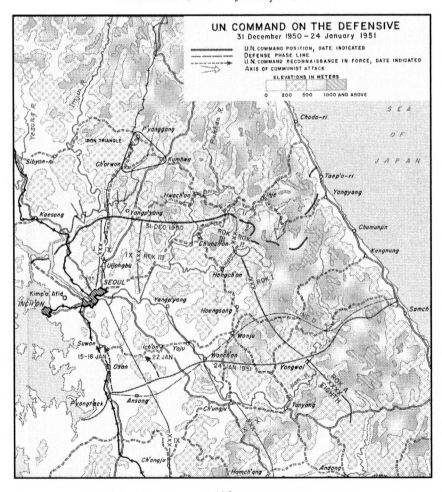

It has often been said that a mother's work is never done. The same might be said for a doctor's work. With a network of aid men sharing bunks with their infantry buddies, it was natural for them to filter medical complaints back through our medical sergeants to me. The Navy doc on the ship was only too pleased to have me help share the on-board sick load with him in the Navy sick bay. We found a few soldiers with coughs (bronchitis or asthma), upset stomachs, vomiting from diverse causes (including seasickness), runny noses, ear aches, bronchitis, diarrhea, gonorrhea, and other complaints.

After several hours of sick call, I retired to my bunk to write a quick letter home, thinking we would soon be getting off the ship.

Dear Folks,   26 Dec. 1950

Today has just been a day of rest. We are still anchored off the shore of Pusan waiting to disembark. We will probably get off tomorrow. Enclosed is another copy of the newspaper published aboard the Randall. *It gives a pretty fair evaluation of the situation.*

The best Christmas present for most of us was getting on the ships and getting a shower and a haircut. We are told there is a lot of mail awaiting us on the beach when we land.

Also enclosed is a North Korean war bond, which I found, abandoned in an old house.

Love, Bob

After finishing the letter, I joined Herrick and Sarka to talk. It was mid-morning on December 26, 1950, and we were wondering when we would be unloaded from the ship. Finally, word was passed down the chain of command to enjoy the rest for a day or so, because the trucks and bivouac area were not ready for us.

Some of our KATSUAs, who had family living in Pusan, had been asking for permission to visit their families. When the ship's troop commander refused, I intervened with the suggestion that he at least permit our Pusan Koreans to visit with their families from sunrise to sunset, but he still refused.

I said, "I've heard far too much griping from some U.S. infantry men about how the South Korean's wouldn't fight; and now, when there's a chance to show a few South Koreans a minimum of respect by allowing them to spend a few hours with their mothers, fathers, siblings, wives, and children in Pusan, you keep them locked up on ship in the harbor. In other words, you treat them like prisoners, instead of like soldiers. As if they have no human feelings." I saw the troop commander was getting tired of my pestering him, so I summed up saying, "I know my KATUSA medics. They are not gooks. They are loyal South Koreans and we have been to hell and back together in North Korea. I will vouch for their return on time."

At that last remark, the ship's troop commander became irritated. But most infantry men don't want to get their doctor mad because they know some day they might be all shot up and praying that he'll keep them alive. So he paused to think a bit.

Finally, the major said, "Doc, I'm tired of arguing with you, so I'll tell you what I'll do. I will let your six Pusan Koreans off when the sun cuts the horizon tomorrow morning and let them back on tomorrow evening when the sun meets the horizon again—but on one condition."

"What's your condition?" I asked.

He smiled.

"My condition is that you get off with them and you don't get back on unless they all return on time."

Before he could change his mind, I put my hand out to shake on the agreement.

"Fine," I said. "I accept your terms."

After we shook hands and saluted each other, he said, "Doc, you don't know much about these people."

"Sir, you don't know much about leading men," I said.

I immediately got Lt. Sarka and Herrick together, told them the plan and got them to gather up our entire medical platoon, both Koreans and Americans, where we could have a meeting, and also try to find a Korean who could speak better English to function as an interpreter.

After we assembled, we still had no competent interpreter, but I began to speak in simple English. Several Koreans tried to translate as I spoke, but with some argument between them over words. I asked the six Koreans who had families in Pusan to come to the front. I asked each one to name the members of his family that he wished to visit. When each of the men had told everyone about their families in Pusan, I asked the entire platoon if they felt these men were worthy of an opportunity to have a daylight visit with their families.

Everyone in the platoon, Americans and Koreans, shouted, "Yes, sir!"

I then told them all that the war was not over and much fighting was still ahead of us. We still had to drive the Chinese out of South Korea and push them back north as far as possible. But I also noted that this was a special moment; we had a little time and the troop commander on the ship had granted me a special pass to get off the ship at sunrise in the morning with the six Koreans who had families in Pusan because of the fine work of our medical platoon in North Korea. At that point, everyone cheered and hugged the six Koreans from Pusan.

I said the next item of business was to prepare a large gift package for each of our six Pusan Koreans to take to their families. For the gift package, I requested that everyone chip in with personal items or money. It would be up to Sgt. Herrick and Sgt. Ogden, assisted by our head Korean, Big Bak, to negotiate with the Navy petty officers in charge of the kitchen stores to see if we had any barter items to exchange for bread, ham, rice, flour, and any other food items that might be appreciated. By late afternoon, the platoon had assembled a lot of stuff, and everyone in the platoon helped decide who got what. They all had a good time playing Santa Claus.

It was a special event for our platoon. There were six Korean families somewhere that were going to see a loved one, and he would be coming home bearing gifts. There were some teary eyes among our platoon members, American and Korean.

Later, I asked Sgt. Ogden how much 200 proof alcohol it took to "buy" all the food gifts from the Navy chiefs.

"Sir, you don't want to know," Ogden said.

He was right; I didn't want to know. I just knew that I wanted some respect for our long-suffering Korean brothers and I wanted our Koreans to respect themselves, as well as their American brothers. After the gifts were assembled and bagged, I told our platoon the rest of the story.

I said that I had promised the troop commander that they were good men, but to get the deal, I had to get off with them and stay in the dock area all day until the sun touched the western horizon, at which time, the boat would arrive to take us all on board again. If anyone failed to return, I would not be allowed back on board.

That information caused a loud, animated discussion among the Koreans that went on for several minutes before they all quieted down. I had no idea of what was said, but I noted that our Pusan Koreans were sweating a bit. Big Bak rose to thank me for my respect and concern for the Korean people and assured me that the six Pusan Korean soldiers would all return at sundown the next day.

Before sunrise, the six Pusan Koreans appeared in clean uniforms, each with a huge bag of presents, including canned goods, wheat flour, rice, powdered milk and eggs, ham, and chocolate for the children. It was really a big event for our platoon, and most of the platoon was there to see them off and shout advice on subjects such as how to make babies—just in case they had forgotten.

As I prepared to leave the ship, a large American infantry sergeant showed up with a lunch box, extra water, an automatic carbine, a pistol with extra clips of ammunition, and instructions from the troop commander to protect me from any and all danger in the port area. I only had my personal revolver with me. As soon as we got off on the dock, our six Pusan Koreans took off and the tough infantry sergeant and I sat down to while away the daylight hours in a little bar near the dock area.

After we had sipped warm beer for about half an hour, one of our Pusan Koreans returned with a pretty Korean girl. He told me that the girl would help me to have a good time all day in a nearby room. I respectfully declined the offer, suggesting that she save herself for her future husband. But as I tried to explain this, my infantry sergeant protector volunteered to attend to the matter for me, so as to not hurt their feelings. I suggested that he keep his zipper zipped up, except for the mandatory discharge of recycled warm beer.

After the Koreans departed again, the sergeant asked me, "Sir, why didn't you take them up on the girl?"

"There are moral limitations clearly stated in the Bible," I answered, "but there's something more involved in this situation."

"What are you talking about?" he asked.

"The Koreans in our platoon feel a sense of obligation to me personally because I interceded for them so they could visit their families," I explained. "They will now do anything I ask because I have respected their personhood and their families. The offer of the young girl was not easy for them, but it was the only way they could think of repaying me. But if I'd had sex with that young Korean girl, they would have felt they had repaid their obligation and they would have thought less of me. I don't want them to repay their obligation this way, but rather to repay me by loyal and courageous service. We have a long war ahead of us, and we will be needing each other again in the future."

The sergeant said nothing more. I knew in my heart I had done the right thing.

After a long day of waiting, our six happy Pusan Koreans returned just as the sun touched the horizon. We boarded the ship together and were greeted by our platoon members seeking vicarious news of their visits with their families. That episode had a bonding influence on our platoon. The news of the Pusan Koreans of the 1st Battalion's medics getting off the ship for a day spread through the infantry. The following day, other Pusan Koreans were allowed home visits with their families. I did not hear of any of them not returning to the ship, and I am sure I would have heard from the troop commander if any had not returned.

From that moment on, we had very hard-working and brave Koreans serving with us. They willingly followed us to hell and some never made it back—but they served with courage and honor.

A few days later, Herrick told me that Big Bak had admitted to him after the platoon meeting that, "Captain Jensen no need worry Pusan Koreans not come back because all Koreans in platoon agree to kill any Pusan Korean who make trouble for Captain Jensen by no come back."

Apparently, Big Bak and the rest of our Koreans had told the six Pusan Koreans that they would all go AWOL to hunt down and kill any of the Pusan Koreans and their families if they embarrassed me by not returning by sunset. I assume that was what all of the loud Korean shouting had been about during our meeting. The one thing our Koreans understood was that their captain had stood up and defended them and their families and their captain was going to do it again by getting off the ship with them. Such an action by a Korean officer was unheard of. For our Koreans to betray such an officer would have been unthinkable for them.

While we rested on the ship, the Chinese received new supplies and fresh manpower in preparation for a new big push to conquer South Korea. By Christmas Day, the Chinese had crossed the 38th Parallel and were heading south for Seoul. The battered U.N. forces continued to retreat with lamentable disorder, while the new 8th Army commander, Gen. Ridgeway, took visible command. But even Ridgeway couldn't immediately turn the demoralized U.N. forces around to stop the advancing Chinese tide.

By New Year's Day, Seoul had fallen again and masses of South Korean refugees again were jamming the roads; suffering frostbite, friendly fire injuries, and exploding mine injuries as they struggled southward hoping to find safety. The sheer number of refugees hindered the much needed reorganization of U.N. forces by Gen. Ridgeway. It was a difficult time for the 8th Army.

Gen. MacArthur granted Ridgeway, who was a wise soldier with steel nerves, complete command of the retreating U.N. forces in Korea, and by the sheer force of his command presence, Ridgeway stabilized the U.N. forces. Through grim mortal combat, the U.N. forces began to push the Chinese back north.

Other changes were made in the command structure. Within the 3rd Division, Col. John Guthrie, the commander of the 7th Infantry Regiment, was promoted to brigadier general and transferred to X Corps, where his steady hand and wisdom would moderate the impulsive Lt. Gen. Almond, a MacArthur pet.

Col. Jim Boswell, who was Guthrie's deputy, became our regimental commander and Lt. Col. Fred Weyand replaced Lt. Col. Toddy as commander of the 1st Battalion of the 7th. We all felt Lt. Col. Weyand was a breath of fresh air and were delighted to have him as our new boss.

While all that was occurring, I was writing letters and having a pleasant rest on board a troopship as we prepared to move out and face battles to come. We were crowded on the ship, but at least we weren't outside in the grimy snow and cold.

Dear Dad and Mother,　　　*28 Dec. 1950*

Believe it or not, I am still on the boat in Pusan Harbor and think we will probably not get off until the 31ˢᵗ at which time we will go about 70 miles north for regrouping and getting replacements. What after that I don't know.

I was off touring around Pusan today. What a crowded, dirty, junky town. It certainly reflects the misery of the Orient. The Orientals are too busy getting three meals a day and a place to not be killed to worry about the difference between democracy and Communism. Any power that will give them peace and the bare necessities of life they will fight for. I am convinced of one thing: that our government has fallen down sadly in our propaganda war.

I haven't received any mail now for two weeks and don't suppose I will get any now until we get to our assembly area. Hope all goes well at home

Love, Bob

As I strolled around Pusan, I was impressed with the poverty, crowding, and squalor, but there was also evidence of vibrant survival efforts. There was much buying and selling of items, from auto parts to food. Even sex was for sale in the back rooms of many shops; South Koreans, as well as U.S. and U.N. soldiers, indulged themselves.

In one street side shop, a Korean woman prepared little green pancakes, about five inches in diameter, on a small charcoal stove. I watched from a short distance away as people stopped to buy the pancakes and other food before hastening on their way. Some ate the pancakes as they walked, others, especially young girls, put the pancakes in a dish or small basket on their heads.

As one young customer hurried away, two GIs walked past. In a carefree mood, one of them put out his hand and tipped the food dish from her head, into the dirt. I stepped from the crowd and called the two GIs to attention. I ordered them to help the girl pick up the pancakes. Guiding them back to the shop, I ordered the two GIs to buy twice the number of pancakes and give the new stack to the girl. I handed the dirty pancakes to the soldiers, shook hands with the young girl, apologized for the soldiers' behavior, and sent her on her way. After she left, I turned to the two GIs who were still standing at attention before me. I told them they could eat the dirty pancakes they held in their hands. Then I asked them a few questions.

"Why do you not have compassion for these poor people?" I asked. "Tell me your names and where you are from. Did you attend church or Sunday school before you entered the Army?"

They admitted they had attended church and Sunday school. I asked them if they thought Jesus would be pleased with their behavior. They said no and one started to cry. Since a crowd was gathering I sent the GIs on back to their unit, still holding the dirty pancakes. I never saw them again, but I doubt they ever forgot our meeting.

When I looked up at the Korean crowd I was greeted with smiles and bows. Some tried to shake my hand, American-style. It occurred to me that these people, who had been so traumatized by this horrible war, were hungry, not just for food, but also for compassion—because compassion gives hope, even in the midst of suffering and squalor.

The following day, we disembarked from the ship, loaded onto trucks, and headed to an assigned area a few miles north. It felt good to get off the ship and into the open air again. We were met by stacks of mail. I sat down to write a letter home again.

Dear Folks,　　　　*31 Dec. 1950, 8 P.M.*

New Year's Eve finds me popping the corn you sent. I received all your packages after I got off the ship. Thank you very much. I appreciate everything, especially the popcorn. We are now situated northwest of Pusan in an assembly and training company preparing ourselves for whatever comes next. I have received a large stack of letters from home and elsewhere, all in one bunch. The last was dated 13 Dec. I should get another stack soon. None had been censored. All the newspaper clippings arrived OK. The general news is about the same as we get but the columnist's clippings are of interest.

Incidentally, if you want to send some more popcorn, it's OK by me. The felt shoes arrived OK. The weather isn't as cold here in Southern Korea as in the mountains in the north.

I have been so stuffed full of candy and rich food the last two weeks that I have gained back what weight I had lost.

Time for bed.

Love, Bob

Dear Folks,　　　　*1 Jan. 1951*

Nothing new to report. We are still regrouping. I received a nice letter from Aunt Esther in which she enclosed a picture of you (and Granny and Granddad) from yesteryear. I am sending some of the pictures home so they won't get lost.

I am going to try to mail home some of my stuff since I have more than I can conveniently carry. The big problem is to get a package wrapped and mailed. Last letter received today was sent 22 Dec. That isn't bad time.

Love, Bob

In between letter reading and writing, we were retraining, in preparation for more war. Our training was both mental and physical. Battalion staff meetings were a pleasure with Lt. Col. Weyand in charge. He did not suggest foolish ideas, and he used his staff wisely. His admonition to forget about Sachang-ni and prepare for the next battle was helpful in bringing old and new soldiers together. We now had a battalion commander we could be proud of. Some thought we had the best battalion commander in the 3rd Division; I tended to agree. It was a good mind-set to have as we prepared for our next battle.

About that time, Bill Herrick got word his younger brother, Don, had arrived in Korea. He wasn't far away, so Bill and I got permission to visit Don at his unit. They had a pleasant reunion before we returned to our units and wrote more letters home.

Dear Folks,   10 Jan. 1951

It's still raining and one wonders how the water will affect the military. We are stripped clean to just what we can carry now so we will be able to go overland anywhere if need be. The big trouble has been so far that we were too heavily loaded and couldn't always move fast enough.

Enclosed (in package to John) are a couple of souvenirs I received from a Chinese prisoner who was wounded. Ring and razor.

The military situation is being well directed, as far as I can see, and all retreats are well planned and orderly and cost the Chinese heavily. We are still not in contact with the enemy.

Love, Bob

As we moved northwest through Taegu to Taejon, we were hit by freezing weather and snow. I learned that we were no longer in X Corps but in I Corps. We were to press north through Chonan to confront the Chinese still coming south from Seoul. It looked like more winter fighting was in store. We started training again for cold injury prevention. An extra pair of dry socks and loose laces on lower boots again became important for every soldier.

Pusan Harbor

4-inch gun on a troopship in Pusan Harbor

Hospital ship in Pusan Harbor

Cpt. Jensen and 2nd Maj. Brown, one of the Protestant battalion chaplains

Chapter Ten
Lt. Gen. Ridgeway stops 8th Army retreat, 3rd Division battles to Han River
January 26, 1951 – March 12, 1951

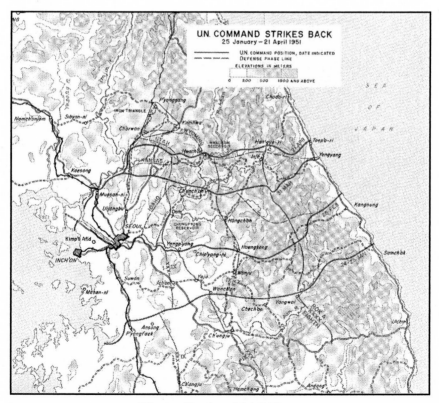

The road back to North Korea

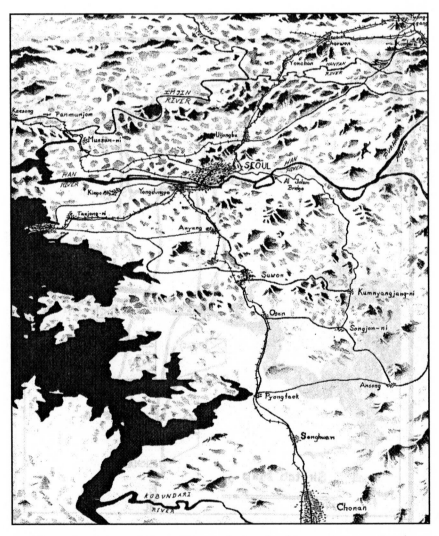

The path taken north from Chonan during the drive to recapture Seoul;
January – February 1951

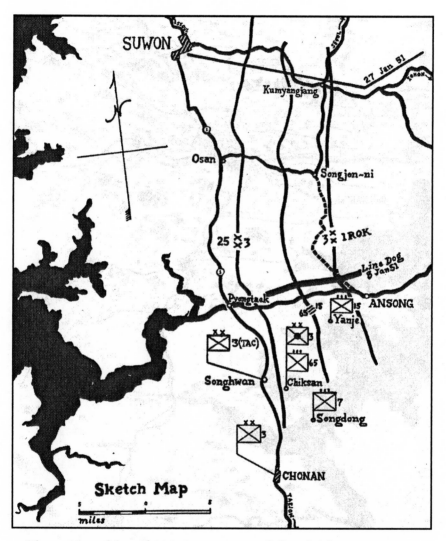

The position of the 25th U.S. Army Division (left), 3rd Infantry Division in (center), and 1st ROK Division (right) during drive to roll back the Chinese; February 1951

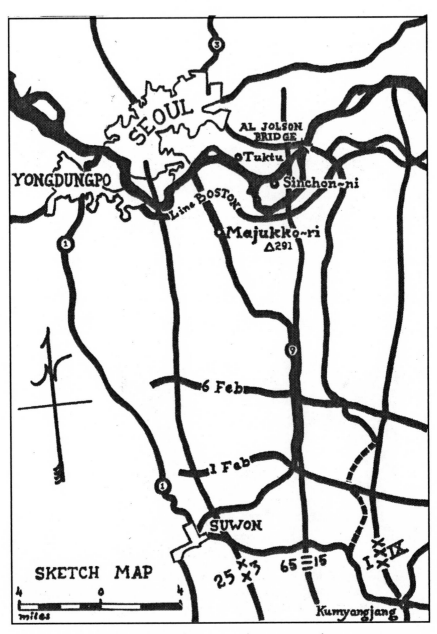

Pushing beyond Suwan to the Han River line

With the death of Gen. Walker in a road accident on 23 December 1950, a new but battle-proven leader, Gen. Matthew B. Ridgeway, was sent to Korea. Ridgeway was acceptable to both MacArthur and Pentagon leaders because he possessed high intelligence, courage, and sagacity beyond most of his star-bearing associates. Ridgeway realized we were entering an age of limited wars, and contrary to MacArthur's views from World War I and II, insisting there was no substitute for victory, Ridgeway knew that future victories might be more limited. The world was becoming too complex to organize grand coalitions willing to stay the course for total victory in an age in which there were atomic weapons in the unreliable hands of potential enemies.

Ridgeway met the challenge of putting new spine into a battered U.N. Army in retreat from the Chinese despite our advantage in air and sea power. The Far East Air Force was unable to stop the Chinese from moving large armies of foot soldiers, who carried supplies for many miles overland, with the aid of mules. The Chinese had perfected the art of night fighting to a point. If they could panic the defenders, as they often did with South Korean forces, they could win the battle. But if we held our positions, if we sighted in and booby-trapped their likely attack routes, and if we used our weapons wisely, we could exact a great toll on the attacking force. If the Chinese did not gain control quickly, before their ammo and supplies were expended, they were likely to become confused and suffer heavy losses from our counterattacks.

Unlike the Chinese Nationalist generals, the Chinese Communist (CC) Army's infantry leaders lived with their soldiers. The CC Armies were battle-hardened, and their entire life evolved around their military unit. If a CC soldier hesitated to engage the enemy, routine discipline was simple and swift. A bullet in the back of the head could be administered by a line officer. CC foot soldiers believed their officers had the right and duty to discipline reluctant soldiers, to the death, if necessary. A court martial wasn't required and there was no need to write a letter home to inform the family. There was no need for the CC officers to worry about a congressional inquiry. That type of discipline would not go over very well in the American Army but it produced results in the Chinese Army

On Christmas Day, 1950, historical forces were in play. The Chinese answered the naive question raised by the U.N.—would the Chinese cross the 38th Parallel and attack South Korea?—by doing exactly that. They had already rejected the U.N. cease-fire offer on 22 December; their POW camps along the Yalu River were filled with Americans and U.N. soldiers; the hills and valleys were strewn with the executed remains of thousands of South Korean soldiers that were considered unworthy of POW status and reeducation; and the Chinese Armies were winning. Why should they stop at the 38th Parallel and allow a festering sore of a Western-style democracy to continue to exist in South Korea? It was China's historic opportunity for some major restructuring in South Korea without having a single bomb fall on China proper.

During the first week of January 1951, Seoul fell under Communist control for the second time, and for the second time, the civilian population headed south, initiating a colossal humanitarian crisis. The Korean people were again caught between two armies in freezing weather. With little food, exploding mines, artillery shells landing among them, and strafing aircraft that could not see who they were shooting at, many refugees were killed, along with North Korean and Chinese soldiers who infiltrated the refugees as they headed south.

It was a sickening situation that the U.N. soldiers on the ground could not remedy. The Communists proved again and again that they would use civilians in small or large numbers to their advantage, and we had to prove again and again that we would not be overrun and slaughtered by infiltrating Communist soldiers, even if we had to shoot the civilians pushed up among them.

Many old men and women, women with babies, and terrified children were slaughtered until the average American soldier would only cringe as he shot at them. While the carnage continued south of Seoul in early January 1951, the 3rd Division prepared to re-enter the fray as soon as the order was given. Some observers thought the refugees were moving south faster than during their first retreat.

The roads were jammed with civilians as we prepared for battle and moved north through the terrified masses. The piles of decaying refugees along the roadside were continual reminders that our killing efficiency had exceeded our compassion. Our medics worked day and night trying to repair the damage done to southbound civilians until we finally reached a place where there were only rotting bodies and no more live refugees. At that point, we began to contend with incoming fire from oncoming Chinese and North Korean forces. We were back in combat. We did not move north with fear and trepidation, but with a desire to move past the retreating civilians and join the battle again on our own terms. But our self-assured bravado was not something to write home about. In my letters, I discussed the weather, the sights along the road, and domestic issues, as we prepared for some serious fighting up ahead.

In January 1950, some people in Washington talked about getting out of Korea, and leaving South Korea to the non-tender mercies of the North Koreans and Chinese. We disliked reading or hearing about those speculations from Washington or Tokyo, because we in the 3rd Division felt we knew how to beat the Chinese. Our men, Americans and KATUSAs, now knew how to stand and fight. Our supply lines were bulging, and the only thing we needed was more ammunition than the live bodies they had to throw at us. Company level leaders in the 3rd

Division that had not stood the first test of war in North Korea had been replaced, and we were ready to go again with better leaders, tested by fire.

Near Taejon—40 miles north of Taegu
Dear Folks,   Jan. 14, 1951
Winter is here in full swing with 10 degree below zero weather and four inches of snow. I am comfortable in my felt shoes and am the envy of all the other men and officers because of them. The aid station is in a little house, which we patched up and now have quite warm. At present we are not in contact with the enemy and I guess no one else in this sector is. Where the Chinese have gone to we don't know, but I am sure they must be cold in this weather.
The road between Taegu and Taejon was a graveyard of American and Russian equipment. There must have been 100 or more Russian tanks knocked out along the road and hundreds of trucks of all kinds. All along the road are streams of shivering refugees with their few belongings on their backs and no place to go.
Continued on 15 Jan. 1951
The weather is mild today, about 20 above, I would say. I was going to order felt shoes for some of the fellows but they are getting in extra overshoes so they can get by. There is little new here. I'll try to get this letter off today.
Love, Bob

On 16 January 1951, our regiment headed north for Chonan. The retreating U.N. forces had stabilized a line just north of us, allowing refugees to filter through and seek food and clothing assistance south of a new MLR. The Chinese forces were striving to build a new support base south of the Han River to facilitate a renewed drive to conquer all of South Korea. But Gen. Ridgeway was not about to let the Chinese have a comfort zone south of the Han River to use as a supply base. Our FEAF and Navy planes were very active and caused great difficulty for the refugees still caught in the area.

As the Seoul refugees moved south toward Taejon and Taegu, the 25th Infantry Division moved north from Chonan and spread out west of the road and rail line toward Suwon and Yongdungpo, which was on the south side of the Han River between Kimpo Airport and Seoul. The 3rd Division advanced north with the 65th Regiment on the left, next to the 25th Division on their left, and the 15th Regiment of the 3rd Division on their right, along with the 1st ROK Division. Together we were called Operation Wolfhound.

Our territorial objective was to reach the Han River; our military objective was to destroy or capture all Chinese and North Korean forces south of the Han River. Initially, the 7th Regiment of the 3rd Division was in reserve, where we didn't have much to do except to prepare for our turn at the front. We continued to run clinics for sick or injured refugees heading south. Our KATUSA soldiers played an ever-increasing role in that freestanding clinic service by bringing to my attention sick and injured refugees.

The pleased smile on the face of a helpful KATUSA soldier in response to my praise for their humanitarian actions assured me that compassion was not dead in Korea; it only required nurturing. I wished I had a fully equipped and staffed MASH instead of a mobile battalion aid station. There was so much work to do helping the battered refugees that I thought it was good and right for God to allow me to be there to serve the needy.

Chonan, Korea
Dear Folks,   *Jan. 17, 1951*
   As you might have noted, there was a little attack launched here by part of the 3rd and 25th Divisions. However, our lot was in reserve so we did nothing but sit around in Chonan by a warm fire and toast our toes. I have had an interesting time the last few days.
   This place looks more like a U.N. Army all the time. Down the street are the Turks and British. The Dutch and French are fighting on the line east of here. The Thailanders are on the line west of here. The Turks have established themselves as ferocious fighters here. I am glad they are on our side. I guess I forgot to mention it, but I stopped in the Swedish hospital before I came up from Pusan. They are very nice and are doing a fine job.
   Everyone wonders what is happening in the U.N. The consensus of opinion here is that we are being damn cowards if we admit the CC into the U.N. Instead we would like to see 1. Hang on in Korea. 2. Bomb and blockade China's coast in an undeclared war and try to undermine the Communist government with propaganda. Chiang Kai-shek is a lost cause and is best left on Formosa where he can do no harm.
   Love, Bob
   P.S. Enclosed is a South Korean coin. It looks like a cheap slug.

I went around to visit the nearby U.N. units. The British Northumberland Fusiliers were keen on trading Scotch whiskey for Kentucky whiskey or Canadian Club, so I said I would see what I could scrounge up. I preferred scotch to bourbon—for slow sipping, followed by water, cheese, and nuts. I never acquired the taste, talent, throat, or stomach to swallow two or three big gulps of whiskey at a time without coming up for air. But just a few sips of scotch on a cold day was a good warmer-upper for me, provided I didn't have medical work to do.

While visiting the Swedish hospital, I made a number of friends who invited me to visit Sweden. I had the opportunity several years later to visit several of the doctors in Sweden and was treated very well. One of those doctors was a sharp young internist/physiologist named Arne Aastrom, who later became a professor at the Karolinski Institute in Stockholm. During lunch one day, he relayed a couple of amusing stories.

First story: An American Army sergeant rushed into the Swedish hospital saying, "I have a full colonel out here that is in bad shape—where shall I put him?"

The Swedish officer responded, "Put him into that closet over there until we can tend to these wounded first."

An odd response? In America, a "full colonel" is a bird colonel, not a lieutenant colonel. But in Sweden, the word "full" is slang for being drunk. So it was reasonable for the Swedish officer to think that a "very drunk" colonel should be put into a closet and out of sight until the wounded soldiers could be cared for. In reality, the full colonel had bullet holes in him that required immediate attention.

Second Story: An American officer called to pick up a Swedish nurse for a date.

Informed of his arrival, the nurse called out, "I will be out just as soon as I finish my douche."

A bit of a culture shock? In Swedish, a "douche" is a shower. In American English, a "douche" is related to feminine hygiene.

As we laughed about those examples of miscommunication, I couldn't help but wonder about all of the misunderstandings, both humorous and tragic, that must be occurring daily between Americans and our KATUSA soldiers.

In the medical platoon, we were saddened to learn that as more American troop replacements became available, many of the KATUSAs in the 3rd and 7th Divisions were being transferred to ROK units, even though they did not want to be transferred. Big Bak and Imm Yung Hee both told me that the transferred KATUSA soldiers would suffer great discrimination in the ROK units. I was able to keep most of our KATUSA soldiers by declaring them to be essential litter bearers or translator/trainers for civilian labor litter bearers.

Our medical platoon received many compliments from the infantry for our efforts toward saving lives. When Bill Herrick was offered a battlefield commission, we were all proud of him. However, a battlefield promotion from sergeant first class to second lieutenant carried with it not just recognition of outstanding soldiering and leadership ability, but also the very high mortality rate of all second lieutenant platoon leaders in Korea, although a battle-wise sergeant had better odds of survival than an inexperienced 2nd lieutenant fresh from the States.

Chonan, Korea
Dear Dad and Mother,   20 Jan. 1951
There is little new to report on the war. We are comfortably situated in a little schoolhouse (one room type). The Chinese are building up north of us, but our patrols

punch them every day or so to keep them off balance. Actually, the morale of our outfit is good and we are as ready as ever for a good fight. The men know how the Chinese fight now and are sure that with anywhere near even odds they can be licked easily. Our tactics and firepower are much superior.

My platoon sergeant, Herrick, received a battlefield commission for outstanding leadership and he is now my new executive officer. Actually, I am very pleased with my medical platoon and believe it is the best outfit of it's kind in the 3ʳᵈ Division. The 35 enlisted men, including 10 ROKs, and two officers, make up the platoon and work well together.

My former platoon executive officer, Lt. Sarka, went to the regimental aid station, where he handles all records and medical supplies for the 7ᵗʰ Regiment. The division surgeon, Lt. Col. Joe Bayne, paid a surprise visit the other day and went away quite pleased with our unit.

I received a package from Aunt Ann and Uncle Ole. There was a large batch of Ann's special cookies, which went over big with the aid station personnel. A letter from John said he got through the quarter OK, which was good news.

Yesterday I received a big batch of mail the last letter dated the 5ᵗʰ of Jan. That's the way it is when we move. The mail collects some place for a week or two and then we get it all at once.

Love, Bob

We continued to have skirmishes daily as we pushed on toward the Han River. The Chinese tended to fortify the tops of hills, where they could not be run over by tanks.

Between WIA, KIA, MIA (missing in action), and transfers, we lost 25 KATUSA Koreans in the previous two months and were down to ten. Many of our WIA Koreans came back to us by going AWOL from the hospital before they could be transferred to an ROK unit. Some had plaster casts, as well as bandages, and walked miles against the flow of traffic to return to our medical platoon. We welcomed them back and put them to work, plaster casts and all, and they served with us as long as I was there.

One day, a KATUSA medic brought an elderly woman to me, riding on a cart pulled by her husband. The old man explained that she had suffered a leg injury two weeks earlier when an American airplane shot at them, presumably thinking they were Chinese. They had been turned away from a Korean hospital that was overflowing with ROK Army casualties. It was a long way to our nearest MASH, which was reported to be sending civilian casualties to the Korean hospital that was turning patients away. It was even farther to the Swedish hospital.

I checked the leg and found a compound fracture of the left tibia from a .50 caliber machine gun bullet. She had a fever and the broken leg was draining foul pus and had become black and gangrenous almost up to the knee. If the leg wasn't amputated soon, I knew the woman would die.

The 3rd Battalion was nearby, so I sent word to Gil Campbell, their battalion surgeon, to come give me some help in cutting off the leg. Gil had more surgery training than I did. He quickly drove over to help out. After inspecting the leg, he agreed it needed to come off ASAP.

We scrubbed our hands and the woman's leg with surgical soap and an iodine solution and started an I.V. drip of saline. Herrick administered open drop ether for general anesthesia. Working in our small aid station tent, we placed the patient on a stretcher with a stack of three footlockers under each end. We put on sterile gloves, applied sterile drapes, and went to work. We had to cut the bone and tie off the arteries and nerves above the knee, but were able to save a flap of tissue from the region of the kneecap. We used a small carpentry saw that we had scrubbed clean to cut the bone.

As we cut through the femur, a runner came from Battalion HQ to tell me the battalion commander wanted me to come right away for a staff meeting. The runner, a 2nd lieutenant, new to the battalion, was a bit taken aback when I told him I would come as soon as I finished cutting off a leg. He peeked over the temporary blanket screen as Gil Campbell turned around and held out the severed lower leg.

"Lieutenant," Campbell said, "don't just stand there with your mouth open, make yourself useful and take this leg out and bury it some place."

I thought the lieutenant would faint, but Sgt. Ogden came to his rescue and helped him sit down on the ground, still holding the leg in his hands.

"Sir," Ogden said, "would you like me to take that leg off your hands? I think I know a nice place to bury it."

The 2nd lieutenant was relieved to be rid of the leg, and after a minute or two, regained his composure and said, "Sir, I will report back to the colonel, sir," and left quickly before someone could hand him another leg.

Campbell was so amused by the shocked look on the 2nd lieutenant's face; I thought he was going to need to sit down before he fell down laughing. But he soon recovered his composure and got back to the serious work at hand. He finished sewing the skin and muscle flaps together and bandaged the leg up while I hurried off to the staff meeting. When I returned, Gil had left for his battalion. Herrick, Ogden, and one of our Koreans were caring for the patient, who rested on the same stretcher, now suspended between two footlockers. Her husband sat near her, soothing her as she came out of the ether sleep. We gave her pain medicine, more I.V. solution, and antibiotics. In the morning, she was given some chicken broth and tea to drink. We kept her in the aid station area for two or three days before we had to move forward again.

I wrote up the operation on a sheet of paper and addressed the envelope:

"To: Any American Army medical officer who sees this Korean man waving this envelope. Please be kind enough to go with this man to see his wife and change the dressing on the leg stump. I cut off her gangrenous leg. See operative report inside envelope. Signed, Robert T. Jensen M.D. Cpt. MC, 1st Battalion Surgeon 7th Infantry Regiment."

When we left to go forward to battle, I gave the husband some pain pills, more antibiotics, and some cans of rations before we helped load the wife on his little cart. They both thanked us profusely. He carefully pinned the envelope inside his shirt. About a month after amputating the leg, an Army truck driver passed on a letter to me:

"To: Dr. Jensen 1st Battalion Surgeon 7th Infantry. A Korean man waving your envelope was brought to me. I read your letter and saw your patient. The stump is healing fine. I changed the dressing. Her husband had made some crutches for her. She is now up and around. Good job. This is a hell of a way to practice medicine and surgery. Hope we meet some day."

The letter was signed by a fellow Army battalion surgeon.

The reason I had to rush off to a staff meeting was because we had orders to move out and to go on an offensive operation. Our battalion attacked a wide area, sweeping scattered Chinese before us. It was cold, but our tanks were effective in some areas, and the Chinese had the choice of fighting or being run over. Some ran, but many surrendered, and that was a good omen.

One day when it was relatively quiet on the front, I decided to pay Gil Campbell a visit. As I drove into the 3rd Battalion aid station area, I saw Gil carrying a Chinese burp gun (picked up on a battlefield) in addition to his pistol. At the time, I carried the Thompson submachine gun (also picked up on a battlefield) in addition to my personal S&W .38 special revolver that I had bought from a policeman friend in Minneapolis, who had assured me it would be less likely to jam than the Army .45 if it was dropped in the mud. Campbell and I laughed as we compared our personal protection weapons.

Gil was finishing up routine sick call. I noticed the last man in line continued to be last, even after others approached. Finally, the crowd was gone and the last man faced Campbell.

"Private Willie Smith," Gil said, "how can I help you?"

"Sir, I have a cold and I think penicillin would help," he replied.

"If you have a cold, why isn't your nose running?"

"Sir," explained the soldier, "I was sleeping on the cold ground and my whole body got chilled, so I don't have a runny nose but I have a runny peter instead."

"Well, then, let me examine you runny peter," said Campbell.

The enlisted man exposed his penis, revealing a purulent discharge.

Campbell paused and said, "So you think you have a cold in your peter, do you?"

"Yes, sir. It was from sleeping on the cold ground," said Pvt. Smith.

Campbell leaned back with a smile.

"Well, Private Smith, you can call this infection in your peter a cold if you wish, but unless your peter starts to sneeze, I am just going to call it plain old gonorrhea. So if you will please turn around and expose your buttocks, I will give you a gonorrhea-size shot of penicillin and some pills to take."

Gilbert Campbell was an upfront, involved battalion surgeon. The infantrymen admired him for his professional skill, but they also loved him for his personal courage and willingness to risk his own life to provide emergency medical care.

I returned from my visit with Gil to write another letter home.

Dear Folks,   1 Feb. 1951

Here it is the first of Feb. and the war drags on with no end in sight. At present we are on the offensive and are slowly grinding the Chinese and North Koreans back toward the Han River. At present we are situated at Yanju, having driven north from Chonan through Kumyangjang-ni to here. Actually, when there is sufficient force, there is no trouble rolling them back, since we have air and artillery superiority. The 1ˢᵗ Battalion 7ᵗʰ of 3ʳᵈ Division and units of the 25ᵗʰ Divisions are in on this drive, along with the British and Turks. The Turks, by the way, are terrific fighters and seem to be extremely anti-Communist. They love close-in fighting. The other day they had a bayonet charge up a hill and air observers said it was the damnedest show they ever saw. The Turks just went wild chasing the Chinese all over the hill with fixed bayonets.

The radio said last night that they at last were bringing before the general assembly of the U.N. a resolution to brand China an aggressor. I sure hope they do, along with all the rest of the GIs here. If the U.N. doesn't, it would remind me of an ostrich hiding its head in the sand to avoid facing reality and thinking it was safe.

We have not been having many casualties recently. That is the usual story. When you attack behind your air and artillery support, your losses are minimal. It's when the enemy attacks and gets behind or inside your lines the casualties mount up. That's what happened in North Korea. Actually, the Chinese suffered staggering losses in their fanatic frontal assaults, but their steady flow of manpower outlasted our ammunition supply in some sectors such as occurred with the 1ˢᵗ Marines and 2ⁿᵈ Division up north.

The horrible side of war is obvious at all times. Civilians, men, women, and children are frequently slaughtered by our air raids. I have taken care of many wounded civilians as best I could, that is, dress their wounds, a shot of penicillin, and send them on their way. There are just no facilities to care for them. The pathetic thing about it is after they have been shot down by one side or the other they are so humble and grateful for any first aid given they seem to be rather docile or numbed by the war that it doesn't seem to matter just what happened. They accept being shot down as part of the war and seem very glad to see us advancing north again.

I am convinced of one thing and that is that war crime trials may be unjust. I have seen and heard of as many atrocities committed by Americans and South Koreans on their prisoners as the North Koreans did to us. After the prisoners get past our front line area, they get fairly good treatment, but all too often the GIs or ROKs may be so angry over losing their buddies that they may shoot prisoners rather than send them back. That is the part of the story nobody talks about, but wars have always been the same and acts of brutality and acts of kindness can be found on both sides.

I received your letter of Jan 18th last. Dad, I would like you to write John for a check to reimburse you for the felt shoes and rubbers. He has access to my accounts.

Love, Bob

At the time the above letter was written, there was little or no information on the atrocious treatment rendered to our prisoners in North Korean and Chinese prison camps.[12] I was not yet fully aware of the extent to which the Communists would infiltrate and use civilian men, women, and children as human shields during movement across roads and in frontal assaults on our forces. And I certainly was not aware that 2,000 American POWs were taken to Russia to be used as guinea pigs for their germ warfare experiments. None of those 2,000 Americans survived.[13]

During early February, there was a lot of fighting. The 2nd Battalion 7th on our right flank found greater resistance to our forward movement. We were told we were facing the 149th and 150th Chinese Communist Divisions, who were digging in on hilltops. Orders had come down for the 7th Regiment to pass through the 15th Regiment on our right to allow them to go into reserve for a spell.

On the second of February 1951, the 15th Regiment was attacking Hill 425, took its summit, and while continuing to advance, took many prisoners. On 3

---

[12] See *Remembered Prisoners of a Forgotten War* by Lewis H. Carlson.
[13] See *Through the Eyes of the Enemy* by Stanislav Lunev.

February, the 1st Battalion 15th Regiment achieved its objective, but the 3rd Battalion 15th Regiment had difficulty securing the high ground northeast of a little village called Sokchon. Lt. Col. Weyand moved the 1st Battalion 7th to the right and pushed up behind the 3rd Battalion of the 15th Regiment just as darkness fell. We could hear shooting and mortars going off on the hill in front of us, so our medical platoon quickly commandeered an empty house for an aid station and got our sergeants, with litter teams, set up for a morning assault. While our aid station was being set up by sergeants Ogden and Prystas, 2nd Lt. Herrick and I went out to scout the area and look for the 3rd Battalion 15th aid station that we thought was close by.

To our surprise, we did not locate the 3rd Battalion aid station of the 15th Regiment, nor did we find any 3rd Battalion 15th litter squads. What we found was a 3rd Battalion 15th infantryman staggering down the hill with wounded, asking for help to bring down more. The Chinese on top of the hill had battered the 3rd Battalion and were pushing down the hill after them. Lt. Col. Weyand assessed the situation and put some of our infantry in position as we sent our 1st Battalion 7th litter teams up the hill with mixed 15th and 7th Infantry teams to secure the area again and search for 15th casualties. One of the wounded was an American infantry major with bullet holes in his side and arm. I wasn't sure if he was the 3rd Battalion 15th CO or his deputy.

While that was going on, our two litter jeeps sped back down a trail with the wounded from the 15th Regiment, searching for the 15th Regimental collecting company. On the way, they spotted the 3rd Battalion 15th aid station along the road—doing nothing. After a string of expletives from our 1st Battalion 7th medics that might be politely summarized as "get your fannies up the road to the fighting to tend to your own casualties," our litter jeeps pressed on farther and found the 15th Regimental collecting company sleeping. Not a good mode during a firefight. Someone had screwed up big time in the 15th Medical Company. Another flurry of expletives by the 1st Battalion 7th medics woke the 15th collecting station's regimental surgeon, who had a reputation as an imbiber of any and all products containing alcohol. As our litter jeeps returned to the front, they were followed by an embarrassed assortment of 15th Regiment medical personnel. The medics from the 15th belatedly made a show of being alert and seen, but by that time, Herrick and his crew had pretty well swept up the hillside and brought down all of the wounded of the 3rd Battalion 15th Regiment.

After midnight, when it was quiet and all of the casualties had been evacuated, Bill Herrick came to me and said, "Sir, our men are exhausted from dodging bullets and climbing that hill to bring out the15th casualties. It's just not right. The 15th medics should be court martialed for not doing their job. And now we have to go at that mountain again in the morning, and we are all pooped out and have rubber legs from climbing and carrying casualties half of the night."

"I agree with you, Bill," I said, "but we couldn't refuse to do the extra work thrust on us to save lives today, and we can only trust the Lord to see us through tomorrow. I'm proud of your work today. Tell the men to get some rest and pray that the Lord will look after us tomorrow."

I knew Lt. Col. Weyand was concerned about the task facing us in the morning. But prayers do help.

The next morning, the 1st Battalion of the 15th was attached to the 1st Battalion of the 7th. The two battalions together went over the hill, and the Chinese fled the area. Taking the hill was a piece of cake. We also had no causalities at all for several days.

Our biggest disappointment came a few months later, when we learned the Medical Company of the 15th Regiment had been awarded the Presidential Unit Citation, but we had not received any recognition for our work. It became clear to our sergeants that our unit was good at everything but public relations. All of the men, including our KATUSAs, were disgusted, disappointed and, to put it politely—ticked off, because a medical company that had provided little or no support for an infantry battalion in dire need had come up with a Presidential Unit Citation a few months later. We thought at the time that the 15th Medical Company might have been written up for the action on the night of February third, when we had done their work. We never did learn the exact date of the action that was cited for their award. Perhaps the 15th medics earned their award for outstanding performance on some other day. The citation below deserves mention.

Award of the Distinguished-Service Cross (posthumous)
to Pvt. 1st Class Robert E. Graf

"Private First Class Robert E. Graf, while an automatic rifleman with an infantry company, (Company F 7th Infantry Regiment) distinguished himself by extraordinary heroism in action against the enemy in the vicinity of Changpyongdong, Korea. On 4 February 1951, Private Graf's company was engaged in a limited withdrawal because of the unrelenting pressure of a numerically superior hostile force. As the friendly troops fell back, constantly harassed by enemy small-arms and automatic weapons fire, Private Graf, with total disregard for his personal safety, moved across the fire-swept terrain to an exposed position in order to provide covering fire with his automatic rifle. He was instantly hit by enemy machine gun fire. Although seriously wounded, Private Graf crawled toward a nearby enemy-manned emplacement and destroyed it with an accurately hurled grenade. His actions drew the fire of a second enemy emplacement and upon ascertaining its location he rose painfully to his feet and fired a burst into the machine gun position, killing three of the four enemy soldiers and successfully neutralizing the weapon. His courageous action was responsible for silencing the enemy weapons which posed the major threat to his comrades."

Not all of our casualties were from enemy fire. On the fourth of February, the U.S. 58th Field Artillery erred by putting three volleys on top of A Company, which was commanded by Cpt. Doug Barrows. That friendly fire accident resulted in the death of nine U.S. soldiers and wounded 22. Among those killed was Lt. Harry Spaker, after whom the Georgetown University Reserve Officers' Training Corps (ROTC) is named.

While the friendly fire mistake was taking its toll on Able Company, the enemy launched a surprise attack, making it difficult to retrieve our wounded. The citation below for a Bronze Star with the V-Device awarded to newly commissioned 2nd Lt. Bill Herrick provides a window of reality into this battle as the Chinese strove to take advantage of our friendly fire tragedy.

Award of the Bronze Star Medal with V-Device to 2nd Lt. William H. Herrick

"Second Lieutenant William H. Herrick 02262601, Medical Service Corps, Medical Company, 7th Infantry, 3rd Division, United States Army. On 4 February 1951, artillery fell on Hill 319, causing many casualties among the third platoon of Company A. The enemy then launched an attack, during which Lieutenant Herrick attempted to move his men forward to the wounded. Although forward movement was practically impossible because of intense enemy fire, he often raised himself in full view of the enemy in order to encourage and direct his men. Through his courageous actions, medical aid was received in a short period of time, which was a major factor in saving the lives of at least four wounded men. Lieutenant Herrick's heroic actions reflect great credit upon himself and the military service. Entered the military service from the State of Arkansas."

While A Company was having its problems, B Company, commanded by Cpt. Ray Blanding, came under enemy mortar and artillery fire. Several men were wounded, including Pvt. 1st Class Chelsie Neal Rood, and were evacuated through the 1st Battalion aid station to a MASH hospital for surgical repair and on to Japan for rehabilitation. Because of Pvt. 1st Class Rood's reputation for courage under fire, he was promoted to staff sergeant when he returned to duty in Korea five weeks later and assigned to A Company, where there were some friendly fire vacancies to fill.

It must have been difficult for the artillery to calculate accurately, not only distance, terrain elevation, and wind, but also when they couldn't tell foe from friend or fleeing civilians. Forward observers and signal panels helped, but friendly fire accidents were a continuing problem. War is a messy business.

The following day, after the dust settled, the bloody gauze had been burned, and the aid station cleaned up, I drafted the following letter. I made no mention of the friendly fire casualties. We felt bad, but most soldiers did not tell the home folks about casualties from our own artillery. On occasion, when an American infantry unit was being overrun, the artillery would be deliberately called in on top of their own position. In the aftermath, the survivors crawled out from under the bodies of attackers to see who had ended up owning that particular piece of real estate.

Dear Folks,   *5 Feb. 1951*

Just a note to let you know everything is OK. At present, we are attacking and have been for last week or so. Too busy to do much writing. The situation is well in hand and Chinese are on the run. We haven't had much trouble with North Koreans in our sector.

Yesterday, I patched up a bunch of civilians caught in an air strike in no man's land. What a pathetic sight, women and kids all shot to hell. I amputated a leg in my aid station again yesterday. It was impossible to get the civilian evacuated so I had to do what I could. Our casualties have been light thus far.

Love, Bob

It was the second leg I had amputated. This time, Gil Campbell was busy elsewhere. The Korean woman had been among refugees infiltrated by many Chinese soldiers, who were shooting at us with small arms and mortars. Our observers called in an air strike. It was horrible. Dead and dying Chinese soldiers mixed in with Korean civilians; men, women, and children, lying in the muddy snow, bleeding. The terrified woman, with a shattered tibia sticking in the mud at an odd angle, was still clutching her live baby. A mother's love is a wondrous thing to behold.

Herrick, Ogden, and I amputated her right leg above the knee to give her a clean stump and hope for survival. One of our medics fed the baby Carnation milk until relatives were found to take the mother and baby off our hands. I left a letter in an envelope, as I had with the previous amputation, but this time I received no response letter passed on from some other battalion surgeon.

At the time, I wondered how much refugee service was being provided in the medical battalion in the 3rd Division. I didn't know what was going on back there. There had been occasional visits to our aid station from the 3rd Division surgeon, but I don't recall ever receiving a visit from the 7th Infantry regimental surgeon or the medical battalion commander of the 3rd Division. While our MASH units treated Korean civilians on a space available basis, our Division Medical Battalion people were pressured to refer civilian casualties to Korean hospitals that were overloaded and under supported. It was a sad situation. Being in an infantry battalion, we were often first in line to sort through the smashed and bloody bodies of civilians, as well as to check body parts left behind after artillery bombardments. We should have mobilized another couple of MASH units for civilian casualties, but I doubt Washington, D.C. would have approved it.

Dear Folks,   *9 Feb. 1951*
   The 1ˢᵗ Battalion attacked a group of hills about 12 miles south of Seoul. The Chinese didn't care to put up a fight and took off over the hills. We had no casualties. Apparently the strategy is to push them back to the Han River and form a defense line there against the many reinforcements they are probably sending.
   The Chinese have had heavy losses from direct fire, cold, and disease. A number of them have been found to have typhoid and all of the prisoners have lice. Thanks to DDT and our typhoid shots, we don't have to worry much about that.
   Everyone was very happy to hear that China was branded an aggressor. I hope they will blockade their ports and bomb Manchuria. If they do, they will destroy the ability of China to wage war without more open Chinese assistance.
   My patient whose leg I amputated in the aid station yesterday was doing well today. The stump looked good.
   Received letters from you written on the 26ᵗʰ. Don't know what will be in store for tomorrow so will have to get to bed. The air mattress has me spoiled now. Before I was just sleeping on the hard ground or on the floor of a local building.
   Love, Bob

While the infantry companies of the battalions were fighting with the Chinese, the 3ʳᵈ Division organized a special task force from each regiment with tanks, a rifle company, mobile AA vehicles, and forward observers for tactical air support. The 7ᵗʰ Regiment established Task Force (TF) Tony, the 15ᵗʰ Regiment had TF Fisher, and the 65ᵗʰ Regiment (from Puerto Rico) had TF Myers.

The purpose of these task forces was to crash through the lines and attack the Chinese from behind. They did a lot of damage and kept the other side off balance.

I used to visit with the medical officers of nearby U.N. units. Maj. Protacio Rizal Sato, the surgeon in the Filipino battalion, became a close friend. I spent time with him explaining how to organize and train Korean laborers to function as backup litter bearer teams. After the Korean War ended, Lt. Col. Sato came to the United States for advanced training at the U.S. Army Medical Field

Service School, and we spent some time together there in Texas. He later became Surgeon General of the Philippines.

I also developed a good friendship with a British major, a supply officer by the name of De Longay. He had been born and raised in France, on an estate owned by his family. He spoke French and English, but considered himself British. We enjoyed tea with crackers and cheese and exchanged a few bottles of Tennessee or Kentucky whiskey for Scotch whiskey.

On one of my visits, a British sergeant tried to warn me.

"Sir, I wouldn't go in to see the major today, sir."

"Why not?"

"Because the major is in a bloody rage today, sir."

We had recently had a pleasant meeting, and I was in a bit of a hurry, so I pushed on and looked inside the major's tent. I was met with a vituperative blast.

"You damn Americans think you own all of the roads in Korea!"

"I'm sorry, Major," I said. "Please tell me what happened that has made you so angry with all Americans."

De Longay responded with a red-faced roar.

"What happened? You want to know what happened, do you? I'll tell you what happened. One of your blasted lorry drivers ran our naffy wagon, with our whiskey and rum supply, off of the road, causing it to roll over and smash all of our whiskey and rum bottles!"

I could see this was not going to be a pleasant tea-with-crackers-and-cheese day, so I apologized profusely for the careless American truck driver and slipped out, leaving him a consolation gift of a couple of bottles of Kentucky whiskey. We got on well thereafter. I presume the Kentucky whiskey soothed his "bloody rage."

During my visits with De Longay, I noticed the British sergeants seemed to be the ones who actually ran their army, so one day I approached one.

"You sergeants seem to run the British Army," I said. "What do your officers do?"

The sergeant thought for a moment and said, "Our officers show us how to die, sir."

One day, I was traveling north near Suwon, with Sgt. Bull Adams driving, when we were rapidly overtaken from behind by a military police (MP) jeep with a bullhorn, telling us to get off the road and out of our jeep immediately. There were other vehicles behind the MP jeep, so Bull drove down into the ditch and stopped. MP jeeps were usually a signal that someone important was coming up the road. I got out and went around to the back of the jeep to stand at attention near the edge of the road. Watching an approaching vehicle with flags, I saluted and as the vehicle passed me, Gen. MacArthur returned my salute. That was my one and only meeting with the general, and there wasn't much conversation. After his vehicle and several others had passed by, I turned to ask Bull Adams why he hadn't saluted.

Bull kept muttering to himself, "Five frikkin' damn stars, and I forget to salute. I ain't never seen so many frikkin' damn stars before."

When we got back to the aid station, the vision of the passing general faded away with the return of patients to tend to. When I got around to writing a letter home, I decided not to mention seeing MacArthur drive by, because I thought the letter might be censored.

Dear Dad and Mother,   *12 Feb. 1951*

Received letter yesterday addressed 1 Feb and also package of cookies, which were very good. Day before yesterday, we assaulted and took a walled city high in the mountains southeast of Seoul, called "Sansong-ni." Everything had to be carried up on packs since there were no roads for vehicles on our side of the city.

It was an amazing place and apparently had been used as a resort town in recent years. The wall was all hand-hewn stone, erected about 700 years ago, and is about 6000 yards around the city. Most of the wall still stands. The Chinese put up a little fight but finally took off. We had only a few wounded and one killed. From the top of the mountain around the city, one could see the Han River, our immediate objective.

Our battalion has had the roughest assignment of the 3rd Division since we have swept over the most rugged terrain. I have climbed so many mountains that I will be quite content to settle down where there aren't any mountains.

My medical platoon has an excellent record and reputation thus far. I am fortunate to have as good a group as I do. My aid men are quite courageous and care for wounded with complete disregard for enemy fire. My assistant, Lt. Herrick (was my 1st Sergeant before battlefield commission), has been terrific in organizing the medical aid on the battlefield. He controls the litter teams and in general coordinates medical support immediately behind the attacking force. I usually follow behind with the aid station on jeeps and a three-fourth ton truck and when they can't go any farther, we use sturdy Korean backs to pack the equipment on "A" frames.

I have not been under direct fire since I left North Korea and the way things are going there isn't too much to worry about.

Today we are driving into the flats south of the Han River and I must admit it seems good to pull out of the mountains. My sleeping bag has been plenty warm, even in coldest weather. The Army has issued down winter sleeping bags, which are excellent for the troops. However, I prefer mine with an air mattress. Food is plentiful but usually consists of C-rations, which get quite monotonous. However, I have made a point of eating everything and consequently I have not lost weight like so many men did here in Korea. I weigh about 175 lb, which is plenty heavy for me.

Love, Bob

"I have not been under direct fire," was a statement made solely to lessen worry on the home front. It was not exactly a lie, because incoming mortars and howitzer shells were considered indirect fire weapons; technically, I was telling the truth. There was usually mortar or cannon fire coming in and going out, some landed nearby, but there had been no direct fire through our aid station tent recently.

While we had few casualties while taking the walled city, the one person killed was Lt. Pat Green. We had difficulty retrieving his body because of continued shooting. Lt. Pat Green was a fine young infantry platoon leader from the West Point Class of 1950, whose father was reportedly a general somewhere. The men in his platoon, as well as the other infantry officers, liked Pat Green. It was expected that Pat would become a general someday—if he survived.

Lt. Arnold Galifa went on emergency home leave just before the Sansong-ni battle. On his return, perhaps because of Green's death, Galifa was pulled off the plane in Tokyo to work under MacArthur as an aid, and later under Ridgeway, as a special assistant.

At Sansong-ni, we had a big problem evacuating the wounded. There were only slippery snow and ice trails down from the city and no clear spots for helicopters to land. I wanted to clear out some trees and part of a rock wall for a helicopter landing area, but approval was denied because the area was a historical place. We had to carry two litter patients down the slippery slopes. It was not accomplished without a few slips and pratfalls. Those wounded who were mobile also found it difficult to walk down with painful wounds. It took eight Koreans, an experienced and capable medic, Sgt. Prystas, and myself more than two hours to get the wounded down the ice trail to the end of the jeep road. The fresh coat of ice deposited overnight made the climb down difficult.

The wounded soldiers complained loudly about the lousy medics who couldn't find a better way to get them down from the "damn walled city." I felt chagrined that I had not found a better way to get them down. I also felt guilty that I had not made a bigger fuss for permission to clear a helicopter pad site up at the top the night before. But I had been overruled and everyone was dog-tired. If the person of authority who had made that decision had been a litter patient that morning, I am sure he would have changed his mind after the first pratfall of his litter bearers.

Once we got the wounded sent off to a hospital, we went back up the hill to try to catch up with our battalion. They were long gone and after an hour's pursuit up and down hills, I realized that we were lost and it would be dark before we caught up, either to our people or to the Chinese, who had been playing a game of hide and shoot with our battalion during the previous couple of days.

Instead of stumbling on as dusk approached, I decided to go back up to the walled city again with my crew, where there was an American military security presence with a radio. After some effort, we managed to get a radio message through to our battalion and were told to sit tight for the night, and in the morning to go back down the trail we had used to evacuate the wounded, where a vehicle would come to pick us up at the bottom. With all that climbing during the day, I was really tired. We spent a cold and hungry night huddled together to share body heat. The next morning, we made it back down the ice trail to a waiting vehicle.

I continued to feel that our attempt to evacuate the wounded from Sansong-ni down that iced path was one of my dumbest decisions.

By late morning, we were back with our unit. Herrick had been worried we'd been lost out in no man's land, until he got our radio message. It was a good thing we had turned back, for there were attacking Chinese and North Koreans in the area we were headed toward, south of the Han River, trying to break into our division rear at night to create general havoc.

It would take another book to record all of the awards given to the fighting regiments of the 3rd Infantry Division or even to the three battalions of the 7th Infantry during the advance to the Han River. I will mention two in order to provide a small window into the action.

Award of the Distinguished-Service Cross to Master Sgt. Joseph D. Dick

"Master Sergeant Joseph D. Dick...a member of Company B, 7th Infantry Regiment, 3rd Division, distinguished himself by extraordinary heroism in action near Chungjang-ni, Korea, on 14 February 1951. His platoon, defending Hill 151, had been attacked by numerically superior hostile forces during the night when the platoon leader was seriously surrounded. Sergeant Dick, who had left the platoon command post to take up a position on the line in order to more effectively direct automatic-weapons fire on the attackers, crawled through deadly hostile fire and carried his platoon leader to a place of safety. The wounded platoon commander ordered a withdrawal, but Sergeant Dick, nevertheless, returned to the line, reorganized the battered platoon, and continued the defense of the position. When an enemy soldier threw a hand grenade into the midst of the staunch defenders, Sergeant Dick quickly picked it up and threw it back at the thrower, killing him and two other enemy soldiers. Leading an inspired counter-attack, he fired continually into the enemy horde until his ammunition was exhausted, then picked up the weapon of a Chinese Communist he had killed and continued to lead the platoon. Again running out of ammunition, he took over the automatic weapon of a wounded man, continued the fierce assault, and succeeded in securing Hill 151. During his daring exploits, he was wounded, but refused medical attention until he had assured the defense of the position."

Award of the Distinguished-Service Cross (posthumous)
to Cpl. Albert C. Erickson

"Corporal Albert C. Erickson...a member of Company C, 7th Infantry Regiment, 3rd Division, distinguished himself by extraordinary heroism in action against the enemy in the vicinity of Chungung-ni, Korea. On 14 February 1951, the 1st Battalion was attacked by an enemy force of numerical superiority and a squad that was serving as an outpost was subjected to an intense volley of fire, which wounded all except one member. As the squad began withdrawing from its exposed vulnerable position, it was harassed by enemy fire that threatened to sever its route. Corporal Erickson, from his position in the battalion perimeter, saw the plight of the withdrawing squad and, with complete disregard for assault fire from an enemy group advancing on his position, shifted his line of fire to cover the movement of the beleaguered squad. This covering fire enabled the squad to withdraw to safety but in the course of action, Corporal Erickson was hit by enemy fire and mortally wounded."

After the experience at Sansong-ni, the 1st Battalion combat team attacked over a wide area. I was somewhere in the middle of the team, following along a trail near a semi-dry creek bed, when we started to receive a few incoming mortar rounds. My driver pulled off the trail on the right side behind some bushes, where there were two GIs who had taken some mortar shrapnel. They were not badly wounded, but as I pulled out a few pieces of metal and applied bandages, there was a big explosion about 50 yards farther up the trail. The jeep that had been following us had set off a large anti-tank mine, blowing the jeep into the air and demolishing it in the process. The two GIs in the front seats were mangled and catapulted into the air. They were both dead when they hit the ground. We could not find the body of the GI who had been riding in the back of the jeep. Sgt. Ogden and I looked all around and couldn't find the third body.

Finally I said to Ogden, "There must be something left of him somewhere."

Ogden said, "I thought I saw him go up in the air, followed by all of the blast, fire, smoke, and dirt, but I doubt he burned up in mid-air."

We then noticed that the slimy surface of a large cement night soil tank had been disturbed, so we ripped off our field jackets and shirts and poked around in the night soil with sticks and located a body. We thrust our arms into the stinking mess and together we pulled out the missing GI.

As we rinsed off his face and cleared his throat, he coughed and emitted the most awful, long animal-like scream I had ever heard come from a human being. By this time, two other medics had joined us, and we moved him gently to a stretcher. As we continued to wash off his face and rinse out his mouth, his eyes seemed to see us, but there was no sign of recognition. He took a breath and emitted another soul-piercing scream.

I could only respond, "Lord, have pity and mercy on this soldier."

As I examined him, I found some voluntary movement of his arms, but both legs were limp, and his pelvis and lower spine seemed to have been mangled and shoved up to his chest like an accordion—severing his spinal cord in the process. I tried to give him some water to drink, but I am not sure he swallowed any. He seemed to have pain all around his thorax, and his pain was aggravated by any movement of his upper body.

There was no helicopter available, as we were well out in front in contested territory. Word came to rejoin the unit ASAP. It was obvious the paralyzed soldier had suffered fatal injuries and would die soon from internal bleeding from the multiple fractures of his hips, pelvis, and spine. I held his hand and prayed for the Lord to take him. We gave him two injections of morphine that put him into a sleep-like status, and then placed him beside his two dead buddies to await the GRO for pick up later. The living wounded we put in our medic jeeps and then hurried up the trail to rejoin our unit.

We were met by an empty half-track with a driver who had instructions from Lt. Col. Weyand to use the half-track as our mobile aid station and to rejoin the unit before we had any more casualties. So I climbed into the half-track with one medic and two GIs who had shrapnel wounds. Sgt. Ogden followed in my jeep, with two litter jeeps following him. We split up so that should mortars rain down, there would be a better chance of having some medics left. A hundred yards up the trail, the half-track turned off the path and drove up the dry creek bed.

I was sitting on top of the gasoline tank, which in the open top half-track is inside the side armor plate behind the driver on the left side.

I leaned down and shouted, "Why are we driving up the creek bed?"

His answer was short and to the point, "Too many mines on the road."

I kept my Tommy gun ready on the left side and my aid man kept his carbine pointed off to the right. The assistant driver on the right front seat had a ring-mounted .30 caliber machine gun, which he was clinging to as we rolled along. We finally drew abreast of our spread-out battalion, which had veered off the road to the left.

Noting that some of the headquarters vehicles and a heavily loaded deuce and a half (as black drivers liked to call their 2 ½-ton, six-wheel drive Army trucks) were carrying GIs and equipment of all types, we moved into the vehicle line on the trail. Our caravan paused as Cpt. McAuliffe from the headquarters staff came by to say we were going to set up a defensive perimeter in the nearby flat area. The HQ, motor pool, tanks, and heavy weapons company would set up in the same area while the rifle companies were going to secure the nearby hills. I was invited to look around and pick an area for the aid station.

I stood up in the half-track and spotted a small (10 x 20 ft.) concrete slab bridge over the dry creek. I thought it would be nice to have six or seven inches of concrete over our heads, in case of incoming mortars. So I asked the half-track driver to back up about 50 feet, in order to take a trail on the right to the little concrete slab bridge. The vehicle immediately behind us was a deuce and a half truck, piled high with bales of barbed wire. A half dozen vehicles eventually obliged us by backing up to give us room to turn off to the right, but it was not done without some griping and teasing, to make the point that they hoped their doc was a better doctor then he was a half-track driver.

As we reached the bridge, there was a terrific explosion, and the frame on the rear end of the deuce and a half carrying the barbed-wire was turned into a steel pretzel, pointing up with the bales of barbed-wire flying in all directions like giant mortar shells. Some of them landed quite close to us. Soldiers closer to the mine explosion had to do some fancy dodging to avoid being hit by the flying bales of wire. Three soldiers were killed by the mine explosion and several others sustained burns and severe injuries from flying gravel. One of them lost both eyes. Ironically, he was a soldier that had been pestering our aid station for a purple heart for some minor scrapes he had received in a foxhole during a firefight. He had been sent away from the aid station with the admonition not to beg for a Purple Heart or he might end up earning one.

When Herrick, who had been with the lead rifle company, came by to help tend the patients overnight, Ogden told him he'd made out a request for a Purple Heart for the solder who injured his face and eyes.

Herrick said, "He earned it, but it's too bad he will never see it."

We were able to get a couple of Bell-13 helicopters at dawn the next day, but I wondered how, twice in one day, the vehicle behind me had blown up on a mine after I turned off to care for the wounded. The three GIs killed in the jeep mine explosion had been picked up by the GRO, including the man with the mangled spine that had landed in the cement night soil pool. Ogden and I each took a soapy, cold-water bath from our helmets that night. We joked about which one of us smelled worse.

There were many battles as we pressed on toward the Han River. All of the regiments were doing their part. The Chinese did not fall back readily, but many began to surrender because of the tenacious fighting of our infantry, the power of our mortars and artillery, and our daytime airpower. Thousands of their buddies had died before their eyes, and the Communist pep talks from higher ups were no longer believable. They began to fight for their units as we did for ours. Our side had the freedom to brag about it, and more artillery and airpower. They had more manpower.

Because of our own continuing casualties, our infantry battalions started building better defensive positions. This became easier as the ground started to thaw. We didn't have any more soldiers shooting themselves in the hand or foot, but I suspected a few men might have allowed their feet to freeze to get evacuated. Frozen toes could usually be prevented, but it took effort.

During lulls, there was always an opportunity to write more letters or sip a bit of whiskey with friendly warriors who kept doing the nasty business of war, day after day. This warrior clan had no racial barriers and transcended rank. For these men, death was not the worst option. Failure to do one's duty was, and to be called a damn coward was the supreme insult.

Dear Dad,   15 Feb. 1951

Another day at the front. We are not moving forward now but rather digging in the high ground just south of the Han River. We have had some little battles lately, but nothing we could not handle.

Last letter received was Feb. 3, '51 from you and Mother. The clippings are enjoyable. Keep them coming. Other fellows are interested in seeing how the news is commented on in the States. The war is pretty much the same all the time.

Love, Bob

I usually heard, but I did not witness, most of the horrific struggles of the infantry platoons doing the fighting. I tried to stay close to the action, to salvage as many lives as possible. A key to survival was to stop the bleeding ASAP, and replace blood volume with I.V. solutions or universal blood. I continued to use a lot of small forceps to stop bleeders, especially pumping arterial bleeders. I would put a pressure bandage over the clamp or hemostat and leave the hemostat attached for the MASH people to remove later. Occasionally, I would put a suture in to tie off a troublesome bleeder or to hold widely gapping wounds together during transportation. I preferred to not use sutures because of the subsequent problem with infection.

It made a big difference if I could get a helicopter, but all too often I was left with land transportation as the only thing available. I heard rumors that more helicopters were coming, but by the first of March 1951, a helicopter evacuation from a battalion aid station was still a rare event and I could not afford to sit around with patients all night in the hope that a helicopter would arrive early in the morning.

Starting patients on a bumpy overland trip at night might seem to indicate that the casualty was fit to travel overland, when in reality, that was not the case. In my heart, I felt the regimental surgeon should be more aggressive in directing helicopters to the battalion aid station and in select situations, even to rifle companies, to snatch a seriously wounded man away.

The little bubble choppers were very vulnerable to ground fire and while most of the chopper pilots I met were brave, they were not suicidal. It was a continuing struggle to keep our wounded alive through the evacuation process.

I failed often enough in my frenzied efforts at resuscitation and evacuation to keep me from feeling really good about my efforts. In my times of disappointment, a few sips of whiskey helped to dull the angst.

The 2nd and 3rd Battalions were heavily involved nearby, as well as the Northumberland Fusiliers, The Royal Ulster Rifles, and the Gloucesters (the units that made up the British Brigade). Some of their casualties would, from time to time, spill over into our area for evacuation.

After the battalion surgeon of the 2nd Battalion, Cpt. Gerry Swab, rotated back to Walter Reed to continue his ophthalmology residency, he was replaced by a young Navy doctor, Lt. John Currin. Another young Navy doctor, Lt. "Jitters," was also assigned to the Medical Company of the 7th Infantry Regiment. It would be a gross understatement to say that Lt. Jitters had difficulty adjusting to the life of an infantry battalion surgeon. He unintentionally provided a measure of comic relief to the unit, because of his obvious chronic anxiety and fear.

The 3rd Battalion of the 7th Regiment was heavily involved in fighting during February 1951. The posthumous award of the Congressional Medal of Honor to Lt. Kyle is copied below to offer another window of reality into the infantry struggles during the forgotten war.

Award of the Congressional Medal of Honor (posthumous) to 2nd Lt. Darwin K. Kyle

"Department of the Army General Orders Number 17, 1 February 1952. To Second Lieutenant Darwin K. Kyle, serving in Company K, 7th Infantry Regiment, 3rd Division, distinguished himself by conspicuous gallantry and intrepidity above and beyond the call of duty in action against the enemy near Kamil-ni, Korea, on 16 February 1951. When his platoon was pinned down by intense fire, he completely exposed himself to move among and encourage his men to continue the advance against enemy forces strongly entrenched on Hill 185. Inspired by his courageous leadership the platoon resumed advance, but was again pinned down when an enemy machine gun opened fire, wounding six of his men. Lieutenant Kyle immediately charged the hostile emplacement alone, engaged the crew in hand-to-hand combat, and killed three. Continuing on toward the objective, his platoon suddenly received intense automatic-weapon fire from a well-concealed hostile position on its right flank. Again leading his men in a daring bayonet charge against this position, firing his carbine and throwing grenades, Lieutenant Kyle personally destroyed four of the enemy before he was killed by a burst of enemy submachine gun fire. The extraordinary heroism and outstanding leadership of Lieutenant Kyle and his gallant self-sacrifice reflect the highest credit on himself and are in keeping with the esteemed traditions of the military service."

The 3rd Battalion had a capable PR team that was alert for awardable actions that merited recognition. This was as it should have been. In other battalions, it was necessary to make a lot of noise to get awardable actions noted, written up, and processed. The next award was given to one of Dr. Gil Campbell's medics in the 3rd Battalion.

Award of the Distinguished-Service Cross (posthumous) to Cpl. Raymond E. Nall

"Corporal Raymond E. Nall...a member of Medical Company 7th Infantry Regiment, 3rd Infantry Division, distinguished himself by extraordinary heroism in action against an armed enemy near Sansong-ni, Korea. On 16 February 1951, Corporal Nall was attached to Company M, 7th Infantry Regiment, as an aid man during an attack on enemy occupied Hill 287. During the attack, a tremendous concentration of mortar fire fell in the area and all personnel in the vicinity were instructed to take cover. Corporal Nall hesitated, saying that he might be needed to render medical aid, but nevertheless moved to cover only when assured he would be called if needed. A few minutes later, a second barrage of mortar fire and intense enemy small-arms fire raked the positions. The cry 'Medic' passed down the line. Corporal Nall grabbed his aid kit, sprang from his foxhole and started towards the wounded soldier. His comrades called to him to wait until the incessant fire subsided, but he replied, 'They need me, I must go.' With complete disregard for his personal safety, he plunged into the midst of the enemy mortar fire and proceeded toward the fallen soldier. He had advanced only one hundred yards when he was killed by a mortar round."

The three battalions in the 7th Infantry Regiment often functioned like pistons in a motor. One battalion would explode over the enemy as another battalion prepared to explode. Where possible, one battalion was in reserve for rest and training of replacements, but at times of great pressure, all three battalions functioned at once, along with attached battalions of Belgians, Turks, Brits, Greeks, Filipinos, French, and other U.N. forces.

The Filipino battalion at times had mobility problems because of their propensity to keep sleeping-bag-warming Korean women with them. A significant number, if not most, of the soldiers in the Filipino battalion had women friends as excess baggage when all combat units were supposed to be mobile and actively involved in fighting the war. This later proved to be a major problem.

Dear Folks,   18 Feb. 1951

The war has quieted down a bit for the last two days. We are situated three or four miles south of the Han; the fanatical Chinese counter attacks have been beaten back, with heavy losses on their side and, unfortunately, some loss to ourselves.

Our boys are getting wise to the Chinese and very adept at booby-trapping the likely lines of night attack. One of our machine gunners stretched a wire about 120 yards to another knoll of ground in front of his position and planted a row of flares. When the Chinese passed over the knoll preparing to attack at night, he pulled the wire and set off the flares and then just mowed them down as they were silhouetted against the flares. He killed 22 and wounded 50. They had enough for that night. Another favorite is to tie a wire to a grenade pin with the pin almost out and both grenade and wire tightened up. With a few of these over a hillside, it makes it pretty hot for a group attacking at night.

The Chinese always try to carry off their dead and wounded. Their care of their wounded is good, considering their resources, and this is one reason probably why the Chinese soldiers preferred the Commies to the nationalist Chinese.

Enclosed is an example of our division's paper and a propaganda piece. The item about the lost N.K. regiment occurred about a week ago. U.S. and South Korean intelligence were feverish about the movement of the regiment and moved up heavy artillery 105 and 240 howitzers to throw a deadly rain of steel into the area where they regrouped. They practically annihilated the outfit.

Last letter received was Feb. 8th, which said the shoes were on the way. They should be here soon. At present, the weather isn't too cold but we expect more cold weather yet before spring. We have packed over some rugged mountain territory so far. My legs are getting toughened in. I usually carry a heavy aid kit, my revolver, and a Thompson submachine gun when protection is needed.

So far I haven't personally returned fire to enemy firing at me since I left North Korea and I hope I don't have to. However, I know how to use all the weapons the infantry has, including heavy machine guns.

Hope all goes well at home. My sleeping bag is quite comfortable with the air mattress. I don't know whether I will be able to sleep on a bed when I get home.

Love, Bob

On 19 February, the 1st Battalion of the 7th Regiment was instructed to hold the center of the line south of the Han, with the 2nd Battalion in a supporting position and the 3rd Battalion in division reserve.

At the time, the captain in charge of the heavy 4.2-inch mortars was chagrined because some of his rounds had been off target. When I observed the heavy mortars being fired, I noticed the heavy base plates would sometimes jump around on the frozen ground. I thought the bouncing might have accounted for his mortars being off target.

There was a level plane extending south of the Han River that looked like it would make a good infiltration route for the Chinese. Because it was a likely attack area, the 4.2 mortar men took their time to dig in their base plates well and then fired off a few rounds to make sure they were on target.

During the next night, a fog settled in the area, and the Chinese decided to use its cover to paddle across the Han River and cross the level plane before dawn in order to infiltrate our position in the foothills. Unfortunately for the Chinese, the fog lifted more rapidly than expected, exposing 200 or more Chinese in the pre-sighted target area.

It was a veritable disaster for them. After three or four rounds had been fired from each of the big tubes, there were no Chinese left running, or even standing. It was a total slaughter. I observed elation on the mortarmen's faces, but some of the celebrants had tears in their eyes. They had slaughtered 200 Chinese. War is much more unpleasant to watch close-up in real life than on a movie screen. Part of the reason for alcohol use in the military was to turn off the regrets and get on with the messy job at hand. I went out with a patrol, to search for any living among the Chinese. There weren't any.

Because of harassing fire coming across the Han River and suspicion that the Chinese may be preparing another sneak attack, a rifle company was sent across on tanks from the 64th Heavy Tank Battalion to disrupt the enemy as much as possible. They ended up in a firefight on the north side of the Han River, with casualties requiring medical support. We knew they needed medical assistance ASAP, but they couldn't release a tank to evacuate the casualties yet, because the two tanks were still engaged with the enemy across the river. With only two tanks, they were both needed to shoot the Chinese off each other's tops.

We couldn't just sit on the south side of the river and allow our wounded to bleed to death, so I said to Sgt. Bull Adams, "We need to get to our casualties across the river now. They can't wait until the fighting is over and the tanks give them a ride back."

Bull smiled and said, "I'll drive as far as I can, and then it's up to you to wade or swim."

With Sgt. Bull Adams driving, we tried to cross the Han, but less than halfway across, the jeep drowned out. While Bull stayed on the hood to flag down any passing tank for a tow out of the river, the two aid men and I waded on across in the icy water, carrying our supplies. We were met on the opposite side by one of our company medics, who took us inland about 75 yards to three seriously wounded men. We could hear the shooting going on nearby, but we were partially concealed by the tall grass.

We saved two of them with blood transfusions and pressure dressings, but the third soldier had gone into shock from blood loss, and in spite of more fluid in his veins and epinephrine, we were unable to get him out of shock. He had several external wounds and may have been bleeding internally, as well.

After the shooting and shouting had died down, a tank came by and gave us all a lift back across the Han. One of the tankers gave Bull a cable hook to pull the jeep backward out of the river. The tanker was a friend of Sgt. Adams, but one would never have known it by the way they railed at each other. The tanker told Bull he made such a tempting target, sitting in the middle of the river, that it was hard not to use him for tank target practice and put him out of his misery quickly, rather than leave him for the Chinese, who liked to eat dogs. Bull responded by telling the tanker the next time he came to the aid station because of diarrhea, he would give him medicine for constipation.

Bull went on to graphically explain how the tanker would end up blowing himself inside out; he would become a jet without wings, and simply disappear out of his rectum. Therefore, he should show more respect for medics if he didn't want to just "poop out." It was amusing to listen to these two old soldiers insult each other within earshot of the enemy. When Sgt. Adams' jeep was out of the Han River, one of our litter jeeps towed him back to our aid station, where Bull got busy draining water out of the jeep's working parts.

Big Jim Boswell, the regimental commander, was visiting Lt. Col. Weyand and after their meeting, Boswell came by our aid station to visit and asked how things were going. I guess Col. Boswell wanted to see how we were doing after wading across the Han to treat casualties. I did appreciate Col. Boswell stopping by, because it gave me an opportunity to suggest that the 7th Regiment's medical support should be leaning toward the 7th Infantry battalion aid stations and not just toward the 3rd Division medical battalion. He seemed surprised, but he listened to what I had to say. I had no idea what he was thinking. He would have been a good poker player. I was glad he didn't stay long, because I wanted to get out of my wet clothes. I was chilled to the bone. I wrote the following letter home.

Dear Folks,   *22 Feb. '51*

Our battalion has been taken off the line and put in a reserve area about five miles south of the Han for a few days rest. The men are pretty tired and needed a change to catch up on letters, clothes, rest, etc. The war seems to be going fairly well. I just wonder where and when it will all end. There is talk of a rotation plan for front line medics after six months in Korea, so I have about two and a half months to go. Actually, I cannot complain. What I have experienced has taught me a great deal about life in general and although I have not advanced scientifically, I certainly feel I have as a person.

One reads with interest over here about the international political haggling. Personally, the views expressed by Sen. Paul Douglas of Illinois in Time Magazine *seem the best to me thus far. I can't see the point of Hoover or Taft's stand, since so many of their arguments have been disproved already.*

At present, I am sitting in a nice warm tent. Actually, it is amazing how comfortable a tent can be. We spread straw on the ground and sleep as comfortable as ever. I don't know if I'll be able to sleep on a bed again right off. My executive officer, Lt. Herrick and I had cots at one time but we threw them away because of the lack of room on our already overloaded vehicles.

There is a leave plan set up now for rotation of five days leave in Japan. Several of the men in my platoon have gone back on this thus far. The rotation is so slow that it would take about two and a half years for everyone to have gone back once. However, it's good for the morale, since each time we get R&R space the men draw to see who the lucky one will be.

The felt boots arrived OK and were passed out to the men. We still have some cold weather ahead but it won't be long now and we will be getting spring rains and be up to our knees in ice and mud.

Incidentally, I think I am probably the first medical officer to have crossed the Han River in the present offensive. We had a patrol on the other side of the Han in a big fight with the Chinese and they radioed back that they had three critically wounded soldiers. They got the wounded out of the middle of the battle on tanks up to the north side of the river a distance of about 150 yards. I got my jeep down to the south side riverbed but was stalled trying to cross, so we waded across in the ice water up to our waists.

Two of the wounded made it OK, but the third was hit so bad I couldn't do much for him. I got his bleeding stopped and gave him plasma to no avail. I felt bad about it since it was the first boy like that I had lost that I got to when he was still alive. I recrossed the Han River with the patients on tanks. The tanks couldn't bring the boys all the way out and across in the first place because they were needed in the fight.

Love, Bob

About a week after the visit from Col. Boswell, I was told to see him at Regiment, where he offered me the job of regimental surgeon. The current regimental surgeon was taking over the job of medial battalion commander in the 3rd Division. I told Col. Boswell that I would do my best for him, but I was sorry about leaving my friends in the 1st Battalion. I returned to the 1st Battalion to prepare to move and write another letter.

Dear Dad and Mother,   *27 Feb. 51*

We are still sitting here in reserve south of the Han River, waiting for something to happen and in the meantime refitting ourselves for more combat.

I have good news. In a few days, I will be on orders to take over a new job, which will of course mean a promotion will follow in about thirty days, since the new job calls for a major. I am to be the new regimental surgeon and will have command of the Medical Company of the 7th Infantry Regiment. This includes the three battalion aid stations of the regiment (I now am just in charge of the 1st Battalion aid station medical platoon) as well as the ambulance section at regimental medical detachment. It also means more responsibility. Apparently the division surgeon and regimental commander figure I have done a good job here in the 1st Battalion and have chosen me for this new job. At least I hope that was the reason.

One thing it will mean is that I won't be in a place where I will be shot at as much as I have been on occasion during the last four months, although I am going to miss the comradeship of Lt. Herrick and the other fellows here at the 1st Battalion.

The spirit, morale, and pride of the individual little platoons will vary with each firefight and as each soldier has a buddy lost. However, the environment builds up close friendship among those who prove themselves brave soldiers and the cowards are soon found out and gotten rid of or at least demoted to the lowest possible rank and more deserving men are promoted. I am also going to miss the new battalion commander, Lt. Col. Weyand. He is outstanding in every way and the rifle company commanders seem to like him. I wish I could have had the opportunity to get to know him better.

I have actually given up hope of seeing the States for a couple of years now unless of course the 3rd Division should be recalled to the States to transfer to Europe. This is only a remote possibility. I would have preferred an assignment to a hospital, but in the Army, one goes where he is ordered and not where he wants.

As a captain, I had a chance of being rotated back at least to Japan but now with majority coming up as regimental surgeon, I will be combat destined for some time. At least I don't have to worry about income tax.

Love, Bob

As usual, mail received generated a new letter home to confirm its arrival and to give updates on what was going on in Korea.

Dear Dad and Mother,   *28 Feb. 1951*

Received two letters today from 17th and 18th of Feb. Nothing new on change of jobs or promotion other than what I wrote yesterday. Enclosed is some North Korean money, which we "liberated" in our recent journey north.

I expect to be given a five-day furlough in Japan soon, probably starting in about four days, after which I will assume my new responsibilities as regimental surgeon, providing of course my replacement arrives on schedule. Actually, one looks forward to furlough in Japan about the way we would think of going to Europe from Africa.

You asked about Kjenaas. He has been in Korea since last July. However, his station is a mobile surgical hospital, which is behind lines of combat at least twenty miles, although on a couple of occasions, the enemy got closer than that, but he has never been under direct fire of the enemy. Kjenaas is now a major. The rotation policy I referred to was for medical officers below the rank of major who had been in front line duty, i.e., battalion aid station for six months

As far as I know, only one of my letters has been censored, however, some of the best pictures I had were not printed. After this, I shall endeavor to print them myself or have friends in Japan print them.

Love, Bob

Battalion surgeons often see things that shouldn't happen. In spite of training, there always seem to be stupid tragedies.

One day, while I was writing a letter, I received a call to come quick to one of our companies. A tragedy had occurred. A group of 13 GIs had been standing around a campfire when one of the soldiers tossed a big armload of wood on the fire but failed to realize a grenade from his lapel had come off and dropped into the fire with the wood. In a short time, the grenade exploded. Two soldiers were killed outright and turned over to the GRO. The other 11 soldiers were wounded. Most required medical evacuation. The soldier had been trying to imitate Gen. Ridgeway; only he forgot to fix the grenade so it could not fall off.

We were aware that some soldiers had marginal IQs. They were a danger to themselves and to those around them. One cold night, soldiers were sleeping near their trucks, running the motors for ten minutes every three to four hours to keep them warm enough to start easily. One soldier decided not only to start the motor, but also to back up a few feet to level the cab so he could sleep more comfortably. He backed over a sleeping soldier—killing him by crushing his head. As battalion surgeon, I was required to file a special medical report and express an opinion about the cause of the accident and how to prevent it from happening again. The most rational answer was more training and more culling of marginally intelligent people to exclude them from combat.

I thought I had seen about every carnage possible when a stretcher was brought in with a dead soldier in his sleeping bag. Both soldier and sleeping bag were shredded and bloody. Apparently, he had a grenade in or on his field jacket. Evidently, in rolling over in his sleeping bag, the pin had been pulled and the grenade went off. We filled out a KIA card and gave the sleeping bag, with body in it, to the GRO.

Soon after that incident, a tanker who rumbled up to the aid station told me his sad story. The tankers had been in a set position, using the cannon as artillery when, because of incoming shells, they'd been ordered to move back to a new position. Unknown to the tankers, two GI truck drivers had crawled under the tank, seeking protection from the incoming shells. When the tank made a quick grinding 180-degree turn from its position, the GIs were crushed. I chose to not go to inspect the two dead GIs. I didn't need to see any more sad sights.

One young soldier from near my home in Minnesota and his Army buddy were in a rifle company in the 7th Infantry Regiment. When their battalion was in reserve, they were sent to the rear area to get supplies, with the expectation they would return the next day. They decided to spend the night in a house of ill repute, where they both got drunk. According to the MP investigation, the two got into an argument about who was the bravest. As the argument grew more insulting, one said the other was such a sniveling coward that he didn't even have the guts to shoot him. The "sniveling coward" pulled out a .45 pistol and shot his buddy. After pulling the trigger, the drunken shooter sobered up quickly to lament his action. The MPs took away the shooter, and the GRO took away the body of his friend. I doubt the family was ever informed of the way their son died. The Army probably sanitized the report by listing the dead soldier as KIA, without providing more details. I don't know what happened to the offending GI shooter.

Two foolish soldiers experimented getting high by drinking gasoline. They both died. Apparently, they had run out of regular booze and wanted a little extra kick. It is hard to explain such gross stupidity. The universal draft may have gathered in some people with limitations, and we were also aware that some local judges tried to get rid of troublesome community youths by having them join the military. I was told that the Marine Corps wouldn't take those who were mentally slow, but our Army seemed pressured to take everyone who could walk and pull a trigger.

On one occasion, an infantry sergeant told me he had a replacement that was supposed to be qualified on the Browning automatic rifle (BAR). When he failed to hit targets, it was found that he was blind in his right eye. Apparently, he had been given a BAR because he was big and strong. The sergeant had him transferred to the heavy weapons company heavy mortar platoon, where he could wrestle the 150-pound base plates. It was the perfect job for the one-eyed strong man. That story had a good ending.

One of the new arrivals in our platoon was a tall youth from North Dakota by the name of Hanson. Because he was over six foot four inches tall and only weighed 140 pounds, we called him "Skinny" Hanson. Skinny was a willing leader of a litter squad, but he often complained that his feet hurt when he walked. I could find nothing wrong with them, except he didn't have much flesh padding on the bones of his size 13 feet.

One day, Herrick and I were watching the air signal panels move up a hill that we were trying to take away from some Chinese when we had a call to bring down two wounded near the right signal panel close to the top of the hill.

Herrick called Skinny and said, "Skinny, take eight Korean laborers up the hill with litters and bring down the two wounded from the location of that signal panel."

Skinny said, "Sergeant, I can't climb all the way up that hill. My feet hurt."

"Skinny," Herrick said, "you are always complaining your feet hurt but I am telling you right now if you don't get going up that hill with these Koreans, your *** is going to hurt ten times worse than your feet have ever hurt—so move out."

Skinny moved up the hill at a quick pace with the two litter squads and had almost reached the marker when a Chinese machine gun team came around the hill's right flank and started raking the hillside, dropping most of the members of the litter squads except for Skinny. Skinny took off running back down the hill while Herrick and I watched. He leaped over rocks, fell, rolled, and bounced back onto his feet as he sprinted down the hill, until, breathless and sobbing, he ran right into Herrick's extended arms. Skinny had bullet holes in his clothes, but no serious wounds.

As he sobbed in Herrick's fatherly arms, Herrick patted his back and said, "There, you see Skinny? Your feet didn't hurt after all, did they?"

The absurdity, as well as the battle wisdom of Herrick's remark, impressed me. In the terror of war, people often recover focus and respond best to funny remarks that seem totally inappropriate, except when spoken in the context of total terror.

Any comment related to the actual terror at hand would only increase the stress, while humor aids recovery from momentary insanity or hysteria. Such remarks may restore orientation enough to enable a soldier to somehow continue to function under impossible conditions.

A few minutes later, a tank rolled up near us, got the Chinese machine gunners in their telescope sight, and blew them off the mountainside. Aircraft came in to rake the ridge ahead of the signal panels, and we sent up more litter squads to bring all the wounded down. Our troops secured the new real estate as the dead and wounded were collected. Another sad casualty day for the medics, but out troops celebrated their victory on the hill.

As Herrick and I prepared to head back to the aid station, we heard the short whine of an incoming heavy mortar round ending with a sickening loud THUNK a few feet away where the shell hit the ground. We hit the ground, expecting an explosion. But it didn't explode. We did a fast worm crawl away from the shell for a few yards before we got up to run. Once again, God had demonstrated His protection. Those 120 mm mortar shells could do a lot of damage.

The next morning, after a sedated sleep, Skinny Hanson was ready to go back to work, but I noticed my hands shaking a bit as I held my morning coffee cup. I thanked the Lord again and asked Him to please take away the shaking in my hands so I could get back to work. Again, that prayer was answered.

I was given a five-day R&R leave in Japan, after which I was to return to my new assignment as regimental surgeon. That meant another doctor would need to be found to be the 1st Battalion surgeon. Navy Lt. "Jitters," who was in the regimental collecting station, was the only doctor immediately available. As a temporary expedience, Jitters was sent to the 1st Battalion aid station, where he soon added to his reputation as a very frightened fellow.

Of course, 2nd Lt. Herrick would actually run the 1st Battalion medical platoon and Lt. Jitters would just be expected to treat patients in the battalion aid station. The division surgeon was already looking for a replacement doctor with steadier nerves to replace Jitters. So with things temporarily quiet in the 1st Battalion, I collected a few things and headed off to Japan for R&R.

It felt strange returning to Japan on leave after five months with the infantry in Korea. After a night cleaning up and resting in an R&R Hotel in Tokyo, I hitched a ride back to the old 128th Station Hospital to see if there was anyone I knew still there. I saw a few old military acquaintances, and some of the Japanese staff seemed glad to see me, but I had no roots that made me to want to stay. My friends and roots were now with the 7th Infantry in Korea.

The highlight of my R&R trip to Tokyo was meeting Lt. Col. Weyand's mother and father, and his charming wife, Arlene. Lt. Col. Weyand told me to call his father, who was a petroleum engineer consultant to MacArthur, when I got to Japan. Mr. Weyand, Mrs. Weyand, and Arlene Weyand were extremely nice. They took Cpt. Baker, an officer who had gone on leave at the same time, Cpt. Fred Snider, my old friend from the 128th Hospital, and me out to dinner at the Tokyo General Headquarters Officers' Club, where we were wined and dined to our heart's content. We had a picture taken at the table. They were kind, erudite, and cultured people. With my background and limited world experience, I felt like a country bumpkin with an M.D. degree.

The following letter was written from Japan before I returned to Korea.

Dear Dad and Mother,   *9 Mar. 1951*

I am writing this letter from Japan. Yes, I am on leave for five days, and coming from Korea to Japan is like going from night to day. At the present time, I am just relaxing in the same room where I stayed when I was at the old 128th Station Hospital. There has been a great deal of change in personnel here, but some of the old familiar faces are still here. I have sent a couple of packages home, which you should be getting in about a month.

I leave again for Korea on the 11th to take up my new job as regimental surgeon. It will be a relatively safer job. Actually, I would rather stay on in Korea, since time spent there counts more than time in Japan as far as overseas time and since the overseas tours are so long now, it may be the only way to get back to the States in less than two or three years.

I shaved off my handlebar mustache that I had been nursing for four months. It got to be quite big, bushy and in the way, so in view of my taking over a new job where it would be advisable to look more presentable, I decided to shave it off. I feel naked without it.

Weather here in Japan is very mild now and in a week or two it will be the same in Korea.

I still have the German, Czechoslovakian-made, 8mm Mouser rifle, which a U.S. soldier got off a Chinese sniper in North Korea. The rifle is in good shape, but the stock needs to be replaced. It was given to me by a soldier that was wounded and couldn't take it with him to the hospital. I hope to be able to mail it home soon. It will probably only be a souvenir, but the Mouser bolt action is excellent and it would make a good hunting rifle.

Hope all goes well at home. The news says there has been a lot of cold weather in Minnesota.

Love, Bob

Miss Zige was still working at the hospital. We spent several hours discussing philosophy and Christianity. She was interested in Christianity only as a philosophy, but seemed torn between two civilizations and ideologies. She was still grateful that I had saved her from Cpt. Laymore and wanted to continue her friendship with me. We parted with a hug.

South Korean ground too frozen to dig foxholes, but good for tanks;
January 1951

Photo taken by Cpt. Jensen of passing Korean civilians traveling south

Photo taken by Cpt. Jensen of passing Korean civilians traveling south

Left to right: Sgt. Ogden, Sgt. Byland, Sgt. Bowie, Sgt. Herrick, Cpl. Heath, Cpt. Jensen, Imm Yung Hee at the 1st Battalion aid station; February 1951

Notice the battered Red Cross flag flying on the right. Aid stations in the rear area were able to safely use the Red Cross symbol (Sgt. Bowie: right)

A soldier resting outside the rear area aid station;
note the luxury of a rough wood floor

Volleyball in the reserve area

The Han River; notice the blown bridge sections in the background

Dr. Cambell (left) and Dr. Jensen (right)
after amputating the leg of South Korean Woman

Roadside aid station in 1st Battalion, 7th medics' 3/4-ton truck;
just north of Chonan

Navy Lt. Curran at the 2nd Battalion aid station

1st Battalion assembly in rear area to witness battlefield promotions;
January 7, 1951

Battlefield promotions of outstanding sergeants to 2nd lieutenants (Herrick: 2nd from right); January 7, 1951

Engineer bulldozer clearing an area for a supply tent

A temporary aid station, 3/4-ton truck, box ambulance, and jeeps

Chapter Eleven
From Seoul to the Iron Triangle for the greatest battle of the war
March 13, 1951 – May 2, 1951

Shortly after I returned to Korea, I got off another letter home. I knew the folks would be worried by my return to Korea and I wanted to reassure them that I was settling into my new job at Regiment.

Dear Dad and Mother,   13 Mar. 1951

Back in Korea again after a very pleasant five days leave in Japan. I shaved off my handle bar mustache while in Japan and when I arrived back in Korea nobody recognized me.

I am getting settled in my new job back at Regiment. I feel so far back in the rear area. I am practically wondering whether the war is still on or not. Actually, we are only about eight miles back, but it seems a long way after being on the front so long.

The offensive at present is going well and the Chinese seem to be withdrawing to the north. Where this war is going to end, I don't know. MacArthur predicts a stalemate so that will mean a permanent tie up of our forces in the Far East. However, there will be a rotation plan out and I expect Korea will be the final training place for the new recruits in the Army.

There is little new to report from here, since the present offensive is going rather smoothly. The 25th has crossed the Han east of us and is pushing west. The 3rd Division is poised to cross the Han soon.

Love, Bob

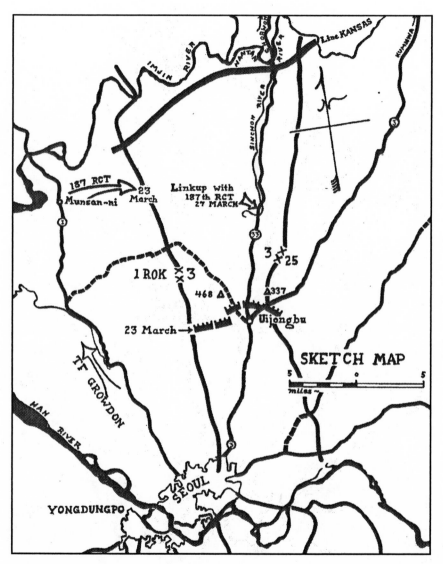

The airdrop of the 187th RCT to link up with the 3rd Division and 1st ROK; 23 March 1951

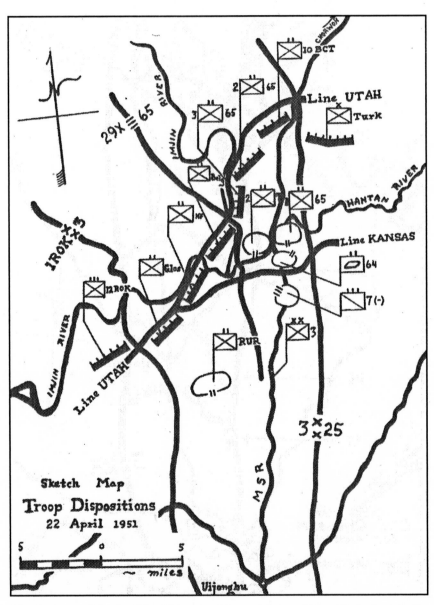

The farthest roll back of the Chinese to Kansas Line and Line Utah along Imjin and Hantan Rivers; 22 April 1951

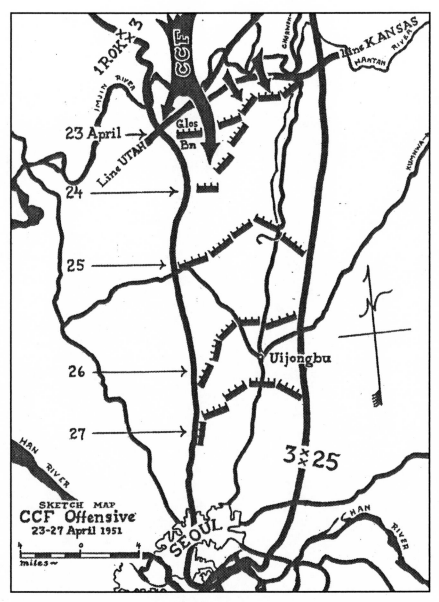

The tidal wave Chinese Offensive started on 22 April 1951, Gloucester
Battalion lost on 23 April 1951

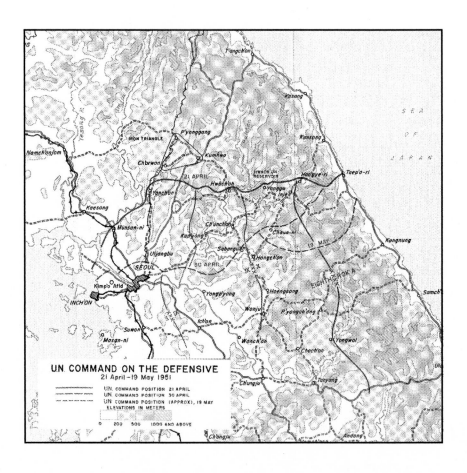

We crossed the Han River shortly after I wrote that letter. There wasn't much of a fight from the Chinese, and I didn't need to wade across this time, but crossed on a pontoon bridge. The retaking of Seoul was relatively easy, because the Chinese did not make a stand there, either. It is likely they were withdrawing to the Iron Triangle area north of the Chorwon to Kumhwa line, where they were reported to be assembling supplies. According to infantry talk and planning, it was in the Chinese interest for us to get as close as possible to their hidden supply catches before they counterattacked in force. When they attacked in mass, they would need to re-supply quickly to exploit any breakthrough. As we moved north, we prepared fallback positions and secondary defense lines, north of which we would have free-fire zones for our artillery and airpower.

In the meantime, the 7th Infantry Regiment spread out and headed north on the right side of the main road from Seoul through Uijongbu, and on north toward the Imjin River.

It was along this journey that the 2nd Battalion 7th had a major problem with food poisoning. They had pushed steadily north over hill and dale, with continued resistance from the Chinese, when command decided they should pause for a bit of rest and some warm food other than C-ration cans. Their mess crew showed up bright and early with a number of marmite cans with hot scrambled eggs, bread, butter, jam, and hot coffee. After breakfast, the troops were off climbing hills, sweeping the Chinese before them.

About noon, the vomiting started. One soldier after another became ill with severe vomiting, and many had diarrhea. Most of the soldiers in the company could not keep any fluids down, and soon became weak and dehydrated. Within two hours, the company was forced to break off contact. Fortunately, the Chinese did not counterattack. The company came stumbling and vomiting back down the hill. One medic called it the worst "puke and poop epidemic" we had ever experienced.

There were about a dozen well soldiers amid more than a hundred very ill ones in the company. The company commander, who was not sick, and the 2nd Battalion commander were considering trucking the sick soldiers back to the regimental collecting station for treatment and using another company to stabilize the line when I received a panicky call from the battalion surgeon, Navy Lt. Currin.

"Help," he said, "I have a company of soldiers collapsing with vomiting and diarrhea. What should I do? Should I send them all back to collecting? We can't manage them all here!"

My answer was short but not sweet.

"No. If you aren't under attack, don't send any of them back. If only one company is involved, it's probably food poisoning. Put them all in a row on a nearby hillside or dry field and if they can't retain fluid by mouth, give I.V. fluids to those showing signs of dehydration. Also have a sergeant do a bit of epidemiology. Use a company roster and make a list of everything both the sick and well soldiers ate and drank in the last 12 hours. You should know what food caused this by the time I get there. I'll call the division surgeon and get him to send a hundred bottles of I.V. fluid in a helicopter, pick me up, and fly me to you. If it's what I think it is—staphylococcus enteric toxin—we should have the soldiers up and around by tomorrow and we'll find a cook's helper with an infected finger. Put out a panel for the helicopter and I'll see you soon."

I was fortunate to get through to Lt. Col. Joe Bayne, the division surgeon, and in short order, he had a helicopter flutter down to the regimental collecting station with boxes of I.V. fluid in each litter pod. We immediately took off and headed north. We didn't need a panel set out. It was easy enough to spot a hundred soldiers lying in rows on the ground. Several of the soldiers, who were still retching, already had I.V. solutions running into their arms with well soldiers holding the I.V. bottles up. The vomiting soldiers were miserable, and those with diarrhea felt even worse. Many would need I.V. fluids to correct their dehydration. Only a few were able to keep fluids down by mouth.

The battalion surgeon was starting more I.V. drips as we fluttered down with the chopper-load of bottles. After I landed, the company commander, Cpt. "Pusher," approached and said he thought it had been the scrambled eggs. He had not eaten any of the eggs, and he was steaming mad because the kitchen crew had transported the scrambled eggs for almost 42 hours as they tried to catch up with the company. When they did, they reheated the eggs, assuming the heat would kill anything bad that might have grown in the eggs.

The kitchen crew was wrong, wrong, wrong, because staphylococcal toxin is heat stable. Cooking does not destroy it. Cpt. Pusher said the battalion aid station sergeants were inspecting the kitchen crews for infected fingers. He wanted to know how we could speed up the recovery process with so much retching, vomiting, and diarrhea going on.

I told him there was one order I had never given since I put on an Army uniform, and I suspected no doctor in the Army had.

Pleased that the problem was coming under control, Cpt. Pusher said, "Doc, I'm curious as hell to know what command you are talking about."

"Is your company top sergeant available?" I asked.

"Sure, Doc," he said. "He's right over there on the ground, but he's in pretty good shape. I'll call him over."

The sergeant came over and saluted.

"Sir, how can I be of help?" he said.

"How do you feel, Sergeant?" I asked.

"A bit weak," he replied, "and I still get the urge to puke and poop a bit, but I've kept a little water down."

"Here's the deal for the next couple of hours," I said. "Any man who can't hold down three ounces, or half a cup of water, every 10 minutes for an hour should get a pint of saline I.V. started in his arm. But you don't want to waste manpower by having soldiers just standing there, holding saline bottles in the air. So I am giving the order to fix bayonets. Every man that needs an I.V. should have his rifle bayonet jabbed in the ground near his head so there's something to hang the I.V. bottle on. We need a slit trench dug downhill from the guys lying on the ground, so they have a place to puke and poop nearby. We also need a water trailer pulled up nearby, and a big can of water heating on a stove so the men can get a helmet of warm water to wash with, starting from the head and working down. They should use blankets to keep warm until they get clean clothes. I want your company clerk to get a pad of paper and print the name of each messed-up soldier on a separate sheet of paper, along with his pants, shirt, t-shirt, and under garment sizes. When the papers are collected, we'll send the helicopter back for clean clothes. You need to designate someone to go with the helicopter pilot and bring back the right clothes for each man, tied in a bundle with each man's paper enclosed in the shirt pocket. And last of all, bring four dozen rolls of toilet paper. If you can fight the Chinese, I am sure you can handle this job, so get started."

"Yes, sir!" said the top sergeant.

I then turned to help the battalion surgeon start more I.V. drips.

The soldiers were weak and miserable, but had all recovered within 48 hours. Not one man was lost or evacuated. I think many of them were ticked off at me for stopping their truck ride to the rear area. The top sergeant took note and told disgruntled soldiers to suck it up, because there were no Purple Hearts for vomiting and diarrhea.

I wished I had a camera handy to photograph the row of soldiers with their rifle bayonets stuck in the ground and I.V. bottles hanging on the stocks. As soon as the water can was hot, the soldiers each got a helmet-full of warm water, scrubbed down in the chill air, and dried off with towels. Washing up helped make them feel better. The next morning, they all received clean clothes.

I never found out who was in charge of getting the clean clothes together or who authorized the return flight of the loaded helicopter the next morning, but I had confidence that a fighting captain and a finagling top sergeant would pull some general's chain of command and the challenge would be met, come hell or water. The 2nd Battalion commander and the regimental commander were only too pleased to stand aside and let medics handle the mess before someone notified a reporter.

I did think my order to "fix bayonets" gave the entire episode a somewhat heroic flare, but I never received any thanks.

After organizing the counterattack against the staphylococcus enteric toxin, I returned to the regimental collecting station to tend other tasks. It had been a real object lesson that gave us the opportunity to clamp down on mess inspections and the cleanliness of the cooks' hands. We never did find the guilty food handler. I didn't mention the food poisoning in my letter home. It would have been something new for my parents to worry about and had it gotten into a newspaper, it could have resulted in a congressional inquiry. We didn't need any more distractions.

Dear Dad and Mother,   *16 Mar. 1951*

There is little new to report as far as the war is concerned. Everything is going fairly well in this sector around Seoul. My new job as regimental surgeon keeps me busy, since I must coordinate medical care and evacuation from the three battalions. This means of course frequent trips to regimental headquarters and also to the battalion as well as back to 3rd Division headquarters. I have a very good staff to work with. There are three medical service officers here to handle administration supply, records, ambulance, and equipment, as well as one who acts as executive officer for me. There also are two dentists and another doctor to assist at collecting aid stations.

I am the youngest officer with captain rank at Regiment. Most of the men are veterans of previous wars, especially the MSCs. However, I am the "old man" and my age is not considered here.

Letters have been coming through fine, as well as packages so far. I haven't received those sent slow mail yet. I don't believe I would send any more by airmail, since the expense is somewhat prohibitive and there is nothing I can think of now that I need in a hurry. Note the change in address—now it's "Med. Co. 7th Inf. RCT."

While on leave in Japan, I picked up a number of things, which I mailed home. I have a fine German Mouser rifle, which I am going to try to mail home if I can. The Chinese have a wide assortment of weapons, chosen helter-skelter from all the arsenals of the world.

The question of rotation comes up. Actually, I don't expect to be home for approximately a year yet. Maybe by next Christmas. Since I am up for a promotion to major, I probably won't be eligible for rotation to Japan until after six more months in Korea. However, I would just as soon stay in Korea as Japan, because the total time overseas is less.

Everyone wonders what is going to happen in Europe. We anticipate a couple of the divisions here being rotated to Europe so they have some seasoned troops to assist training there. I rather think it is just a rumor.

Love, Bob

A letter from home usually got a quick response if I was not otherwise occupied.

Dear Mother and Dad,   18 Mar. 1951

Received your letter of Mar. 9 today. I'll try to answer a couple of your questions. I have only done two leg amputations in my aid station and both were doing well when I last heard at three weeks and two weeks post operative in each case. Actually, one would have trouble getting results as good as that in a hospital, but these Koreans are very hardy and give them half a chance and they will heal up.

My boy, Imm Yung Hee, is here at Regiment with me, where he takes care of the officers' tent, sets the table for the officers' mess, helps with the Korean patients in the aid station, and generally makes himself very useful. He was very happy when I brought him along with me. I see the fellows at the 1st Battalion frequently, since my job includes keeping tabs on the medical platoons in each of the three battalions of the regiment.

At present, the war is rather quiet in our sector. It will probably be 60 days before I can get promoted, since I find the regulation states that captains must fill the job of a major for 60 days during a war before he can be promoted to that grade. However, I am content to wait. Time for bed.

Love, Bob

When I came back to regiment, Navy Lt. Jitters had been sent forward to take my place as the 1st Battalion surgeon. Dr. Jitters was an excellent primary care physician, but he was unable to mask his fear of being in an infantry battalion. He knew a number of American infantry battalions had been overrun during Chinese attacks, and several doctors had been killed or captured in the war. It was not an unrealistic fear. The problem was a matter of fear management.

I asked Bill Herrick once how he kept going day after day, crawling out under fire to drag or carry back wounded. He thought for a minute.

"Sir, there are things worse than death."

"And what might that be?" I asked.

"To look at my face in the mirror while shaving and know that I was looking at a cowardly bastard who hadn't done his duty," he said. "For me to know that I had not saved someone I might have saved—that would be worse than death."

"Bill," I said, "that is why we get along so well together. You tell it like you feel it in your heart and guts."

Lt. Jitters joined the Navy reserve under pressure from the doctors' draft, in order to have a nice clean bunk on a nice clean ship, if he couldn't get shore duty. He was overweight and not athletically disposed. He wanted to finish his residency in internal medicine and go into practice with friends who had the same roots, in New York. He was a kind and likable person, as well as a good doctor.

But his carefully planned, secure world fell apart when the defense department called excess Naval Reserve doctors to active duty and loaned them to the Army for placement wherever the Army needed them. Dr. Jitters entered the Army world of outdoor grime and killing fields with great reluctance and obvious trepidation. His outward comportment was such that the most frightened recent draftees felt relatively brave in comparison. I spent a lot of time orienting and reassuring Lt. Jitters, to no avail.

As with many Jewish people, he had family ties to holocaust victims, an historical reality that evoked my sincerest sympathy. Moreover, I was aware that according to scripture, God said, in reference to the Jewish people, "I will bless those who bless thee and the one who curses you I will curse" (Genesis 12:3).

Because of that, I was disposed to be helpful to the Jewish people. Moreover, I had enjoyed my association with Jewish students and professors in medical school and I admired their love of scholarship and excellence in providing medical care.

But despite his professional excellence, Dr. Jitters was not endowed with a warrior's spirit. I suggested he pray for courage, but he was more bound by tradition than faith, so praying didn't seem to be an option for him. Moreover, the silent witness of six million Jews, murdered by Hitler, seemed to discount the effectiveness of prayer and left unanswered the big question: "Why, Lord?"

I planned to pull Lt. Jitters out of the 1st Battalion and bring him back to the regimental collecting station as soon as I could get another doctor to replace him, because his chronically frightened countenance was becoming a bit of a battalion joke, and that was not a good influence.

The first night Lt. Jitters slept in the medical platoon squad tent, he noticed no one else had a cot; the other officers and enlisted men slept on the ground. He asked why. The reason was because an infantry unit had to travel light in a mobile war, and even our temporary use of a squad tent was a luxury. But one of the jokester sergeants told Lt. Jitters the reason they got rid of their cots was because of the "Chinese bouncing mortar shells" that bounced when they hit and then exploded horizontally, decimating people sleeping on cots. No one said anything to correct this blatant lie. Everyone just rolled over and went to sleep on the ground, except for Lt. Jitters.

A little later, when some exploding shells were heard nearby, Lt. Jitters abandoned his cot and moved his sleeping bag to a slight depression on the ground, inside the tent. In the morning, he noted the jokester sergeant waking from a good night's sleep on his nice new Navy cot.

A few nights later, it became clear that Lt. Jitters was afraid to go outside to urinate. To accommodate this essential function, he kept a tall coffee can near his cot to use as a urinal. During the night, some of the soldiers crept up to Lt. Jitters' cot and urinated in his empty coffee can until it was filled to the brim. When Lt. Jitters tried to use it, he couldn't quite figure out why the can was full and running over his fingers.

It provided some comic relief, but it was unkind and didn't help unit morale, so I passed the word down to stop picking on the new Navy doctor, because he was a good doctor and they should help him and not make his life more miserable. I believe the admonition may have helped some. Actually, the troops warmed up to Lt. Jitters as they found him to be a sympathetic and helpful doctor.

Soon afterward, a young soldier came to see Lt. Jitters in sick call because of recurring nightmares. When Jitters asked about the bad dreams, the soldier explained he'd had the same dream several times, in which he was shot between the eyes, and killed. Jitters used his best counseling to reassure the soldier that dreams had no basis in reality.

Two days later, the soldier's body was brought to the aid station. He had been killed with a single shot between the eyes by a North Korean sniper. On seeing the dead soldier with the prophesied bullet hole between his eyes, Lt. Jitters suddenly lost his disbelief in supernatural forces and sniper rifle fire was added to Lt. Jitters' fear of being hit by bouncing mortar shells.

Dear Dad and Mother,   *24 Mar. 1951*

Haven't written for two or three days now because I have been pretty busy. Not so much because of casualties but rather because we are situated just south of Uijongbu, which is about half way between Seoul and the 38th Parallel.

The 3rd Division has been having a bit of a fight for this area but as of tonight, things look pretty good. The 7th RCT now has the Belgium battalion attached. I was up and visited their aid station and doctor this afternoon. They are a good bunch of soldiers, but are very expense conscious. Too bad we don't have a few people like that in our government.

The destruction in this country is almost complete. Nearly every building in Seoul has been gutted with fire and I must say, Seoul surprised me. It was a very beautiful city, with modern buildings, ancient palaces, temples, and gardens. What a pity it is such a mass of rubble now. Enclosed is an example of North Korean money, which we liberated. The last letter received was Mar. 15, so the mail service hasn't been too bad.

Love, Bob

P.S. You undoubtedly heard about the airdrop. Part of our regiment was in the armored spearhead, which went through from Seoul to meet them.

My 25th birthday, on 19 March 1951, had come and gone unnoticed, and without the usual cake and celebration, apart from the sounds of guns around us.

I got a late birthday card from my parents and one from my brother. The only other person who remembered my birthday was Miss Zige. I answered her letter and then mailed it home, which is why her letter was included in my mother's collection.

Dear Dr. Jensen, 17 Mar. 1951

I was very glad to see you. How have you been? I was very anxious about you. When I last see you I could not tell you things. I kept them to myself. Did you have a nice vacation? You were looking very fine as well as you looked here and are putting on weight. Your eyes shine, showing full to peace of youth, hold everything human.

I am learning from you. I thank you very much for your good advice to us. We find many scholars in it. These are what we lack. You told me how to get happiness when I heard this from you it caused me agony. It is very difficult for me and discouraging. The happiness foundation is an affection.

Affection is moved with environment each person different but mostly the same. What do you think about affection? This is very difficult for me to explain. I think on the philosophical it is complicated and reason leads this one. Many intelligent do not know and find themselves very unhappy.

A literary man says, "Love is best." I know that but just on impulse or reason— which leads to affection. If somebody were to ask me I would say that reason leads. Many famous books show me though about the end of affection. I do not believe in affection it only shows on the surface.

My thoughts are on the pessimistic side and I do believe them. I told you before about Mrs. Matsutani (Diet Member). She is very unfortunate now because of her husband I am really afraid of affection, as I do not know the reason that leads to affection.

Many happy returns on your birthday and I hope you become major very soon. That is very wonderful and I am very happy to hear it. I have never seen a major as young as you. It amazes me. I know your wonderful personality has a lot to do with it. I admire you for your wonderful human interests and I am always learning from it.

My school is very hard. My result this year (from Apr. 50 to Mar 51) was all superior. I am very happy with my teacher and girlfriends. I will study hard this year too. I must study for two (at University) more years (economics and politics) then I am very anxious to continue on for one more (we call a University hall) year if I graduate from there I can get my doctors degree very easy. I do not know sure because there are very few girls that finish the school and need a lot of money too. After then I will get a new job it is very much values in Japan and world and I must study hard to finish school.

My parents are worried for my marriage (the man say he likes me very much but I still dislike him) but I do not care for that. My happiness will come from the living of my ideas. I will do one's endeavor until I reach my object. Will you please always teach and guide me?

Yesterday we visited a Japanese house with Major Jernigan, Lt. Gwinn, Lt. Senter but I did not enjoy it because of missing you. Spring has come to Japan and soon there will be Cherry blossoms. It is very beautiful but it brings back memories of my nice garden and house, which was destroyed by the B 29 in the last war. I really miss them. Then there were my lovely gold fish and tortoises in the pond in the garden. They were killed in the bombings. When will I enjoy these things again? I must try to forget them but it is hard when I have such fond memories.

How sad a conquered country is! The conquered and the conquerors. I never think of that because it makes me very sad. I hope you come back to see me again. I feel it will be very soon. Please take good care of yourself. I hope this letter is not lost and I pray for it's safe arrival to you.

Sincerely, Zige

In the recurring skirmishes, some of our troops were isolated from returning to their battalion by road because the Chinese had brought the road under fire. Our troops had a couple of causalities, and the direct overland evacuation root covered difficult terrain. But there was a more round-about, secondary trail on the west side by which a litter jeep might reach the casualties. Thus, while I was trying to call a helicopter, Lt. Sarka volunteered to take a litter jeep by that longer secondary trail to try to reach the casualties. It seemed like a good option, since HQ had reported that the round-about trail was in friendly hands and we weren't sure if or when we might get the chopper.

Fortunately, we were able to get a helicopter quickly, and I went with the chopper to pick up the two litter patients.

As we were loading the patients and starting blood, I mentioned that we had a litter jeep that should be coming to them from the west and the squad leader said, "Hell, Doc, there isn't anyone coming to us from either the east or west. The Chinese have cut us off on both sides. We don't have vehicles with us, so as soon as you leave we are walking overland straight south."

They did, and they made it out.

I told the pilot to go straight to our collecting station and unload the patients; then we would head down the western trail to try to catch Lt. Sarka before he ran into a Chinese ambush or our own artillery, trying to take out the Chinese in that area. As soon as we unloaded, we located the trail and followed it as fast as we could, flying low with our hearts in our mouths, praying and hoping we would catch up to them in time. Our problem was that we had no radio communication with our litter jeeps.

We finally spotted Sarka in his litter jeep and swooped down over him. I hung out of the bubble door with my helmet off so Sarka could recognize my face as I signaled them to turn around and head back to the collecting station. He got the message clearly and responded immediately. We didn't see any Chinese and didn't receive any bullet holes, so there was nothing to write home about. It was just another day along the ever-shifting frontline.

Sometime in late March 1951, Herrick returned from rescuing wounded on the line and found Lt. Jitters agitated and demanding they move the aid station because, as he said, "they are shelling the hell out of us."

Upon receiving this information, Herrick asked, "Where have the shells been landing?"

"Two mortar shells landed about 50 to 100 yards to the right of the aid station, and then two more shells landed about 50 to 100 yards to the left of the aid station."

Herrick said, "Doc, if they landed two shells to our right and two shells to our left, it seems to me the aid station is in just the right spot not to be hit, so I don't think we should move in any direction. Besides, I'm dog-tired because I've been working all night, so I'm going to take a nap."

Lt. Jitters threw up his hands and said, "I now know what's the matter with you, Herrick."

"And what is the matter with me?" Herrick said.

"Your problem, Lieutenant Herrick, is that you are insane!"

"Oh, is that all?" Herrick said. "Well, I still need some shut eye."

Jitters declared that he was going to see Col. Weyand, but Herrick ignored him and climbed into his sleeping bag.

Lt. Jitters made his way to the headquarters tent and, after being given permission to speak his mind, he gave an account of his conversation with Herrick, ending with his clinical diagnosis that Herrick was insane.

Col. Weyand said, "Dr. Jitters, you are a trained medical man and you've been working with Herrick for a month, and you only now figured out that he is crazy? I've known he was crazy since we first met, but he also is a damn fine soldier. Is there anything else you wanted to see me about?"

"No, sir," Lt. Jitters said.

As he trudged back to the aid station, he muttered, "Everyone here is crazy. This entire country is an insane asylum, and all the crazies have guns!"

Now it so happened that the aid station crew had dug a 5 x 5 x 5 foot trash-burn-pit a short distance from the 1st Battalion aid station, which was behind a low hill. The Chinese knew we were dug in behind that hill, and had tried lobbing mortars over the hill, without much effect.

Unfortunately, the Chinese decided to take the camouflage cover off a high velocity 57 mm cannon, which was mounted on a two-wheel carriage and dug in. According to Cpt. Dick Anderson, the 7th Regiment Tank Company commander, this 57 mm cannon had dueled with some of our M-4 tanks with 76 mm cannons, from its protected and semi-concealed position near a crossroads about two miles north.

One of the Chinese 57 mm shells bounced off the low hill and careened down near the 1st Battalion aid station, making a fearsome noise as it tore through the area, exploding as it went. That exploding high velocity shell burst caused Lt. Jitters to jump headlong into the trash pit, and the terrifying, strange new noise that was definitely not a mortar woke Herrick up. He wandered out of the aid station and found Lt. Jitters' head peeping out over the edge of the trash pit.

"What the hell are you doing in that filthy trash pit?" Herrick asked.

Before Jitters could answer, another 57 mm cannon round came bouncing down the muddy road to the left of the aid station and Herrick, without hesitation, joined Jitters in the trash pit.

Jitters turned to Herrick and, shaking his finger in the second lieutenant's face, Jitters said, "You see? You see? I told you they were shelling the hell out of us, and you wouldn't listen. You just went to sleep. And now another shell went off and you just jumped into this garbage hole with me. You see? You see? They really are shelling the hell out of us!"

Herrick was speechless but only for a moment.

He soon explained to Jitters in a calm voice as follows, "The only reason I jumped into the pit was to help you to get your fat *** out of this deep hole."

Lt. Jitters' facial expression slowly changed from total terror to inane hilarity and they both burst out laughing so hard that neither was able to help the other to climb out of the garbage pit. Fortunately, the Chinese did not fire another round precisely between the first two rounds.

It so happened that my driver, Cpl. Heath, and I were just returning from a visit to the 3rd Battalion aid station and were passing through the 1st Battalion shortly after the 57 mm cannon shells exploded on either side of the 1st Battalion Aid Station. We were en route to the regimental collecting station when we saw Herrick and Jitters laughing and trying to climb out of the garbage pit. Not knowing why they were in there, I thought I'd would add to the humor of the moment and offered them a few unopened C-ration cans so they wouldn't need to eat in the garbage pit any more that day.

I sent Cpl. Heath to the Battalion HQ, where he found out that we couldn't get back to regiment the way we were going because the Chinese had placed a cannon at the road junction up ahead and were shooting at vehicular targets. One of our tanks was on the way from the south to knock out the Chinese cannon. Heath also found out that I was needed at the regimental collecting station ASAP.

My immediate problem was to find a way to get myself back to the regimental collecting station without taking the road being held by the Chinese cannon. As we looked at the map and the terrain features, it seemed that the best way for me to get back to Regiment was to walk about a mile straight across some dry rice paddies. The path I would need to take was within two miles of the 57 mm Chinese gun, but I didn't think they would waste precious ammunition by shooting at one lone soldier running across a rice paddy two miles south. So I left my jeep and driver at the 1st Battalion aid station and took off at a fast jog across the fields.

As I approached the halfway point, I heard the whine of an incoming round, followed by the bark of the 57 mm cannon as I threw myself flat on the ground. The shell exploded behind a bank of soil at the edge of the dry rice paddy. Immediately, I was up and running again, until I heard another incoming whine, and again threw myself flat on the dried mud, and heard the cannon bark again as I hit the ground. I shouted in the direction of the Chinese gun, telling them to stop shooting because I was only one person. I started to get up to run again, and noticed my helmet was missing. I spotted it about twenty feet away, crawled over to retrieve it, and found a dent in one side. Apparently a fragment from the second shell explosion had hit my helmet as I threw myself to the ground.

I rested for a moment before thinking the Chinese might send a runner out to see who they'd hit, so I got up again, and sprinted forward until I heard a third incoming shell and threw myself flat again. The explosion landed about 30 feet away, and before the dirt had settled, I was up and running. As I ran, I saw one of our tanks coming from the south across the fields, going north. Perhaps the Chinese saw the tank coming too, because no more shells came in my direction.

At the spot where the tank would pass me, there was a low hedge topping a vertical berm of earth separating two rice paddies. The berm was designed to retain water at a level four feet higher than the rice paddy to the north. Knowing they could not see the drop off, I tried to signal the tanker as they roared past, but they were buttoned up and didn't see me. The tank must have been traveling about twenty-five miles an hour when it crossed the berm and became airborne for about two seconds.

Take it from me, tanks do not fly well. Fortunately, the tank's 76 mm cannon was aimed backward; otherwise, they would have plunged their cannon into the ground when they landed on their nose. Tanks being tanks, it gradually chewed its way forward to a level position in the lower paddy, where it stopped and a soldier opened the hatch.

I climbed on top of the tank and helped a tanker climb out through the hatch. He was moaning with pain, holding his right shoulder. I identified myself as Dr. Jensen, 7th Regiment surgeon. Finding a doctor on top of his tank was a bit of a surprise for the tanker, and he remarked that it was nice to have such prompt tank-top medical service. He had injured his right shoulder when the tank dropped onto its nose, throwing him forward with his right arm still slung over the cannon loading mechanism. I opened up his shirt and saw that he had dislocated his right upper arm from the shoulder socket.

As an intern at the Minneapolis General Hospital emergency room, I'd seen an orthopedic resident demonstrate the Kocher Technique for rotating the arm behind the patient in order to reinsert the ball-head of the humerus bone back up into the shoulder socket. So right there, on top of the tank, I tried the Kocher maneuver with the tanker's arm, and with the Lord's assistance, and to my surprise, his arm popped back into position. I trussed it up in a sling and advised him to see an orthopedic surgeon and get an x-ray at the nearest MASH hospital for follow up.

After thanking me profusely for my tank-top medical service in a dry rice paddy, the tanker crawled back into the tank and I hopped off. The two other tankers were battered and bruised, but still able to function. I couldn't resist offering a parting bit of advice and reminded them that tanks were not really designed to fly. They laughed and roared off to finish their assignment of demolishing the Chinese cannon. I heard some cannon shots up the road, and I was told they did indeed knock out the Chinese cannon, but I never saw those tankers again. Later, a story circulated around 7th Regiment about some crazy doctor providing tank-top medical service.

I spoke with Dick Anderson, currently retired in Louisiana, and he remembers well the duel his M-4 tanks had with that Chinese cannon and the weird noise made by the 57 mm cannon shells. He did not recall hearing about one of his tanks landing on its nose or about a tanker with a dislocated shoulder. But I guess not all tank commanders report every rice paddy misadventure to their tank company commander, if all ends well.

When I reached the collecting station, I was delighted to find the division surgeon had sent us a new Army doctor, Cpt. Henry Barnes. Hank Barnes was a quiet, likable fellow who didn't hesitate to do whatever needed to be done, regardless of the circumstances. He seemed to be an ideal battalion surgeon. After a few days' orientation at Regiment, I took Cpt. Barnes to the 1st Battalion, exchanged him for Lt. Jitters, and brought Jitters back to the regimental collecting station, where he would not be as close to the fighting. Lt. Jitters was happy to make the move back to Regiment with his cot. He wanted nothing more than to get as far south as possible in Korea, and back to New York as soon as his tour of duty was over.

We continued to move north past Uijongbu. There were some firefights, but nothing major to cause us much concern. Father Carroll came down with bronchitis, associated with shortness of breath. I thought Carroll had what doctors at the time called "Pickwickian" syndrome, which occurs in obese people with reduced pulmonary ventilation. I wrote it on his tag, with the recommendation that he be rotated back to the States. He had been wounded three times in World War II and exposed to enough enemy fire in the Korean War to have earned a rest.

He was so sick I was afraid I was going to loose him. I had to get him back to an oxygen supply. We hugged each other as we said goodbye. We'd become close friends. He gave me his best Roman Catholic blessing as I bid him farewell. I told him Jesus loved him. He nodded, wheezed, coughed, and departed in a box ambulance.

I was saddened by his departure. We had talked of many things during our time together: salvation by faith in Christ through the grace of God, the disciples and of their varied ministries in the first century, the sacraments of baptism and communion, the gospel message, and the authority of scripture versus the authority of the church. I would miss his companionship.

I never saw Father Carroll again, but I did receive a letter from him two years later. He was living in a home for retired priests.

I found that soldiers who became dysfunctional or zombie-like from near misses of multiple shells exploding around them recovered quicker if given a day's rest in the environs of the battalion aid station. Food, rest, a shot of whiskey as a tranquilizer, along with encouragement and reassurance, helped most soldiers who had become shell-shocked.

A shell-shocked soldier may be unable to function rationally and purposefully during a firefight, but he often would recover his nerves and ability if kept near his unit, where his buddies could come in to see him. If he was separated far from his unit and put into the medical evacuation chain, he seldom returned, for two reasons: First, he felt guilty about being medically evacuated when he had no bullet holes or shrapnel wounds to show for it. Second, emotional paralysis in a firefight was somehow equated with cowardice, and undermined his self-esteem. In many cases, I am sure soldiers on the verge of becoming emotionally dysfunctional under fire were grateful when a non-fatal bullet wound gave them a more honorable way out of the war.

Soldiers nearing a breaking point did not wish to discuss it with a psychiatrist in the rear area, because it made them feel cowardly. While many soldiers could not bring themselves to prefer death to cowardice, they still despised cowardice, which only reinforced their emotional trauma. If we kept the psychologically traumatized soldier near the aid stations and close to his buddies, most would go back to their units doing their messy war chores again. If the overstressed soldier stayed dysfunctional for more than 72 hours, they usually needed a longer rest and a new assignment.

One of our litter squad leaders ended up in a hospital in Japan for a month as a result of shell shock and emotional trauma. When he returned to the 3rd Division, I received a call from Maj. Jennings MC in the division medical battalion, who explained that the sergeant was on his way back to us, but was fearful he might "lose it" again. The sergeant hated the thought of letting his people down a second time. I asked Maj. Jennings if he could give him a job in Division where he could help train others, and send me a new soldier as a replacement. A switch was made, and it worked out well for all concerned.

There were continuing battles as all of the regiments of the 3rd Infantry Division pushed forward with artillery and tank support. There were numerous engagements with mines laid by the Chinese, making progress hazardous. When the pressure on the Chinese became great, they withdrew farther north at night to a new hilltop or ridgeline positions favorable for defense.

The zigzag trenches the Chinese dug on ridges were vulnerable to napalm drops from Marine Corsairs and from the Navy carrier-based AD dive bombers. The latter single-engine airplanes could carry a huge load of bombs and napalm. When a napalm tank landed in a zigzag trench, the fire would zigzag down the trench, roasting everyone in its path. It was hideous to watch, but effective.

Marine pilots had to be smart and jink (zigzag) into their targets, because a straight-in bomb run could give the Chinese heavy machine gunners time to get the Marine pilot in their sights, with fatal results. A shot by the Chinese toward the side of our planes was less dangerous, because the Chinese were like inexperienced duck hunters—they didn't lead their targets enough.

As I watched the aerial activity over a nearby hill, I was reminded of hunting ducks on Lake of the Woods. As a boy, I would try to lead the first duck by several feet, but still would miss. Then, on one occasion, I aimed ahead of the leading duck again and hit the last duck in a formation of five or six ducks. I learned then how much lead and elevation for bullet drop, as well as adjustment for wind, must be taken into consideration to hit flying objects. It is easier if the bird is coming straight in or going straight away. I suspect the Marine support pilots who had been duck hunters probably invented the jink approach, and they probably had the best survival rate in Korea.

I had the opportunity to learn something about Marine Corsair pilot flying tactics after the war from my brother-in-law Lt. Col. Don McEachern USMC (retired). He had flown in combat in Korea.

Having watched the Corsairs in action around us, it was interesting to hear about his experiences from the cockpit perspective. On one flight, he was set on fire by Chinese gunners but managed to fly his plane upside down far enough south before the fire forced him to bail out. Fortunately, Don was picked up by South Korean soldiers.

Tex Atkinson's book *From the Cockpit: Coming of Age in the Korean War* provides many more details about the life and experiences of these flying warriors.

The awards below indicate the type of involvement of the 3rd Infantry Division Regiments' soldiers in their steady effort to push the enemy out of South Korea.

Award of the Distinguished-Service Cross to 1st Lt. Richard W. Durkee

"First Lieutenant Richard W. Durkee...a member of Company L, 65th Infantry Regiment, 3rd Infantry Division distinguished himself by extraordinary heroism in action against the enemy in the vicinity of Uijongbu, Korea. On 23 March 1951, while attacking well-defended enemy positions on Hill 221, the 1st Platoon of Company L was subjected to intense small-arms fire and pinned down. After ordering the remainder of the platoon to furnish covering fire, Lieutenant Durkee led the 1st Squad in an assault on the enemy entrenchments. When his ammunition was expended, Lieutenant Durkee single-handedly assaulted an enemy position and killed the occupant with his bayonet. Unable to remove his bayonet from the dead soldier, he went unarmed to another hostile position, seized an enemy soldier's rifle by the bayonet and wrested the weapon from his hands and clubbed him to death. Although his hand was seriously lacerated during this action, Lieutenant Durkee continued to lead the assault against the enemy and his men, inspired by the fearlessness of their leader, overwhelmed the hostile troops and secured the objective..."

Award of the Distinguished-Service Cross to Sgt. Woodrow L. Weaver

"Sergeant Woodrow L. Weaver...a member of Company C, 15th Infantry Regiment, 3rd Infantry Division, distinguished himself by extraordinary heroism in action against the enemy near Uijongbu, Korea. On 23 March 1951, Company C had the mission of attacking and seizing Hill 155, located in the vicinity of Uijongbu, Korea. Due to the intensity of enemy fire, the attack faltered and the friendly forces were temporarily halted. Sergeant Weaver, with complete disregard for his personal safety, left his position of cover and advanced alone toward the enemy emplacements. As he approached the hostile positions, intense grenade and rifle fire was directed at him. Pressing forward despite the extreme danger, he tossed grenades into the hostile positions and engaged several of the enemy in hand-to-hand combat, killing them. Sergeant Weaver then continued to move toward the crest of the hill, neutralizing other enemy positions as he advanced. His actions were so inspiring to the remainder of the company that his comrades stormed the hostile positions, overwhelming the enemy troops and securing the objective...."

Award of the Distinguished-Service Cross to 1st Lt. Daniel W. Dotson

"First Lieutenant Daniel W. Dotson...a member of Company C, 15th Infantry Regiment, 3rd Infantry Division, distinguished himself by extraordinary heroism in action against the enemy in the vicinity of Uijongbu, Korea, on 24 March 1951. Lieutenant Dotson's platoon moved with Company C in an assault against a well-entrenched and camouflaged enemy force, which was fiercely defending its position on Hill 337. With his platoon spearheading the attack, Lieutenant Dotson observed one of his squads pinned down by a heavy mortar barrage and intense small-arms fire. Quickly he reorganized them and maneuvered them to within fifty feet of an enemy emplacement. Lieutenant Dotson then led them forward in a bayonet assault and, with utter disregard for his personal safety, jumped into the enemy dugout, bayoneted one of the enemy soldiers and killed the remaining two with a burst of fire from his carbine. Shortly thereafter, Lieutenant Dotson charged another emplacement and moved close enough to throw grenades that killed four of the enemy. Throughout the ensuing action, he fearlessly and aggressively destroyed many enemy strong points to secure the objective...."

Award of the Distinguished-Service Cross to Sgt. J. E. Bales

"Sergeant J. E. Bales...a member of Company C, 15th Infantry Regiment, 3rd Infantry Division, distinguished himself by extraordinary heroism in action against the enemy in the vicinity of Uijongbu, Korea. On 24 March 1951, the 2nd Platoon of Company C was given the mission of attacking and securing a well-defended enemy-held hill near Uijongbu. As the attack commenced, the 2nd Squad, led by Sergeant Bales, moved out as the lead elements of the platoon and after advancing approximately 75 yards across open, fire-swept terrain, encountered the first enemy position. Deploying his squad to furnish covering fire, Sergeant Bales secured eight hand grenades and single-handedly charged the position, hurling grenades into the entrenchment as he approached it. Then, assaulting the position with his rifle, he killed five enemy soldiers and captured two. Although constantly exposed to intense hostile fire, he signaled his squad to advance and then led his men in systematic assaults on the remaining enemy positions. On one occasion, Sergeant Bales boldly advanced within 15 feet of an enemy position and fired a rocket launcher from a point blank range into a fiercely defended dug-out, forcing three enemy troops to surrender. The personal bravery and aggressive leadership of Sergeant Bales resulted in 63 enemy killed and in the complete dispersal of a numerically superior hostile force...."

Award of the Distinguished-Service Cross 1st Lt. Ralph H. Barnes

"First Lieutenant Ralph H. Barnes...(then Second Lieutenant)...a member of Company C, 15th Infantry Regiment, 3rd Infantry Division, distinguished himself by extraordinary heroism in action against the enemy in the vicinity of Uijongbu, Korea on 24 March 1951. Company C, given the mission of securing Hill 337 from a well-entrenched and determined hostile force, was temporarily pinned down by intense enemy small-arms, automatic-weapons, and mortar fire while moving toward the objective. Lieutenant Barnes, leader of the 1st Platoon, realizing the necessity of seizing the objective to alleviate the pressure being exerted on other friendly units, courageously led his men forward in a frontal assault until forced to take cover. Observing that a machine gun emplacement was blocking the platoon's advance, Lieutenant Barnes ordered his men to cover him then fearlessly charged toward the enemy position, but was knocked to the ground by an exploding grenade. Although stunned, he regained his footing and, disregarding the intense enemy fire being concentrated on him, continued his single-handed assault. Hurling hand grenades into the hostile emplacement, he killed the four enemy occupants, permitting his unit to renew their attack and preventing the casualties, which the enemy-manned machine gun undoubtedly would have inflicted. He then led his men in an assault which terminated with the seizure of the objective and resulted in heavy losses to the enemy in both men and equipment...."

Award of the Distinguished-Service Cross to Master Sgt. Ronald E. Callahan

"Master Sergeant Ronald E. Callahan...a platoon sergeant with an infantry company, (Company C, 15th Infantry Regiment) distinguished himself by extraordinary heroism in action against the enemy in the vicinity of Uijongbu, Korea. On 24 March 1951, Sergeant Callahan's platoon was assigned the mission of attacking and securing a group of heavily fortified hill positions from a numerically superior hostile force. As the friendly force advanced, it was subjected to a heavy volume of enemy automatic-weapons fire. Upon reaching a point some seventy-five yards from the hostile emplacements, the enemy fire became so intense that further forward movement was impossible and the friendly troops were forced to seek what cover they could on the bare slope. Realizing that his men faced possible annihilation in their present untenable positions, Sergeant Callahan, without regard for his personal safety, left his position of cover and single-handedly charged toward the key enemy emplacement from which most of the devastating fire originated. Despite the fire being concentrated on him, he steadfastly moved forward, alternately firing his rifle and throwing grenades. Sergeant Callahan's deadly accurate fire was responsible for the destruction of the enemy weapon and his bold assault enabled him to kill two of the hostile soldiers with his bayonet and to capture three. He then signaled his men to move forward and distributing captured enemy grenades among them, he led them in an assault against the remaining enemy positions. Throughout this action, Sergeant Callahan remained where the fighting was heaviest, constantly urging them forward and inspiring them by his personal example of fearlessness until the objective was secured...."

Award of the Distinguished-Service Cross (posthumous) to Pvt. Knots Gilmore

"Private Knots Gilmore...as a member of Company K, 7th Infantry Regiment, 3rd Infantry Division, distinguished himself by extraordinary heroism in action against the enemy in the vicinity of Hill 347, Korea. On 30 March 1951, a numerically superior enemy force launched a fierce attack against the defensive positions held by Private Gilmore's platoon. During the engagement, a grenade thrown by an enemy soldier landed within a few yards of Private Gilmore's emplacement. Realizing that the grenade was a serious threat to the lives of two of his comrades, who were nearby and unaware of the danger, Private Gilmore, with complete disregard for his personal safety, unhesitatingly attempted to seize the grenade and throw it from the position. As he did this, the grenade exploded, mortally wounding him...."

During March, I was getting used to my new job as regimental surgeon, which was good because for the following three months, we would battle the Chinese and North Koreans from Uijongbu to the Iron Triangle and across the Korean Peninsula. In my job, my focus was on the support needs of the three upfront infantry battalions of the 7th Regiment and the attached battalions of Brits, Belgians, French, Filipinos, and Turks. The Medical Company headquarters collecting station was the funnel through which all of the casualties from the three battalion aid stations would be sent for evacuation, either through the clearing stations of the medical battalion of the 3rd Division, or directly to the nearest MASH unit.

Col. Boswell was supportive of my efforts to "lean forward" to help the fighting battalions, but working closely with the battalion aid stations was not a popular idea with some of the MSC officers stationed at Regiment. Many of them preferred the old way of putting as much distance as possible between the regiment and the battalions. I soon realized that I had to both lead and push support forward to the battalions that were most heavily engaged with the enemy. Pushing included ordering some of the MSC officers with ambulances and additional medics to forward locations to provide immediate assistance to embattled battalion aid stations.

My philosophy was that no battalion aid station that we supported should ever wonder where to evacuate their casualties. The regimental Medical Company was put where we were needed and when we were needed, day or night. Some in the regimental Medical Company and in the 3rd Division medical battalion ambulance platoons thought I was nuts for putting them at risk. They were right in thinking I sometimes put them at risk, but they were wrong in thinking I was nuts, because the division surgeon, Lt. Col. Joe Bayne and his successor, Lt. Col. Bill Yuckman, both tried to get the regimental surgeons of the 15th Regiment and the 65th Regiment to adopt the 7th Regiment's method of forward medical support. It was clear that foot-dragging couldn't be cured unless the regimental surgeon himself showed up at every reinforced battalion aid station hot spot. But the battalion medics and the infantry loved the support we provided. I was fortunate to have superb NCOs in the Medical Company who understood what I was trying to do and kept the unit running smoothly, even when I was helping out up forward.

As helicopters became more available, it became easier for me to co-opt one to take me to the hot spots where extra help was needed. Our new medical support tactics required the following:

(1) Close coordination with S-4, Maj. Dick Lee, for approval of selected and trained men from Korean labor forces to serve as litter carriers under medics' supervision on the way back from delivering ammo and other supplies to fighting front-line troops. The medical evacuation training usually took place the day before the action was to happen. Maj. Roland Fraser, the regimental headquarters company commander, was also fully attentive to the needs of the medics.

(2) Attendance by the regimental surgeon to regimental staff meetings conducted by Col. Boswell, especially those with battalion commanders to determine when, where, and which battalions would next be involved in fighting, in order to plan ahead for their medical support.

(3) Dividing the resources of the regimental medical collecting unit into two echelons; one or more forward units, commanded by myself or MSC officers from the regimental Medical Company to support the battalion aid station most heavily engaged with the enemy, and a rear unit, to function near the regimental HQ as the central collecting station.

(4) Assign one MSC officer, usually Lt. Sarka, the tasks of obtaining supplies (including type O blood), and maintaining close contact with the box ambulance units of the division medical battalion, as well as with the Bell-13 helicopters available for evacuations.

(5) Assign another MSC officer and a staff sergeant the task of continual training of litter squads of Korean laborers, supervised by our Korean and American medics.

(6) Assign another officer, usually an Army dental officer, to review medical evacuation cards and make sure records were properly kept. Dentists made good triage officers for new casualties.

(7) Assign the senior MSC captain to substitute for me in regimental staff meetings if I was occupied with medical tasks in the forward echelon. I later discovered that could be a problem. I found one senior MSC captain who couldn't be trusted to not lean toward the rear area when I was not there to stiffen his spine. I came to think of him as Cpt. "Foot Dragger." He was efficient and smiling when I was around, but in my absence, he seemed to find a lot of excuses to attend to some urgent administrative matter in the rear area, especially when fighting was going on up front.

(8) Assign myself the task of keeping the division surgeon aware of what was going on in the 7th Regiment and how we were dealing with current medical requirements. By keeping a running telephone contact with him, he would be more effective and have more clout with other division staff, because he would be better informed about ongoing operations and able to make intelligent contributions to the division commander's staff meetings. Both Lt. Col. Bayne and his replacement, Lt. Col. Yuckman, appreciated being informed. In turn, they were responsive to my needs.

Some civilians moved back to Seoul with its retaking, but there was not much to go back to. Governmental function occurred south of the Han River until some temporary bridges were set up.

Many of the leading South Korean citizens and their families in Seoul had been systematically hunted down and slaughtered by the Communists. Only the poorest were allowed to live and become slaves or Communists through forced reeducation and relocation.

The systematic culling of populations not considered worth saving was a practical matter. In the Communist way of thinking, new populations could always be produced from the compliant masses. Power was kept in the hands of a self-selected central committee, since the masses could not be trusted to make decisions.

The Filipino Battalion was on one of our cross-country trips, and had more troops than expected for each truck. Maj. Dick Lee, our capable S-4, was baffled by the situation. Previously, when I visited the Filipino battalion surgeon, I noticed quite a few Korean women with short haircuts in Army uniforms. These women provided every sort of comfort to the Filipino soldiers.

When I drove by, Maj. Lee asked for my opinion on the matter. I think Dick had already figured out the cause of the overload, but wasn't sure how to remedy it. I suggested he order all the women out of the trucks, and if they didn't offload, he had two choices: (1) have everyone unbutton their shirt and then load on the trucks only the soldiers without breasts, or (2) have everyone drop their pants and load only those with male external parts. I think Dick used option one. Having given my best advice, I continued on about my business. I presume the offloaded women went to a Filipino support unit somewhere in the rear area.

About the same time of year, somewhere around Easter, Lt. Col. Fred Weyand surprised his troops by being baptized into the Christian faith by the division chaplain at a Sunday Protestant service with all of the troops in attendance at the church service. Since the 7th Regiment's three chaplains were two Baptists and one Catholic, Lt. Col. Weyand had discussed his desire for a believer's baptism with the division chaplain, who was a Lutheran. Lutherans generally do not believe that total immersion is essential and, besides that, there wasn't any river nearby that was not cold, muddy, and shallow.

As I watched, I was reminded of Cornelius, the Roman Centurion soldier, who was baptized by Peter. I thought then that it would have been great if the baptismal ceremony had taken place in front of a British Centurion tank. But I doubted anyone would have noted the symbolism, although it would have been a great prop for a sermon based on the book of Acts chapter 10 in the Bible. I was very happy for Col. Weyand.

On 31 March, a special attack unit named Task Force Hawkins, after Lt. Col. Wilson M. Hawkins, CO of the 64th Heavy Tank Battalion, and two platoons each from the 15th and 65th Tank Companies with supporting elements, were organized to clear out pockets of resistance and strong enemy positions up to the Imjin river at the 38th Parallel near Chorwon. While the tankers were busy, I tended to some routine medical work in the collecting station and found time for another letter home.

In the visiting of one of the battalion aid stations, I found that the battalion surgeon, Navy Lt. John E. Currin, had gone forward on a road leading to a rifle company because two casualties had been reported there. I told my driver to follow the road they had just taken, to see if we could be of any help. As we were driving alongside a low hill, we heard several incoming mortar rounds explode just ahead of us. Just around the hill, an ambulance jeep had stopped. Lt. Currin was busy trying to stop the bleeding of a large scalp wound of an infantry soldier that had been standing near the ambulance jeep when the mortar shells landed. Fortunately, most of the mortar wounds were not life-threatening, but they did need care. I observed Lt. Currin attempting to pack Vaseline gauze under the large scalp wound next to the exposed bone of the skull in a vain attempt to stop the bleeding. That was not the place to use Vaseline gauze. I looked at Currin's face and saw a vacant zombie-like stare. He was essentially out on his feet. He seemed to be suffering a blast injury without much evidence of shrapnel injury.

I just talked reassuringly to Dr. Currin and had him lie down on one of the jeep litters. I put the scalp-injury soldier on the other jeep litter and pulled a yard of Vaseline gauze out from under the scalp, checked for evidence of skull injury, and applied a pressure dressing to the scalp to stop the bleeding. When everything seemed stable, the ambulance jeep with the wounded soldier and the shell-shocked Navy doctor headed back to their aid station while I continued on the road in an attempt to reach the casualties that Currin had started out to find before they were bracketed with 82 mm mortar rounds.

We arrived near the backside of a slightly higher hill, near the top of which, our troops were in holes, observing a number of enemy spread out before them. These enemy soldiers were apparently the ones lobbing mortar shells over the hill now in front of us. Unfortunately, the dirt trail had been deeply rutted in a recent rain and our jeep became hung up, with all four wheels spinning in the deep ruts.

I sent the driver up to the nearest bunker to find out where the casualties were located while I tried to find some rocks or logs to put under the jeep wheels. As the driver reached the bunker near the top of the hill, three 82 mm mortar shells landed just over the ridge near them, with about 30 yards or so between each shell explosion. Then, after about 30 seconds, three more shells landed spread out before me. This prompted me to start calculating my options.

At the rate the salvos of shells were moving in my direction, I thought I should stay where I was until the next three rounds landed, probably just short of my position. But if they kept reaching out at the same rate, the following rounds would probably bracket the jeep where I was standing. Since the jeep trail was in a low spot, I decided to wait where I was and, after the explosions, I would dash forward and then lie flat and wait for the following volley to go over me. The next three rounds landed closer, as expected. I then dashed forward, just beyond the line where the last three rounds landed, and hugged the ground. I waited and waited; however, no more shells landed. I had been hugging the muddy ground like a fool for no reason.

I guess the Chinese had used up their quota of shells. If it had been Americans shooting our 81 mm mortars, they would have popped off two or three rounds from each position. But then again, we didn't have to carry our ammunition on our backs.

As I sat up in the mud, I wondered what time it was, so I pulled the old gold pocket watch, which had belonged to Zige's father, from my shirt pocket and tried to flip open the lid to see the watch dial. However, the watch had gotten rather muddy and the top wouldn't flip up. So I wiped my hands and the watch on some grass and then tried to use my fingernail to pop open the cover. Much to my surprise, I popped open the back cover instead of the front and there, inside, I found the word "COMRAD," under which there was the number "85026."

I wondered about the significance of this inscription, but simply closed up the watch and put it back in my pocket as my driver returned, unscratched, with some help, as well as with two walking wounded. With some pushing and shoving, we got the jeep turned around and headed back to the 2nd Battalion Aid Station.

I found that Lt. Currin was still a little foggy in his thinking, but seemed rational and able to talk. He did not have any flesh wounds. Apparently, he had been near some sort of concussion round and was suffering some type of shock injury. I suggested he be written up for a Purple Heart and take a sedative for sleep. We then loaded up the walking wounded and headed back to Regiment with the litter jeep.

Dear Dad and Mother,   31 Mar. 1951

The war goes on with considerable vigor in this sector. The 7th is attacking now and the poor doughboys up front are catching a lot of hell. The collection station was busy most of the day. Fortunately, most of the wounds were not serious and will require only short hospitalizations.

The weather is mild now and that makes things a lot more comfortable. There has been some rain, but not too much. The new job is going well, but it entails a lot more details to worry about than the battalion aid station. I received the box of candy and popcorn and sent one of the bags of popcorn up to Herrick and his crew.

Last letter received was when you were visiting Uncle Ole—glad to hear he is getting along so well.

Love, Bob

After checking with HQ and finding things relatively stable, Sarka and I drove by Division, stopping at the medical battalion to chat, and then drove on to the nearest MASH unit to see how some of our casualties were doing. The soldier with the big scalp injury was all stitched up and resting well.

I wanted to talk with a doctor who knew more than I did about a soldier being functionally impaired but still on his feet after some nearby shells exploded. I didn't gain any special insight on managing such a case, except for the necessity of rest and observation. The thinking then was that if the casualty seemed normal after a night's rest, don't worry about it.

In general, it was best to keep these types of stress injuries in or near their units. If emotional or mental stress injuries were evacuated, there was a danger of them becoming stress/anxiety dependent for avoidance of further combat duty and their residual guilt over this sham might keep them chronically ill for a long time.

Much to my surprise, I found Maj. Dutch busy interviewing some wounded Chinese soldiers in the MASH. We had lunch together and laughed about our "sake-wacky" train trip in Japan.

I then told Dutch the story about Cpt. Laymore, Miss Zige, and the gold watch. He was curious about the inscription in the watch, so I pulled it out of my shirt pocket and opened the back cover. On reading the inscription, Maj. Dutch started to laugh. According to Dutch, it was likely the Miss Zige's father had been a secret member of the Communist party. I thought at the time that this was an "O Henry" type ending to the Miss Zige story.

Casualties were not heavy in our regiment during the first week of April, so there was an opportunity to get in some training of replacements, and to visit other units in our areas. I was always glad for an opportunity to visit the 1st Battalion again, to swap news and humorous stories. I also wanted to make sure there was a continuing training program for civilian Korean laborers before each engagement. It was a never-ending task, because labor companies were always changing. Both sides in the war used Korean civilian laborers near the front line.

On one occasion, I met a Korean laborer who spoke German. He was an older man and appeared tired, so I invited him into our aid station tent for a cup of coffee and some food. He spoke of the recent tragedies in his life and also about early Korean history. I wish my German had been as good as his. It was a cool night, so I gave him an Army blanket as he left to rejoin his labor battalion. He was a cultured and educated gentleman, reduced to heavy manual labor and recurrent battlefield threat to life and limb. I wished I could have given him employment in our collecting station. I wished I could have gotten to know him better. But, as before, my personal wishes lacked command authority. Many people had passed my purview, almost as apparitions, during the war, but my authority to succor or befriend them was painfully limited.

Dear Mother and Dad,   5 April 1951

Received your letter today concerning arrival of linens and PJ's. Was happy that they arrived in good shape so soon. Linen is one of the better buys in Japan. Another good buy is silver.

I would like you, Mother, to see if you could dig out some elementary books somewhere between 7th and 9th grade level which I could use in helping to teach my #1 boy Imm Yung Hee to read English. I also am interested in a very bright young boy, 15 years of age, that some of my ambulance drivers have picked up and keep with them. He is nicknamed Jerry. Jerry is small for his age but a good student and is picking up English well. I am sure his IQ is far above average. In fact, I would like to bring him home and educate him and let him return to help his country out. If America took as much interest in proper education of the youth of a country, we would have less trouble with Communism. As it is, the Russians wisely work the hardest here and we ignore it completely, even in our own country to a great extent.

Most of the Korean youth who have any education speak Japanese fluently, but no Chinese. The writing is quite complicated. The basis for the writing is Chinese characters, so even a Korean who speaks neither Japanese nor Chinese can communicate with either by writing notes if they are reasonably well educated.

I wouldn't send Imm Yung Hee a watch, since it is difficult to keep anything over here. The war has quieted down here somewhat. We are taking defensive positions south of the Imjin River, which is north of Mason and Uijongbu. The last week or so, the 7th has been engaged in relatively heavy fighting with the inevitable flow of casualties. We have crushing air and artillery support. I would hate to think of fighting as the Chinese do with their only superior weapon just being their manpower.

I have received the 2nd of two packages you mailed. The one today contained cookies, dried fruit, etc. Actually, at present our rations here in Korea have been exceptionally good lately.

Tomorrow I am giving a seven-day leave to Imm Yung Hee so he can go home. He hasn't been home since we came to Korea nearly five months ago. He lives in Yangdong, which is a little town between Taejon and Taegu.

I am sending home a picture I had taken while on leave in Tokyo. Col. Weyand had me call his father, who is a petroleum-engineering consultant to MacArthur. Mr. Weyand was extremely nice and took Captain Baker, another officer who went on leave at the same time I did, and my old friend Fred Snyder out for dinner at the SHG officers club, where we wined and dined to our hears content. We had a picture taken at the table.

Time for bed.

Love, Bob

P.S. I have 30 days more to go before I will be eligible for promotion. The ruling is 60 days in the job calling for major in combat before an officer can be promoted from captain to major. But it has to be approved by 8th Army after that, so it may be awhile.

I was not aware on April 5th that the 64th Tank Battalion was about to spring a big trap on a bunch of Chinese. Our observers discovered the enemy positioned in a bend near the Hantan and Imjin River junction. It was a horseshoe-shaped area of rolling country—ideal for tanks. A Company and C Company of the 64th Tank Battalion performed a pincers movement and had a field day crushing the emplacements and dropping grenades in the holes of the Chinese. Our tankers and engineers had to explode mines along the way, but in the end, it was a complete rout of the enemy. It was later said the Chinese learned a lesson that day, and never again put their infantry in such a vulnerable position without effective anti-tank weapons. Forty-eight prisoners were taken. The death toll probably numbered several hundred.

We didn't know at the time that the Belgian Battalion would soon occupy some of that same territory near the junction of the Hantan River and the Imjin River. We also had no idea a huge number of enemy troops and military supplies were being hidden in the Iron Triangle.

While Ridgeway had us attacking north, he also had us preparing a series of secondary defensive positions 20 to 40 miles to the rear, as fall back positions, north of Seoul and the Han River.[14] Ridgeway also knew that in spite of our air attacks, steady streams of Chinese supplies and manpower were flowing in just north of us.

We knew it was only a matter of time before we would be hit again by several hundred thousand Chinese soldiers, coming in waves, assisted by many thousands more in refurbished North Korean units. So as we moved north, all of our units had elements preparing fall back defensive positions for future use. All of the U.N. units were preparing to slaughter masses of attackers, even as the Chinese prepared to overwhelm us with their sheer manpower. We knew what was coming and we talked about it. But in the midst of it all, there was time and a need to let the folks at home know that I was still okay.

Dear Mother and Dad,   *postmarked April 10, 1951*
Another short note. Nothing new to report. We are just digging in and making our tents as comfortable as possible. The weather here has been beautiful recently, cool and clear. We have taken off our winter underwear now and are ready for the expected summer heat and rains. As it is, we are now enjoying a pleasant transition period.

Enclosed are the pictures I had taken on leave in Japan. At that time, I had my mustache trimmed from the large grotesque handle bar it was previously. As you see, I am in good health. Weight 175 lb. I am also sending a small packet of pictures, which are the last of the pictures I had taken in North Korea. I sent most of the black and white pictures to John and I imagine he forwards them on.

---

[14] See the map on the I Corps defense of Seoul from Line Wyoming (never fully established south of Chorwon and Kumhwa) and the Kansas Line (where horrific battles occurred), back to a line north of Uijongbu, (where the Chinese thrust was exhausted), to No Name Line north of Seoul (which was never again reached by the Chinese).

The Army talks about a rotation plan. I have a month to go yet before my six months in Korea are up. However, there are a great many who will be in line before me. However, with the present rotation plan I should be getting home in mid-summer if things continue as is.

Love, Bob

The news that Truman had relieved MacArthur came as a shock to all of us. Many soldiers wrote home to get their friends to raise hell about it. It was difficult to keep fighting when we had so little respect for the pompous political nerds who played at leadership in Washington, D.C. The following letter expressed my initial reaction to MacArthur firing.

Dear Dad and Mother,   11 April 51

The tragic news has been received here about the idiot Truman relieving MacArthur of his command. The morale of the men here has suddenly dropped to zero because of the profound faith everyone here has in MacArthur. Everyone here still believes Mac to be right both in his international political views and for the military.

Of course, Ridgeway is an excellent military strategist, but he knows nothing about politics, which apparently is one reason Truman appointed him. However, Mac was the only thing that stood between the feeble effort of democracy and the flood of Communism here in the Far East. I hope he goes home and lets the country know what really is going on now that he has his hands untied. Many feel Truman should be impeached along with the rest of his crony friends.

The military situation here has reached near a stalemate now and one wonders what is going to happen next. MacArthur said it was a war neither side could win— just a matter of pouring more men and supplies in and using them up.

If I were not in the service, I would write a few letters, but men in the service by law can be sent to jail for expressing sentiments against the government.

Time to hit the sack.

Love, Bob

As I gradually learned more about MacArthur and his palace guard sycophants, I felt Truman was right in relieving him of command. However, Truman was so petty, so prejudiced against the West Point and Annapolis brass, and so worried about political backlash that he was not willing to simply order MacArthur home for face-to-face consultations before taking final action. It should have been managed more politely.

Dear Dad and Mother,   21 April 1951

Received your letters of the 13th today. Have also received package containing canned pineapples, etc. The news magazines are coming through too. Also Time *magazine finally got my address straightened out so I am getting it direct from Japan now. The supply of food and little luxury items is pretty good now. I can think of nothing in particular that we need.*

Enclosed is an example of our regimental paper that we put out when we are in reserve. We had an impressive formation, at which Col. Boswell presented the combat medical badge to all members of the Medical Company who had carried out medical aid work while under direct enemy fire—such being the necessary qualifications to earn the badge. I certainly feel I have earned mine and I know the men of my company have earned theirs.

The back of the paper has an amusing letter which has a sarcastic twinge to it, since elements of it are not uncommon to letters some of the fellows get over here. The newspaper clipping is from Stars and Stripes. *I have often mentioned my former Sgt. Herrick, who became Lt. Herrick. He is still with the 1st Battalion, doing a good job as you can see by the newspaper clipping.*

Everyone here was greatly impressed by the speech of MacArthur before the Senate. The big question is whether we are going to face reality or drift along doing nothing by just trying to antagonize no one. That is the big question of foreign policy. Over here, I scarcely know what to expect now.

There is a strange lull, comparatively speaking, on the front now. This lull is not a good sign.

Love Bob

By the time I wrote that letter, we had reached the Imjin River and pushed across in a few places. We seemed to have a formidable force as we moved north, but the Chinese had only engaged in delaying actions in March and early April, and we knew something big was going to happen soon. It was just too quiet.

The strange lull was indeed the calm before the storm of a major spring offensive by the Chinese—a titanic battle, in which the Chinese hoped to simply overwhelm U.N. forces by the sheer number of their attacking soldiers. Much has been written about that battle.[15] No one knows how many thousands of Chinese were mowed down by our infantry or slaughtered by our artillery, yet they kept

---

[15] See schematic maps on pages 245-247 with military units and successive defense lines.

coming, in wave after wave. If there were Korean civilians nearby, whether men, women, or children, they would be driven in front of the Chinese to stop bullets and explode mines. How great is the insanity of war! Yet history has proven that those who choose not to fight will be consumed.

Once a war starts, there is a continual attrition of the expendable and of the courageous. A leader's most treasured assets are the willing and courageous soldiers in his unit. The loss of two or three good men can damage the effectiveness and cohesion of an entire company of soldiers. I realized that, without thinking about it, I had been giving leadership and responsibility to the brave, willing, and thoughtful leaders, while ignoring those who whined, griped, and complained.

There were no letters written between 21 April and 29 April 1951. I drafted an unpublished account of the action just one year later, in order to explain the operational deployment and function of a regimental Medical Company during actual battles. There were no official records available at the time, and the Korean War cease-fire had not yet occurred. My paper was entitled "Observations and Recommendations on the Employment of the Medical Company of an Infantry Regiment in Combat." It was submitted during the Army Medical Service Officer Advanced Course (8-0-3), Class Nr. 5, at the Medical Field Service School at Fort Sam Houston, Texas. As far as I am aware, my paper received little attention. However, I kept a carbon copy of that paper in a file drawer for 53 years, and pulled it out while writing this book to supplement deeply etched, but now fading, memories of that epic battle.

The general situation previous to the Communist's spring offensive from 22 through 29 April 1951 was as follows: The Chinese winter offensive wore itself down during the months of February and March in 1951. The U.N. forces succeeded in pushing the invaders back north of the 38th Parallel. Operation KILLER, as the counter offensive was called, was very successful, in that the overextended Chinese suffered heavy losses in men and material. But north of the 38th Parallel, the resistance stiffened, and each hill was fought over savagely. There were well-founded reports that the Chinese were preparing to launch another major offensive. The enemy amassed large quantities of supplies, in spite of our Air Force. The so-called Iron Triangle area, formed by Chorwon and Kumhwa, 30 miles north of the 38th Parallel, and Pyonggang, 60 miles to the north, as the top of the triangle, was the scene of the heaviest enemy buildup.[16]

The U.N. troops were arranged as follows: On the far western side of the corridor, north of Soule, was the 1st ROK Division, an excellent fighting force. They prepared defensive positions on the south side of the Imjin River. Next to

---

[16] Refer to map on page 245.

the 1st ROK Division was the 3rd Infantry Division. Situated on their west flank was the attached British Brigade, commanded by Brig. Gen. Tom Brodie, and composed of the Gloucester Rifles, Northumberland Fusiliers, and Royal Ulster Rifles, from west to east, respectively. Attached to the British was the Belgium Battalion, situated on a patrol base north of the Imjin River. Tied in with the Royal Ulster Rifles on the east was the 7th Infantry Regiment, with the 3rd, 1st, and 2nd Battalions from west to east. North and east of the 7th Infantry Regiment was the 65th Infantry Regiment, with its three battalions, plus the Filipino Battalion. The 65th Regiment was tied in on the 3rd Division eastern flank, with the Turkish Brigade, which was attached to the 25th Division, on its right.

The Kansas defense line was planned along the Imjin River, roughly in the vicinity of the 38th Parallel. Because of the width of the area, each regiment may have had three battalions on the line, with no immediate available reserve.

On the twentieth of April, a POW captured in our area said the Chinese were going to launch a major offensive in the full moonlight on the night of the twenty-second. That proved to be accurate G-2 information. The Chinese launched massive attacks along the entire western sector. There were numerous minor penetrations, but the lines held during the night. During the daylight hours on the twenty-third, the Chinese succeeded in driving a wedge between the Royal Ulster Rifles and the 3rd Battalion, 7th Infantry Regiment, which had moved north to reinforce and relieve the 65th Infantry Regiment. That Chinese penetration cut off the Belgian Battalion north of the Imjin and Hantan River junction. The rest of the British Brigade was heavily engaged, and could neither effect relief of the Belgians nor maintain contact with the Gloucester Battalion to the west.

The 65th Regiment withdrew south of the Imjin River. The 3rd Battalion 65th was attached to the 7th Infantry Regiment. The 1st Battalion 7th was given the mission of rescuing the Belgians, who were in a desperate situation by that afternoon. Using a plan devised by Cpt. Fred Long S-3 (now Col. retired), the 1st Battalion 7th (commanded by Lt. Col. Fred Weyand) made a 13-mile end run south around a ridge line, and then north through the British sector, to directly attack a larger Chinese force sitting on the hill south of the looping junction of the Imjin and Hantan Rivers.

From their elevated position, the Chinese were blocking the exit of the Belgian Battalion, but they were forced to cease their attack of the Belgians in order to defend themselves from the determined assault of the 1st Battalion 7th from the south. At the same time, the 7th Regimental tank company, with infantry attached, fought their way to the Belgians from the east by crossing the Hantan and Imjin Rivers in low water areas. After several hours of heavy fighting, the tanks finally broke through, brought out the wounded, and covered the retreat of the remaining Belgian infantrymen. One of the tanks, commanded by George Taylor, straddled and drove directly over a wounded Belgian soldier, causing him a moment of additional terror until the trap door was lowered and he was pulled to safety in the tank, to his great relief.

With the Belgians out of the trap the 1st Battalion 7th returned from the British sector, and the 3rd Battalion 65th was relieved on the line to rejoin its unit several miles to the south, and regrouped as a reserve counterattack force. The 7th Infantry gradually withdrew to positions farther south of the Hantan and Imjin Rivers.

In the early hours on the twenty-fifth, the Chinese launched major assaults and continued daylight attacks all along the line. In spite of staggering enemy losses resulting from aircraft, artillery, and infantry, the Chinese continued their attacks. The number of Chinese bodies on battlefields was beyond belief, yet new Chinese units were thrown into battle to keep the offensive rolling.

In the far west, the 1st ROK Division fell back slowly, fighting for every yard of ground lost. Meanwhile, the British Gloucester Battalion was surrounded and cut off from the rest of the British Brigade, as well as from the ROK 1st Division on their west flank. The Fusiliers and Ulster Rifles had suffered such heavy casualties; they were unable to reform their lines or help the Gloucester Battalion as it withdrew to a hilltop defensive position west of them. It might have been better if the Gloucesters had withdrawn with the 1st ROK Division on their left flank, but that didn't happen—probably because they had no interpreters to effect good coordination. Instead, they would try to hold out on a hilltop, with the many wounded they undoubtedly hoped to bring out with them if they could be rescued from the south or east. But the Chinese armies flowing around their flanks blocked their exit south. The Chinese probably believed that the more U.N. deaths they affected, the sooner the U.N. forces could be induced to withdraw from Korea.

The Gloucester Battalion was besieged on every side. Unfortunately, their eventual designated rescuers were not trained to coordinate with tanks in attacking a fanatical foe. The troops that might have rescued the Gloucesters, the 1st Battalion 7th Infantry, were already committed elsewhere, rescuing the Belgian Battalion. When Gen. Soule belatedly ordered the rescue attempt, he picked the Filipino Battalion and a Battalion of the 65th Regiment. As they began to fight their way to the Gloucester Battalion, the Filipino Battalion received casualties and stopped in their tracks, rather than fighting on through with the tanks blasting the way.

When the Gloucester Battalion was captured, the walking British soldiers were quickly separated from their wounded. The wounded Brits that could not walk were probably executed as soon as those walking were out of sight en route to a prison camp.

About 40 Gloucesters did manage to fight their way through to friendly forces, but some of them were killed by American tanks that misidentified them as Chinese. Our errant tank cannon fire ceased only when one of our light spotter aircrafts swooped over a tank and dropped a hand written note, asking the tanks to please stop killing the few remaining Gloucesters trying to escape from the Chinese. There were some apologetic American tankers when they finally reached the remaining Brits and gave them a lift back to the rest of the British Brigade.

It was unfortunate that the spotter plane could communicate with the artillery people but not with our tankers, who could not communicate with our infantry or with the medics without making special adjustments. Because of poor communications, very unfriendly friendly-fire accidents were inevitable. In retrospect, when flanks are cut off, it's time for a planned orderly fighting retreat, to survive and fight another day, rather than defend a hilltop with dwindling hope of rescue.

Some of the British Centurion tanks operating in the area found themselves covered with Chinese soldiers, making it necessary for the tanks to sweep each other with machine gun fire in order to remove the swarming Chinese soldiers. One isolated report said that a Centurion tank crashed through a house in order to scrape the Chinese off of the top. I do not know if that story is true or not, but it was being widely circulated.

Other Centurion tanks protected the west flank of the 1st Battalion 7th as they fought to spring the Belgian Battalion. According to the 1st Battalion 7th S-3, their protecting Centurion tank cover withdrew at tea time to join up with the rest of the British forces moving south, leaving the 1st Battalion 7th battling the Chinese alone until the Belgian Battalion crossed the Imjin and Hantan Rivers, with the fording assistance of a 7th Regiment tank platoon.

Unfortunately, Col. Weyand was not immediately notified when the Belgians were safely out of the trap. Later, I wondered whether Weyand's 1st Battalion 7th, with all of their available tanks, might also have rescued the Gloucesters if he had been directed to that task immediately after the Belgians were freed. However, Weyand's warriors had been in a vicious fight most of the day. To send them on another tank/infantry task force battle to rescue the Gloucesters would have been stretching them thin, but I think they would have made it, because the bulk of the Chinese were, by that time, south of the Gloucesters and a passage to them from the northeast was relatively open.

I now personally feel, aided by all of the hindsight intuition that I can muster, that the responsibility for the loss of the Gloucesters rests partly with the stiff upper lip propensity of the British leadership to not call for help sooner. But the major failure was on the part of Maj. General Soule of the 3rd Infantry Division for not keeping close enough tabs on the swirling battles engulfing not only his own 7th, 15th, and 65th Regiments, but also the attached units of British, Belgians, Filipinos, and Turks. Certainly the existing inadequate military communication systems of 1951 were a major part of the problem. In fact, Brigadier Brody, the commander of the British Brigade, should have been kicking in Gen. Soule's tent flap, demanding that a special task force be set up immediately, in which his Centurion tanks and a survivors unit made up from the Northumberland Fusaliers could have taken part. As far as I know, this was never suggested or considered by Gen. Soule. To belatedly send the Filipinos, with unfamiliar tank support from the southeast, as an attacking spearhead to rescue the Gloucesters was a decision doomed to failure.

But the only reasonably open path to rescue the Gloucesters, at that moment, was from the northeast. That would have required combing the British Centurion tanks with a platoon of the heavy tanks of the 64th, as well as trucks following, for infantry, wounded, and close air support. If Lt. Col. Weyand of the 1st Battalion 7th had been put in charge of that task force immediately after the Belgians had escaped across the Hantan River, it might have worked. It would have made for an interesting war game to play out in the Army war college.

During the swirling April 1951 battle in the eastern portion of the 7th Infantry Regiment sector, the U.N. forces were also very hard-pressed. The 2nd Battalion 7th was overrun in the early morning hours of the twenty-fifth. The battalion surgeon's assistant, Lt. Dudyk, and about half the 2nd Medical Platoon, were missing. I made a quick trip north with two litter jeeps to a point south of the Hantan River, to establish a temporary collecting station for the 2nd Battalion 7th and to look for wounded stragglers from all battalions. After the Belgians started coming out, we returned to our main collecting station near the fork in the road where Route 11 branched off to the east.

Our temporary north collecting station unit was withdrawn, bringing casualties south as the 1st Battalion 7th followed the 3rd Battalion 7th out of the hills and down the MLR. The Turkish Battalion, a little farther east, was hard-hit and scattered. The 35th Regimental HQ and collecting station was overrun, and stragglers from their units drifted into our overworked collecting stations.

By mid-afternoon on 25 April, the 3rd Battalion 7th had lost all contact with the Royal Ulster Rifles and was being outflanked by the Chinese from the west. Evacuation was then impossible, except through the 1st Battalion 7th that had moved back east after the breakout of the Belgians.

The following is an after-action interview with 1st Lt. Harley F. Mooney, then commander of Able Company, 1st Battalion of the 7th Regiment of the 3rd Infantry Division on 7 September 1951. Defense by Platoon and Rearguard Action—the date of the action discussed was 25 April 1951. With the permission of Brig. Gen.

Harly Mooney the after action report of 1st Lt. Mooney below is as transcribed, except for minor editing.

"The April Offensive by the Chinese began on the night of 22 April 1951. On the twenty-third the 1st Battalion 7th Infantry was ordered to attack to relieve a Belgian Battalion which was in difficulty. Since an estimated three enemy battalions were opposing this move, Cpt. Fred L. Long, S-3 of 1st Battalion 7th Infantry, suggested that the battalion attack toward the north against the larger enemy force, which would draw away some of the pressure against the Belgians to allow them to slide off toward the right, and pull back through the positions of the 65th Infantry. This was done and finished on the evening and night of the twenty-third.

"On the morning of the twenty-forth, the 1st Battalion was ordered to effect the relief of the 3rd Battalion 65th Infantry on Line Kansas. This was accomplished by 1600 hours that day.

"On the line that night, Able Company 7th held a ridgeline approximately 1400 yards long and, in addition to this, there was a gap of about 700 yards across a low saddle that linked the left flank position, with a lower hill just behind the right flank position of Item Company 7th Infantry which was on the left flank of Able Co. To cover this gap, Lt. Mooney put a ten-man squad, under Sgt. 1st Class Thomas, on this hill as an outpost, with instructions to make physical contact with Item Co each half hour and Item would make contact the other direction each hour. There was a sharp bluff between the two positions, but the gap was not more than 75 yards.

"On the night of 24 April, both Item Co and Baker Co, 7th Infantry, which was on Able's right flank, were heavily engaged from shortly before midnight until soon after first light, when the enemy withdrew. More than 600 counted bodies were in front of Baker Co the morning of 24 April. [2nd Lt. MSC Bill Herrick on inspecting this battle scene looking for wounded to rescue called the place 'Ray Blandin's slaughterhouse.']

"On the twenty-forth, at 1600, Mooney moved onto the hill, after three and a half hour walk and climb, and took up the positions dug by L Co, 65th Infantry, which Able Co was relieving. Mooney had such a wide front that he committed all three platoons on the line, leaving him only his command post (CP) group, a force of eight men, including Mooney, his executive, and his weapons reserve. On the left of the line was his 1st Platoon, under Master Sgt. Joseph H. Lock, and from this platoon, Mooney took his second in command and nine other men to outpost the small hill to the front of this platoon. In the center was the 2nd Platoon, under 2nd Lt. Jonas A. McCall. The 3rd platoon was on the right flank tied in physically with Baker Co. This platoon was under 2nd Lt. Paul R. Kennedy, a former Air Force enlisted man and a recent ROTC graduate, newly arrived in the theatre, who was not acquainted with infantry tactics.

"The 4th platoon, weapons, was under 2nd Lt. John N. Middlemas, and he had his mortars located at the limiting point between the 2nd and 3rd Platoons and just about 15 yards behind the Co CP. As soon as he was in place, Mooney had Middlemas go to each platoon to concentrate fire. He kept the mortars close, since he could then draw on the men there for support, if necessary.

"During the night of the twenty-forth, there was no activity, although the men could hear the heavy firing on both sides and the men were alert and expecting action in their sectors.

"About 0700 on the morning of 25 April, a large enemy force attacked an outpost (OP) that CO 3rd Battalion 7th Infantry had on the left flank of Lock's platoon. Lock reported this to Mooney and said he could see the OP group leaving and, soon after, several men from this group came up to Lock's position. To help them get out, Lock gave them some machine gun (MG) fire and fire from a .57 recoilless rifle (RR) to help them get down. This placed a large enemy force on an extension of the hill Mooney occupied, although on a lower hill, and directly behind the 3rd Battalion.

"While the 3rd Battalion OP group was leaving, Cpt. Fred Long, the 1st Battalion S-3, called Mooney and told him, 'You and Baker Company are to cover the withdrawal of the 3rd Battalion and to be prepared to move out Able Company at 1000.'

"He explained that they would move to new positions. He told Mooney that he had told this to Cpt. Ray Blandin, the Baker Co commander. Able Co was to take the rearguard for the move.

"After receiving this message, Mooney and his executive officer, 1st Lt. Leonard Haley, walked over to see Blandin and worked out the coordination with him. Mooney also wanted to find out what damage Blandin had suffered during the night. The plan at that time was for the 3rd Battalion to pull back through Able Co, then Baker Co would follow the 3rd Battalion, and Able Co would go last. The three companies of the 3rd Battalion were on line, and these three companies had to pull out through Able Co, since this was the only easily accessible route by which these companies could move out and take their wounded with them.

"For some reason, which Mooney does not know, and for which he does not blame Cpt. Blandin, with whom he has always worked well, Baker Company started moving out soon after 1000. The first Mooney knew of this was when Haley called him to say that Blandin was moving out. Haley had talked with Blandin, who told Haley that he had been ordered to move out. At this time, Mooney still figured that he could expect his trouble to come against his left flank, and was hoping that he could keep Lock's platoon in place. He told Haley to take a few men and put them on a small knob, just on what had been Baker Co's left flank as an outpost, and to have Kennedy refuel their flank. Haley and Middlemas personally supervised this.

"At 1100, the activity began to build up again. The forward observer (FO), meanwhile, had gone out to Teti's position, where he believed he could observe the enemy, which Teti had reported 'cold trailing' the 3rd Battalion. Mooney felt that he had gotten himself out of position by moving over to the left end of his flank and that his FO was also out of position. The second company from the 3rd Battalion was just about through the position, but moving very slowly. Mooney got the executive of that company on the telephone as he came past Teti's position and asked him to hurry up his company. The executive explained that he needed some more litters and that his men were tired. Mooney furnished the litters to him and told him he'd 'better hurry or all of us will be up here and damn tired.'

"Meanwhile, Baker Company had reached the bottom of the trail and had met Lt. Col. Fred C. Weyand. He ordered Blandin to immediately get one platoon back up on the hill to help Mooney hold his right flank. Blandin sent back a platoon under 2nd Lt. Eugene C. May and 1st Lt. Fred Ferris, the executive of Baker who accompanied the platoon up the hill. This platoon reached the top of the hill again about 1130 and was going into position on the right of the 3rd platoon to protect the right of the 3rd platoon and also to protect the trail. The last company from the 3rd Battalion was moving through the area and is about halfway through. About the same time, Mooney had realized that his FO was out of position and called to tell him to get back up on the top of the hill, where Mooney was staying with the 1st Platoon.

"The activity along the company front suddenly fell off to a quietness; the fire on the left flank subsided for a short while. Mooney called Middlemas to tell him that everything was quiet and asked him what was going on where he was.

"'It is so quiet here I'm just about ready to read some adventure stories for excitement,' said Middlemas.

"Just then, there was the sound of scattered fire against the outpost on the right flank, where Sgt. 1st Class Joseph T. Dotty had about four men placed after Baker had pulled back.

"Suddenly, Dotty came running back down hill toward the 3rd Platoon, yelling in a voice loud enough to be heard at the company CP, 'They're coming! They're coming! Millions of them! They'll banzai us!'

"Middlemas heard this and immediately took off running toward that flank. Dotty was on Hill 283 at the time. This was about 100 yards away from the right flank position. Middlemas caught Dotty at a small knoll just beyond the 3rd Platoon right flank and physically tackled him, stopping him. The four other men with him were following 'just as goslings follow along after a mother goose.'

"Middlemas told him to 'get the hell back on your position.' Middlemas yelled for Master Sgt. Dixon, platoon sergeant of the 3rd Platoon, to send up one squad, then Middlemas took off running and chasing the outpost back on the knoll, trying to get there before the Chinese did. These men just made it first, since there was one Chinese within 50 yards of the knoll when Middlemas and his men reached the knoll between Hill 283 and the right flank of the 3rd Platoon. They shot this Chinese with a rifle. Eight more men of the 3rd Platoon followed immediately and built up a base of fire. Almost immediately, 1st Lt. Robert Burt, platoon leader of the weapons from Dog Co, realized that trouble was coming toward this position and shifted his heavy machine gun (HMG) from the 3rd Platoon position to the same knoll, where it could fire down against the enemy force. Within ten minutes after Dotty had come running down from Hill 283, Middlemas had organized a heavy base of fire and the HMG was up on the knoll with 22 boxes of ammo. This action developed very fast.

"At the left end of the line, the FO was moving back toward Lock's platoon and was almost there when he was hit in the leg by small arms fire. Mooney heard this and then, in another minute or two, heard the sudden burst of fire on the far end of his line. He took off to investigate and see what was happening (since there was no activity of consequence on the left flank) and found the trail clogged with men from the 3rd Battalion who had squatted on the trail as soon as the first firing commenced. No one was moving.

"Mooney kept telling them to get moving, found the platoon leader of the 2nd Platoon down in a hole and said, 'Get out of the damn hole now and keep these men moving.'

"He also met Haley on the way back, who was starting up the trail toward Middlemas' action. Mooney told him to strip all of the ammo from the men from the 3rd Battalion as they went through. (The day before, Able Co had brought up 300 extra bandoliers, in addition to the basic load and these 300 bandoliers were still intact when this action commenced.) Haley got the command post (CP) group out and had them carry the ammo up.

"The Chinese worked up within grenade range soon after the firing commenced on this knoll. The very heavy volume of fire soon drove them back beyond the next knoll between them and Middlemas' knoll, a distance of 70 or 80 yards away.

"Meanwhile, Dotty had recovered his composure and had organized the men and went along assuring the men, 'We're holding them, by God. We're holding them.'

"Middlemas kept walking along the line, telling the men to hold down their rate of fire, watch where they were firing, and to fire aimed shots and make them count. Ferris moved his platoon from Baker Co up on this knoll almost at once, so that within a very few minutes, there were approximately 30 men from this platoon, eight men from the 3rd Platoon of Able Co, and the original five-man outpost. It was the sudden and very heavy base of fire that was built up during the first ten minutes of this firefight that saved the flank, according to Mooney. This drove the Chinese back and never let them get close again during the 40 minutes during which this fight lasted. Mooney had cautioned Middlemas that he would have to make the ammo last until everyone got out and had told him to hold down the rate of fire. This action commenced immediately by Middlemas.

"While Mooney and Haley were over making these plans with Baker Co, Middlemas had moved a 57 mm RR over to fire upon the OP hill the 3rd Battalion had just left, to ease the pressure on the group that had been run from that hill, and Lock had his MG firing at the Chinese on the hill. The machine gunner, Cpl. Pedro Colon Rodriquez, had zeroed his light machine gun (LMG) in on a trail the Chinese had to follow and as one appeared, he would click off one or two rounds from a range of approximately 300 yards. When the Chinese went to get the wounded man, Rodriquez would fire again and hit another. Then he would let the Chinese go out and get one wounded man, or two, then hit the next few. He kept giving them a few as encouragement, but during that morning, about four to four and a half hours, Rodriquez hit 59 Chinese. He was never greedy about this; he just played it cagey.

"Meanwhile, Mooney had returned from Baker Co, and he and Haley had made the plan for the movement of Able Co and when it was to commence. To keep his line solid throughout the move, Mooney decided to peel off his line from the left. The outpost with Teti would follow the last element from the 3rd Battalion and as he passed through the 1st Platoon, this platoon would then move through the 2nd Platoon. Then the 2nd Platoon would move through the 3rd Platoon, which would stay until the rest of the company was on the trail down the hill, then take the rear of the company. Mooney went to each of his platoon leaders and explained the move, stressing that they had to move out in that order to keep a blocking unit in place.

"From 0800 to 0900, the action on the left flank increased from the hill vacated by the 3rd Battalion OP group. Mooney, accordingly, believed that the next action would be against his 1st Platoon and went over to that end of his line, to be in a position to watch this situation develop. And, by this time, no part of the 3rd Battalion had yet come through his positions. Mooney did not know the situation with the 3rd Battalion and was anxious to find out, knowing that the Battalion CO had lost control of it when he left his OP. Mooney called Teti and asked him to grab the first officer who came through his outpost and ask him to call Mooney and advise him of the situation. During this time, there were increasing amounts of enemy rifle and MG fire from the OP hill on the left and, at the same time, Teti reported to Mooney that he could observe enemy activity over in the zone of the 3rd Battalion. Mooney employed his mortars against this position.

"It was about 0915 when the first men from the 3rd Battalion, these from K Co, came through Mooney's area. These men were following the narrow trail, moving slowly, and it took 45 minutes for this company to clear Mooney's positions. These men were tired from the night and day before, and sat down when they got a chance to rest. Mooney urged them to hurry up and when he could, contacted the officers with them and asked them to hurry the movement up.

"Realizing that he would be in no position to move out at 1000, just before that time, Mooney had Haley call the Battalion S-3 to get a confirmation of his orders to stay in position until the remainder of the 3rd Battalion and Baker Co were out. Battalion S-3, Cpt. Fred Long, said that was correct.

"Haley kept working along the line from the 3rd Battalion and got those men to move on. Then, according to the original plan, Teti followed the last elements of the 3rd Battalion and went back to join the 1st Platoon. When this was done, Mooney ordered the 1st Platoon to start down.

"Just about that time, as the last elements of the 3rd Battalion started down the trail, Mooney called Lt. Col. Weyand to tell him of the situation and that his FO was hit and that he desperately needed artillery (Arty) fire. Mooney told Weyand that he wanted this Arty on the hill formerly held that morning by Baker Co. Weyand wanted to know if Mooney had any troops on 283, but Mooney didn't know.

"'I don't know what hill I'm on, but I'm with the forward elements of the company and no one is beyond. Put a round out somewhere and maybe I can hear it.'

"The colonel, who, fortunately, had been all over the terrain and knew it well, put out one round—asked if Mooney could hear it, but he couldn't. The colonel then gave the order for the Arty to 'drop 100, right 200.' This round fell right on the Chinese and the men from Able Co could hear them scream. This round landed just behind the position the Chinese were trying to reach and they evidently had troops down there. At the time, Mooney wasn't sure if this screaming was to signal another Chinese attack or not, but when the troops heard it, they immediately took it up and they began yelling all along the line—a regular rebel yell. This yelling, together with the Arty fire, apparently affected the Chinese fire, because it dropped off noticeably right then.

"Mooney yelled over the radio, 'That's beautiful, that's beautiful. Keep it up and walk it around out there.'

"More shells then landed in battery volleys. By this time, Haley informed Mooney that Lock was moving his platoon. The colonel had the Arty continue and fire approximately 150 rounds in the area, all with excellent effect and, throughout the firing, Mooney and his men could hear the Chinese screaming.

"Meanwhile, Mooney had revised his plan for moving his company out. The 1st and 2nd Platoons were moving out and they were not affected, but Mooney ordered the remainder of his force, which now had become a mixture of the 3rd Platoon, his headquarters group, and the platoon from Baker Co, to move out, one man at a time, strictly peeling off right to left. This would keep men along the trail to protect that, and would take away those least needed by that order.

"The machine gun had fired up the 26 boxes of MG ammunition (26 X 250), so Mooney sent that section out. The other two platoons moved through and down the trail, then the last of the company started down, one man at a time, as planned. Meanwhile, the battalion had sent in a flight of planes and these had been circling overhead for a few minutes. Col. Weyand had told Mooney that he would call them in on his order. Mooney couldn't use them yet because the enemy was too close and he would have to lift the Arty to use the planes and the Arty was too effective at the time.

"As the last group moved out, the Baker Co Platoon would be placed at the rear. The entire situation was getting pretty tight as time was running out and Col. Weyand had urged Mooney several times to move out as soon as he could. Finally, just about the time the first of the squads from the 3rd Platoon (it was about 1200 now) started moving out, Weyand again called Mooney and told him to hurry since the supply of Arty ammo was about gone and he'd have to move fast. Mooney told him that his last platoon was beginning to move, and asked for smoke to screen the movement of those men as they started to break contact. The Arty, with a mixture of smoke, replaced the rifle fire and Mooney's last group peeled off, Indian fashion.

"That movement was very rapid—not more than five minutes elapsed from the time that the first men from that group started off until the last man was on the trail. The entire action on the right flank had lasted not more than 45 minutes.

"There were four machine guns firing in the right flank section—two .30 caliber HMGs from Dog Co, which had been moved from the 2nd and 3rd Platoon positions just as soon as the firing there commenced. Then the 3rd Platoon had its LMG, and the Baker Co brought its LMG up again. The two heavies were sent back when they ran out of ammunition after firing 26 boxes. The two LMGs were taken out when the rest of the men left.

"The first 150 yards of the trail were subject to long-range small arms fire. As the men went down that trail, Middlemas and Mooney were fourth and fifth from the end of the column on the way out. As the last man got 75 yards down the trail, one single mortar round landed on the trail just in front of them. The round fell at the feet of one man, who was killed by the burst; both Mooney and Middlemas were injured, Mooney in both legs and Middlemas in the leg, also. Right after that, a few rounds of small arms fire came from the top of the hill, where a few men at the tail of the column moved down, firing back at the Chinese.

"Four men were wounded seriously enough that they had to be carried down and, in addition, there was the one KIA whose body had to be carried out. Down the hill about 50 yards, Cpl. John P. Kierwan heard that Mooney had been hit and went back up to get him, bringing up several other men to help carry out the other wounded and the KIA. In addition to those five, there was Middlemas, who got down by himself. Then there were the FO and two killed by small arms fire during the action on the right flank."

When Herrick was asked in the Aid Station how A company was doing, he replied, "As long as Loony Moony is standing, Able Company will keep fighting. Mooney and Middlemas are two of the best soldiers in this Army."

The following are some of the awards given to outstanding soldiers involved.

Award of the Medal of Honor (posthumous) to Cpl. John Essebagger, Jr.

"Corporal John Essebagger, Jr., Company A, 7th Infantry Regiment...distinguished himself by conspicuous gallantry and outstanding courage above and beyond the call of duty in action against the enemy near Popsu-dong, Korea, on 25 April 1951. Committed to affect a delaying action to cover the 3rd Battalions withdrawal through Company A, Corporal Essebagger, a member of one of two squads maintaining defensive positions in key terrain and defending the company's right flank, had participated in repulsing numerous attacks. In a frenzied banzai charge, the numerically superior enemy seriously threatened the security of the planned route of withdrawal and isolation of the small force. Badly shaken, the grossly outnumbered detachment started to fall back and Corporal Essebagger, realizing the impending danger, voluntarily remained to provide security for the withdrawal. Gallantly maintaining a one-man stand, Corporal Essebagger raked the menacing hordes with crippling fire. With the foe closing on the position, he left the comparative safety of his shelter and advanced in the face of overwhelming odds, firing his weapon and hurling grenades to disconcert the enemy and afford time for displacement of friendly elements to more tenable positions. Scorning the withering fire and bursting shells, Corporal Essebagger continued to move forward, inflicting destruction upon the fanatical foe until he was mortally wounded. Corporal Essebagger's intrepid action and supreme sacrifice exacted a heavy toll in enemy dead and wounded, stemmed the onslaught, and enabled the retiring squads to reach safety. His valorous conduct and devotion to duty reflect lasting glory on himself and are in keeping with the noblest traditions of the Infantry and the United States Army."

Award of the Medal of Honor (posthumous) to Cpl. Clair Goodblood

"Corporal Clair Goodblood, Company D, 7th Infantry Regiment...distinguished himself by conspicuous gallantry and intrepidity at the risk of his life above and beyond the call of duty in action against an armed enemy of the United Nations near Popsu-dong, Korea, on 24 and 25 April 1951. Corporal Goodblood, a machine gunner, was attached to Company B in defensive positions on thickly wooded key terrain under attack by a perimeter, rendering the friendly positions untenable. Upon order to move back, Corporal Goodblood voluntarily remained to cover the withdrawal and, constantly vulnerable to heavy fire, inflicted withering destruction on the assaulting force. Seeing a grenade lobbed at his position, he shoved his assistant to the ground and, flinging himself upon the soldier, attempted to shield him. Despite his valorous act, both men were wounded. Rejecting aid for himself, he ordered the ammunition bearer to evacuate the injured man for medical treatment. He fearlessly maintained his one-man defensive, sweeping the onrushing assailants with fire until an enemy banzai charge carried the hill and silenced his gun. When friendly elements regained the commanding ground, Corporal Goodblood's body was found lying beside his gun and approximately 100 hostile dead lay in the wake of his field of fire. Through his unflinching courage and willing self-sacrifice, the onslaught was retarded, thereby enabling his unit to withdraw, regroup, and re-secure the strong point. Corporal Goodblood's inspirational conduct and devotion to duty reflect lasting glory on himself and are in keeping with the noble traditions of the military service."

Award of the Distinguished-Service Cross to Cpt. John T. Monaghan

"Captain John T. Monaghan...Commanding Officer, Company E, 7th Infantry Regiment, 3d Infantry Division, distinguished himself by extraordinary heroism in action against the enemy in the vicinity of Taepon-ni, Korea. On 24 April 1951, Cpt. Monaghan's company, occupying defensive positions, was suddenly attacked and encircled by an overwhelming enemy force. Despite the heavy volume of fire pouring into the area, Cpt. Monaghan constantly moved about the perimeter, encouraging his men and supplementing their fire with his own weapon. When an enemy machine gun began to fire at the position from a distance no greater than 40 yards, he single-handedly rushed the emplacement in the face of intense fire and destroyed it with grenade and rifle fire. Given permission to move his men at his own discretion, Cpt. Monaghan then ordered all platoons to prepare to withdraw and, keeping complete control of the unit, led them to safety through the surrounding enemy's lines. The inspiring leadership and outstanding courage displayed by Cpt. Monaghan in this action reflect great credit on himself...."

Award of the Distinguished-Service Cross to 1st Lt. John N. Middlemas

"First Lieutenant John N. Middlemas...a member of Company A, 7th Infantry Regiment, 3d Infantry Division, distinguished himself by extraordinary heroism in action against the enemy in the vicinity of Tosong-ni, Korea on 25 April 1951. On that date, the defensive positions of Company A were attacked by a fiercely determined and numerically superior hostile force. The positions were successfully defended, but Lieutenant Middlemas realized that the overwhelming numbers of the enemy would soon make the position untenable. Cognizant of the fact that the hostile troops were preparing for another assault, he unhesitatingly rushed across 150 yards of exposed terrains in an effort to secure reinforcements for his hard-pressed men. As he returned with the friendly troops, he was hit and knocked down by the enemy fire. Undaunted, he arose and led the reinforcements to the friendly positions where he stationed them. When the enemy attack came, heavy casualties were inflicted among the hostile troops. Upon receiving the order to withdraw, Lieutenant Middlemas began to fall back to the friendly lines but observed a wounded soldier too weak to walk. Despite his own wounds, he helped the stricken man back to the friendly position...."

Award of the Distinguished-Service Cross to 1st Lt. Charles A. Fitzgerald

"First Lieutenant Charles A. Fitzgerald...a member of Company L, 7th Infantry Regiment, 3d Infantry Division, distinguished himself by extraordinary heroism in action against the enemy in the vicinity of Tongmang'ni, Korea. On 25 April 1951, Company L's positions were attacked and overrun by an overwhelmingly large enemy force. Realizing the seriousness of the situation, Lieutenant Fitzgerald voluntarily exposed himself to the heavy volume of enemy fire in order to shout encouragement to the small group of men around him. Quickly organizing the men into rifle squads, he deployed them in a skirmish line and then personally led them in a counterattack against the hostile elements, successfully recapturing vital equipment, which had been left behind when the positions were overrun. Throughout this entire action, Lieutenant Fitzgerald remained in an exposed position, effectively directing the fire of his men. When the company was finally ordered to withdraw to new defensive positions, Lieutenant Fitzgerald personally assured himself that the wounded and dead were evacuated...."

The account by Lt. Mooney was only a part of the massive attack of the Chinese along the I Corps front on the twenty-fourth and twenty-fifth of April, 1951. Major assaults continued in daylight all along the line. The plan of the

Chinese generals was to overwhelm the U.N. forces by sheer numbers of combatants and to insert Chinese forces over the top of and between defending units to try to overwhelm the U.N. infantry and supporting artillery units. In the far west, the 1ˢᵗ ROK fell back slowly, fighting for every yard of ground. The ROK unit did not panic, cut, or run, as the Chinese had expected, but there was no way the 1ˢᵗ ROK could remain tied in with the Gloucesters on their right after they withdrew to defend a hilltop position. It was an audacious Chinese plan, but it failed to destroy any U.N. battalion other than the heroic Gloucesters, who defended their hilltop position to the end. In spite of staggering losses, the Chinese attacks continued for the next 48 hours, as our artillery, defending infantry, and air strikes drained the life-blood out of thousands of Chinese attackers.

The action was not without loss to ourselves. The 2ⁿᵈ Battalion 7ᵗʰ was overrun, but not without a fight, as the Medal of Honor citation for Cpl. Hiroshi H. Miyamura bears witness. Despite his severe wounds, Cpl. Miyamura made the journey to a POW camp, survived to the end of the war, and was repatriated. The U.S. Army withheld news of his Medal of Honor until he had returned home. Miyamura's citation is given below.

Award of the Medal of Honor to Cpl. Hiroshi H. Miyamura

"Corporal Miyamura, a member of Company H, distinguished himself by conspicuous gallantry and intrepidity above and beyond the call of duty in action against the enemy. On the night of 24 April, Company H was occupying a defensive position when the enemy fanatically attacked threatening to overrun the position. Cpl. Miyamura, a machine gun squad leader, aware of the imminent danger to his men, unhesitatingly jumped from his shelter wielding his bayonet in close hand-to-hand combat, killing approximately ten of the enemy. Returning to his position, he administered first aid to the wounded and directed their evacuation. As another savage assault hit the line, he manned his machine gun and delivered withering fire until his ammunition was expended. He ordered the squad to withdraw while he stayed behind to render the gun inoperable. He then bayoneted his way through infiltrated enemy soldiers to a second gun emplacement and assisted in its operation. When the intensity of the attack necessitated the withdrawal of the company, Cpl. Miyamura ordered his men to fall back while he remained to cover their movement. He killed more than 50 of the enemy before his ammunition was depleted and he was severely wounded. He maintained his magnificent stand despite his painful wounds, continuing to repel the attack until his position was overrun. When last seen, he was fighting ferociously against an overwhelming number of enemy soldiers. Cpl. Miyamura's indomitable heroism and consummate devotion to duty reflect the utmost glory on himself and uphold the illustrious traditions of the military service."

The 2nd Battalion 7th eventually regrouped farther south and was defending the east side of the MLR near our collecting station. The 7th Regiment HQ was farther south. Late in the afternoon of the twenty-fifth, the regiment moved south, bringing all casualties and equipment, and after several delaying skirmishes, followed the remainder of the British Brigade and the 65th Infantry Regiment, to set up a new defense line a few miles north of Uijongbu. On the twenty-sixth, the 7th Regiment moved south of Uijongbu, and the next day moved into the defense line north of Seoul.

That defense line around Seoul was never broken or even tested. We expected them to make another assault on Seoul, but it did not occur. Instead, the Chinese shifted the weight of their attack to the eastern sector of the peninsula.

During this time, the Medical Company of the 7th Infantry Regiment was fairly well up to strength. Of the authorized 199 enlisted men and 13 officers, we had 163 American enlisted men, 35 KATUSA soldiers, and about 20 semi-permanently attached civilian Koreans, who served as extra litter bearers and general laborers. The Medical Company was short one MC and one MSC at the start of the engagement.

When the Chinese attack started on the 22nd, the service elements of the regiment, including the medical administrative officer, with all administrative and supply elements of the Medical Company, were moved to the training area about ten miles to the rear, leaving only the tactical collecting unit forward. That unit consisted of one squad tent, all the litter squad section, litter jeeps, collecting station personnel, and an ample quantity of medical supplies. A three-quarter truck and a two and a half ton truck were kept with the tactical collecting unit for transportation and hauling jobs. Each of the battalion medical platoons was stripped of any excess gear and relocated to the battalion supply trains in the rear.

The evacuation of the forward 7th Regimental aid station just south of the Hantan River was carried out by the ambulance company of the division medical battalion. One platoon of box ambulances was in support of each regiment. To effectively control the ambulances, the ambulance platoon leader stayed with the collecting station most of the time when the action was the heaviest. On special occasion, box ambulances and even the Medical Company two and a half ton truck were sent forward to help the overworked litter jeeps evacuate casualties. With the warning of an imminent attack, an MSC officer was sent to the rear to retrieve lockers of 25 or 30 bottles of whole blood and other supplies we might need.

Throughout the night of the twenty-second and morning of the twenty-third, casualties were light. But in the afternoon of the twenty-third, the 1st Battalion was suddenly removed from the line and sent into the British sector. The

Route 11 road junction into the British sector was near our collecting station, and the nearest 3rd Division medical clearing platoon was only five miles south on the main road, Route 33. I decided to attach extra litter bearers, three litter jeeps, and three box ambulances to the 1st Battalion, and evacuate straight to the clearing station. A few bottles of whole blood were given to the battalion surgeon, Cpt. Barnes, for the special mission to help extract the Belgian Battalion.

In the meantime, casualties came into our collecting station from the 3rd Battalion 7th, from the 2nd and 3rd Battalions of the 65th Regiment, and from the Filipino Battalion. The 65th Regiment, with the attached Filipino Battalion, had been in exposed positions north of the Hantan River crossing, in the broad area between the Imjin River and the Hantan River where they flowed north. I had no idea where the collecting station of the 65th Regiment was located. I assumed they were south of us, along Route 33.

Sometime in the morning of the twenty-fourth, with the assistance of the 7th Regimental tank company, the Belgians crossed the Imjin and Hantan Rivers while the Chinese guns on Hill 257 were diverted by the attack of the 1st Battalion 7th from the south. When Weyand was informed that the Belgians were out of the trap, the 1st Battalion 7th returned south to the junction with Route 11, and then north to cover the withdrawal of the 3rd Battalion 7th.[17]

In anticipation of further retrograde movement, a new location for the collecting station was picked a few miles south of the junction of Route 11 and Route 33. But we didn't move until later. Our current location by the fork in the road was crucial, although it became increasingly exposed.

Early in the mornings on the twenty-fourth and twenty-fifth, the heaviest Chinese attacks were launched. The 2nd Battalion 7th was overrun. The MSC officer and about half the 2nd medical platoon were reported missing. The MSC in charge of the litter squads at collecting was sent to the 2nd Battalion to help the battalion surgeon, Navy Lt. Currin. The 2nd Battalion was regrouped to defend the east side of the MLR. Throughout the day, stragglers and groups of men from the 2nd Battalion fought their way through to friendly territory. By nightfall, nearly three-fourths of the 2nd Battalion was back in action. A tank task force was sent on a probing attack into the area the Chinese had overrun and rescued the battalion surgeon's assistant and several medics with wounded who were hiding in the hills. Two litter jeep drivers in the 2nd Battalion area were lost in a Chinese grenade ambush.

---

[17] More details on the crucial role of the 7th Regimental tank company in this operation can be found in an excellent article by Col. George O. Taylor, Jr. (retired). "Fighting Retreat from the Imjin River" in the Spring 2004 *Military History Quarterly*.

By mid-afternoon on the twenty-fifth, the 3rd Battalion 7th was outflanked from the north and west, and all routes of evacuation were cut off except through the 1st Battalion. Because of the situation, the litter squads from the 3rd Battalion 7th were sent into the 1st Battalion 7th area and the battalion surgeon's assistants from the 1st and 3rd Battalions operated with the rifle company commanders. With a seesaw battle, only very close medical support could prevent casualties from being left behind in a withdrawal.

The influx of casualties to the collecting station was overwhelming. It was impossible to do anything other than to tie on a tag with name, rank, date, time, and type of injury. The casualties were unloaded onto a field in front of the collecting station by the scores. Our efforts as medics with such a mass of casualties was to triage for visible bleeding, check the pulse, and blood pressure. Those with more serious injuries or signs of shock requiring circulatory support were placed closer to the aid station, where I.V. solutions were started and bleeders clamped. Lt. Jitters was proficient at starting I.V.s and once again, we fixed bayonets on rifles and used them to hold the bottles.

In spite of the tension, and his own fear, Lt. Jitters worked steadily to meet the needs of the wounded. He gave his best to his patients. I thought he should have received a Bronze Star, for, in spite of his high level of anxiety, he worked hour after hour on dozens of patients, and that enabled me to tend to emergent command chores.

We attempted to call for helicopters, but were told none were available because the MASH units were preparing to move farther south. The lack of helicopters was a serious problem. I called the division surgeon, Lt. Col. Bayne, who was aware of the hospital "bug-out" decision made by the Army surgeon, and he was mad as hell about it. We ended up sending a great many severely wounded soldiers overland to Kimpo Airport, which was across the Han River, west of Seoul. I have no idea how many survived the journey.

By late afternoon, there was a general withdrawal, and Route 33 heading south was a solid mass of vehicles and men. Returning ambulances found it nearly impossible to travel north again against the two-lane southbound traffic, forcing some of them off the roads and into the fields. Fortunately, it was fairly dry. As I looked at the flat fields south of us, I wondered why no one had thought to build a 3000-foot airstrip there.

During that time the remains of the British Brigade withdrew, their ambulances and vehicles filled with dead, wounded, and dying soldiers. In an attempt to salvage as many lives as possible and to maximize the use of southbound medical transportation, the British casualties were unloaded, checked, given blood, plasma, or albumin in saline to maintain blood volume, and bandages as needed, before they were reloaded and instructed to head for Kimpo. A separate British lorry was commandeered for the dead. It was overloaded with bodies from the British Brigade. A British Army doctor turned up during that hectic period and gave valuable assistance in our collecting station. He and his aid men pitched in and did a great job. I wish I could remember his name. As I looked around, I thought it was like D-day in reverse.

In the midst of the controlled chaos at the collecting station, who showed up but the 3rd Division Surgeon, Joe Bayne. He immediately pitched in, checking casualties and preparing them as best as we could for the rough ride to Kimpo. We didn't talk about the absent helicopters, but I think we were both churning inside as we tended patients we knew had little chance of making it overland. Bayne worked until dark and then left in his jeep. Our paths never crossed again. I couldn't help but think that if Joe Bayne had been Army Surgeon, the MASH Hospital would have remained at Uijongbu, the Evacuation Hospital would have gone to Kimpo, and the Navy Hospital Ship would have been kept busy with helicopters flying between us.

The furious rate of casualties was exceeded only by the mounting tension we all felt, since Chinese were known to have infiltrated the immediate area. Small arms fire could be heard a few hundred yards to the east, where they had broken through our forces. Our artillery had backed up and was being protected by soldiers from the 2nd Battalion and the 35th Regiment. With spotter plane assistance, the artillery had a field day slaughtering Chinese caught in the open. Occasional puffs of smoke from enemy mortar shells were visible in nearby fields to the east of us, and our squad tent gained new holes in the roof, so we took it down.

A couple of heavy tanks with 90 mm guns from the 64th Tank Battalion of the 3rd Division rolled up to protect our eastern flank. One of the tanks fired a round about 50 yards from our squad tent and I was practically deaf from the noise. One of our sergeants ran to the tank and demanded they move farther away before the medics and all our casualties became deaf. Not only that, but the tank might attract countering fire; not an issue for those with inches of steel around them, but we had only our field jackets for protection. The heavy tanks crunched farther to the northeast, where we could still hear them blasting away.

After the majority of the British had been evacuated, we continued to receive a steady flow of casualties from our own battalions, as well as stragglers from the Turks, the 35th Regiment, and neighboring units.

Late in the afternoon, the order to withdraw was finally received by the 7th Infantry Regiment. The 3rd Battalion withdrew through the 1st Battalion to the MSR, but the point where the casualties from the 1st and 3rd Battalions were brought to the MSR was seriously threatened by Chinese infantry. There was a race between our infantry, withdrawing from the hills, and the Chinese, attempting to cut them off from the road. Under the protecting guns of the tanks from the regimental tank company, all the litter jeeps of the Medical Company, two box ambulances, as well as the two and a half ton truck were able to evacuate all the wounded brought down from the hills. The tankers had a field day of shooting as they kept the Chinese from preventing our withdrawal down the road.

The regimental executive officer designated another area about five miles south where a delaying stand would be made, and a portion of our collecting station was sent to the area in the three-quarter ton truck to set up another collecting station, as the old station was cleared out. All litter jeep and ambulance drivers were directed to the new collecting point. The rest of the collecting station joined the medical platoon of the 1st Battalion 7th as it withdrew south.

The Chinese tried desperately to outflank the rear of our retreating column, but were decimated by our artillery and tanks. About 1,000 yards east of the MSR, I saw the Chinese coming toward us from what had been the British sector. The division M-16 and M-19 AAA provided excellent protection and prevented them from closing in.

When we reached the new area of defense, we found the collecting unit, sent south earlier, was set up with the 2nd Battalion 7th aid station and in operation, although casualties were light at the time. As regimental surgeon, I received staff briefing from the ambulance platoon leaders concerning the status of the clearing company and evacuation problems. The 1st Battalion MSC reported their three-quarter ton truck had a broken axle, and had to be towed to its current position. I sent the three-quarter ton truck from our collecting company to replace it. It was of the utmost importance that nothing hamper the mobility of the battalion aid stations. Our mechanics got to work scrounging parts from wrecked vehicles along the road to repair the broken three-quarter ton truck.

The regimental commander, Col. Boswell, stopped by and gave the order to continue moving south to a newly designated area just north of Uijongbu. As darkness closed in, the regiment dug new positions and prepared to defend the area for the night. The Chinese were unable to move as fast as our mechanized troops and our exhausted men were able to get a little rest.

The job of cleaning equipment, replenishing medical supplies, and servicing our vehicles was completed on the twenty-sixth. By the night of 27 April, we had withdrawn again—to a defense line just north of Seoul. During the retrograde movement on those days, the Chinese were never able to exert much pressure, and casualties were light.

Confusion is a salient feature of any hard fought, rapidly moving battle, and the dangers inherent in confusion are much greater in a retrograde movement. It was mandatory that I maintain intimate contact with the regimental commander and also with our own 7th battalions and attached infantry battalions. This could not be done by relying on messages from litter jeep drivers, telephone, or the personal reconnaissance of the litter section leader of the collecting platoon. Throughout the engagement, I felt compelled to make personal trips to all the battalions to exert my command authority to effect maximum medical support. Casualties had to be stabilized, tagged, and prepared to travel on the first available transportation, which might be on any truck going south.

As regimental surgeon, I was expected to plan and direct the medical support of the regiment, and this fact was understood by all concerned, making it possible to achieve the best cooperation not only from all members of the regimental staff, but also from the battalion commanders' staffs and from the tankers that provided periodic fire protection. I was fortunate to have a regimental commander who gave me freedom of action and excellent backing. As long as Col. Boswell knew the wounded were being retrieved, treated, and evacuated rapidly, he was free to tend to the fighting needs of the regiment. I was occasionally asked for information about the status of different casualties, but I was never chewed out by Col. Boswell. I took that as a compliment, since others were upbraided. But there were times when a compliment would have brightened my day.

Col. Boswell reminded me of my father, who expected people to do their job and doing an expected good job never seemed to earn a compliment. I was used to just getting on with the work, but I tried to compliment others for jobs well done. But I should have said thanks more often, because some died without receiving even a pat on the back.

The unique relationship I had with Boswell didn't seem to be repeated in some of the other regiments, where regimental surgeons served as figureheads far from enemy lines. It was little wonder some inadequacies in front line medical support were reported from other units.

The key factor that made a successful fighting withdrawal possible without leaving wounded men behind, was that our MSC officers, our medic sergeants and our Korean litter squads functioned closely behind the rifle companies. The MSC had with him albumin or plasma, as well as saline I.V. solutions and extra medical supplies, carried on a pack board by one of our loyal Koreans. The all-around close medical support not only saved lives, but also was a tremendous morale booster for the infantrymen. Each aid station by then had become equipped with tow SCR 300 radios, one with the battalion surgeon and one with the MSC officer in his forward position. In the regimental Medical Company, 1st Sgt. Andrew Koschak and Master Sgt. Clifford May kept the Medical Company administration functioning smoothly and they kept me informed so I could do other needed tasks.

The use of whole blood in the collecting station and aid stations was limited to cases so severe that more than plasma or albumin with saline was required. Although some of the blood we received was outdated, we used it if it wasn't too hemolyzed. The blood was procured from the clearing stations and carried in cool wooden reefer boxes, which held about 25 to 30 bottles. A few bottles at a time were sent forward to the battalion aid stations as needed. I rarely left my base without some blood and I.V. kits.

Occasionally, mild chill reactions were noted after transfusing blood. The reactions could have been treated if we had been provided with a preparation of antihistamine for I.V. use. But the Army only gave us oral antihistamines, which were of no use to a man in shock. Cross matching the blood, of course, was impossible. Only type O blood was used.

The clearing platoons from the division medical battalion that supported us did a magnificent job, and by leapfrogging their teams, managed to move back and still evacuate us.

The support from the MASH and evacuation hospital was another matter. The 8055 MASH was located at Uijongbu, which was about 25 miles south of our collecting station and the 121st Evacuation Hospital was in Seoul, about 20 miles south of Uijongbu. When the retreat started on the 25 April, these two hospitals moved south, but instead of stopping a reasonable distance behind the line, they were sent to Suwon and Chonan, which were 35 and 65 miles south of Seoul, respectively. It was impossible for our casualties to reach them. The result was that hundreds of serious casualties were unloaded at the Kimpo Air Strip. Those that lived were flown to Japan for surgical treatment that should have been given by MASH and evacuation hospitals in Seoul.

Although the hospital ship Consolation was in Inchon Harbor, just 15 miles from Seoul, I was later told by the Naval medical officers that they received very few casualties from the Chinese spring offensive. The Army surgeon told them they were no longer needed, since the Army could handle its own casualties. It's little wonder a number of medical officers working with divisions felt bitter toward the individuals at Army level that were responsible for such errors in judgment.

There are statistics that show remarkable survival rates of battle casualties in hospitals in Korea. I wonder what the statistics would look like if we added in all those who died between the collecting stations and the hospitals. Rough roads can be fatal to severely wounded soldiers.

When we reached the Seoul defense line, the 7th Infantry was placed in reserve, and I had time to write a long overdue letter home.

Dear Mother and Dad,   29 April '51
Undoubtedly you have been worried about the news of late. The 7th Infantry certainly saw its share of the Chinese tidal wave, but I am proud to say we earned the name "the fighting 7th." Incidentally, the RCT stands for Regimental Combat Team

which means the 7ᵗʰ Infantry RCT is a complete fighting unit with its own artillery, tanks, air liaisons, etc.

The Chinese hit our lines in waves on the night of the 23ʳᵈ and kept coming night and day for three days. The 1ˢᵗ Battalion had them piled up like cordwood in front of their position. One could look down the hillsides for miles and see nothing but Chinese bodies. One company in the 1ˢᵗ Battalion counted 350 bodies around them after the first night attack.

The 2ⁿᵈ Battalion of the 7ᵗʰ didn't do so well and got overrun by the Chinese. However, most of the men in the second fought their way back in groups and got reorganized and have done well since. The 3ʳᵈ Battalion did as well as the 1ˢᵗ. I had a tremendous job with casualties. The first day, I must have evacuated 250 wounded. The British and Belgians were on our left flanks and were hit extremely hard. They put up a whale of a fight but suffered heavily. I evacuated about 150 British through my collecting station one day. I don't know for sure, but I think the British and Belgians suffered from 20% to 40% casualties.

We pulled back under cover of tanks and are now in reserve near Seoul. Where we go from here, I don't know. However, the morale is high and the men feel they can whip the Chinese anytime.

One of my officers, Lt. Paul Dudyk, was missing with eight of my aid men, but they all worked their way back through the enemy lines, with the exception of three aid men. I am afraid they don't have much chance. I am very proud of my Medical Company. They are a wonderful, courageous bunch of men and have the praise of the entire regiment for their outstanding work.

Herrick and the gang at the 1ˢᵗ Battalion are all ok. Things look pretty well organized now, so don't worry. The Chinese pay a tremendous price in human life for every yard.

Love, Bob

The following day, someone brought around a box of Mothers' Day greetings cards with the Cottonbalers emblem of the 7ᵗʰ Infantry Regiment on it. So I sent a brief note home.

Dear Mother,   April 30, 1951
A little card from the 7ᵗʰ Infantry. All is well here. I hope to be home sometime this summer on rotation.
Love Bob

It had been sunny for a day or two, but then it turned cool and started to rain. We moved farther south over the next two days, looking for shelter from the rain. We found a scattering of buildings that had probably been a school in the pre-war days, when children could go to school in South Korea. I picked a big room at the end of a long building to use as the new regimental collecting station and office for the Medical Company.

Everyone else seemed to disappear after we moved our aid station materials in from the rain. I wondered where everyone had gone, but I was tired. I just wanted to stretch out on the floor, take off my boots, write a letter home, and go to sleep in some dry clothes. I assumed everyone else was doing the same and were giving me some space. So I wrote the following letter.

Dear Dad and Mother,   *May 2, 1951*

Things take a long time in the Army but my decoration, Silver Star medal, was finally ordered for my work in North Korea. The order states the specific occasion for which it was awarded.

I am sending home a few of the newspapers, the Front Line *printed by the 3rd Division and the* Cottonbalers *by the 7th Infantry Regiment. They give a little account of this unit's action by citing little instances here and there.*

At present, we are in reserve just west of Seoul. All is quiet at the front now. The Chinese offensive has stopped. Perhaps they are awaiting the rainy season. I received the package with the two books for Jerry. I sent Jerry, one of the orphan boys, back to the supply train where he would be safe when the big push started. Of course Imm Yung Hee (my number one boy) stayed with me at all times. I don't think he even thinks about getting scared.

Actually, the Chinese suffered such losses I think all immediate danger is over. The weather is warm. I was out sun bathing today.

Love, Bob

After writing the letter, I strolled outside in the rain to try to figure out where everyone else had gone. I could hear noise and laughter, but saw no one. I soon discovered why I had been abandoned. The school buildings contained many ladies of the night, and everyone else seemed to have found something else to do, and someone to do it with, when they came in out of the rain.

Forward collecting station near Uijongbu; April 30, 1950

"Weary doughfeet from Company L, 7th Infantry took a break on Hill 717 after having captured the place twice in three days." (*The History of the 3rd Infantry Division*)

"Pvt. Ricardo Lopez, Cpl. Raymond Zimmerman, and Cpl. Charles L. Brown were the only unwounded survivors of the 2nd Squad, 2nd Platoon, and three banzai counterattacks." (*The History of the 3rd Infantry Division*)

"A wounded Cotton Baler was lifted gently to a stretcher for the long trip down the hill." (*The History of the 3rd Infantry Division*)

"Walking wounded and the unhurt stopped for a breather." (*The History of the 3rd Infantry Division*)

The 187th Airborne's first pay jump north of Uijongbu to link up with the 7th Infantry Regiment on their way to the Iron Triangle; 23 March 1951

Marine corsairs, our helpful friends

The 7th Infantry Regiment Headquarters; note the logs around the squad tent for protection from mortar rounds; South Korea

Cpt. Jennings (left) and Cpt. Jensen (right) at Regiment

A rugged hill being fought over

Two soldiers standing next to a sign that was probably their own handiwork;
Chorwon

White phosphorous shell exploding in background on hill being fought over

Bull Adams (sitting front) with two KATUSA soldiers (standing on right)
training Korean laborers to be litter bearers

Korean laborers learning to make a blanket stretcher

Mountains in the Iron Triangle area

Cpt. Jensen with a mustache during R&R in Japan after the Chinese were
pushed back north

Frank D. Grothe after Chinese
Offensive; April 1951

Frank D. Grothe with wire team,
note the empty C-ration box on
the ground

Bloody Snow

Chinese prisoners being
questioned by I&R

Wounded Chinese soldier

The 7ᵗʰ Infantry Headquarters; near the 38th Parallel

Chapter Twelve
Che Cha Ja finds a new father for one night
May 3, 1951 – May 4, 1951

As the 1ˢᵗ Battalion surgeon, and later as the regimental surgeon of the U.S. 7ᵗʰ Infantry Regiment, my primary task was to preserve the fighting strength of our armed forces and to minimize the carnage of war. In my spare time, I found myself providing medical aid to the battered civilian population that managed to survive the ebb and flow of battles. But after six months of war in both North and South Korea, I had become numbed by the sight of hundreds of dead, dying, and mangled American, Korean, Chinese, British, Belgium, Turk, and Filipino casualties. The sight of uncounted and unlamented piles of slaughtered refugee civilians scattered along roadsides added to the visual and olfactory horror. In winter, the stench was muted by the freezing weather. In summer, the triad of rotting flesh, night soil on fields and in concrete 'honey' tanks near houses, and garlic-laden food added to the aroma of our un-bathed bodies and filthy clothes. In the end, we smelled nothing at all.

For me, the worst sight was the hundreds of slaughtered Korean civilians, especially the children, who grotesquely draped hilly battlefields where they had fallen among the Chinese and North Korean soldiers, who had driven them mercilessly ahead in battles to absorb the bullets, shells, and mines of the defending U.N. forces.

When I set up the small aid station in a room at the end of the rambling school building, I was surprised to find the sex business going full steam. Soldiers occupied every room in the building and the prostitutes moved from one battle-weary soldier to the next, providing sexual release in exchange for money or military commodities. As I observed all this, a soldier passed by, pulling a small girl along with him.

I stopped him and asked, "Are you planning to have sex with that child?"

For a moment, the soldier hesitated, and then said sheepishly, "She was the only girl left, and I didn't want to have sex with the other bigger girls when they'd already had a dozen or more soldiers in one night."

"So," I said, "You thought you would just rape an unde -aged child? How would you like it if some soldier did that to your little sister?"

He dropped the little girl's hand and walked away, leaving her standing there before me, wet, shivering, and frightened. Her name, I found out later, was Che Cha Ja. According to Imm Yung Hee, Che Cha Ja could still remember her eighth birthday in late 1950. She lived with her father, mother, 14-year-old brother, and 12-year-old sister in their farm home near Sibyon.

Sibyon is located in the central part of Korea, two days walk north of the border between North and South Korea, west of Pyonggang, which was the apex of the Iron Triangle. In that area, China's third and forth great offensives savaged, but failed to eliminate, the U.N. forces. Che Cha Ja was one of the survivors.

Her family members were Christians, but for as long as she could remember, they had been careful to not reveal their faith, because Christians were considered enemies of the people in North Korea. The churches had been closed by the government. Her father and mother tried to maintain themselves on their small farm and not cause problems for the authorities. They feigned loyalty to the Communist government to survive.

In the spring of 1950, there were increased military activities near their home. Her father and brother were called to provide labor, transporting supplies south. They knew war was coming, but dared not speak about it openly. To be suspected of disloyalty in North Korea could result in death.

When the war began, the early victories of the North Korean armies brought official jubilation in the cities, but after the Inchon invasion and the recapture of Seoul by the Americans, life became extremely difficult for them. Che Cha Ja's father managed to return home from the labor unit in the confusion of the retreat of the North Korean Army. But her brother had become separated. Her father tried to find out what had happened to her brother, but without success. Che Cha Ja never saw her brother again.

The retreating North Korean soldiers took her family's meager supply of rice and vegetables, as well as their cow and pigs. They used their house and animal shelters to hide from enemy airplanes. Che Cha Ja's parents dug a cave in a hillside near their farm for shelter. Her mother tried to make her sister appear younger and ugly so the soldiers would not use her. But they were unsuccessful. Che Cha Ja remembered her mother and father crying as they tried to comfort her older sister.

As the South Korean and American armies pushed north, they passed through Sibyon. After some hesitation, her father and mother went out in a field near a big rock and dug up a box containing their most prized possession, a Korean Bible.

They had hidden the Bible, knowing it would be seized and burned, and they might be punished.

Feeling secure behind the advancing Americans and South Korean armies, her father gathered several neighbors who had been Christians before 1945. They opened up a storage-shed building and held their first church service in five years. It was a joyful time.

But the celebration was short-lived. When the Chinese armies entered the war in October 1950, the U.N. forces were driven south again. Her parents decided to flee to the south, because they had revealed their Christian convictions and welcomed the American and South Korean Armies as they came north. They were in great danger from the advancing Communist armies of China and North Korea. In every city and village, there were people who would testify against Korean Christians who opened up their churches and celebrated their new freedom.

A great migration of North Korean civilians took place spontaneously from every city and village liberated by the American and South Korean Armies. Che Cha Ja started south with her parents, but the roads were so jammed with military vehicles they decided to walk overland with other refugees. It wasn't easy. When her sister became ill and couldn't walk any farther, her father sent Che Cha Ja on with some relatives. They agreed to meet at a Christian Church in Wonju in South Korea. Che Cha Ja never saw her mother, father, or sister again.

Wherever one looked in central Korea, there were North Korean refugees, men, women, and children, with their meager possessions carried on their heads or on A-frames on their backs, struggling to stay up with retreating American and South Korean forces. Many were killed and wounded in their effort to flee south or east to the ports of Hungnam or Wonsan. Others were turned into expendable assault forces, to carry supplies and to run ahead of the Chinese in battles. Che Cha Ja and her relatives were overtaken by the Chinese and North Korean military forces before they could reach the U.N. forces near Wonju.

But by January 1951, Seoul was again captured by the Communists. The Chinese offensive was finally stopped at a line between Pyongtaek and Wonju. Slowly and methodically, the Chinese forces were pushed back across the Han River, Seoul was retaken again, and the U.N. forces advanced across the 38th Parallel and into the Iron Triangle.

The social support services provided for civilians caught up in the battlefield were non-existent. Men of military age were usually conscripted directly into the South Korean Army. Many boys below the age of military service became mascots and were carried along with the American forces. Korean girls caught in the ebb and flow of battles often established themselves in the business of prostitution south of the battle line, where they bartered their bodies for food and shelter.

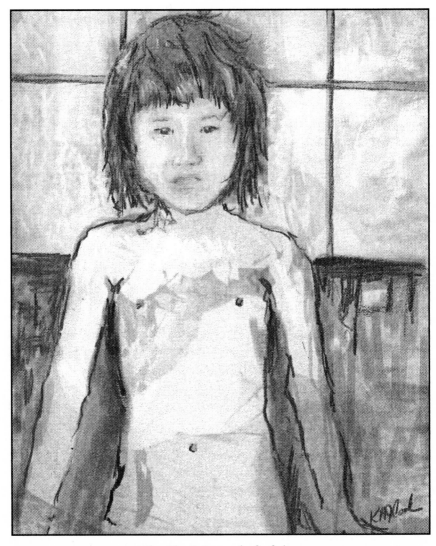

Che Cha Ja in need of a father.
(drawing courtesy of K.A.J. Cook)

In the aftermath of one of the many Iron Triangle battles, Che Cha Ja emerged from hiding in the rubble of war to find herself alone on the American side of the battle line. An older Korean girl, working as a prostitute, unofficially adopted Che Cha Ja as her washing girl, in exchange for food and clothes. In due time, she would be expected to provide sexual services.

I took her into my temporary aid station room, where I gave her a blanket. I lit a candle, and set it on a medical chest. I spread out an Army blanket for her on the floor on the far side of the room by a window that still had a few unbroken panes of glass, and another for myself near the door, and searched my pack for dry clothes and some food ration cans. I paused, looking outside at the falling rain. The dirty panes seemed etched with distorted faces crying raindrop tears.

As lightning flashed, I turned to see Che Cha Ja standing naked and submissive before me, eyes filled with tears. It broke my heart. I pulled out a dry tee shirt from my pack and helped her put it on. The shirt came down to her ankles.

I wrapped the blanket around her, opened two ration cans of stew, and handed one to her. She swallowed in gulps, as people do when they are very hungry. I patted the floor beside me and she sat down. I gave her a gentle hug and wiped away her tears as I cast about for some way to relieve her anxiety and fear over what might happen next.

I pulled out a pistol bullet to draw stick figures of a man and a woman on the wall. I joined the stick figures with a line and then drew two stick figures of two boys under the figures of the man and the women. I then pointed at the man and said "father," and to the women and said "mother." I pointed to the first boy and said, "Brother John." I pointed to the second figure and said "Bob," pointing to myself. She seemed to understand immediately.

I pointed to her and handed her the bullet. She drew stick figures of her mother, father, brother, sister, and herself before crossing them all out, leaving only her own figure. She pointed to the remaining stick figure, and then to herself, and started to cry.

I redrew the stick figure of her father, and pointed to myself. I told her I would be her father for that night. She didn't understand my words. Again, I pointed to the stick figure of her father and then to myself. I then pulled her close to me and fashioned a pillow for her head from clothes in my pack, gave her a drink from my canteen, wiped the tears from her face, and kissed her on the forehead. She looked up at me, smiled for the first time, and slowly relaxed and fell asleep in my arms.

I slept fitfully that night, because I knew the 7th Infantry would be reorganizing in the morning and probably back on the line fighting within 48 hours. What would I do with Che Cha Ja? I couldn't take an eight-year-old girl with me into combat. We already had three orphan boys with our unit. I could cut her hair short and dress her like a boy, but she would soon be discovered.

I needed to round up my medical NCOs early in the morning and not ask where or how they slept. The men who managed to get out of the rain in the old school building were lucky, as far as the weather was concerned. It remained to be seen how many of them would come down with gonorrhea, syphilis, or chancroid. I expected to see a minor rush in the sick call clinic in the morning. There would be many requests for no-sweat morning-after antibiotics.

By first light, the Medical Company NCOs were putting up a squad tent, had two stoves heating water for coffee and drying clothes. I located Imm Yung Hee and told him to talk to Che Cha Ja to get her family history and protect her until I could arrange transport to the rear area for her. I hoped to get her to a nurse in a MASH hospital who would look after her until some orphan's home could be found. I felt so helpless.

I reported to the regimental CP and found out a stripped down regimental combat team was being formed to occupy an outpost in front of the 25th Infantry Division on our left flank. We would be the first to meet the Chinese if they continued to advance on Seoul. The outpost unit would consist of the non-wounded survivors from the 1st and 3rd Battalions of the 7th Regiment, with added support from regimental artillery, tanks, mortars, and medical units.

The regimental commander, Col. Boswell, assumed, as did I, that I would head up the medical unit in this new regimental task force. The survivors from the 2nd Battalion would be supplied with replacements and equipment in regimental reserve. The regimental Medical Company would be divided with half, including Lt. Jitters, going into the reserve position, and the other half joining me in the regimental task force. We would be leaving in three hours to occupy the blocking position to the north to prevent the Chinese from launching a new offensive before our forces could be regrouped and re-supplied. We were expected to buy time.

I rushed back to divide up the Medical Company as ordered. After deciding who and what equipment would go into the regimental task force and who and what would go to the rear area reserve, I hurried back to the temporary aid station in the school building and found Imm Yung Hee.

"What happened to the little girl?" I shouted.

"Trucks from 3rd Division with MPs come and pick up all girls. The little girl, Che Cha Ja, they take her. I tell them you want to help, but they not listen. One MP say you should not use little girl like Che Cha Ja. They all laugh and say she too young for girlfriend. Che Cha Ja cry. She say you father. Nobody listen. I talk to Che Cha Ja about family. She thinks all dead. I tell Che Cha Ja you good man. You no call us gook. But MP no listen me. MP say bad to use little girl. MP take Che Cha Ja away. She cry for you as truck take women away."

I felt devastated and helpless. I was also angry to be suspected of molestation of a child.

I just prayed that the Lord would be Che Cha Ja's father and look after her. I had wanted so desperately to save her and protect her from harm. But it was not within my power to do so. I never found out what happened to her. Today, whenever I see raindrop faces on a dirty window, I think of Che Cha Ja.

When the 7th Infantry Regimental task force pushed off into no man's land to occupy the strategic blocking position in front of the 25th Infantry Division, the Chinese Army unexpectedly pulled back. I guess they were licking their wounds, just as we were. For five days, there was no fighting or casualties. We thought we'd be going on a suicide mission to buy time for our forces to regroup. Instead, we were given five days of unexpected rest in an outpost position in front of the MLR. I thanked the Lord for the rest, but wept because I could only be a father to Che Cha Ja for one night.

Chapter Thirteen
From I Corps to X Corps, 3rd Division rushes east to disrupt, stop, and repel a major Chinese breakthrough into Central South Korea
May 5, 1951 – May 30, 1951

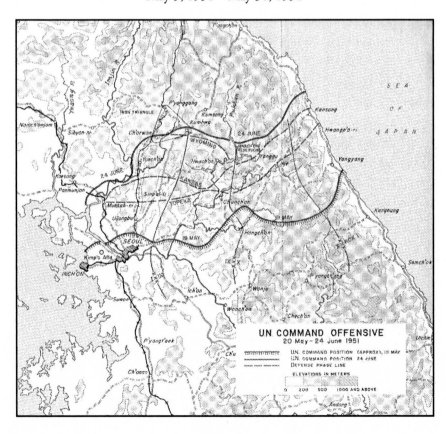

U.N. COMMAND OFFENSIVE
20 May - 24 June 1951

U.N. COMMAND POSITION (APPROX), 19 MAY
U.N. COMMAND POSITION 24 JUNE
DEFENSE PHASE LINE

ELEVATIONS IN METERS
0   200   500   1000 AND ABOVE

At the start of the big offensive on 22 April, the Chinese announced that they would be celebrating May Day in Seoul that year. Little was heard about that prediction as the first of May came and went. The Chinese had gained territory and inflicted casualties, but they had paid dearly for those gains, and they were not yet at the gates of Seoul. Would they try to capture Seoul again? We had to prepare for anything.

Just before I left for the outpost line of resistance (OPLR), I walked into the regimental collecting station tent and heard a cheerful voice shout, "Hey Doc! Over here!"

I found 1st Lt. John Middlemas, lying on a stretcher, waving his arms. Both his legs were bandaged and he was tagged and ready for evacuation. He's been hit with a bullet and mortar fragments. He'd been injured about the same time Lt. Mooney had been hit in both legs on 25 June. Mooney had to be carried off and evacuated, first to the 155th MASH, then to the 121st Evacuation Hospital that moved south to the region of Chonan South Korea. From that location, Mooney was taken to the nearest airport, and flown to the 382nd General Hospital near Osaka, Japan.

Because Middlemas could still walk, he had refused medical evacuation and tried to carry on for another two or three days. But his wounds became so infected that Dr. Hank Barns, the 1st Battalion surgeon, finally insisted that he be put on a stretcher and evacuated before the infection got into the bones of his right ankle.

Because Lt. Mooney had been evacuated several days earlier, I thought Middlemas might have been hit again. As I looked down at my favorite warrior friend, I couldn't resist kidding him a bit.

"Johnny, you old son of a gun," I said. "It looks like the Chinese finally got to you."

"They sure did, Doc," he said, "but they only shot me in the legs, so I can't walk now and my legs still hurt."

"Okay, Johnny, you just wait here and I'll get you something to ease your pain a bit."

"Why are you bothering to tell me to wait here, Doc? I sure as hell can't walk away."

"That's a good sign Johnny," I said.

"What's a good sign, Doc?" he asked.

"The good sign, Johnny, is that the Chinese didn't shoot away your sense of humor—so you are going to get well."

I bent down, gave him a drink of water, and handed him a flask of brandy to sip on to his heart's content. Johnny liked that pain medicine, so I slipped a little bottle of brandy into his pocket and gave him another swig of water to chase the brandy he had sipped. Then I was called away to tend to other problems. When I returned, Johnny had disappeared in a box ambulance. I was rather sad that Middlemas had been evacuated; we hadn't finished talking. We had been good friends since our time together at Sachang-ni and enjoyed swapping stories.

Middlemas eventually landed in the 382nd General Army Hospital in Osaka, Japan, one floor above where Lt. Mooney had landed. These two outstanding infantry leaders were good friends, but one might not realize it by the way they talked to one another.

Middlemas and Mooney were both pipe smokers. During their many exposures to enemy fire, the pipe in Middlemas' shirt pocket had been smashed by a bullet or shell fragment. Because there was no PX around that sold new pipes, Mooney offered to lend Middlemas his pipe to smoke whenever they were together. It so happened that the last firefight they were involved in, Middlemas was using Mooney's pipe.

Thus, when Mooney was told by a nurse that there was a man named Middlemas from his own unit on the floor above him and asked if he had a message for Middlemas, Mooney answered, "I do have a message for Middlemas, which is give me back my pipe and buy one of your own."

Middlemas returned the pipe and bought himself a new one.

After more than two months in the hospital, Johnny Middlemas felt more than ready to return to duty, but the hospital dawdled in releasing him. So Johnny, being Johnny, just went AWOL and returned to Korea to rejoin his unit without clearing the hospital.

On the third of May, our regimental commander, Col. Jim Boswell, was ordered to establish an OPLR patrol base out in front of the 25th Division. According to rumor, the 25th Division commander was having difficulty finding the forces within his division ready and able to mount their own OPLR.

The immediate move back to frontline duty was not sucked up with great enthusiasm by the 7th troops. But it was a rational decision by the I Corps commander to select the 7th Infantry. The 1st and 3rd Battalions of the 7th were still in reasonably good condition and able to fight. To give our new OPLR Regimental Combat Team more punch, the all-black 58th Field Artillery Battalion (FAB) was attached to the 7th Infantry, and both units were attached to the 25th Division. It was a comfortable arrangement for the 25th Division, because we were the guys sitting way out in the front to face any new tidal wave of Chinese. The unknown factor was whether the Chinese generals would try to recapture Seoul or seek a softer target. If they did go for Seoul, they would need to go over us first.

I had split the 7th Regimental Medical Company into two units, a forward echelon, with a lot of medical supplies and myself in charge, and a rear unit, with Lt. Jitters and our two dentists, Cpt. Colden D. Raines and 1st Lt. Conrad Rioux, who spoke French —which was useful when the French or Belgian Battalions were nearby. MSC Cpt. Cohen was put in charge of the rear echelon of the 7th Medical Company. As Lt. Jitters and I parted, I guessed from the expression on his face that he thought we were going out on a suicide mission and he would never see us again.

The 2nd Battalion 7th was left behind in reserve, to absorb replacements and prepare to fight another day. The 2nd Battalion medical platoon, including Lt. John R. Currin MC and Lt. Paul P. Dudyk MSC, had had a rather harrowing time when they were overrun by masses of Chinese. But by keeping their heads, they'd been able to sidestep the passing Chinese, to regroup and fight their way out. But now they needed time to reconstitute themselves before getting into more fighting. Lt. Dudyk received a Silver Star for his leadership under fire.

The battalion surgeons of the 1st and 3rd Battalions, Dr. Barnes and Dr. Campbell and their assistants, Lt. Bill Herrick and Lt. Sebastian Cennamo, went forward with us. I couldn't ask for better teams of MC and MSC officers. While they had been recently stressed, they had not been overrun and were ready to go at it again.

The 7th Infantry Regimental Combat Team received the command to move out early on the fourth of May. We were told to actively patrol to the north and to hold on as long as we could if and when the Chinese launched a new frontal attack to recapture Seoul.

We made ourselves comfortable in semi-prepared bunkers and foxholes to await developments. As it turned out, we had five days of sunshine and rest out in no man's land. Some of the men were very unhappy the Military Police had taken all the Korean women away. I wondered and worried about Che Cha Ja.

I wished I had some reading material, but my duffle bag was heavy enough without adding books. But I did have my pocket New Testament, with Psalms and Proverbs over my heart in my left shirt pocket at all times. It was a continuing source of comfort and eternal insight. It was always comforting to be reminded of who was really in charge of the universe. The easy duty out front on the OPLR was also a good time to write letters home, to think through a lot of things, and to enjoy some sunshine.

Dear Mother and Dad,   7 May 1952

Nothing much new to report here. We are back on the front again, but there is no heavy contact. The weather is warm and most of the men are getting suntans. I got a little pink myself, so I put my shirt on. I have to take it slow and easy, as always.

Jerry was very pleased with the books you sent. I think he could take a little more difficult ones. Imm Yung Hee is bright, but not as interested in learning. He will have no trouble after the war. He used to work as a telephone pole wireman before, and there

is plenty of that work needed here now. Jerry is the boy I am primarily interested in. Jerry is now 15 and Imm Yung Hee is 21 years old.
     Love Bob

By the end of April 1951, the Army had started to notice that the wounded from the 3rd Division arrived in hospitals better prepared for survival of needed surgeries than those from other divisions. We attributed that difference to our front line use of blood, plasma, and albumin in saline to replace blood volume, and to our extensive use of hemostats of every size and shape to clamp bleeders, and then cover the clamp with a bandage. We started these life-saving routines in the 1st Battalion of the 7th in North Korea, but it is likely that the desperate inge-nuity of many battalion surgeons working in isolation came to many of the same conclusions as they fought to keep people alive and stabilize them for rough over-land journeys that were arduous enough for the healthy soldier but jolting and strength-sapping for riddled, torn, and fractured soldiers.

While helicopters were considered a godsend and their pilots were uniformly spunky soldiers, choppers were as scarce as hen's teeth at the beginning of the Korean War and strangely hard to obtain when there were hundreds of casualties streaming back from aid stations, collecting stations, and clearing stations. It was my conviction that we should have had a company of medical helicopters at-tached to our division medical battalion as a part of our regular TO&E, with one or two of these choppers at each Regimental Collecting Station, just as we had box ambulances for forward deployment from our location.

The incongruent and simultaneous battles being waged around us to kill and disarm the enemy and salvage the wounded of both sides, as well as the mangled civilians caught in the meat grinder of war, continually challenged our resolve and ingenuity. While we couldn't stop the crazy Communists without killing a lot of them, we knew the closer we were to falling soldiers of either side, the better their chance of survival. Thus, the terse message painted on Bill Herrick's jeep—"you fall, we haul"—signified the need to lean forward to catch, gather, and succor the wounded, when and wherever they fell. After I had amputated the second leg, one of our sergeants painted "SAWBONES" below my jeep windshield. Someone from the rear area sent an order prohibiting unauthorized lettering on vehicles. It remained to be seen how long the "you fall, we haul" message would last.

The following *Pacific Stars and Stripes* article, "With 3rd Division Wounded," is from page 205 and 206 of the History of the 3rd Division in Korea.

"The 3rd Division troops have been receiving the best 'medical field treatment possible' according to doctors at the 8055th Mobile Army Surgical Hospital. Of-ficers at the 'MASH,' which has handled cases from as many as four divisions at the same time, have said wounded from the 3rd consistently arrive there in better shape than any others.

"The statement was made recently by Cpt. Rod Smith, commander of the division's 2nd Clearing Platoon who worked at the MASH for over a month, 'It got to be standard comment there,' he said, 'that this division has set up a nearly perfect system in picking up wounded, caring for them, and speeding them back.'

"He pointed out two practices employed by the 3rd Division medics which are largely responsible for the successful evacuation of wounded: the use of whole blood on a regimental level, and accompanying wounded all the way back to the main hospital.

"'Plasma has been invaluable in the field,' Smith said, 'but it takes whole blood to build up a man fast to the point where he is able to travel.'

"Smith said he believed the 3rd is the first division to stock its regimental collecting stations with whole blood. Large electrical refrigerators are used to store the bottles.

"'In nearly every battle casualty, the loss of blood is the determining factor between life and death,' Smith said. 'And it's impossible to over-praise the company medic—the man who applies the initial tourniquet and administers the first transfusions.'

"Since the last war, medical science had developed an extract called 'serum albumin,' which comes in a small, four-inch long bottle and can be fused directly into the body. It has to a large extent replaced the use of plasma, which requires the mixing of fluid and powder from two large bottles.

"'We have found by getting the man from the field through battalion aid station as fast as possible, then building his resistance with whole blood, we can save many more lives,' Smith went on. 'Then when he is back to the clearing company and ready to move, we send an experienced man to the hospital with him. A blood supply and oxygen respirator is kept in the ambulance to maintain his strength, which is liable to be knocked way down from the rough ride, otherwise.'

"Smith pointed out that one other advancement in evacuation of the wounded since World War II is the growing use of the helicopter. 'All that is needed on the ground is a telephone and identification panel,' Smith said. 'A call is put in to the division surgeon, and in a short time the pilot has coordinates and is on the way.'"

We in the 7th Medical Company enjoyed that favorable newspaper report. I had cut out the article to send home in a letter. It was a nice pat on the back. But we were sobered by the fact that we knew there were many KIA that we were not able to help. That fact and the GRO work that continued daily around us tempered any real sense of satisfaction that we might have had. A lot of people were still being killed.

When we returned from the patrol base out in front of the MLR and rejoined our forward and rear collecting stations, I was perturbed to find that Lt. Jitters was neither in the 7th Regiment nor in the 3rd Division medical battalion. On further questioning, I found that he had requested a driver take him to a supply center and then sent the jeep and driver back to Regiment with supplies, but without him. I wondered if he was ill or just scared out of his wits. From what I could gather, the latter seemed to be the case. But he was also AWOL, and in wartime, that is considered desertion.

I called the division surgeon to ask for a replacement doctor, and he promptly sent me a new doctor by the name of Duffy, who proved to be both competent and unflappable. What a joy it was to have Duffy after Jitters. I didn't need to cover for Duffy or daily pump him up with enough courage to carry on with the tasks at hand. Duffy had trained for the priesthood, but before ordination, he fell in love, got married, and decided to go to medical school. As a new doctor, he was yanked away from his wife and sent to Korea, courtesy of the doctor draft. But he never complained. We had many good conversations about a wide range of subjects, both philosophical and mundane. But that still left me with the "Jitters" problem to settle.

The division surgeon then made a few more calls and found out Lt. Jitters was volunteering his professional services way back at the replacement center, where he was much appreciated, since they needed a doctor. He also provided them with a bit of entertainment by telling war stories.

I was truly ticked off when I got the news. But I didn't want him smashed by a court martial or shot for desertion. I knew he just did not have enough courage, and in his insecure state, he was not cut out for duty with the infantry. But in spite of his chronic high anxiety, he had done a good job caring for casualties during the recent big Chinese push. At that time, he had proven to be a real asset. Moreover, I liked the guy.

I needed to get Lt. Jitters out of the mess he was in before the ponderous Army administration caught up with him, ground him up, and spat him out. I called Joe Bayne again to thank him for sending me Duffy, and I suggested that he arrange to have Lt. Jitters placed on temporary orders for a month in the replacement center. Then I would go down to have a talk with him as soon as I had some free time. Bayne agreed with the plan, because he did not want to create a stink for the Army Medical Corps or the U.S. Navy. Bayne had also observed Jitters doing his professional duty in an acceptable manner when the Chinese were creating havoc nearby. Since I would soon be writing Jitters' efficiency report, I wanted to clear up the matter. I also knew in my heart that without the Lord, I might have been a Dr. Jitters.

In the meantime, there was training to be done, and I was glad to have the new doctor. With the "Jitters" matter temporarily defused, I settled down to write another letter home.

Dear Mother and Dad,   May 13, 1951

Nothing much doing here now. The 7th had been back on the line for the last week, but there is very little activity. Every day we sent out tank and infantry patrols, but there were no heavy engagements with the enemy.

At present, I am just sitting outside my tent, getting a suntan. Everyone talks rotation but it looks like it may be a long time before the officers will be sent home. There are so many whose enlistments are up that the rest of us will be stuck for some time. It looks now as if I can expect another six months here.

I am sure there are more doctors, but they aren't in the service and those that are in the service are in the wrong places. Oh, well, things may change by summer when they get in a new crop of doctors.

Love, Bob

On 16 May, I had a wake up call. The Chinese launched a new mass offensive, not at Seoul, but in the east. Twenty Chinese Communist divisions struck the X Corps and the five ROK Divisions on the right flank of the X Corps. By the following day, the 3rd, 5th, 6th, 7th, and 9th ROK Divisions had ceased to function as coordinated Army units, and some of them were in rapid retreat, leaving their weapons behind. The U.S. Army 2nd Division was left fighting on three fronts as the CCF swept south, hoping to disrupt our rear area and capture supplies. It was a move doomed to failure, for the CCF had not counted on the speed with which our 3rd Division could move, nor on the killing efficiency of the U.S. artillery.

Lt. Gen. Almond asked for help from the 8th Army when the ROK section of the line collapsed in his X Corps. Almond also had some good practical suggestions about just what to do next. Both Gen. Van Fleet and Gen. Ridgeway agreed with Gen. Almond's plan, and it was implemented quickly. First, the U.S. 187th Airborne troops moved in behind the X Corps in the Hoeng-san area to counterattack east, directly into the side of the Chinese phalanx. Next, the 3rd Division moved across the Korean peninsula with the 15th Regiment, pushing out from the right side of the X Corps area. Meanwhile, the 7th Regiment had one wild night ride across the country with the Battalion and Regimental medics, including our Korean litter teams, moving with our infantry. Our artillery, except for the self-propelled 8-inch howitzers, could not keep up the pace. The big howitzers were the most accurate artillery weapons we had, and great support weapons to have with our mobile infantry.

Col. Boswell had gone on leave in Japan, leaving Lt. Col. Weyand, the 1st Battalion commander, in charge of the 7th Regiment. When we arrived at our eastern battle station, Brig. Gen. Mead, the assistant 3rd Division commander, showed up and ordered Lt. Col. Weyand to attack immediately.

Weyand tried to explain that attacking would not be wise until our artillery arrived, but Gen. Mead persisted with his direct order until Lt. Col. Weyand rose to his full height, stood over the shorter Gen. Mead and said clearly, "Bull**** General! Bull****, bull****, bull****!"

That stopped the discussion.

Faced with the option of relieving a top field commander for insubordination and vulgar impertinence, Gen. Mead considered the fallout, turned, and walked away. Lt. Col. Weyand had just put his career on the line for his troops. He refused to implement an unwise order from the deputy division commander, especially when Col. Boswell, the regimental commander, was on leave.

The 7th Regiment went on the attack when all systems were ready. Weyand used his men and all support systems in a coordinated manner, like a veritable combat battalion symphony concert director. Lt. Col. Weyand, who was not a West Pointer, went on to become a four-star general and the chief of staff of the United States Army.

The 7th Regiment pushed northeast into the mountains, clearing the area of Chinese and North Koreans. Our medics went on foot wherever the troops went, but on that occasion, we were able to get helicopters and blood as needed. We were part of a coordinated infantry, armor, artillery, and air force counterattack symphony of death. Our infantry forced the retreating Chinese into the valleys, where our artillery could be more effective, and flights of B29s could carpet-bomb them. The loss in Chinese manpower was enormous, because we had FOs in place to coordinate air and artillery weapons with tanks and infantry. The Chinese never tried a multi-division sweeping attack deep into Korea again.

Our medical support was often difficult to implement. We gathered information from any and all sources, from patients on litters, to S-3s and S-4s, sweating to stay up with the battles. Our wire crews went out in all types of weather, including enemy firefight storms. There were many unsung heroes among the communications crews as stated by Communications Sgt. F. D. Grothe below.

"The wire used at that time was usually not strung over one or two miles. In May of 1951, the 7th Infantry was assigned to the X Corps on the opposite side of Korea and we moved on one hour's notice. When we arrived in the X Corps area, we went into the mountains and left all of our vehicles. During this operation, we laid over ten miles of wire from the rear area vehicle park to the battalion perimeter in the mountains. The wire section was able to give the 7th Regimental commander telephone communication with the battalion commanders and the rifle companies and attached units.

"While stringing wire to B and C Companies, the wire team was attacked by a force of NKPA soldiers trying to escape through our outfit. In stringing a wire line, a line phone was always carried to test the line back to the switchboard. As soon as the NKPA soldiers began to fire on our team, I called C Company and requested any assistance they could give us. I did not think the volume of fire from our two carbines and two M-1s was going to be enough against ten to twenty of the enemy. C Company gave us immediate support with their 57 mm RR and then sent two squads of Infantry to our aid. This strong response forced the few remaining enemy to make a hasty withdrawal and my team completed its assignment of getting phone communications for Lt. Col. Weyand, the battalion commanders, to all of their units."

As battle changed from a tidal wave Chinese invasion to large groups of Chinese surrendering or frantically trying to get back north and avoid being cut off, we saw hundreds of ROK troops debugging sheepishly down from the hills. Efforts were made to fit them into units again, and new ROK leadership training was initiated shortly thereafter. Many young ROK officers from all strata of South Korean society were sent to U.S. Army officer schools in America, where they learned and matured into first class combat officers. It is important for the political leadership in a free society to have self-discipline, moral character, and respectable maturity, if they expect their soldiers to continue to fight and die for their country.

In the midst of that cross-country, Chinese-chasing, I answered a letter.

Dear Dad and Mother,　　　　*Post marked May 24, '51*

I received your letter of 14 May today. I am not quite sure just what day this is, since we have been on the move so much the last few days. 21st or 22nd I guess.

Our reserve time in Seoul was cut short and we trucked 135 miles across Korea to north of Wonju, where we plugged the gap left by the Chinese breakthrough in the ROK division's sector. Everything is going quite well now and casualties are not too heavy.

This part of Korea is extremely beautiful—green, wooded mountains with waterfalls, clear streams, and pleasantly cool weather. We have had some rain but it is not too heavy as yet.

Right now it is quite noisy in the valley where I am sitting, since we are surrounded by a battalion of 105 mm howitzers on the right and a battalion of 155 mm howitzers on the left. It all makes good protection.

I can sympathize with you, Dad, about city folks sitting on their fannies instead of helping on a fishing trip. We have a few people like that here, only I have the authority to boot them in the rear (verbally that is).

Love, Bob

There is much more that could be said about the battle action in the X Corps area, but the net result for the Americans was a leap in battle confidence as American units attacked and out-maneuvered the Chinese and NKPA forces, causing their early victories to turn into traps, and thwarting their efforts to maintain their supply lines.

By 28 May, the Communist forces were in a disorganized retreat and a number of South Korean units had gained new confidence fighting side by side with, and at times under, American divisional control.

The battles that unfolded between 16 and 28 May would make excellent war game studies in military schools. The 3rd Infantry Division gained warrior confidence within units and between cooperating units. I believe that it was this battle that caused the Chinese generals to realize they could not conquer South Korea as long as Americans were there. They also realized that they needed better weapons and tactics. If our casualty totals had come anywhere near Chinese casualty totals, our U.S. Congress would have had convulsions.

According to reports, all of the 3rd Division forces were in high spirits as they traveled back across Korea, having accomplished their mission of coming alongside other U.S. units and battering the Chinese and North Korean Armies back north with heavy losses once again.

When we returned to I Corps near Seoul, I remembered my unfinished business with Lt. Jitters. I did not look forward to it. But first I sent another letter home.

Dear Folks,   30 May 1951

Nothing new on rotation. I hope to make it sometime this summer. My promotion is pending in Tokyo. The people there keep regular office hours, so only God knows how long it will take them wading through the paperwork before they get to it.

The 2nd wave of the Chinese offensive has been thrown back. We were pulled from reserve in Seoul, where we had been for five days, and rushed 160 miles across the peninsula to plug a hole in the line where we were engaged for about six days. Yesterday we came back west again and are now going back into the line north of Uijongbu, which is familiar territory.

Just where this rat race is going to end, I don't know. The reports from the front say the Chinese are routed. I hope so.

Love, Bob

332

Close friends of Cpt. Jensen: Maj. McAoliffe (left) and Cpt. Piaseczny (right);
May 1951

Left to right: Dr. Jensen, 2nd Lt.. Herrick, Dr. Barnes, and Dr. Jasper (USN)

"The Flying Boxcar," aircraft for troop movement and airborne drops

Left: ROKs that bugged out and we detained

Right: A typical switchboard location

Chapter Fourteen
Return to I Corps battles in Iron Triangle. Troop Rotation?
June 1, 1951 – August 2, 1951

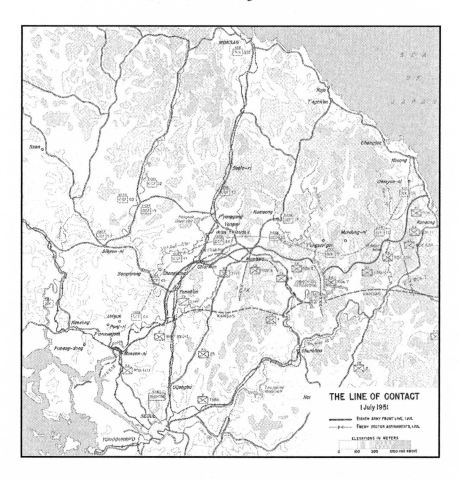

THE LINE OF CONTACT
1 July 1951

ELEVATIONS IN METERS

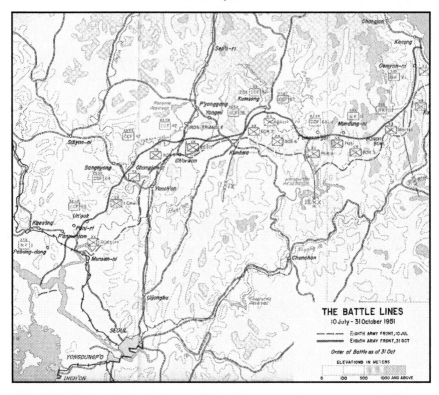

THE BATTLE LINES
10 July - 31 October 1951

There was little rest after the 3rd Division returned from X Corps to I Corps near the city of Uijongbu. The idea was to hit the Chinese and push them back north while they were still recovering from the surprise drubbing they had received after their thrust into central South Korea through the ROK Army in the X Corps area. There was hardly time to get off a letter before heading north toward the Iron Triangle again.

Dear Mother and Dad,   June 5, 1951

The war goes on at its usual dreary pace. We are attacking again now and are again north of the 38th Parallel in the west.

The rotation plan has set in here. I will be sending home 25 of my most deserving men this month. However, unless I get a few replacements with some medical training, it will be difficult to send that many good men next month. There is no word on medical officer replacements as yet, but I expect there may be some by July or August. I hope to have a replacement for my job by the 1st of Sept. Only time will tell. I am still waiting for my majority to come back from Tokyo. They take forever on their routine paperwork.

The papers didn't say much about the mad dash the 3rd Division made across Korea to stop the last Chinese offensive break through of ROK divisions located next to the 2nd Division. We were in the fight immediately after a 140-mile ride from Seoul and stayed in it for six days when we rushed back to the west again and joined the attack north.

The enemy is certainly confused by the 3rd, they never know where we are and half the time I don't know myself.

Time to go to staff meeting.

Love, Bob

The 7th Regiment advanced north of the Hantan River Bridge via the muddy Route 33. This was familiar territory. We were to relieve the 25th Division, to which the 25th Canadian Infantry Brigade was attached. The Canadian outfit was known as the Princess Pat Brigade. We were never informed who Princess Pat was, but we were pleased to see the Canadian contingent as we passed by to become a part of Operation Piledriver. Our job in Piledriver was to hammer the Chinese in the Iron Triangle and occupy Chorwon, the southwest anchor city of the Iron Triangle.

We thought the Chinese must be surprised to see us back in the I Corps area, attacking them around Chorwon, since the last they had heard of us, we were in central Korea. Whether the Chinese were as off-balanced as our brass hoped was debatable. They had acquired some new antitank guns from Russia, as well as mortars and some real artillery, and were preparing to go head-to-head with some U.N. forces. Their new equipment may have been some help to them, but they had another consistent advantage: they were less concerned about battle casualties than we were.

They had been instructed to kill as many Americans as possible to induce our Congress to stop supporting the war. The Soviets seemed to be supplying enough mortars and artillery to the Chinese to make a real difference, but it was up to the Chinese to get the weapons to the battle line by using trucks, mules, and indentured, expendable Korean laborers, working long nights. Perhaps that was why the Iron Triangle was so named. There was an awful lot of iron located there, throwing hot steel back and forth. It was not a good thing to write home about.

Dear Dad and Mother,   10 June 51

Received your letters of May 31st today. At present, we are just outside the gates of Chorwon on the west central front. The 7th has had some hard battles getting here but we are now scheduled to go into reserve tomorrow for a long overdue rest. Our last reserve was cut short by our mad dash to the eastern front to plug the hole in the line between the ROKs and the 2nd Division and once that was stopped, we got on trucks again and rode 170 miles back to join the attack here. The men are almost exhausted, mentally and physically.

Between and during all the activity, we have been giving immunization shots for typhus, cholera, Jap B Encephalitis, and others. It is quite a problem trying to work it all in.

The problem of rotation looks a little better now. I sent 25 of the enlisted men home this month. I do not know what the quota will be for next month, but it will be a little more difficult to meet if I do not get a few trained replacements. Most of the enlisted men replacements have been raw recruits. I still have hopes of getting home before September, maybe sooner.

Love, Bob

Some of our medic sergeants were being rotated home by that time, which opened up a space for medic corporals to be promoted to sergeants. One of our corporals was a black soldier and, as I recall, his name was Harold Murphy, which was a bit unusual, I thought, for a black man to have an Irish name. He came to see me because he felt it was his time to be promoted. I had the feeling he was worried that I might be prejudiced about promoting blacks. Actually, we had very few blacks in our medical company, except for box ambulance drivers. I had a cup of coffee with Murphy, to put him at ease, and explained to him that the criteria for being promoted to sergeant was to demonstrate a closeness and concern for the welfare of the men he was leading. I also added that I did not give a hoot what color the skin of a soldier was. The corporal that would be promoted to sergeant had to be able to lead his men and they should have confidence in him.

A week or so later, Corporal Murphy was killed by a sniper while leading his litter squad to retrieve casualties on 10 June, 1951. I felt terrible about Murphy, especially when I realized that I had not taken the time to pray for him. I also thought that if I had not encouraged him to lead his men, he might not have been picked off. But I could not allow myself to be tortured with such "what if" thoughts if I was to do my job. It was just a miserable war, and I had not started it. Corporal Murphy was later awarded the Bronze Star with V-Device.

Among the enlisted replacements to our medical company were several Hispanics who I found made excellent medics. It was my impression that they had gentle hands in dealing with the wounded. I was pleased to have them in the medical company.

There was another source of replacements that has been often overlooked. That most valuable source was the wounded in action, who returned to duty with their units on the battlefield after being hospitalized and recovering from their war injuries. We often think that a soldier hospitalized for war wounds has earned a ticket home, but many are returned to their units if they are capable of soldiering again. It may surprise some people that many, if not most soldiers actually desire to return to their units, because that is where their close friends are and they have taken pride in serving their country. Even the majority of our KATUSA soldiers tried to return to their American Army units after being wounded; most were successful. The bonding of soldiers, one to another, is a powerful force. Any leader that does not understand that bonding can never be a good leader of soldiers. But there is an emotional downside to that, because some of the WIA returnees from the hospital became WIA again, and some even became KIA.

One such soldier was Henry Franklin West, who was born in Kingsport, Tennessee, on 25 December 1932. I managed to place Henry on a Marine Helicopter in Sachang-ni, North Korea in November 1950. He was made to sit up, despite pain from his wounds, but he was not a complainer. I put another slender soldier beside him in the seat and then placed a stretcher patient across their laps.

Henry returned to duty in his unit in Korea from a U.S. Army Hospital in Japan in February 1951. He was later nicknamed "Cast-Iron" by his new platoon Sergeant, Chelsie Rood. He was awarded the Bronze Star with V-Device for heroic action on 8 June 1951.

Award of the Bronze Star Medal with V-Device (posthumous) to Pvt. 1st Class Henry F. West

"On 8 June 1951, near Sam Ywie, Korea, Company A was advancing in the assault upon Hill 786 when it was suddenly subjected to enemy machine gun fire from the front and both flanks, forcing Private West and three comrades, two of them wounded, to seek cover on the forward slope of the hill. Realizing the wounded men were in desperate need of medical aid, Private West left his position of cover, crawled up the slope, which was under a constant hostile barrage, located a medical aidman, and led him back to the slope, which was under a constant hostile barrage of continuing enemy fire. Private West's audacious heroism and genuine concern for his comrade's welfare were instrumental in saving their lives and reflects great credit upon himself and the military service. Entered the military service from the State of Tennessee."

Henry West was killed in action on 3 July 1851. He was still only 18 years old.

There was another young soldier named Flint, who was found to be only 15 years old. He apparently had not told the truth about his age when he joined the Army. The unit was in the process of trying to have Flint sent home, even though he did not want to go. Flint had become a close a friend of West and was sort of under West's protection. The two had become almost inseparable. They were both killed by the same heavy mortar shell explosion. We were all saddened by the loss of Henry and his young buddy, who had found a home in the Army with people who cared about him. May they both now rest in peace and be at home with the Lord.

I had rather hoped someone in West's hometown might name a school or a post office after him as a remembrance. He was a fine soldier who lost his life in the service of his country, but more than that, he represents many WIAs who returned to duty after recovering in a hospital, only to become KIA the next time he was hit. We owe much to those young men or boys, who found a new home in the Army.

In June and July of 1950, there were hundreds of vicious battles for hilltop positions, and if we were not willing to expend lives for a particular hill, the Chinese would take it and then contest the next hill farther south all along the battle line. Many have likened this phase of the war to the trench warfare of World War I.

One of our old soldiers with China experience reminded us of the World War II story of a battle in which the Japanese army lost 3,000 soldiers and the Chinese army lost 15,000 soldiers.

After the battle, a Chinese general was supposed to have opined, "We are winning. At this rate there won't be any Japanese left to fight us."

The epic struggle for control of the Iron Triangle area continued throughout the two years of the cease-fire talk.[18]

In the midst of those battles, a new disease, Korean Epidemic Hemorrhagic Fever, appeared on the scene. It struck individuals without warning and caused the death of many after they had been incapacitated for a week or more. There was no specific treatment, other than careful physiological support in an intensive ward. Eventually, it was suspected that the disease was spread through the urine of rodents that had come to occupy the trenches where food was left by soldiers. We presumed that the enemy soldiers were being made sick, as well, but I know of no statistics on that. It was a continuing burden to bear during the remainder of my time in Korea.

On the fourteenth of June, the entire Medical Company, including all of members of the regimental collecting units and the three battalion medical platoons, were assembled near Regimental HQ. This was the first time the Medical Company had been all lined up in a row by platoons in front of me. Master Sgt. May knew all of the proper orders and procedures for me, so I wouldn't make some foolish military protocol mistake as I presented the company to Col. Boswell. I may have been Medical Company Commander, but I had no military troop presentation experience, and I didn't know beans about parade formations.

---

[18] For more details on these battles, read of Clay Blair's excellent thousand-page tome *The Forgotten War —America in Korea 1950-1953*.

Nevertheless, it was my job to present the troops smartly for their awards. I was more nervous about that military formation than I was about taking care of wounded under fire. I did make one verbal order error, but everyone was quite forgiving of their doctor as he was trying to play spit-and-polish soldier. Most of the troops knew I was out of my element. But that was not what I had been sent to Korea for.

All of the men in the company who served honorably in their medical tasks under fire were awarded the Combat Medical Badge (CMB). Those who already had earned the CMB in World War II, were awarded a CMB with a star on top to signify that it was their second wartime award. Bill Herrick had received his first award for crossing the beach on D-day in France, and Sgt. 1st Class Jack Cobb got his first award serving under Gen. Patton in Europe. All of our other sergeants had received their first CMB awards in Europe in World War II. I was proud to serve with them. There was not a person in the company that was not proud to be there that day, but there was also sadness for our friends who had not survived to stand there with us. I felt regret that Lt. Jitters was not there to receive a Combat Medical Badge. The "Jitters" matter was unfinished business that I still needed to attend to, as soon as I had some time without casualties.

The faithful KATUSA that had not been released to the ROK Army also stood there with us, as did little Tommy, the orphan, in a uniform prepared by Sgt. Byland just for the occasion. Tommy properly saluted Col. Boswell as he inspected the troops. Col. Boswell managed a smile as he saluted back and overlooked the little irregularity. There were Silver Stars and Bronze Stars with V-Devices presented that day, as well. Most of the men in the Medical Company felt we deserved a special unit citation for continuing excellence is combat, but that never came. Perhaps it's a bit of sour grapes, but sometimes we felt we were medics doing a good job but lacking a PR agent.

Dear Dad & Mother,   *15 June 51*

Today we are in reserve, resting, getting cleaned up, and giving shots for cholera, typhus, typhoid, tetanus, Jap B Encephalitis, and small pox. The medic's job is never done. Sick call is very heavy, with the men coming in with all sorts of complaints they didn't have time to think about before.

Yesterday we had a presentation of awards at Regiment. There were 9 Silver Stars given out in the Regiment. See Cottonbaler.

The first group of enlisted men to leave on rotation left yesterday. Those with the best record went first. I hope to get enough replacements to send a like number next month.

No official word yet as to when the medical officers will be rotated, but it should be this summer some time.

Love, Bob

Having a little time available, I had my driver, Cpl. Heath, drive me far south of the Han River, to the replacement station where Lt. Jitters was reported to be working. Leaving the driver outside, I found Lt. Jitters and we went to a quiet corner of the tent where we could sit down and talk. He appeared anxious as I started to speak.

"Lt. Jitters, I know that this war business has been especially difficult for you, and I have tried to cover for you as best I could. I brought you back to the collecting station at Regiment from the 1st Battalion aid station. In spite of your fear of being wounded or killed, you did a good job tending to dozens of casualties under difficult circumstances during the big Chinese offensive in April. You did the job of a real combat surgeon, and I was proud of you. Then when we were ordered out on the OPLR in front of the 25th Division, I headed up the medical team there and left you in charge of the rear echelon of the regimental Medical Company. I realize you might have thought the Chinese would attack again and that perhaps the troops out on the OPLR would be wiped out and you might never see me again. But when I returned five days later, you were not at your post in the regimental collecting station rear echelon. As far as anyone knew, you were AWOL, and in wartime, AWOL is considered desertion."

I paused to let the matter sink in.

"Lt. Jitters, do you understand what you did?"

His eyes filled with tears as he muttered, "But I'm just not like you. I just couldn't go on anymore. I just could not face any more war."

I felt only sorrow for Jitters, and tried to explain as gently as I could.

"When I finally found out where you were, I asked Joe Bayne to cover you by having orders cut for temporary duty in the replacement center. Your professional services here seem to be much appreciated. Neither Bayne nor I wanted you to be hit with a court martial. Bayne was willing to cover for you because he saw you doing a good job up north when the Chinese were coming from all sides. He felt you were exhausted, but you continued to work. But now we must clear up this matter.

"I would like you to feel good about yourself in the future. You should know that it is okay to be frightened while you are doing a difficult job in dangerous circumstances. It is also okay to be emotionally exhausted after a period of stress in war. But it is not okay to run away. I want you to come back with me. I can arrange for you to work in the division medical battalion for the last month of your tour with the Army. It should be quiet there and you will receive honorable credit for your combat service. You will not be court martialed. But if you don't return with me, I cannot give you a satisfactory efficiency report. If you do return with me, you'll receive a good efficiency report and perhaps a commendation for your work with casualties during the big battle in April. I am perhaps exceeding my authority by giving you a choice, but for your own sake, I urge you to return with me now. Since you are only here on temporary duty, I can clear up the matter with whoever your superior is here."

After a long pause Lt. Jitters said, "I would rather have an unsatisfactory efficiency report than return to the infantry."

I suppose I should have expected that answer, but I didn't. I was surprised and disappointed. I had wanted him to be able to go forward in life with dignity and with the demon of fear vanquished.

I looked at him sadly for a moment, and then I said, "I am sorry you made that decision. I like you as a person, and I respect you as a physician, but it seems there is nothing more I can do for you. Goodbye and good luck, wherever life takes you. If you change your mind and show up at the 7th Regimental collecting station during the next three or four days, I will welcome you, but after that time, I will turn in your efficiency report to Lt. Col. Bayne, and you will officially be out of the 3rd Infantry Division."

We parted and I never saw or heard from him again.

In his efficiency report, I praised his work as a physician and his likeability as a person, but I rated his deportment in combat as unsatisfactory because of poor control of his fear under very stressful situations. I did not mention his going AWOL.

The Navy was not pleased that one of their officers had a less than satisfactory efficiency report. From Navy correspondence received, I learned that Lt. Jitters defended himself to the U.S. Navy by pointing out that he had excellent efficiency reports before and after this one unsatisfactory report. This prompted the Navy to write to me to further explain or amend my report. I chose to do neither. I just let stand what I had written and that, as far as I know, was where the matter rested. I half expected a visit from a Naval officer to find out the "rest of the story," but no one came.

Looking back, I realize that at the time I rated him as unsatisfactory, I was functioning with the mind-set of a soldier, and I was thinking of all of the officers and men who were scared, yet did their duty without running away. Today, I wish I had been more compassionate, and had simply made permanent his temporary duty in the replacement center. Today, I probably would even grade his deportment under fire as satisfactory, because he did the best he could. I had a heavy heart after that last meeting with Jitters, but there was still a war to fight, so I chose to focus on other things.

Dear Dad and Mother,   17 June 1951

Nothing much new to report. We are still in reserve. Although this is supposed to be the rainy season, we have been enjoying beautiful weather. The area we are in is high, dry, green, and has beautiful rolling hills.

The men are all getting rested up. We have gotten fresh rations in, which makes things a lot easier. I have gained back the weight I had lost and am now up to a plump 180 lbs. again so I guess that Korea agrees with me.

I cannot understand what is taking so long for my promotion to come through. It has been resting in Tokyo for 30 days now. I still have hopes of getting home sometime in August if all goes well.

There are a lot of mules running around, left behind by the Chinese. The men are having a lot of fun riding around on them.

Love, Bob

Shortly after our fun with Chinese mules, the 7th Regiment was back in battles in the Iron Triangle. As the battles for hilltop positions continued, many of us reflected on the stalemate-status of the war. If we had put forth greater effort, and taken more casualties, we could have moved the line farther north, but that would have made the Chinese supply lines shorter and their counterattacks more desperate and forceful.

It became apparent that the Chinese were not going to abandon the Iron Triangle without shedding major quantities of blood. Although the objective of Operation Piledriver had been achieved, the re-conquered territory could not be held without the continual spilling of blood on both sides, and the Chinese and North Korean leaders cared less about loss of life than we did.

To put it in more graphic terms, even with our air and artillery advantage, if we only continued to match their five gallons of blood with our one gallon of blood, they might have recaptured Seoul and pushed us back below the Han River again. Then, because of their more extended supply lines, we might have extracted 10 gallons of their blood for one gallon of our blood. On the other hand, if we were willing to spend an equal amount of blood, we might have pushed them back to the narrow Korean waste line between Pyongyang on the west and Wonsan on the east. But if we chose not to fight continually in pitched battles, we might have eventually been back to the Pusan Perimeter.

Moreover, if we had refused to continue fighting because of congressional and voter fatigue in America, all of South Korea could be lost. China was unlikely to face internal problems unless they had more than a million casualties or their ports were bombed. Eventually, they did have more than a million casualties, but we never retaliated against their ports. They in turn never retaliated against Hong Kong.

But, fortunately, we did choose to fight on to at least save South Korea, and had we not done so, there would have been mass genocide in South Korea. If we had pulled out of South Korea, every South Korean who had supported the South Korean cause would have been executed

During that time, there was a growing air war along the Yalu River to be considered. Despite their denials, the Russians were flying their MIG jets against our F86 Saber Jets along the Yalu River, and young flyers on both sides were losing their lives.

As the air game was played, the Russian planes had not attempted to go farther south, as they might have done against our carriers and supply bases if we had attacked their support centers in Manchuria and Siberia. Gen. Ridgeway, who had replaced Gen. MacArthur in Tokyo, agreed with Truman that there should be no widening of the war in Asia. Ridgeway had a good sense of current and possible future trends in world history, and he was not unduly burdened with lessons from past history when those lessons were no longer applicable. But there were times when Ridgeway had to stand up to Truman, lest he fail to defend South Korea adequately. We heard rumors that Truman had entertained the thought of firing Ridgeway but had decided the political cost would have been too high to fire a second general and also to lose South Korea.

But the question remained, how could we stop the war, leaving an independent and free South Korea, if neither North Korea nor South Korea wished to stop fighting for their much-desired unification of Korea—with each side wanting very different terms?

Fortunately, Eisenhower won the next election and he was under no illusion that diplomacy with Communists would ever succeed at a bargaining table without a credible U.S. threat. After the defeat of Germany, Eisenhower had learned from a Soviet general that the Russians often ordered the Soviet infantry across mine fields, to the surprise of both Germans and Americans. The Chinese were just as harsh.

By mid-June, the Chinese and North Korean forces had been pushed out of South Korea and the cities of Chorwon and Kumhwa. With the base of the Iron Triangle in U.N. hands, Ridgeway rightly sensed it was a reasonable time to put a lid on the Korean War, because to continue as we had been going left many different escalations possible on either side, making things more unmanageable, and possibly drawing in Taiwan, Japan, and Russia. But shutting down a war is not an easy task.

There was an additional hope for peace because Russia finally abandoned their boycott of the U.N. when it was their turn to serve as chairman of the U.N. Security Council. In spite of continuing Soviet bluster and bullying tactics, on 23

June 1951, Soviet U.N. Delegate and Deputy Foreign Commissar of the Soviet Union, Jacob Malik, proposed a cease-fire in Korea.

On 30 June 1951, acting on orders from Washington, D.C., Gen. Ridgeway broadcast to China the U.N.'s willingness to discuss an armistice in Korea. It proved to be only the beginning of a frustrating two-year haggling process, during which there would be continuing insults from the North Koreans and continual blood-letting assaults in Korea, while China continued building up their military potential, including artillery, and used every opportunity to push the boundary line farther south in Korea.

It was not a good faith cease-fire, as suggested by Malik. Instead, it was a malevolent new Communist war stratagem to build up their supply base and to push their propaganda. It was truly a Faustian deal for the Communists to continue killing indefinitely, because they thought they could outlast us if they could bring in more supplies during a temporary cease-fire. But at least we were talking.

Lt. Col. Joe Bayne was rotated in late June and replaced by Lt. Col. Bill Yuckman. Bill Yuckman was the type to drop into a busy regimental collecting station to see how things were going. I don't know what he found in the 15th and 65th Regiments, but after a while I, noticed we were obtaining new replacements, including MC and MSC officers, for two or three week tours of duty before they were pulled out and sent to the other regiments as replacements. So I called Bill Yuckman to ask why we were getting replacements for only two or three weeks.

Bill Yuckman explained that the Medical Company in the 7th Regiment seemed to have a forward collecting unit just hovering over and helping whatever infantry battalion was under the greatest stress at the moment. He liked that way of providing medical support. Therefore, he was sending MC and MSC replacements through the 7th Medical Company for a bit of on-the-job training before sending them on to other regiments. We had become an unofficial battle line training camp for division medical replacements.

I was not sure at that time that Bill Yuckman realized the only reason that our "leaning forward system" of medical support worked was because the regimental surgeon positioned himself with the forward collecting unit that was busiest. It served to keep our medical support system focused on the main job at hand. But if the regimental surgeon stayed in regimental rear, the system collapsed, no matter how much on-the-job training replacements were given.

When I later explained that to Lt. Col. Yuckman, he said he was working on the regimental surgeon end of the problem in the other regiments, and I should just keep doing what I was doing and train replacements for the division. Shortly after that conversation, Yuckman founded the 38th Parallel Medical Society, where both medical and combat leadership issues could be discussed among doctors and other medical personnel.

By early July 1951, the entire line had been pushed north of the old defense line on the Imjin River, past the 38th Parallel. The object of the U.N. drive was to wrest control of commanding high ground in the center of the Iron Triangle and prevent the Chinese from using it.

The Hills 717 and 682, and smaller adjoining ridges a few miles south of Pyonggang, were held by well-entrenched Chinese. The plan of attack was for the 3rd Battalion 7th Infantry, to attack Hill 717 from the west and the 1st Battalion 7th to attack Hill 682 from the south and east. The regimental tank company would penetrate behind the hills from the northeast and provide supporting fire.

During the early hours before dawn, the 1st and 3rd Battalions moved into position. Because of poor roads and long distances, a section of the collecting platoon moved forward to set up a tactical collecting station at a road junction about two miles from the aid stations. The use of a forward tactical collecting station had become standard operating procedure for us. It consisted of a medical officer, standard collecting platoon equipment and personnel, one squad tent (not always used in fair weather), box ambulances from division, colored panels and smoke grenades for helicopter signals, radio and telephone communications, a locker of whole blood, and a reserve force of Korean civilian litter bearers. We had everything except our own helicopter. I had not been able to figure out how to get a helicopter with a pilot reassigned to our medical company. All the equipment was usually carried on a two and a half ton truck. The MSC in charge of litter squads and the regimental surgeon worked between the tactical collecting station and the forward battalion aid stations to coordinate and expedite medical support.

We were fortunate to have a regimental communications officer who gave us excellent support in laying telephone wire. The SCR 619 radio was unsuitable in hilly country, but we were able to secure an ANGRC 9 radio from the division medical battalion. With the ANGRC 9 radio, we were able to monitor the regiment and battalion command net at all times, staying abreast of the tactical situation and always available for contact, even if the telephone wires had been knocked out. Of course, the main method of communication was still with messages by litter jeeps and personal reconnaissance.

The attacks jumped off at dawn on 2 July 1951, preceded by an air strike and artillery preparation. Repeated assaults throughout the day produced heavy casualties, but failed to dislodge the Chinese. At nightfall, the 1st and 3rd Battalions withdrew and formed a perimeter defense near the base of the hills. Because of a lack of local protection, the tactical collecting station withdrew behind the main line for the night. Casualties during the night were kept within the battalion perimeter until morning or sent out with armed escort.

On the morning of the third, the tactical collecting unit moved back into position as the attack jumped off. The 1ˢᵗ Battalion succeeded in taking their objective, Hill 682. The tank infantry team on the northeast had several wounded, two of whom were critical. The only accessible road for litter jeeps to the area was under fire from Chinese to the east. Overland evacuation would take several hours. A helicopter was called to the forward collecting station, and as senior medical officer in the forward collecting station, I went with the helicopter, taking whole blood along. With the aid of ground assistance and terrain maps, the helicopter landed safely behind enemy lines, where blood was given to the two most critical casualties as they were quickly loaded for transport back to the forward collecting station and then on to a MASH unit.

The same procedure was used repeatedly in the following months. Sometimes the battalion aid station crew couldn't reach a company that was temporarily cut off from an overland route, but they could be reached by a helicopter hopping over a ridgeline to land on a panel in the rifle company area for a quick pick-up of casualties. We were out of there before the Chinese knew what was happening.

The helicopters had often been instructed not to fly in front of the regimental collecting station without special clearance. But we frequently brought a helicopter to our forward regimental collecting station near the action, where the pilot would be somewhat reassured by seeing the regimental surgeon there. The pilot would be briefed on the safest route to the casualties, whether in a Battalion aid station or in a rifle company over a ridgeline somewhere. It was usually necessary to send a medic with the helicopter who knew the landscape, who could evaluate quickly, start blood, and get out before becoming a target. Since I made a habit of studying the terrain maps and battle plans, I often went myself, since the pilots felt more reassured that they were in the environs of the regimental area if the regimental surgeon went along for the ride. It was the best way I knew to get fast service near the front line—and the infantrymen loved it.

On one such occasion, the helicopter pilot pulled out a bottle of whiskey and offered me a drink as we were flying up a valley hugging a ridgeline. Only then did I notice he was a bit intoxicated.

"Have you been drinking from this bottle of whiskey?" I said.

"Just a few swigs, Doc. Only enough to steady my nerves so that I can control this damn contraption in the up-drafts when flying near these ridges."

So I took a sip and tossed the bottle out of the helicopter.

"Hey," he said, "why did you throw out my bottle? I need that for my nerves, in case we fly over the Chinese."

"I think we're over the Chinese now," I said, "and your bottle was our only bomb. So let's see if you can land this contraption, as you call it, by that panel just ahead of us down there."

We landed safely and took off quickly, with a casualty in each pod, to the cheers of the GIs on the ground. On the third day of fighting, the entire hill masses of 717 and 682 were in our hands.

A couple of weeks later, I ran into the same helicopter pilot again in the mess tent at a nearby MASH. He said he thought we had met before, but he wasn't sure just where. I didn't remind him. After all, I might have needed him again in the future.

As we entered July 1951, Bill Herrick was overdue for rotation, but we were having difficulty getting a good replacement. Bill had become an institution on the front in the 1st Battalion 7th. Most new young MSC officers wanted to specialize in hospital administration, and the new 2nd lieutenants of hero potential and inclination from the ROTC schools or from West Point who wanted to become a general some day were more likely to select a career in the infantry than in the medics, where the doctors took up all of the slots for stars.

So in order to obtain a replacement for Herrick, we had to make a new 2nd lieutenant by the battlefield promotion route. Sgt. 1st Class Jack Cobb in the 3rd Battalion was a brave and competent NCO, willing to become an instant 2nd lieutenant and extend his tour, in spite of the dangers inherent in the job. He'd done a good job under Gil Campbell as the NCO boss of the medical platoon in the 3rd Battalion 7th. There was no problem getting him approved for a Battlefield Commission when he indicated he would be willing to extend his tour. We all felt we had just the right man for the job, but I never heard what his wife, Doris Cobb, thought about Jack's extension. However, he did survive the war and rejoined his wife a few months later.

As soon as 2nd Lt. Jack Cobb reached the 7th Medical Company, I put in a call on a field phone to Bill Herrick and, as usual, found him up on a hill on the battle line with his good friend 1st Lt. Fred Ferris, the Baker Co commander, and another first lieutenant, who was a FO for air and artillery. I told Bill his replacement had arrived and that he should gather all his stuff at the 1st Battalion and report to Medical Company HQ at Regiment. Because it was already afternoon, Herrick suggested he spend the night where he was and come down in the morning.

As I thought about his request, I experienced a heavy discomfort in my gut. I could not shake the feeling that Herrick was in danger.

So I said, "No, Bill, I want you here now, today, and not tomorrow, do you understand me?"

Bill was not happy about being called off the hill so abruptly, but he gathered his personal stuff and said goodbye to his infantry friends. When he reached HQ, he discussed a few things with 2nd Lt. Jack Cobb, then came to me with the suggestion that there was still time for him to go back up the hill and introduce Jack Cobb to his friends, and they could all spend the night in the B Company command bunker and return back down in the morning. Again, I experienced a real twisting in my gut.

I said, "Bill, I have not given you a direct command order since the morning after our first night battle in North Korea. But since you are being persistent, I am giving you a direct command order now. You will not go up that hill to B Company again. You will stay here in the Medical Company tonight. And you will start your journey home to see your wife tomorrow morning. Is that understood?"

As a good soldier Bill came to full attention immediately, saluted, and said, "Yes, sir!"

The matter was settled.

That night, there was a big battle, involving B Company. In the morning, the bodies of Bill's two friends were brought down. A direct hit by an artillery shell had penetrated the command bunker roof and killed everyone inside.

Cpt. Ray Blanding came by the medical collecting station to kneel by 1st Lt. Fred Ferris' body, to remove his first lieutenant bars, and to pin on his shiny new captain bars. The promotion had come through the day before he was killed. Cpt. Blanding, Lt. Herrick and I stood around the stretcher to say our final farewells to Fred Ferris—a great soldier who was also a believing Christian. Why did the Lord call him home then? I do not know the answer, but I know God is sovereign.

It was comforting to remember what the apostle Paul said in Philippians 1:20-21, "It is my eager expectation and hope that I will not be at all ashamed, but that with full courage now as always, Christ will be honored in my body, whether by life or by death. For to me to live is Christ, and to die is gain."

A few minutes later, when Bill and I were alone, he turned to me and said, "You knew this was going to happen, didn't you? Today Jack Cobb and I would have both been dead there on the ground beside Fred if you hadn't ordered me down off that hill. You knew that whether on offense or defense, I usually stayed beside Fred, because he had communication with the platoons and with the other companies to tell me where there were casualties to carry off."

"Bill," I answered, "I didn't know what was going to happen, but I had a strong feeling in my gut that you were in danger, which is why I ordered you not to go back up the hill. On several occasions, God has given me warnings and I have had to try to figure out what He was telling me. Sadly, it seems he was telling me that your time for being protected by Him was up. You've done your duty and it's time to go home. And that is why I ordered you not to go back up the hill. Soldiers on the line have been saying you've led a charmed life. I don't believe it was a charmed life, Bill. You've had a protected life—perhaps it was because of the special bond we've had ever since Sachang-ni. I don't pretend to understand such things—but so far, neither of us has shed a drop of blood in Korea, and if you think about what's been happening around us, doesn't that seem unusual? We have both been protected."

Bill pondered for a moment about the miracle of not being hit and then said, "I don't understand these things and I don't understand God. I just feel that from now on, I'm living on borrowed time."

As Bill Herrick passed through the 3rd Division HQ, he was called into Lt. Col. Bill Yuckman's office. Yuckman offered Bill a choice training job in the medical battalion with the assurance of a promotion to captain if he would extend for six more months. Bill declined the job.

"My time in Korea is up," he said. "I'm now on borrowed time. I'm going home to my wife."

And he did.

Cpt. Fred Ferris' body was sent home for burial in America.

Award of the Distinguished-Service Cross (posthumous) to Cpt. Fred Ferris

"Captain Fred Ferris...while commanding officer, Company B, 7th Infantry Regiment, 3rd Infantry Division, distinguished himself by extraordinary heroism in action against the enemy in the vicinity of Chich-on, Korea on 3 and 4 July 1951. On the evening of 3 July, Captain Ferris' company, given the mission of attacking and securing an enemy-held hill, launched a determined assault against the hostile positions. As the friendly troops reached the slope of the objective, a devastating volume of enemy fire pinned them down. Exposing himself to the intense fire, Captain Ferris, with complete disregard for his personal safety, moved among his men, reorganizing them in a skirmish line. Then, shouting words of encouragement to them, he led the friendly troops in a fierce assault that drove the hostile troops from their positions and secured the objective. In the early morning hours of 4 July, the defensive perimeter set up by Captain Ferris was attacked by the fanatically determined enemy. Again he exposed himself to the hostile fire in order to bring direct artillery fire against the on rushing enemy troops Captain Ferris directed an artillery barrage to within a short distance of his own position. In the ensuing action, the enemy assault was crushed by the heavy volume of artillery fire, but Captain Ferris was killed by shrapnel from an artillery's shell which fell near his command post...."

A few days later, we were placed in reserve again, a little distance away from the fighting, and I was offered the opportunity to go on R&R. While I had no great desire to go on R&R again, I thought it would be my last trip to Japan before I was rotated home and I wanted to check out the possibility of a hospital job in Japan after I left Korea. I didn't know that the Army already had plans to send me to Texas. I don't know why the Army could not have told me about my next assignment before I reached America.

Dear Dad and Mother,   *14 July 1951*

While the diplomats are trying to figure out a peace proposal, the war has quieted down somewhat and I am on leave in Japan for five days. I have bought several things, which I am mailing home. I will let you guess what they are until they arrive. There is nothing new to mention as far as rotation goes. I still hope to get home sometime in August or September.

I was out to a Japanese doctor's home last night for supper. We talked long into the night. He knows a little English, which, with my scant linguistic ability in Japanese, we were able to communicate quite well.

The Japanese are very interested in the coming peace treaty for Japan. The efforts of the U.S. to secure a lasting and fair treaty are well appreciated here. Most of the Japanese still consider MacArthur as the source of everything good that has happened to Japan and to a large extent, I am inclined to agree.

Hope all goes well at home.

Love, Bob

When I returned to Korea, I dashed off another letter home while waiting for my driver to pick me up. I mailed it before traveling north again. I didn't know what I would find when I got back to my unit.

Dear Dad and Mother,   *17 July '51*

Back in Korea again, to find no change in the tactical situation. The front is quiet except for patrol skirmishes.

We have been able to get some of the MSC (Medical Service Corps) officers home on rotation and hope to get more home soon, but there are not enough replacement doctors as yet to start any of us home, but there should be soon. There were quite a few doctors whose enlistment was up and doctors were being returned to the Navy. These vacancies have taken up all the MD replacements.

Everyone was of course quite interested in the Japanese peace treaty, but the greatest interest is in the present peace talks about Korea. I am very suspicious that it will only be a temporary stall for another offensive to build up.

Of course, maybe Russia is so alarmed at our war preparations they are going to sing real peace overtures for some months in order to slow down our rearmament while they keep increasing theirs until it is their time to strike. Only time will tell.

The weather here is very warm, with occasional showers to cool things off a little. Time for chow.

Love, Bob

Sometime near mid-July 1951, Cpt. Gilbert Campbell MC had finished his most commendable tour as 3rd Battalion surgeon. He was much admired by the infantrymen because he was a fearless and competent surgeon. Gil also liked to party and imbibe a bit of whiskey now and then. It so happened that Gil was in a festive party mood with infantry friends in the officers club near the rotation center in South Korea when the very corpulent 8th Army surgeon, Col. "Fellow," entered the club, expecting to meet Col. Page, his replacement. But before Col. Fellow could greet Col. Page, a very agile, but tipsy, Cpt. Campbell stepped up to address him.

As Campbell approached the Army surgeon, Col. Fellow, he said something like the following in a loud voice,

"Well, if it isn't Colonel Fellow, our Army surgeon. This man has the body of Sydney Greenstreet and the brains of Mortimer Snerd. This is the man that hid behind nurses' skirts to bug out to south of the Han River with our MASH and Evacuation Hospitals, taking with him all of the helicopters, so that we had to send all of our wounded by trucks and box ambulance to Kimpo airport and fly them to Japan for emergency medical care. This action by this fat colonel caused needless deaths and was undoubtedly the worst screw-up in the history of the U.S. Army Medical Corp!"

After Gil Campbell's verbal assault, Col. Fellow bellowed, "Arrest that man for insulting a superior officer!"

An overweight major MSC, who was an aid to the fat Army Surgeon, made a lunge for Cpt. Campbell, who dashed up the stairs to an elevated deck lounge area. Gil Campbell was a bit of a scrapper and was not exactly a follower of the Marquis de Queensbury rules for pugilistic encounters. As the overweight Major MSC reached out to seize Campbell, he found himself deftly dusted off, and falling flat on the floor. Campbell vaulted the handrail, landed spryly on his feet, and dashed through the door into the night air. By that time, he may have started to sober up and consider his options, none of which was very promising.

But some things worked in Campbell's favor. There were many hardened infantry officers of all ranks who had enjoyed the show that Campbell had just put on and who would be more than happy to testify on his behalf and verify Campbell's statements in any inquiry.

There was also some anger about the collapse of hospital suport caused by the Army Surgeon's movement of the hospitals too quickly and too far away.

In addition, Col. Page followed Campbell out into the night and spoke with Campbell privately, saying something to the effect that he was not unsympathetic to the views Campbell had expressed in the club, but that he was in a lot of trouble unless the matter was settled quickly. Page wanted to avoid having the matter raised to the level of a court martial after Campbell's excellent service on the front line in Korea. Moreover, Col. Page did not want mud splattered over him just as he was assuming the job of Army Surgeon.

I can only speculate about what happened next. My best guess is that Col. Page interceded with Col. Fellow to have him withdraw all charges and prevent the embarrassment to the U.S. Army Medical Corps from a bunch of decorated infantry offices testifying that the basis of Campbell's verbal assault was essentially true.

According to Campbell, he soon found himself on an infantry officers' plane, flying from Korea to Japan, where he entered the rotation line for the United States. He returned to civilian life with two Silver Stars, a Bronze Star with V-Device, and a Purple Heart, all earned during his stint as battalion surgeon for the 3rd Battalion of the 7th Infantry Regiment. He later became a chairman and professor of surgery and retired in Arkansas.

As the month of July rolled on, I realized that most of the people I had entered Korea with had been rotated, promoted to new positions, or evacuated as KIA or WIA. But I continued working as before, without a clear end in sight.

The battles over Hills 717 and 682 were repeated many times during the month of July on other hills. In one three-day battle, the enemy had 575 counted KIA with another 200 estimated dead and 39 Chinese had been taken prisoner. Our Division's losses were 26 KIA and 170 WIA. During July, the 3rd Division's 64th Tank Battalion had nine tanks put out of action by cleverly placed new anti-tank guns. Our tanks were later recovered and repaired while the new Russian anti-tank cannons were vulnerable to napalm and bombs from our planes. The battles clearly revealed the need for balanced weaponry and flexibility in deployment by well-trained soldiers.

It was time to write another letter home. I always got a response.

Dear Dad and Mother,   23 July, 1951

Nothing much new to report. The front is quiet and everyone is wondering what is going to happen next. The Chinese have postponed the peace talks for a few days. One wonders if it's just more of their tricks to build up for new offensive.

Got in a set of new replacements today, all newly drafted. I couldn't help but feel sorry for them. They were quite a forlorn group. Everyone here looked at them with covetous eyes, hoping they would be their replacement for rotation. As yet, there have been no doctors from the 3rd Divisions rotated, except for those whose tour of enlistment was up. I am quite high on the list, if and when they ever start rotating Army doctors.

Some of the MSC officers have been rotated Bill Herrick (Lt.) has been started on the trip home. The only way we got him rotated was by getting field commissions for other high caliber enlisted men and thereby provided a new officer replacement. However, we can't get battlefield commissioned doctors.

I hope the good fishing lasts until I get home.
Love, Bob

One of the many valiant soldiers during the Korean War who after being WIA, hospitalized, and returned to duty, became KIA; Pvt. 1st Class Henry West, 7th Infantry Regiment

Left to right: Maj. Jensen, Tommy, and an infantry officer; Tommy had been recently orphaned after his parents were killed by crossfire, we picked him up, lost and hungry, along the road heading north to the Han River

Tommy with an ambulance driver; he looked pretty good after he felt safe and had a full belly; he quickly became the beloved mascot of the Medical Company

Maj. Jensen (center) at troop presentation for an award ceremony;
14 June 1951

Troop presentation for award ceremony; note Tommy in uniform on the left;
14 June 1951

Awards for June 14th presentation

A newly-promoted Maj. Jensen, background: box ambulance (left) and
collecting station in squad tent (right)

Maj. Jensen (2nd from right) with three new officers of the Medical Company; the squad tent in the background was used for an aid station; July 1951

Vehicle bunkers south of the demilitarized zone in the Iron Triangle leading to underground shelters; July 1951

Chapter Fifteen
A delay of my rotation and a chopper flight over the MLR to rescue Love
Company casualties on Hill 284
August 3, 1951 – September 10, 1951

In early August 1951, the rains were heavy, turning roads into slippery mud streams, making the life of foot soldiers difficult and re-supply on the high hills even more challenging. Most of the Iron Triangle was under our control at the time, and when we controlled the dominant hills in the northern region, it could not be used as a troop and supply assembly area by the Chinese, allowing our troops to move freely throughout the Triangle and to observe the enemy's movements north of us. The net result was a new line of demarcation north of the 38th Parallel. It also meant more time to write and, hopefully, less blood lost fighting.

Dear Dad and Mother,   3 Aug. 1951

Very little activity, except training of replacements and waiting for something to happen. As yet, there have been no doctors for rotation purposes. So far, all the replacement doctors have been used to replace those whose extended enlistments are up or else those doctors going home to Army residencies. If they don't send doctors over any faster, I don't expect any replacement until Sept. Then it will take a month to get processed and home by boat, etc. So you shouldn't expect me until sometime in October. I hope things get speeded up a little for the incoming doctors.

Everyone is watching the truce conference but nobody is very optimistic. Most people expect another offensive. Personally, I am very pessimistic. I wouldn't be surprised at all to find Russia sweeping across Europe and Yugoslavia or Iran this fall. I hope I am wrong.

I will try to get a picture of myself and send home.

Love, Bob

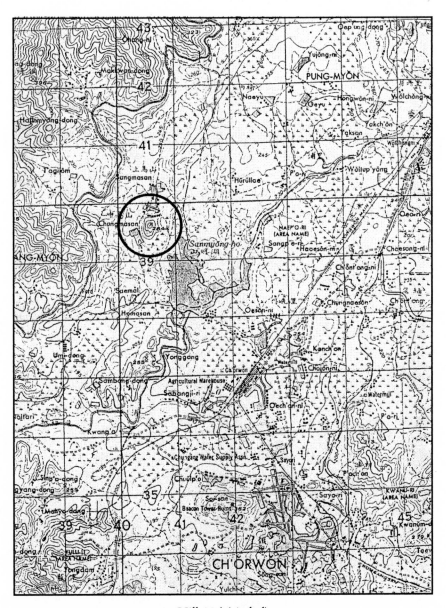

Hill 284 (circled)

The cease-fire talks in Kaesong, combined with the continuing rains, probably slowed the war activity in August. But there was little optimism, and soldiers on both sides used the time to improve their military positions and prepare for the next fight.

Dear Dad and Mother, 9 *Aug. 1951*
The rains came. For the last week there have been sporadic heavy showers every day. The mountains are good watersheds and the small streams in the valleys rapidly swell to overflowing but just as rapidly again recede. The engineers have done a good job on the roads and for the most part, travel is normal.

The lull over the front continues. It is anyone's guess what may happen. We have prepared permanent fortification about 20 miles south of here, where we can scurry to if need be and really give the Chinese a bloody nose if they try to break through here and there. That's one reason we aren't anxious to retreat to the 38th Parallel. We would lose our best positions.

Nothing new on rotation. As usual, the doctors will probably be last. They have a new point system out now for rotation, however, they won't say how many points are needed for rotation. I have about 40 points now and that is equal to 40 months of duty in Japan. There are not many with more points.

There is a Norwegian hospital about 45 miles from us but I haven't been able to get away to visit the place and see what it's like.

Love, Bob

Shortly after writing that letter, I did get a little free time, so I drove south to find the Norwegian MASH, about which I'd heard favorable reports. I hadn't gone very many miles before I saw a new MASH unit with a Norwegian Flag flying over it and I stopped for a visit. Since I had relatives in Norway, I thought I'd introduce myself in Norwegian and see if anyone was from Skien or Ulefos, Norway, where some of my father's family was located. My Norwegian wasn't good enough to get much past the introduction stage before they switched to English and invited my driver and myself for a meal. They were a friendly group, busy caring for casualties from all sources.

An orthopedic surgeon, from Oslo, Dr. Bernhard Paus, appeared to be very interested in my job in the infantry, and expressed a desire to visit me at the front. Usually, normal people don't want to visit places where fighting is going on, because it is viewed as a hazard to health and longevity. But Bernhard Paus was a sturdy Viking, who accepted prudent risk as a small price to pay for expanding the scope of his life experiences. I gave him our last location and told him to search for the 7th Regiment HQ and then ask for the regimental surgeon, Maj. Jensen. I also suggested he look for box ambulances from the 3rd Division because they might be able to lead him to me. Dr. Paus was delighted and said he would come to see me when he had a chance to get away for a few hours.

He took me around to see all of the patients in their hospital. When I saw the fine work they were doing for Korean civilians and ROK soldiers, as well as for some American GIs and other U.N. soldiers, I told them that they were a godsend, especially for the suffering civilians caught up in the war. So many thousands of Korean civilians did not receive the care they needed. After touring the MASH, we toasted each other with a nod and the traditional word *skoal* as we lifted some fine Norwegian brandy to our lips. Then I was on my way back north again.

A week or so later, who showed up in our collecting station but Dr. Bernard Paus, ready and willing to see anything and everything that I cared to show him. He seemed unconcerned about flying metal.

I took Dr. Paus to two of our battalion aid stations and introduced him to some of our infantry NCOs and officers. They were pleasantly surprised to have a visitor from a MASH unit. No one could remember that ever happening before, and some wondered what a MASH doctor was doing up in our battalion.

When I explained that he was from the new Norwegian MASH, one infantry officer laughed and said, "Well that explains everything, Doc. Our visiting doctor here is one of your cousins from Norway, and he doesn't have any more sense than you do to go sightseeing and visiting around infantry units on the line during a stinking war."

That remark caused a bit of a laugh.

The infantry officer continued, "You are both welcome at any time, and just keep up the good work in patching us all up."

Dr. Paus seemed to enjoy his infantry welcome and his brief inspection visit to the line. He returned to his MASH before nightfall.

From official Norwegian records I later read that the Norwegian MASH was set up close behind the front line from July 1951 to November 1954. They treated a total of 90,000 patients of which 14,755 were hospitalized. Dr. Paus had several tours of duty in Korea.[19] Dr. Paus and those who served with him represented Norway very well, indeed.

Things remained quiet around the Iron Triangle during the April rains as we speculated about the future, cleaned our weapons, and wrote letters. What we should have been doing was praying for peace, rather than just speculating about it. But I knew that at least my mother was praying for the war to end.

---

[19] In 1952 and 1962, I had the pleasure of traveling to the Paus private island in the Oslo Fjord, where I enjoyed visiting with his delightful family.

Dear Dad and Mother,   *19 Aug 51*

The problems connected with rotation are multiple. At present, I feel sure I will have a replacement for myself by the middle of Sept., if not before. However, there are a lot of points to consider.

I am afraid that because of my combat experience, I may be stuck in a training unit in the States and then after six months, be sent to Europe. If I come home to the States on rotation, I may have no choice of assignment and until next spring I wouldn't be eligible to apply for discharge.

I have been seriously considering applying for a six-month extension in Japan if I can get in one of the larger hospitals, such as Tokyo General. This way I would be coming home next spring, at a time when I could apply for discharge and it would be more favorably considered than if I were in the States as an essential part of a division trained and ready to go overseas.

I don't know what the best cause to follow is, but you may be sure that whatever I do it will be after careful consideration of all angles. Another thing to consider is that if an all-out war comes, I would be better off in Japan than in the States because I would be sure to be shipped off with a combat unit to Europe or wherever the conflict was if I were in the States. The war here is very quiet now. Everyone wonders what the peace talks will bring.

Love, Bob

It wasn't long before Bill Yuckman sent me a doctor, a newly drafted but mature major MC, direct from the Army Medical Field Service School. He was being considered as my replacement. That was something to celebrate and write home about.

Dear Dad and Mother,   *27 Aug. 1951*

The situation in Korea now looks good from the replacement standpoint. I have my replacement now and will spend the next two weeks getting him acquainted with the many responsibilities of being a regimental surgeon.

In my last letter, I mentioned the possibility of going to Japan. I made a flying trip to Japan to feel out the situation there. Here are the facts. Because of my combat experience, there is a very good chance I would be assigned to a training unit in the States. In this position, I would get no medical experience and would very likely be going to Europe within a month. I know that doesn't sound fair, but that's the way the Army does things. I have gotten word back from some of the doctors in the States who have met such a fate after being rotated from Korea. Also, if I were in such a unit I would have very little chance of being able to resign.

On the other hand, if I extend for six months in Japan, I may be given my choice of hospital assignment and by the time I would be coming home next March. I would be eligible to apply for discharge and if this were not accepted, I would be in a far better position to get a hospital assignment having come from a large general hospital in Japan. When everything is added up, I believe it would be wiser for me to serve six months in Japan.

Love, Bob

I started to introduce my replacement around Regimental HQ and took him back to visit the medical battalion of the 3rd Division. I was a little concerned about his adaptability to service with the infantry, but was hoping for the best. He had a number of years in private family practice and also had emergency room experience that would be of great benefit, but he seemed shy and didn't ask many questions. I showed him around the Medical Company and explained how forward collecting stations were used to support the battalion aid station most in need at any particular time. But it was all theory that could only be conceptualized by visiting the three infantry battalions of the 7th Infantry Regiment.

The plan was to brief him, show him around the three battalions to familiarize him with his future supervisory duties, and introduce him to Col. Boswell at Regimental HQ. At the time, we didn't have any U.N. battalions attached.

I had one of our medic sergeants drive us around in a jeep to visit each battalion, including those on the line. During this drive, I noted that the new major become rather anxious. There was some scattered incoming mortar fire, but it wasn't much to be concerned about because it wasn't landing close to us. But as we talked to the battalion surgeons about their ongoing activities, I observed the new major become increasingly nervous and I started to worry a bit, thinking we might have another "Jitters" on our hands. Except it would be much worse because as regimental surgeon he should set a good example by getting to know the battalion people and he should not be quaking in his boots in the rear area whenever a stray shell went off.

As the tour progressed, it became clear that he didn't enjoy conversing with gung-ho types, so I shortened the tour and sped back to the regimental Medical Company to have a private talk with Maj. "Quak-in-Boots." It seemed that he had been under the impression that the role of regimental surgeon was more ceremonial than command, and more rear area than forward leaning.

According to his visit schedule, I was supposed to introduce my replacement to Col. Boswell after our tour of the Battalions. I began to question whether he was the right man for the job. But as we stood up, I realized he had made the decision easy for me. He had just wet his pants. I could never introduce him to Col. Boswell in that condition, nor could I recommend him as my replacement. I suggested that he look around the collecting station and talk to some of the men while I made a phone call at the division surgeon's office.

When I got Lt. Col. Bill Yuckman on the phone, I asked him to send me another candidate for Regimental Surgeon.

"What happened, Bob?" he asked. "Has he been killed already?"

"No," I responded. "But he wet his pants after I showed him around the infantry battalions and that disqualifies him for a leadership position in this regiment."

"Send him back to me," Yuckman said, "and I'll try to find someone with more courage and better bladder control, but you may be stuck there for another month."

"Sir," I responded, "send me a captain MC with a bit of gumption who wants to be promoted to major, and not a middle-aged doctor who was drafted as a major because of his years of clinical experience in a small town."

That was the last I saw of Maj. Quake-in-Boots, my first replacement candidate for the job of regimental surgeon.

By that time, the orphan Jerry had learned enough English to write my mother to thank her for the books and personal items she had sent him. There were no stamps available, and he had no money to buy them, anyway, so he stuffed his letters in the Army mailboxes, wrote corporal or sergeant in front of his name for a return address, and mailed the letters for free. Since he kept changing the rank, my mother wrote, asking about it, prompting the letter below.

Dear Mother,   *31 Aug 51*

Your wondering about Jerry's rank is natural. Why Jerry keeps changing from Pvt. 1ˢᵗ Class to Sgt. to Cpl. I do not know, except as a boy will do, he selects the one that suits him at the moment he writes. He has no actual rank, since he is not in any army officially. He only stays with the U.S. Army as a very useful civilian unpaid employee. But in order for him to use the Army mail system, it is necessary for him to appear as a military person on the return address. Therefore he uses a rank when he mails a letter.

I received a letter from the little Japanese nurse, Miss Teruko Zige, whom I had other letters from. She wants to try and get a scholarship in this country (USA) and work on her master's degree in economics and then return to Japan. She is a very bright student. I will send her letter on for you to see after I have answered it. I am checking on the possibilities of a scholarship. She has completed the equivalent of a bachelor's degree and then some with a very superior rating. I hope I can help her.

I am glad to see that Dad is home. It will take many weeks before he will regain full use of his legs after being hit by a car, but I am sure it will all end up well. As for the Vets Hospital at Fargo is concerned, I had thought of that but I have had a few poor reports about it and was not too fond of the idea of his going there. The Vets Hospital at Minneapolis is very good, however—the difference being that it is associated with a

medical school, which makes it keep higher standards. I hope your game old hip doesn't give you much trouble. Heat and rest are the best for it, and maybe a little massage.
   Love, Bob

I had received a couple of letters from home dealing with the accident. My dad's car had broken down and while he tried to flag down a passing car for assistance, he was sideswiped and suffered injuries in both legs, which put him in the hospital for a while. I wrote no letters home between August 31 and September 11, 1951 because it was a busy and unsettled time period. While I was dealing with the problem of my replacement, Col. Boswell also received a replacement for one of his battalion commanders. But on arrival, the lieutenant colonel was obviously sobering up from a drinking spree. He was shaking and smelled of stale whiskey.

When I ran into him, I heard him say in a tremulous voice, "I want to get up to my battalion now."

I thought, *I can't believe Col. Boswell would let this uninspiring lieutenant colonel become a battalion commander!*

After Col. Boswell got off the phone with higher authorities, the shaky lieutenant colonel left in a jeep, with his bags, heading for somewhere in the rear area. At the time, it seemed to me to be a gross injustice that a drunk lieutenant colonel with a tremor received the same pay as a brave and intelligent lieutenant colonel, successfully commanding a battalion in combat.

Col. Boswell solved that replacement problem by making Maj. Walter Turner a battalion commander. Maj. Walter Turner had been the S-1 in Sachang-ni. Walt extended for six months, and did a good job as a battalion commander but, sadly, he did not get the expected promotion to lieutenant colonel for his extra effort.

As I waited for my next replacement in early September 1951, I reviewed a list of organizational and tactical changes that had been instituted to improve our recovery and stabilization of casualties for evacuation. The most important lesson we had learned was to stay up to date on the ongoing operations in Regimental HQ and focus our medical support and evacuation effort where it was most needed. There wasn't a book solution—only continual flexible improvisations.

There was a continuing problem in getting helicopter evacuation from outposts in front of the MLR. I was still waiting for a replacement when the outpost battle of Love Company on Hill 284 occurred.[20]

---

[20] The story was first published as "The Medical Saga of Hill 284" in the Summer '97 *Cottonbaler*, pages 6-8. I have rewritten it here to include more details.

Love Company had been placed in a defensive observation position about a mile in front of the MLR. The area around Hill 284 was defended by an extensive minefield. According to a sketch by Frank Hiek, the top of Hill 284 was shaped like a crescent, with the elevated portion facing north. There was a sharp escarpment on the northwest side, which overlooked the broad plain to the north. This corner of Hill 284 was held by the 3rd Platoon. The 2nd Platoon occupied the northeast sector and the 1st Platoon the southeast. Between the first and second platoons was a low area with only a shallow escarpment, covered by machine guns, wire and mines. Hill 284 had an excellent view of all likely attack routes from the north, but under cover of darkness, the enemy could attack from any side. As it turned out, the heaviest Chinese attacks on Hill 284 came from the east-southeast, and not from the north.

As Regimental Surgeon, I was concerned about the difficulty in providing medical care for outposts that were far out in front of the MLR. To reach Hill 284, it was necessary to follow a winding two-mile trail through a minefield and over a dam that was probably mined and under Chinese surveillance. Helicopters were still in short supply and because of recent helicopter losses, an order was issued by an I Corps general that prohibited medical evacuation helicopters from flying in front of the MLR. Medical evacuation from places like Hill 284 was going to be difficult. Everyone at 3rd Division HQ understood that preplanning and prepositioning of medical support saved lives, but none of it would apply if I could not persuade a helicopter pilot to fly out to Hill 284.

We listened in on the field radio talk during the battle over Hill 284. It was grim. On the night of the sixth and the morning of the seventh of September 1951, the Chinese attacked L Company in waves, with little heed for the exploding mines and machine gun fire. The Love Company commander called down our own artillery around their positions, while the men fought with bayonets, bullets, and grenades to prevent attacking enemy soldiers from jumping into their defensive bunkers and foxholes in order to avoid the artillery explosions.

After suffering staggering casualties, the Chinese attackers withdrew before dawn, leaving dozens of their dead and injured strewn across the slopes and summit of Hill 284. Love Company also had dead and wounded and, as expected, they called for evacuation of wounded and a re-supply of ammunition, food, and water.

We already had box ambulances parked next to my jeep and a cooler of type O blood from a MASH at the MLR near one of our battalion aid stations. Knowing I would need a helicopter to get out to Hill 284 before dawn, I had already scheduled a pre-dawn helicopter visit to our forward collecting station, neglecting to mention that we were sitting on the MLR.

Early on 7 September 1951, before the sun kissed the horizon, a Bell-13 bubble chopper, with two litter pods, fluttered down to our signal flare. I was glad to see that the pilot was Joe, a man I had flown with before because it was going to require some negotiation.

Joe hopped out of the chopper with a cheery, "Hi, Doc. Good to see you again. Got your casualties ready to fly?"

"Sure, Joe," I said, "they're ready to be picked up, but they aren't here. They're on a hill about a mile north of here, and I need you to take me to them with this case of blood. Some of them need it bad. I can show you the way."

"Well, Doc," he said, "why didn't you just drive out there and bring the blood to them?"

"I couldn't do that, Joe, because there are no roads through the mine fields between here and there."

"Mine fields!" Joe exclaimed. "Where in hell are we? And where in hell are they? They must be way the hell out in front of the damn MLR, and I have orders to not fly in front of any MLR. If I get shot down out, there I would be in deep kimchee from some general and up to my *** in land mines!"

"Well, Joe, look at it this way," I said. "If you are shot down, I will be with you and can give you blood if you need it. And if we make it and save our soldiers lives, you will be a hero, and no general wants to pick on a hero getting a medal for valor."

"But, Doc, you don't seem to understand. I was given a specific order to not fly in front of the MLR," Joe said.

At that point, my patience was about gone, so I said, "You know, Joe, if that general was standing here right now and knew our soldiers were bleeding to death out on Hill 284, he would immediately amend his order and tell you to stop stalling and take me out there without further delay. Moreover, Joe, it's fairly safe now because there's a haze over the valley, so if we take off over that haze, no one is going to see us until we get to Hill 284."

"What haze are you talking about?" Joe said. "I don't see any haze."

I pulled my S&W .38 Special out of its holster and dragged the barrel across Joe's belly for added emphasis before I pointed north, drawing a bead on Hill 284 in the distance.

"Look where I am pointing, Joe," I said. "And then look at the haze covering the valley. We have some cover. No more delay. The time to go is now, Joe. Now! Now! Now!"

Joe eyed my revolver and said. "To hell with what that general said back in Corps. What the hell does he know about this spot? If he was here now, he would tell us to go, right?"

"That's right, Joe," I said. "In fact, we should already be out there, so let's get this whirly bird going."

We took off without further argument, still well before the morning sun broke the horizon.

On the way, Joe asked, "How many wounded do you have out there, Doc?"

"I don't know," I said. "But I suspect there are three or four in very bad shape and maybe a half dozen more that don't have life-threatening wounds. When we get there, I'll do a quick triage, start blood, and try to stop the bleeding on the most seriously wounded while you shuttle the first load of the less seriously wounded back to the aid station we just left. Then return immediately for the very seriously wounded, and if we have them stabilized by the time you return, you must rush them straight back to the nearest MASH. Then gas up and return immediately back out to Hill 284 for the rest of the wounded. If the Chinese start shelling the place, we'll wave you off."

"But, Doc, how will you get back if you wave me off?" Joe said.

"That's not something to be concerned about now. Let's just get all the wounded off that bloody hill first."

By the time we finished shouting over the chopper noise, we had landed on the south side of Hill 284, to be greeted by a bunch of dirty, bloody, and bedraggled smiling faces. I asked the company medics to bring three soldiers with serious, but not life-threatening, wounds, to send off on the first trip, and to help me get blood infusions going in the worst casualties. I was immediately led to Pvt. 1st Class Jerry Crump, who had been blown out of a fighting bunker that he had occupied with three or four others. In the heat of battle, an enemy soldier had managed to hurl a grenade into the bunker.

Crump had shouted, "Grenade!" and threw himself past his friend Earl Brown in an effort to cover the grenade with his helmet and body.

As the grenade exploded, Crump and Brown were blasted backward. Crump landed unconscious on top of Brown, who, though stunned, was sickened to find his left hand laying inside Crump's abdominal cavity. Two seconds later, a concussion grenade exploded in the same bunker and the explosion catapulted the soldiers up and over the rim of their bunker.

Crump's sacrificial action inspired an immediate bayonet, bullet, and grenade counterattack from the surviving L Company soldiers. Marion Goslin, Bob Klebart, John Myrich, Eugene Owen, John Scott, Frank Hiek, Gene Warshawsky, and Richard Bowman were among those who rose to the challenge to repel the invaders. Master Sgt. Bowman was among the dead.

My biggest concern was to keep Crump alive. Although I could not find a pulse, I managed to find a vein in his right arm, and started blood running in. He was lying in a twisted position and was the color of ash. When we tried to roll him onto his back to free up his left arm and straighten out his legs, a part of his intestines and blood flowed out of a large gash in the left side of his abdomen. I surmised that the rim of his helmet had been blown back, gouging the wound in his abdomen.

I poured some sterile saline on a large belly bandage and folded his intestines over the top of this wet-pack. Underneath the abdominal cavity was a sea of fresh blood. Unable to see the source of the bleeding, I used my hand to scoop blood out of his abdomen until I saw the outline of his left kidney. Then I saw a slow, but very weak, agonal pulsing of blood that seemed to be coming from a torn left renal artery. It was clear that his gallant heart was in the last throes of pumping the last of his blood into his abdominal cavity. Immediately, I pulled out a large curved hemostat, and, pressing blindly near the abdominal aorta at the mid region of the left kidney, I squeezed the clamp shut. The slow agonal pulsing stopped. I then noticed a weak spurting of blood that could have been an artery to the mesentery or spleen. I used a second smaller clamp to stop that leak.

With his aorta still pulsing slowly, and finding no other blood spurting, I carefully folded his intestines back into the abdominal cavity. I used another sa-line-soaked belly pad to cover the abdominal wound. We slipped a third belly pad under his back and used the ties around the front of it to hold the pads over his abdomen. There were multiple fragmentation holes in his intestines, stomach, colon, liver, spleen, and lung, but they weren't big wounds or spurting blood. Crump's helmet had apparently protected his heart and most of his lungs.

All I could do for the many external wounds was apply pressure dressings and give more blood. In order to make the blood run in faster, I had two soldiers hold the bottles as high as they could, and when the bottles emptied, two more were started as the helicopter returned from its first trip behind the MLR.

Jerry Crump and his friend Earl Brown were loaded into the pods. Each had blood or saline with albumen running into their veins. A lightly wounded soldier sitting next to the pilot had the task of keeping the life-sustaining fluid running into the veins of the wounded soldiers lying in the pods. Just before they took off, I detected a pulse in Crump's neck and Brown was regaining consciousness. On the second trip, the pilot went directly to the nearest MASH unit. As they lifted off, I breathed a prayer to Jesus to look after Jerry Crump, for he had sustained enough injuries to kill two or three soldiers. I would have liked to have been in the MASH operating room to hear the discussion when they found two clamps in the belly under his guts.

I imagined them asking, "What idiot clamped the renal artery out there on the battlefield?"

After the pilot left with the second load, I examined the rest of the dead and injured among the Chinese and Americans. I saw one Chinese moving, a little way away. I asked the company commander if it would be possible to bring in the wounded Chinese soldier.

A sergeant answered, saying, "Hell, Doc, why don't we just put him out of his misery from here with a bullet through the head? He's in a mine field."

I asked if he knew a safe way through the mines.

He said, "I know the way because I set out the mines, but I wouldn't ask any of the soldiers to go out there with me to rescue a Chinaman after the bad night we have had."

"Could we bring the Chinaman back together if I went with you?" I asked.

The sergeant thought for a moment and said, "Doc, you came out here for us, so I will go out there with you if saving that damn Chinaman means that much to you."

"Sergeant," I said, "It's just the right thing to do."

So the two of us walked carefully out to the wounded Chinese soldier and carried him back between us. I was careful to step only where the sergeant stepped.

The Chinese soldier had been shot in several places, including an abdominal wound. We carried him back to the helicopter landing spot, where I gave him blood and morphine for pain and dressed his wounds. There was some murmuring from a few soldiers about rescuing the "chink." I didn't discuss the matter further, but I thought I'd made the point that, as Americans, we should try to rescue all wounded. I also thought about the wounded Chinese prisoner in Sachangni who had insulted one of our KATUSA soldiers and paid for it with his life. In a way, I felt that rescuing that last Chinaman was an atonement for the Chinese prisoner that was shot while in my custody in North Korea. I never learned whether the wounded Chinese soldier survived, but if he did, he was part American, because he had some American blood running in his veins.

Sometime later, the helicopter returned for a third load. I loaded the Chinese soldier into one pod and a soldier with a leg wound into the other pod. A walking wounded soldier went into the seat next to the pilot. By that time, the fog was lifting. I told Joe to go straight to the MASH again and suggested he try to make a return trip for the remaining walking wounded, but if there were signs of enemy incoming mortars or artillery, to go back without landing, since he would only draw more enemy fire.

As the chopper lifted off, Col. Jim Boswell walked in with food, water, ammunition, and replacements. He was a bit surprised to see me on that hill, clearing out the last of the wounded. Boswell talked with the men and officers to congratulate and encourage them. As the supply group prepared to walk back through the minefield trail, some incoming shells overshot us by about 50 yards. The soldiers immediately took cover and we waved off the returning helicopter. Joe saw the shells explode, and probably would have turned around, even if we hadn't waved him off.

As I walked back overland with Col. Boswell and the others, I remarked that his visit to L Company was an encouragement for the men. Big Jim Boswell stopped in his tracks and faced me.

"Doc," he said, "I am the S.O.B. that put Love Company out here on this hill. Seeing me did nothing for their morale. The real morale booster for the men was seeing you arrive out on that bloody hill before the break of day to tend to their wounds. What I want to know, Doc, is how in hell you got that helicopter not only to fly out here, but to then make three trips? I sure as hell couldn't get a chopper to bring me out here."

"Sir," I said, "after getting the chopper up to the MLR, the pilot and I had a discussion, and after that, I simply pointed out the direction to go, he brought me out here, and we started shuttling casualties."

I didn't mention that I had pointed the way with my revolver. That might have raised some eyebrows. I think Col. Boswell already knew more than he wanted to, so he changed the subject.

"Doc," he said, "do you think Crump will survive?"

"I don't know, sir. He was as close to being dead as a man can be without being dead. I was able to stop the loss of blood from a major internal artery and fill up his circulatory system again with more blood. But if I had been delayed another 15 minutes by arguing about not flying in front of the MLR, Private First Class Crump would have been dead. If his parents are praying for him, he has a chance of making it."

Fortunately, they were, and their prayers were answered.

By word-of-mouth reports from the MASH, I learned that Crump had to have his left kidney, his spleen, and parts of his intestines removed, and multiple holes in his intestines, liver, lung, side, and hip cleaned up and sutured. For days, his life hung in the balance, sustained only by prayer and the vigilant care from the MASH staff. Six months later, to our great joy, we learned that Cpl. Jerry Crump had lived to receive the Congressional Medal of Honor from President Harry Truman in the White House. Jerry stayed on in the Army for a full career, married his sweetheart, fathered two daughters, and retired as a master sergeant.

I had seen a lot of blood and misery between Sachang-ni and Hill 284. I knew the infantry commanders had to keep their focus on the fighting men. They didn't often tell us what to do or how they felt about us. Our job was to be where we needed to be and do whatever needed doing. And that is what being a combat medic is all about.

On our walk back, I told Boswell that my rotation replacement was expected soon at Regimental HQ and that Hill 284 may have been my last little battlefield adventure. He laughed for a moment before lapsing into silence. I knew he was thinking about turning over his command to another infantry colonel. It's not an easy thing to turn over command in the middle of a war. It would have been so much nicer to have finished the war before all of the rotations started.

I never had the chance to meet Master Sgt. Richard E. Bowman. He was already dead when I arrived on Hill 284. I wondered why there was no mention of Hill 284 in his award. Chorwon was five or 10 miles south of us and was already in our hands. Sometimes award writers selected the nearest town big enough to be found on a map, but the families of the people who fought and died on Hill 284 might have preferred to know the exact location.

Award of the Distinguished-Service Cross (posthumous) to Master Sgt. Richard E. Bowman

"Master Sergeant Richard E. Bowman...while a member of Company L, 7th Infantry Regiment, 3rd Infantry Division, distinguished himself by extraordinary heroism in action against the enemy in the vicinity of Chorwon, Korea, on 6 and 7 September 1951. During the night of 6 September, Company L's defensive positions were attacked by a numerically superior and fanatically determined hostile force. Advancing under cover of a smoke screen, wave after wave of enemy troops hurled themselves against the friendly defenses. After the battle had raged for two hours, with each enemy assault being successfully repulsed, the hostile force suddenly shifted its attack to a different sector of the defense perimeter. Under the terrific pressure of this attack, the perimeter was breached and the enemy began to pour through the gap. Realizing the dangerous threat posed by this break in the friendly lines, Sergeant Bowman immediately moved across the fire-swept terrain, organizing men for a counter-attack. He then fearlessly led them forward in the face of the devastating enemy fire and engaged the hostile troops in hand-to-hand combat. Early on the morning of 7 September, with the friendly forces fighting fiercely, Sergeant Bowman observed a fresh enemy force poised to attack his squad from the flank. Without hesitation, he charged the enemy troops single-handedly, effectively delaying them and diverting their fire from his men until he fell, mortally wounded by the intense hostile fire concentrated on him. His aggressive action so inspired the friendly troops that they successfully executed their counter-attack and drove the enemy from the area...."

Award of the Congressional Medal of Honor to Cpl. Jerry K. Crump

"Corporal Jerry K. Crump, member of L Company, 7th Infantry Regiment distinguished himself by conspicuous gallantry and outstanding courage above and beyond the call of duty in action against the enemy near Chorwon, Korea, on 6 and 7 September 1951. During the night, a numerically superior hostile force launched an assault against his platoon on Hill 284, over-running friendly positions and swarming into the sector. Corporal Crump repeatedly exposed himself to deliver effective fire into the ranks of the assailants, inflicting numerous casualties. Observing two enemy soldiers endeavoring to capture a friendly machine gun, he charged and killed both with his bayonet, regaining control of the weapon. Returning to his position, now occupied by four of his wounded comrades, he continued his accurate fire into enemy troops surrounding his emplacement. When a hostile soldier hurled a grenade into his position, Corporal Crump immediately flung himself over the missile, absorbing the blast with his body and saving his comrades from death or serious injury. His aggressive actions so inspired his comrades that a spirited counterattack drove the enemy from the perimeter. Corporal Crump's heroic devotion to duty, indomitable fighting spirit, and willingness to sacrifice himself to save his comrades reflect the highest credit on himself, the Infantry, and the United States Army."

Jerry Crump, wearing his Congressional Medal of Honor awarded by President Truman; 1952

Chapter Sixteen
Thanksgiving dinner at home, bloddy snow by the blulder, then off to Texas in January 1952 for training and to meet the love of my life, Rosemary
September 11, 1951 – February 20, 1954

There is a special type of loneliness that sets in when one no longer sees familiar faces. All of the original sergeants and officers in my Medical Company had rotated. Amazingly, they had all survived the war. The division surgeon had collected several new MSC and MC Officers into a working team that would soon be coming in to take over the Medical Company of the 7th Infantry, and I would be free to rotate home. A Cpt. William F. Wagenbach MC, had been picked to replace me as Regimental Surgeon. Even Col. Boswell and Lt. Col. Weyand were leaving, or gone as well as other commanders. I felt the rotation loss of familiar friends and comrades.

As I wrote another letter home, it seemed that I would soon be replaced, but it had not happened yet. Perhaps the division surgeon wanted me to finish training the last bunch of replacements before he sent in the new team. I could never be sure what was happening at division level, because there were also rotation considerations in the medical battalion at 3rd Division and in the 15th and 65th Regiments.

Dear Dad and Mother,   11 Sept. 51

Time drags on. It looks as though the peace talks will come to nothing and I don't think anyone thought they would, except possibly Harry Truman. The tempo of things at the front has been stepped up during the last two weeks with sharper clashes along the front than there have been for the past two months. It looks to me as if another week may see the onset of another CC offensive, although I don't think they will have any better luck then they did with their last two big offensives.

I imagine you are wondering whether I will ever be rotated. Well, I sometimes wonder myself. I expect to be out of Korea at least by the end of the month, if not before.

At present, I am busy training new men. It seems odd to be considered an old veteran but that's the way things go. At least two-thirds of the men in the company are not of the original bunch that came over. Many of the officers here were enlisted men when they came over. I now have three battlefield commissioned officers in the company. I am not sure yet whether or not I will stop for a few months in Japan before I come home. I won't decide until I get to Japan and then see which way the wind blows. So many things can happen to change the picture.

Love, Bob

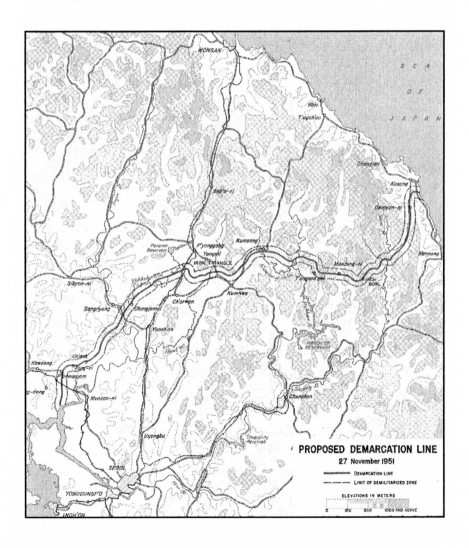

There was a bit more activity of the 38th Parallel Medical Society at that time, with even a professional conference being held occasionally. Lt. Col. Bill Yuckman was trying to generate a bit more medical *esprit de corps* among the doctors. The 8ᵗʰ Army command decided that an award should be given to the regiment with the lowest venereal disease rate. After gathering some statistics from all of the U.N. forces, it was announced by the 8ᵗʰ Army HQ that the Canadian Princess Pat Brigade had the lowest venereal disease (VD) rate, and the award was to be presented to the Canadian surgeon at one of the meetings of the 38th Parallel Medical Society, which was attended by some rear area infantry brass.

The Canadian surgeon was a crusty sort, not given to making something out of nothing. According to my memory, which is not infallible after 50 years. when the Canadian surgeon came forward to receive the Lowest VD Rate Award and say a few words about his stellar achievement, he bellowed out something as follows: "Fellow soldiers, I am pleased to accept this singular honor. However, as to how we honored Canadians achieved the lowest VD rate among all of the U.N. forces, I must credit the physical location of the Canadian force, for we are in the middle of the line in a depopulated, denuded mountain area, and there is not so much as a single vagina within fifty miles of our location. And if this award turns out to be my singular claim to fame in the Korean War, I am, of all men, most miserable."

The Canadian surgeon's choice of words sounded somewhat familiar. He had used a phrase that could only have come from the King James version of the Bible. The apostle Paul wrote in the New Testament, I Corinthians 15:19, "If in this life only we have hope in Christ, we are of all men most miserable." Probably most of the men did not catch his King James phraseology, but the Canadian doctor received a hearty applause, with laughter, from all the doctors.

However, some of the busy-work brass in attendance thought his remarks were miserable and his reference to the non-availability of vaginas was neither appropriate nor funny. But that VD rate award conference did provide the Army doctors in the 38th Parallel Medical Society with a bit of comic relief.

I did not mention that bit of comic relief in my next letter home, since I thought my mother would consider the Canadian's distortion of scripture sacrilegious.

Dear Dad and Mother,   Oct. 6, '51

I am not doing much now but waiting for the red tape to clear away for me to leave Korea. I hope to be on my way in a week, but the way some things have dragged out I don't believe anything until I see it. As far as a stay in Japan is concerned, I have not decided as yet. If I can get the choice job I want in Tokyo Army Hospital, I will take it for six months, otherwise I will come straight home and take my chances on a decent assignment in the States. I had long since hoped to have my next letter tell of my departure from Korea but as yet I can't set a definite date.

I am glad you got the package OK. Silver set, binoculars, etc. They are some of the better buys in Japan. There are some excellent buys in other things, such as pearls, hand-carved furniture, and cabinets, etc. I am thinking of getting a couple of hand-carved cabinets made to mount my radio phonograph in.

Love, Bob

After Cpt. William Wagenbach arrived to replace me, Bill Yuckman asked me to stay on as medical battalion commander in the 3rd Division for six months, with the promise of a promotion to lieutenant colonel. I was flattered by the offer and started to say I would think it over, but my gut told me no, so I said no. It was time for me to go home. I didn't even want to stopover in Japan.

But I rejoiced that I'd had the best support possible from two fine division surgeons—Lt. Col. Joe Bayne, who rotated in June 1951, and his replacement, Lt. Col. Bill Yuckman, who didn't rotate until April 1952. I would have enjoyed working for Bill Yuckman at division level and, as was pointed out to me, it might have been a good steppingstone to becoming a medical corps general some day, but my gut told me that was not the Lord's will for my life.

Before I went overseas, I prayed that the Lord would give me courage to do my duty, no matter what happened to me. The Lord faithfully answered that prayer during my time in the 7th Infantry Regiment. Now that my replacement had arrived, I was weary, perhaps even fearful of going beyond the Lord's tether. I trusted that God would pick me up again at the time, place, and work of His choosing. The following letter was one my parents had been waiting to receive.

Dear Dad and Mother,   11 October 1951

Well, the long-awaited news has arrived. I am now in the 3rd Division Replace-ment Center in Seoul. It will probably be a week before I arrive in Japan. I believe I will come on home instead of staying in Japan for a few months.

At last, after eleven long months, I am getting off the front. My next letter will probably have a stamp on it.

Love, Bob

There was one last indignity rotating soldiers had to endure before we were allowed to get on the plane for Japan from the replacement depot in Korea. All of the men were lined up for a short arm inspection, and no rank was excluded from the need to assure the home folk that no sexually transmitted diseases were being brought home to America. I suspect the Army MASH nurses were able to opt out of the SAI routine.

Dear Dad and Mother,   19 Oct. '51

I am now in Japan, awaiting transportation home. I expect I will get a ship in about a week and another ten days to two weeks for the trip to the States, so if all goes well I should be home between the 10ᵗʰ and 15ᵗʰ of November.

I still do not know where I will be assigned in the States but if necessary, I will make a trip to Washington, D.C. to the Army Surgeon General's office to try to get a good assignment.

Enclosed is an example of Chinese money. I am using Middle River as my forwarding address, so you will probably have some mail waiting for me when I get there.

Love, Bob

Dear Dad and Mother,   21 Oct. '51

I will be leaving Japan for the States tomorrow. I should arrive in San Francisco sometime between the 5ᵗʰ and 17ᵗʰ of November, depending on whether the ship will have numerous stops or go straight across. I will send a wire when I get to San Francisco. Upon arrival at San Francisco, I will probably go by train to Minneapolis for a 30-day leave. See you soon.

Love, Bob

No sooner had I found my assigned bunk on the troop ship than I was visited by a young Navy doctor, who had found my name with an MC attached on the ship manifest. He wanted assistance in running sick call and, as a reward, I could have a bunk in sick bay. So I volunteered to work with him. He was quite busy and it turned out to be a full-time job for eleven days as we traveled from Yokohama to San Francisco.

We had barely cleared Yokohama Harbor when a young soldier showed up with a hot appendix—ready to rupture. He'd been hiding it for three days, fearing he would miss his ship home. We gave him a spinal anesthesia, but soon ran into a storm. The ship was pitching and rolling so much that we had to operate on the patient partly sitting up to keep the spinal medication from causing paralysis all the way up to his neck. But it turned out well, and by the time we reached San Francisco, he had his stitches out and was able to walk off the ship and catch a bus home.

The reception in San Francisco consisted of a brass band and a very short welcome home speech, broadcast over a loudspeaker as we tied up to the dock. Those who expected more ceremony with a parade, confetti, and girls to kiss were sadly disappointed. Hundreds of U.S. troops filed off the ship to form lines in alphabetical order in a huge warehouse, where we received orders for leave and our next duty assignments. My orders were to report in at Fort Sam Houston in

San Antonio, Texas, to attend an Advanced Officers Training Course, starting in January 1952 at the Army Medical Field Service School.

As expected, I couldn't get a flight, but managed to get a train reservation to Minneapolis. On 2 November, I gathered my duffel bags and sent a Western Union Telegram from San Francisco to my dad at Middle River, Minnesota:

"Arrived in San Francisco today. Proceed to Minneapolis tonight. See you in a few days, Bob."

I also called my brother, John, at the Phi Rho Sigma Medical Fraternity in Minneapolis, to alert him that I was on my way.

I remember nothing about that train ride. I don't even recall if I slept all the way. I was depressed, not because of leaving friends and the continuing challenge in Korea, but because I hadn't yet adjusted to reentering life in America. I didn't exactly know how to behave in a land where there was so little awareness or concern over the life-and-death struggles going on in Korea. But it was good to see my brother again after 17 months away. John helped me to unwind. He had experienced a similar depression reaction after returning from World War II.

While in Minneapolis, I went to visit Professor Cecil J. Watson, chairman of the Department of Medicine, to see about entering the Internal Medicine Residency Program. Dr. Watson was surprised to see me, because he had recently heard I'd been killed in Korea. I was pleased to tell him that the report of my death had been exaggerated. He was very gracious and offered me a residency spot in July 1952, or later if I couldn't get out of the military that soon.

But after going on medical rounds in the University Hospital, I felt as if I was in a foreign land, and very much left behind in the art and science of medicine. Medicine is a time-consuming continual study of ever-changing information. In addition, there was a subtle anti-war and anti-U.S. military manner of thinking in some of the people at the University of Minnesota, including the assumption that our military leaders were not trying hard enough to stop the war and make peace. I felt like speaking up and calling those people idiots, but I held my tongue. Perhaps those naive attitudes had been there all along and I'd just not noticed before. But faced with that sort of mental garbage after returning from Korea, I felt defensive for the honor of the U.S. military. I didn't think I could happily put up with such political nonsense.

I also found myself thinking that if some of those superior-sounding sophists had followed me around in Korea and had to do what I had been trying to do to save lives, most of them would have wet their pants. And if they had been put into an infantry squad, they would probably have been the first to shoot themselves in the foot to get out of combat. I soon realized that most people didn't wish to hear war stories and any polite request for information was just to be polite. Few wanted to hear a truthful response, and most didn't want to be troubled with stark realities that defied simplistic solutions.

The real problem was that I had not yet adjusted to life in America. Even my speech pattern had become a simplistic English that could quickly switch into a pidgin mix of English-Japanese-Korean for use with our KATUSA. So after a couple of days of touching base around the University of Minnesota Medical School and Hospital, I decided to visit a wider circle, listen more, and talk less. To facilitate traveling, I bought myself a new Dodge car, which helped to lift my spirits.

On the way to northern Minnesota, I stopped by St. Cloud for a pleasant, but not heart-throbbing, visit with Rachel and her mother. There were no welcome home hugs or girlish squeals of delight that let a boy know his presence is really appreciated at the heart level. I was aching to love and be loved, but it was clear that I would just need to be patient until the right young lady came along.

After the short visit, I drove north to Middle River, where my dad had purchased a house. Dad was still teaching agriculture and farming to a group of veterans under the GI bill, and Mother was teaching English and other subjects on the nearby Indian Reservation. It was a happy reunion, with a lot of talk but no deep probing. I read newspapers and several books in the next couple of days while waiting for my brother, John, to arrive for Thanksgiving Day and the weekend holiday. I was happy to see John drive in, because we still had a lot of talking to do.

The Thanksgiving Day dinner was a time of abundance, with the traditional turkey and all of the trimmings and the enjoyment of being together again. We put the camera on a tripod and set the timer to get a picture of the four of us. In order to see all the faces, John and I sat on one side and Mother and Dad sat on each end of the table. This, of course, left one side of the table empty, but we decided that big space was for Jesus to be present at our table. The Thanksgiving dinner with my mother, father, and brother was truly a time of thanksgiving to the Lord.

During the dinner, my mother asked if I had received any medals besides the Silver Star. I said no, but that there was a rumor in 1st Battalion Headquarters that I was being considered for a Bronze Star with V-Device for wading across the Han River and hiding in the grass to care for wounded while fighting was going on around us. There was another rumor in Regimental Headquarters that I was being considered for a second Silver Star for flying out to Love Company to treat our casualties and for carrying a wounded Chinese soldier out of a mine field on Hill 284. But I heard nothing more about those proposed citations after I left Korea. As so often happens, nothing ever came of the rumored awards. Probably the fact that I had never been wounded in action was the reason that no more awards were given. In fact, it is actually rather difficult to get medals without having been wounded in action. It may also just have been the fact that there were so many people being rotated in September and October of 1951 that the paperwork may just have gotten lost or just didn't get done.

Later in 1952, I received a generic Bronze Star with Oak Leaf Cluster for meritorious service in Korea after I reached my next duty station in Texas. That seemed strange, because there was no record of the original Bronze Star with V-Device. However, my greatest reward was the close friendships I had made with the clan of infantry warriors and medics who served our country so faithfully.

My mother's expressions of thankfulness to God for my safe return during mealtime prayers and on Thanksgiving Day helped me to focus on some unfinished business I had neglected with the Lord. Therefore, after John left to go back to the university, I decided to drive up to the home by Lake of the Woods, to the prayer rock.

My dad pointed out that it was freezing outside, the lake had frozen over, and the house was closed up and cold. It was not a good time for a two hundred-mile round trip with the snow blowing. But my parents understood it was some type of pilgrimage for me. I started out with food and drink in a cooler, warm clothes, and a few heavy concrete blocks in the trunk for better traction. It was typical winter gear for cars in northern Minnesota before the advent of four-wheel drive SUVs.

It was a pleasant trip, even with the light snow. I reached Williams, Minnesota, without problem, and visited old friends as I gassed up. Then I stopped at Lundsten's General Store to chat with Melvin and his Uncle Jimmy, who'd been a lieutenant in the infantry in World War I. Jimmy Lundsten's son, Leslie, had also become a doctor. There was no problem swapping stories in Lundsten's store.

I thanked them for sending the boxes of felt shoes with rubbers to Korea and assured them they were much appreciated. They were delighted to hear a first-hand report and hastened to let me know that my father had paid for all of the felt shoes. They said my parents had both been worried, but proud of me.

My father had told everyone that would listen, "Bob is working as a doctor in the thick of the fighting in Korea."

When I got to the lakeshore, I parked by the house, but didn't go in. Instead, I walked about two hundred yards down the lakeshore, climbing over some fallen trees and heavy ice slabs that had pushed up on shore before the lake had frozen all of the way across. There on the beach, encrusted with ice, was the big granite boulder on which I had sat and had prayed for courage to do my duty in spite of personal danger, before I left for Korea. I knew that God had answered that prayer over and over again in Korea.

But I had also promised God to return to this very rock to thank Him for bringing me home. Now, seventeen months later, I was at last back to give thanks and worship as I had promised to do if He brought me home safely from Korea. It was unfinished business I should have attended to sooner. It's not good to keep the Lord waiting for one to keep promises made.

So I called out to God, "I'm back from Korea, Lord, and thanks to You, Lord, I'm all in one piece."

But then it occurred to me that God knew who and where I was at all times and at that moment, I was not demonstrating proper reverence or humility before the Lord God Almighty. So I thought I should climb up on top of the big boulder and assume a more reverent position. However, it was now winter on the Canadian border of Minnesota.

I tried to pull myself up to the top of the boulder by gripping a projecting ice slab with my bare hands. The ice slab suddenly broke from my weight. I tried to stop myself from falling by grabbing the newly-broken edge of ice and, in doing so, I cut the palms of my hands on the sharp edge of ice as I slid down the side of the rock and into the snow. I looked down at the bloody snow. I remembered well what bloody snow looked like in Korea. Only this time, and for the first time since I left home, the blood on the snow was my own. I had not lost a single drop of blood while I was in Korea.

God was giving me a wake up call. Not only had He given me courage to do my duty, but He had also protected me, and even protected those around me. I realized that I shouldn't have tried to climb on top of the rock; it was now more appropriate to just lean against it, as I had leaned on Jesus, the real Rock, for strength to do my duty in Korea.

I used the snow to wash the blood off my hands and constrict the bleeding before wrapping handkerchiefs around my hands. I thought about what Jesus' blood on the cross has done for all who believe. I had taken advantage of the Lord's goodness and had not yet rendered Him due worship. I was still a sinner and totally dependent on His death on the cross and resurrection for my salvation. Feeling very unworthy, I could only revert to the 23rd Psalm, only this time, I made it more personal, specific, and confessional, putting some of the verbs into the past tense and inserting a few extra words in parentheses, thinking of what the Lord had done for me in Korea. And thus I prayed:

"The Lord is my shepherd; I **did not** want (in Korea). He **made** me to lie down in green pastures (as well as in snow and mud); He **led** me beside the still waters, (across oceans and rivers). He **restored** my soul (in spite of my failings); He **led** me in the paths of righteousness for His name's sake (Jesus my Lord and Savior).

"Yea, though I **walked** through the valley of the shadow of death, I **feared** no evil; for Thou **wast** with me; Thy rod and Thy staff they **comforted** me (and gave me courage). Thou **prepared** a table before me in the presence of mine enemies (and shielded me and my close associates from shrapnel and bullets);

"Thou **anointed** my head with oil (a protective blessing while on the battle field); my cup runneth over (and I now belong to You forever!). Surely goodness and mercy shall follow me all the days of my life; and I will dwell in the house of the Lord forever."

I stood a while, reflecting on the bloody trails in Korea and the many who had died and were still dying. I received no explanations of imponderable events—only a growing sense of the magnitude of God's sovereign grace for me personally.

For how else does one explain turning over in a jeep and landing in a rice paddy with only a posterior dislocation of an index finger that I reduced by simply pulling on it? How else does one explain working on wounded soldiers in a small house for five days without being hit by the same mortar fire that had leveled every other house in the area? How else does one explain a 120 mm mortar shell that failed to explode when it landed right next to me? How else does one explain an airburst of an artillery shell directly overhead that sent multiple pieces of hot shrapnel screaming down through the canvas roof of our mess tent into our mess table without hitting any of the six people sitting around it? How else does one explain a sniper who continued to fire, but failed to hit any of us loading patients into a Marine helicopter? How else does one explain two occasions when I turned off of the road to attend casualties while the vehicle behind went on to be blown up by a mine? How else does one explain a shrapnel dent in my helmet and no shrapnel dent in my head? How else does one explain Bill Herrick's "charmed" life on the battlefield, rescuing soldier after soldier under fire without so much as a scratch? How else does one explain the survival of Jerry Crump, who covered a grenade with his body to save others? How else does one explain lifting his bleeding intestines to clamp a hemorrhaging torn renal artery on the battlefield of Hill 284?

How else does one explain the ability to function day and night for months in war-torn Korea, except for God's answer to a simple prayer for courage to do one's duty in all circumstances? One cannot explain such things, apart from God's sovereign grace and mercy. And that is why I have survived to tell this story about surrendering personal will to God's will.

I was, and still am, grateful that I was permitted to return home to give thanks at the same spot from which I had left. I felt blessed by His presence. The big boulder is still there by the shore of Lake of the Woods but the real rock of my salvation is Jesus Christ, the only begotten Son of God, who exists as one within the most Holy Trinity.

I closed that private time by the boulder by singing two hymns, "My Jesus I Love Thee I Know You are Mine" and "Fairest Lord Jesus."

I trudged through the snow, back to my car, and drove back to my parents' home in Middle River with an unburdened heart. I stayed at home until after Christmas in 1951.

After Christmas, I loaded all of my personal belongings into my new Dodge, set out for San Antonio, Texas, and the Army Medical Field Service School. I reported in before the first of January 1952 to take the ten-month-long advanced officers' course. It was a good way to unwind and become familiar again with traffic signs, stopping to get out of my car on a military post when the flag was being raised and lowered, and other rules of civilization. I could also attend medical conferences at Brook Army Hospital without being responsible for patient care, and it gave me time to catch up on my medical reading.

After the completion of the Advanced Officers Course at MFSS, I hopped a flight to Germany for a visit with old Army friends. I then went up to Norway to visit uncles, aunts, and cousins, and traveled around, visiting people I had met in the Norwegian MASH and the Swedish Hospital in Korea. I returned home in time for Christmas in 1952 in Minnesota before heading back to San Antonio.

I entered the internal medicine residency program at Brooke Army Hospital in January 1953, learning how to be a doctor again in a civilized world with technical resources to aid in diagnosis and treatment. I was delighted to find my good friend Bill Herrick working as the club officer at the Brooke Army Hospital Officers' Club. I was even more delighted when the U.S. Army Medical Department started training an elite group of female college graduates who were brand new second lieutenants. They would become Women's Medical Specialist Corps officers in physical or occupational therapy. I thought that was one of the best ideas the U.S. Army Medical Department ever had.

Then one evening in early September 1953, a friend and fellow bachelor doctor, Cpt. Bob Hardy, and I went to the Brooke Army Hospital Officers' Club. It so happened there was a bachelor/bachelorette dance at the club that evening. To our mutual delight, there were a bunch of attractive new second lieutenants swirling around the dance floor. Not being much of a dancer, I stood on the sidelines and watched until I saw a beautiful young lady with dark hair jitterbugging with some young officer that knew how to dance a lot better than I did. But the more I watched, the more determined I became to cut in, for truly that young lady seemed far too wonderful to waste on the U.S. Army. I made my way over and cut in. Unfortunately, before long, someone else cut in on me, but it was not before I had learned the name of 2nd Lt. Rosemary Elizabeth McEachern, an occupational therapy student from Florida. She had been a high school English teacher and was also a Christian. That was a good basis, and I was determined to learn a lot more about Rosemary Elizabeth McEachern.

When I returned to the sideline, my friend, Bob Hardy, a neurosurgeon, who had been dancing with someone else, spotted Rosemary and said, "I think I'll cut in on that attractive young lady."

"I don't think you should do that," I said.

"Why not?" Bob said. "It's an open dance, isn't it?"

So I said, "The dance may be open, but I saw her first. I've already danced with her, and I plan to try to get a date with her."

"Well," Bob said, "you're not going steady with her, so I don't see why I shouldn't have at least one dance."

I responded, "Bob, aren't you going to be doing surgery in the morning?"

"Yes," he responded, "but what has that got to do with anything?"

"Well, Bob," I said, "how could you do surgery with a broken arm?"

Bob reflected on the matter for a moment, and then asked, "Are you serious?"

"Not about breaking your arm," I said. "However, I would like to get to know that young lady better and I don't want to be in competition with a good friend and handsome guy like you."

Bob thought for a moment, and then said, "Okay, I'll give you some leeway, but only for a little while, and then we'll see what happens."

What happened was that after steady courting and repeated proposals, Rosemary and I were married on February 20, 1954. And that was when I really started to live and think of the future as wonderful. We recently celebrated our fiftieth wedding anniversary with our three daughters, their husbands, and our nine grandchildren.

The last fifty years have included many more adventures, all of them more uplifting than the story told here. But the pre-Rosemary story, detailed in this book, has been recorded so that we do not forget the sacrifice of those who fought and died, and the lessons we may still learn from the Korean War as we try to meet the challenges that lie ahead in our war with terrorism today.

rtj

The new crew takes control of the 7th Infantry Medical Company

Maj. Jensen homeward bound at Rotation Headquarters

The reception in San Francisco; note the brass band

Lundsten's store in Williams, Minnesota; the store was the source of the felt shoes sent to Korea for the 1st Medical Platoon

Thanksgiving dinner in Minnesota (right to left: Dad, Bob, John, Mother);
November 1951

"Got love?" Bob and Rosemary Jensen's 50th Wedding Anniversary; February
2004; back row, left to right: Kathy (Jensen) Cook, D.C. Cook, Annie (Jensen)
Thorp, Jim Thorp, Israel Kreps, Tova (Jensen) Kreps; front row, left to right:
Rosemary and Bob Jensen

"Got love?" Bob and Rosemary Jensen's 50th Wedding Anniversary; February 2004; back row, left to right: Lindsey Kreps, Lauren Thorp, James Roach, Tiffany (Cook) Roach, Joel Cook, Jenna Thorp, Whitney Thorp; front row, left to right: Jay Cook, Bob Jensen, Alyssa Kreps, Rosemary Jensen, Bobby Kreps

Epilogue

This epilogue contains three parts. The first part is a brief recounting of personal life events between 1952 and 2005, the year this book was published. The second part considers the problem of the American military men still listed as missing in action (MIA) and American prisoners of war (POWs) that haven't been accounted for following the Korean War and other wars. There is a real possibility that some of our missing military men from the Korean War and the Vietnam War have been used as human guinea pigs to test the effects of NBC (nuclear, biological, and chemical) weapons. The current national security threat from NBC weapons is also considered in part two. The third part considers what may be happening in this world today, from God's perspective.

Part One
A summary of personal events in the last half-century

After returning home from the Korean War, my next military assignment was at Fort Sam Houston, Texas. In January 1952, I started the ten-month Advanced Officers Course at the Medical Field Service School (MFSS) located in San Antonio, Texas. I had never been to Texas before, but I thought it had to be a change for the better, especially if I used my recent Korean assignment as the measuring rod. I'd heard that Brooke Army Medical Center (BAMC) was also located at Fort Sam Houston. As I drove south to Texas from Lake of the Woods, on the Canadian border of Minnesota, I thought I would have preferred to go directly into the residency program in Internal Medicine at Brooke Hospital rather than go to an Army Officers Advanced Course. But, as usual, I didn't have much choice in the matter.

However, in retrospect, I came to realize that I needed time to decompress a bit from my year spent with the 7th Infantry Regiment. Most of the Medical Corps and Medical Service Corps officers who attended the Advanced Officers Course were also just back from Korea. It didn't take long to realize that some officers had alcohol problems that created family problems. The Korean War experiences of the group were as varied as their names and faces. But it seemed that a majority of the officers in that class had had hospital or rear area assignments. I don't remember any other doctor in the class with me that had actually served as a battalion or regimental surgeon. What had happened to all the doctors that had been assigned to the infantry? I've seen no figures on that, but I wondered if the doctors that had actually served in infantry battalions or regiments used the first opportunity they could find to get out of the military and disappear into towns across America. They were starting over from scratch professionally, and as for the infantry, they'd been there and done that and they probably didn't want to think about that anymore.

But there was still a lot of camaraderie, with swapping of stories and frequent friendly deflation of inflated war stories—all of which was a healthy catharsis for reentering normal life again. It was a common joke at MFSS that we would now be taught everything that we should have been taught before we were rushed off to war without being taught anything.

One of my assignments during the course was to write a thesis from my then-recent memories about the field medical support provided during several infantry battles in Korea. I don't know where the original copy of that thesis landed at MFSS, or even if it was ever read. However, I kept a carbon copy. The thesis was, entitled "Observations and Recommendations on the Employment of a Medical Company Infantry Regiment in Combat." That old carbon copy was useful in writing this book a half century later.

In January 1953, I entered the Internal Medicine residency program at Brooke Army Medical Center and set about the daunting task of becoming a skilled internist. I had a lot to learn. Whenever a medical doctor spends a year or two away from bedside medicine and a teaching environment, his professional skills regress. However, the scientific cutting edge of medicine doesn't stop progressing when a doctor steps off the medicine train into another type of work. It just means that a doctor must work even harder to catch up again, because the medical progress train has left the station.

But having returned alive and in one piece, I had no regrets about serving with the infantry. I'd been young and acquainted with hard work in the north woods, so I'd found it easy to identify with the infantry officers and enlisted foot soldiers. I tried to meet their obvious medical needs in combat and, in so doing, I'd just become a part of the active infantry battlefield force. The only thing I was sure about then, and now, was that God exists and Jesus Christ's work on the cross was completed. I know because He was with me then and, by His grace and mercy, he has been with me since that war. Otherwise, I wouldn't be scribbling to finish these stories about ordinary but young Korean and American soldiers now, 55 years after the Korean War happened.

The Korean War fighting ended about the time I met Rosemary in San Antonio, Texas, in September 1953. That was the start of a wonderful new life for me. Probably if my mother hadn't saved all of my old letters from Korea, and if I hadn't met many fine old infantry friends from the Korean War era, this personal bit of history would never have been written down.

Today, the events of my life that I consider most memorable all happened to me after I met Rosemary. Rosemary brought meaning, color, flavor, sunshine, joy, companionship, love, wholeness, Godly wisdom, and holiness into my life, and in all these things, she gave more to me than she received from me.

We were separated on our first wedding anniversary because I was sent to Nevada from the Walter Reed Army Institute of Research (WRIAR) with a small group of Army doctors to watch an airplane drop an atom bomb. It turned out that the leaders of that group of Army doctors decided we should all travel from Washington, D.C. to Nevada by Pullman Rail. I'm not sure how they ever got that whisky-wacky, poker-playing train ride approved. Not being either the leader of that bunch of doctors or a poker player, I spent most of my traveling time reading the books I'd brought along, including the inexhaustible Bible. I never did acquire an interest in playing poker, although back in those days, I didn't mind sipping a bit of Scotch.

The observation of even a small parachute-dropped atomic bomb was impressive, even from a distance. I well remember standing in a line with others behind a shallow defilade, or berm of dirt, with dark glasses on and with my back in the direction of the explosion. It was a bright, sunny day. Even with very dark glasses on, I could see a telephone pole about 60 feet in front of me. The shadow of the telephone pole was to the left from the sun on my right.

While we were instructed to keep our eyes closed at the time of the detonation, I allowed my left eye to be open just a slit. Then suddenly, in spite of the darkness of the eye covering and the bright sunlight of that day, there was a brief, overpowering whiteness caused by the atomic explosion. The white brightness of the bomb explosion overpowered all other light and caused the sun's shadow from the telephone pole to vanish and a new shadow appeared, perpendicular to the pole. Gradually, over a few seconds, the white light became less bright and the sun's shadow from the telephone pole reappeared. A few moments later, a blast wave rushed over us, but it wasn't severe enough to blow us over, because we were a mile or two away. Actually, I don't know exactly how far we were from the site of the atomic explosion. We were informed that it was a relatively small blast. If it had been a hydrogen bomb explosion, we would have been incinerated. I remember thinking "even a small nuke could kill a lot of people—what a horrible weapon."

That was also the date of our first wedding anniversary. Rosemary and I had planned a little celebration together for February 20, 1955. But the big blast, fireball, and mushroom cloud on that day were a bit much, even for our first anniversary. We've now been married fifty-one years and, fortunately, without another atomic explosion.

Col. Viney, who wrote a piece about his 10 November 1950 patrol contact with the Chinese, took part in an atomic bomb test in 1953. Viney and other soldiers had been placed in foxholes, but without dark glasses. He reported a dazzling and dancing white light, even down in his foxhole, from the fission weapon explosion. One can only speculate that the creator God may have used a bit of fission power when he blinded Paul with white light from heaven on the road to Damascus (Acts 9:3). I agree that out nation must be prepared to continue to live under the MAD doctrine of mutual assured destruction, but I also agreed with Joshua 24:15, where he's recorded as saying, "But as for me and my house, we will serve the Lord."

Our first daughter, Annie, was born on 13 October 1955, in the Fort Mead Maryland Station Hospital. After repaying with more military service for the time I'd spent in internal medicine residency training, I resigned from the Army in 1957 in order to go to Africa as a medical missionary to serve the Lutheran Church in Tanganyika.

After an additional five months of training in the London School of Hygiene and Tropical Medicine, we traveled from London in a four-motor propeller plane, stopping in Cairo and Khartoum, before landing in Nairobi. From Nairobi, we flew in an East African Airline DC-3 to Arusha, Moshi, and eventually landed in Mombo, where we stepped off of the plane into muddy grass. It didn't take long to adjust to living in a whitewashed mud brick house. That was the beginning of a new lifestyle in Africa.

The time we spent (1958-1961) as missionaries at the Lutheran Mission Hospital and Medical Assistant Training Centre at Bumbuli in the Usumbara Mountains among the Sambaa people were busy and happy years. It was also the exciting period in which Tanganyika gained its independence from colonial rule.

But from a family standpoint, the most important events at Bumbuli were the birth of two more healthy daughters, Kathy, on 29 September 1958, and Tova, on 23 January 1961. These daughters were, in later years, pleased to have been born in Tanganyika, which later became known as Tanzania after the merger with Zanzibar.

From 1962-1966, we lived in Moshi, Tanzania, where Rosemary taught school and I worked as an assistant to the African Lutheran Bishop, Stephano Moshi, for the planning and founding of the Kilimanjaro Christian Medical Centre (KCMC), a 425-bed reference and teaching hospital. After getting the construction of KCMC underway, I returned to the United States, to take advanced work in Public Health and to become a bit more up to date in medicine again before taking on another new task overseas.

KCMC now has a Medical School attached and at least a dozen other educational programs, with students drawn from many countries in Africa. Students from medical schools in Europe and America also go there to gain international experience. Today there is a great need for funds for student scholarships and for a medical school building at KCMC, yet KCMC continues, despite their chronic poverty. They're impelled to carry on by the needs of patients and students, and by continual prayers. It's a story of service and of hope for a better future. Indeed, the Kilimanjaro Christian Medical College has now joined with other Christian educational centers in Tanzania in Tumaini University. (*Tumaini* is the Swahili word for *hope*.)

After I was enrolled in the School of Public health at Johns Hopkins in Baltimore, we were visited by three Army doctors who were old friends from the Korean War period. It turned out that their surprise visit wasn't entirely a social call. They wanted me to return to active duty in the Army as a Colonel, to teach Tropical Medicine at the Walter Reed Army Institute of Research (WRAIR). At the time, the specific job that I was thinking about in Tanzania had been filled by another person, so I was willing to listen. In the end, the Army agreed to pick up the cost of my MPH education at Johns Hopkins if I would agree to serve at least two years at Walter Reed. Since we'd be stressed financially on the $7,000 per year U.S. Public Health Service scholarship, I agreed to return to active duty in the Army as a Colonel, for $19,000 per year.

The year I spent (1966 – 1967) at Johns Hopkins School of Hygiene and Public Health earning an MPH degree and the next two years (1967 – 1969) teaching tropical medicine at WRAIR were professionally fulfilling and enjoyable.

That service at WRAIR was followed by an overseas tour in Okinawa (1969 – 1971) as the Chief of Health, Education and Welfare (HEW) in the U.S. High Commission of the Ryukyu Islands. That was the period in which the Ryukyu Islands were prepared for reversion to Japanese administration. During that tour, I prepared a paper showing the very positive impact of 25 years of U.S. military administration in lowering the disease levels of malaria, filariasis, tuberculosis, and leprosy. I also noted the significant increase in the height, weight, and aptitude of the school children on the islands. However, I wasn't able to get that paper published. Probably, if the statistics had shown a negative impact on the people of the Ryukyu Islands by the U.S. military occupation forces, most of the university presses in the United States would have been delighted to publish the paper. But during the Vietnam War, no good deed by the U.S. military was likely to be published, least of all by the American university presses. I believe this anti-USA bias was in some way related to the Soviet KGB/GRU anti-USA propaganda effort.

The Vietnam era was quite different from the Korean War era, in which the U.S. military was generally ignored by the U.S. media. But, in retrospect, it was better to be ignored than maligned. Today the U.S. Government and the people in the U.S., since the time of the Vietnam War, are still largely unaware of the large cash investment that was made by the Soviet Union to directly subsidize and facilitate anti-USA front organizations and demonstrations in and around American centers of higher education. The KGB and GRU efforts even made it a shameful thing to serve in the U.S. military. [See *Through the Eyes of the Enemy*, page 170, by Stanislav Lunev, a GRU Defector from the Soviet Union.]

After returning to the United States in 1971, I was appointed Chief of the Public Health Division at the U.S. Army Medical Department's Academy of Health of Sciences in San Antonio, Texas. I served there for five years before I retired from the Army on December 31, 1976. That, of course, was the time period when our three daughters were going to high school and college, and it was good to have more school stability and some family financial resources available.

It was also the time that first Rosemary, and later I, became a teaching leader in the Bible Study Fellowship (BSF) program. After the retirement of Miss A.W. Johnson, the founding director of BSF, Rosemary became the Director of BSF, a position she held for 20 years. Rosemary felt that the BSF program should, and could, be taken to Africa.

Fortunately, I didn't have a great desire to go into private medical practice. Rather, I was content to work for a salary where I could provide medical care for the poor. I could work for less because I had a military pension. Thus, I worked at the San Antonio State Chest Hospital and then with a Rural Health Initiative program near San Antonio, where I saw a lot of poor, elderly people. My work with the elderly led to an invitation in November 1984, by the Chief of Family Practice, to join the faculty of the University of Texas Health Science Center (UTHSC) at San Antonio as an Associate Professor of Clinical Medicine. My job was to teach, see patients, and establish a geriatric program—which I did.

I also received an appointment to teach International Health for the UTHSC at Houston School of Public Health extension branch in San Antonio. Later, I worked directly with adult HIV/AIDS patients in the Family AIDS Clinic sponsored by the Department of Pediatrics in the UTHSCSA. That gave me an opening with Africa again, where the HIV/AIDS epidemic has been spreading rapidly and now is a major concern, with millions of deaths of young adult workers and with millions of AIDS orphans and street children now needing help.

In 1985, Rosemary and I, along with two others, established the Rafiki Foundation as a 501C3 organization to serve as an agency to receive donations, send missionaries, and support special projects overseas in Africa. [Note: *Rafiki* means *friend* in Swahili; see the website www.rafiki-foundation.org.] Rosemary, who directed the affairs of the Rafiki Foundation from its inception, as well as Bible Study fellowship until she retired from BSF in 2000, now spends full time as the director of Rafiki. She's the inspiration behind the current Rafiki programs in Africa, which have become focused on the problem of AIDS orphans and street children. Now, in January 2005, at age 75, Rosemary continues to lead and expand the work of building Rafiki villages in ten nations in Africa. I enjoy contacts with new Rafiki missionaries and also enjoy helping out in some of the Rafiki community clinics in Africa.

Part Two
The unsettled matter of missing American prisoners from the Korean and other wars

This is an important and long unsettled question. Please allow me to tell you what I have heard and read. After I entered medical residency training at Brooke Army Medical Center in January 1953, I found many returned American POWs from the Yalu River prison camps on the Brook Hospital medical and surgical wards. All needed compassionate care, and some needed socially restorative interventions. Having recently been in that war, I had a non-authoritative point of contact that was useful for their venting their feelings without their having to worry about being charged with collaboration with the enemy by talking too much with an official army debriefer. Some of the American POWs back from Korea were reluctant to talk, depending on the severity of their prison experience and the non-critical understanding of the listener.

For many POWs, their emotions were a mixture of resentment over their brutal debasement with feelings of guilt because of occasional unpatriotic survival compliance with their prison bosses' frequent demands under starvation and torture conditions.

The North Korean and Chinese prison camps along the Yalu were nothing like the POW camps run by the Americans or Germans in WWII. And even though the POW camps run by Japanese had some brutal taskmasters, there wasn't the incessant ideological torture of the oriental Communists. Many of the Communists believed the class warfare bilge they'd been taught, or at least they were afraid not to pretend they believed it. Many Chinese became angry when they found that most American POWs considered Communist ideology to be nonsensical. But eventually all prisoners had to more or less comply or die. Even worse would be to watch a friend beaten or starved to death as punishment for someone's failure to cooperate with the Communists' planned and scripted propaganda efforts. It was a brutal no-win situation for the American POWs in Korea.

It soon became apparent to me that some of the former American POWs in Brooke Army Hospital in 1953 and 1954 were self-dividing themselves into easy collaborators and resistant collaborators. We dealt with that problem by moving some of the reputed easy collaborators to a separate ward for their own safety.

In so far as I could discern, few, if any, strong American non-collaborators returned home to America. According to our POWs, some of our strong POWs simply disappeared out of the prison camps. In retrospect, I now think, but can't prove, that those strong resisters were either killed outright or shipped to Russia, to be used as guinea pigs in Soviet biological, chemical, or other types of warfare experiments. According to rumors, noted by Lunev in Russia on page 167 in *Through the Eyes of the Enemy*, some American Korean War POWs finally ended up as slave labor in secret lead (uranium) mines—which was an assured death from radiation exposure.

It may be logically hypothesized that resistant non-collaboration by American POWs was considered a measure of special inner strength and those specimens were considered by the Russians to be worthy animals for biological experimentation. There is, of course, no hard evidence to prove that such bio-experimentation ever took place.

Moreover, as Lunev explained to me on the phone, "Any Soviet citizen who actually took part in such work would never be allowed to leave the country."

They'd be forever locked into the secret recesses of their vast country.

However, there is an interesting bit of corroborative evidence that inadvertently comes to us via Iraq. Colonel Matthew Dolan M.D., of the USAF Defense Institute for Medical Operations, gave a lecture on Wednesday June 23, 2004, (0800 – 0900) at the Medical Grand Rounds at the University of Texas Health Science Center at San Antonio, Texas (UTHSCSA). I happened to attend Col. Dolan's lecture, which dealt with the U.S. military's search for Iraqi weapons of mass destruction and their interviews with Iraqi scientists involved. Colonel Dolan noted in his lecture that it gave him a strange feeling after he asked one Iraqi scientist how they tested their biological and chemical weapons.

The immediate, almost casual, response was, "We used the prisoners in Abu Ghraib Prison."

It should be noted that those Iraqi scientists had been trained by the Russians. They were simply following the procedures prescribed for testing the potency of biological and chemical weapons. I can only wonder why that information hasn't yet been reported in the American press. My immediate reaction at that point in Dr. Dolan's lecture was that the casual confession by a leading Iraqi scientist to Col. Dolan was a confirmation of the truth of the many shop-talk type rumors heard by Col. Lunev from within the Soviet intelligence community concerning American Korean War and Vietnam War prisoners being used to test secret Soviet biological and chemical weapons.

It also confirmed the drunken confession of Boris Yeltsin (later denied) that the Soviet government held American POWs from the Korean and Vietnam War. It isn't an uncommon experience for alcoholics to be more truthful when they're drunk than when they're sober. Just ask the wife of an alcoholic.

Another view on the matter of missing POWs was addressed in the following letter, which appeared on page 19 of *The Cottonbaler*, the newsletter of the 7th Infantry Regiment Association, Volume IX, No.1, Winter 1999. It is reprinted with the permission of the President of the 7th Infantry Regiment Association.

"THE POW/MIA ISSUE: The following letter appeared in a recent issue of the *Hartford (CT) Courant* in response to a letter that had appeared in that paper earlier.

"Dear Editor, I am a Desert Storm veteran. Long before that battle, I served in Vietnam, Laos and Cambodia from 1969 until the fall of Indochina in April 1975. I also experienced Cold War conflicts in a dozen other countries. Throughout, I was involved in special operations, including 23 years as a CIA clandestine services officer. After I retired from the CIA, but before I retired from the Navy, I spent 1995 and 1996 as a POW Special Investigator for the U.S./Russia Joint Commission on POW/MIAs.

"What I saw and experienced in Indochina, the Cold War, and as a POW investigator causes me to take issue with Tom Condon's viewpoint, "Lower Flag on Myths of POW-MIAs." I cannot say, based on hard evidence, that any American POWs are still alive in Indochina, North Korea, China or Russia. Neither can I say all are dead. Two Japanese WWII POWs, well into their 80s, and three Korean POWs have turned up alive in the past three years.

"But that's not the point. What does matter is that an estimated 9,000 'unrepatriated POWs' were alive at the end of various wars, not just Vietnam, and were not allowed by their captors or circumstances to return home. This is why the POW/MIA flag still flies.

"Many of these men survived years, even decades after the wars were over, only to die in Soviet Gulag camps, and possible prisons in China, North Korea, or North Vietnam. The fact that they might all be dead does not mean the truth about the immense sacrifices and untold heroism should not see the light of day.

"My research as an intelligence officer, and the investigations of other professional investigators and historians, indicates that approximately 9,000 American POWs were illegally detained or taken into the USSR over a period of 57 years (1918 – 1975). Moscow never accounted for any of these detainees, which it exploited for intelligence and political purposes along with at least a million other foreign POWs it harbored in the midst of 30 million of its own citizen-prisoners.

"Beginning with the 1918 – 1920 North Russian and Siberian Expeditions at the end of WWI, to suppress the Bolsheviks, between 43 and 200 American POWs were secretly detained and not returned. It was the first time Moscow had kept American citizens and learned that it could get away with it.

"In the 1930s, American citizens ranging from leftist sympathizers to American intelligence agents were kidnapped in Moscow and imprisoned 'incommunicado.' One of these agents escaped in 1941 after five years in Siberian camps and walked 4000 miles to safety in India. It took him a year. I had the opportunity to debrief the only known survivor who escaped with him.

"At the end of WWII, the Soviets secretly incarcerated, until they died, 7,000 American GI's that they obtained from German Stalags. Stalin's motive was revenge for the tens of thousands of Soviet citizens that the Allies would not repatriate (against their will) back to Moscow. U.S. Army documents from 1945 admit that the missing POWs were placed in the 'MIA column' of accounting (joining the total 78,000 missing from that war) so the numbers would balance.

"During the Cold War, 134 American pilots and airmen were shot down over the USSR—some killed, some captured. Because the United States did not admit to violating Soviet airspace, Moscow did not need to account for the fate of the detained captives or return the remains of those killed.

"In the Korean War, an estimated 2,000 POWs were transferred to Siberia via Manchuria. A Hungarian military officer reported seeing 200 of these American POWs as late as 1964, working on a road-building project. Another 200 were transported to Moscow from Korea via Prague and East Berlin, where they were subjected to a series of psychological, biochemical and other medical experiments. An eyewitness to this operation, former Czech General Jan Sejna, testified before Congress to this in 1996. He swore to the truthfulness of his statements to me on his deathbed in August 1997.

"The transfer of American POWs to the USSR continued, he said, in lesser numbers into the Vietnam era. General Dmitri Volkogonov, head of the Russian side of the Joint Commission, knew this, but was not allowed to reveal what he knew while he was still alive. Instead, he revealed part of what he knew in his just-published autobiography, *Reflections*. [Note: I have been unable to obtain a copy of *Reflections* through normal book-search methods. rtj]

"As for the unrepatriated POWs, alive or dead in Indochina, it does matter that the truth about what happened to these men comes out. I knew two men personally who were captured and held after Saigon fell. One was Jim Lewis, who was released nine months later and died in Beirut. The other was Tucker Gouglemann, who died in late 1976 in an NVA prison. His remains were eventually returned, and forensics verified that he had been tortured and killed.

"Somewhere in the neighborhood of 200 American POWs were reportedly executed around the same time Gouglemann was killed; there are indications that another 20 survived at least until 1979, just before Bobby Garwood came out.

"Having spent more time than most in Indochina, I too am skeptical of most of the live-sighting reports. However, I also know that Indochina is an excellent place to cover up what really happened to the unrepatriated POWs, and it is this information—the fate of these men—that we need to determine."

In spite of many testimonies and papers such as quoted above, there has been no concerted effort made by our government to insist on a public accounting of all American "guinea pig" POWs utilized in the Soviet Union. It's also an outrage that we apparently allowed Kissinger to negotiate away our rights in the Vietnam peace treaty to continue asking and searching for missing American POWs in Russia, China, or elsewhere. This treaty, which Kissinger signed, was our ultimate betrayal of American POWs. Today it may still be the main reason our diplomats haven't pressed the issue. We simply signed away our right to ask.

Kissinger also should be grilled about why he pressed Nixon to propose an unenforceable worldwide treaty ban on biological weapons. Anyone with a modicum of knowledge of microbiology research should realize that any secure building or tunnel under the Urals could be used for bio-warfare experiments or production and remain undetectable for years unless someone talked. If an enemy were to calculate the number of people that could be killed per investment dollar, bio-weapons would be cheaper than nuclear weapons. Moreover, the infrastructure would be left ready for invading new owners as soon as the bodies could be gotten out of the way. Gas or coal-burning electric power plants could be modified to accept millions of human bodies as a supplemental fuel source after a major bio-warfare attack.

I realize that this sounds horrible, even incomprehensible, but perhaps not for diabolical criminal scientists and power-crazed commissars. We need to remember that six million Jews were gassed and burned by German public servants after the Jews were stigmatized as being less than human. Today in the Middle East, many Arab Muslims refer to the Jews as cockroaches. In the Muslim *Hadith Bukhari*, vol. IV, no. 524, page 333, it's claimed that the prophet (Muhammad) was informed through inspiration that a group of lost Israelites had been transformed into pigs and monkeys. Such writings form a militant Islamic excuse for de-humanization, unreasonable hatred, and violence against the Jews that continues to this day.

To gain a fresh view of East/West relations after the collapse of the Soviet Union, it's recommended that the reader who would like to be informed, at the expense of being somewhat disconcerted, should review the writings since 1999 of Christopher Story, editor of *The Soviet Analyst: A Review of Continuing Soviet Global Revolutionary Deception Strategy.*

The Soviet Analyst generally supports the views of Anatoliy Golitsyn, except that Story digs to greater depths into the ongoing plotting of international Communism. [Note: Story's U.S. Office is 280 Madison Avenue, New York, NY 10016-0802, Fax 212-679-1094.]

Suffice to say here that Christopher Story considers many of our experts to be uninformed or duped. He also feels that Gorbachev is an active Communist, still plotting World Revolution by other means. I've had several telephone conversations with Story concerning his views on GRU (military intelligence) agents that have defected. [Note: from *The Soviet Analyst*, Volume 28, Number 10, January 2004, GRU is the acronym for *Glavnoye Razvedyvatelnoye Upravlenie*.]

Biohazard: The chilling true story of the largest covert biological weapons program in the world as told from inside by the man who ran it, Ken Alibek. [Note: Alibek was formerly known as Kanatjan Alibekov.] This should be required reading for all CIA officers and U.S. diplomats. Alibek mentions the use of monkeys as test subjects for biological weapons, but never mentions the Soviet use of humans in testing. However, humans could also have been used by a secret KGB or GRU POW research units, working alongside the cages of monkeys. The human test animals would, of course, be retrieved separately before the monkey cages were picked up. It's unlikely that a basic science virus researcher would have known if POWs were also being utilized as test subjects. An entirely different top-secret KGB unit would have had control of the POWs. It wouldn't have been in the best interest of Soviet bio-warfare scientists to know that American POWs or other prisoners were being used in virulence tests. But it also seems unlikely that the Soviets would be storing thousands of pounds of weaponized biological agents without first verifying the aerosol dose of the agent needed for a 50% kill rate on humans.

Alibek, however, did provide a lot of very valuable information on the Soviet bio-warfare program, as did Vladimir Pasechnik, who defected in 1989, almost two years before Alibek defected. One of Pasechnik's successes was the use of a powerful blast of air to turn viral or bacterial mixtures into fine powder and obviate the need for heavy milling. Pasechnik also modified cruise missiles for the delivery of biological agents. Because of their sea launch potential from submarines or ships at night and low altitude flight, cruise missiles would revolutionize bio-warfare. [See *Biohazard* page 140-141.]

The unanswered questions about American POWs being used for testing bio-weapon agents in Russia should have been brought up by U.S. diplomats. But American diplomats are usually polite, and the Russians and Chinese have come to depend on our doing nothing to provoke them lest they have a temper tantrum. The truth is that we're not prepared to fight either Russia or China today, and certainly not both at the same time. Thus, it is probably best not to provoke them, but rather to try to change them from the inside, which seems to be what President Bush is trying to do.

One might have hoped that some of our American POW guinea pigs and uranium miners might have been released in exchange for the billions of dollars of foreign aid that Clinton gave to Russia after the Soviet Union breakup. I wonder if anyone even thought to ask Russia about our missing POWs while Bill Clinton and Strobe Talbot were pushing money into Russia.

The sad personal accounts of the former American Korean War POWs at Brook Army Hospital in 1953 and 1954 made a lasting impression on me. We simply haven't done right by our missing military POWs in the past. Perhaps we should start now by questioning Iraqi germ warfare scientists about the protocols they received from the Russians for testing chemicals and germs out on human prisoner guinea pigs. We need to know exactly what Iraqi scientists did and who provided their instructions, and then it should be made public information and not remain buried forever under diplomatic cover.

It should be noted that when I returned to medical residency training in January 1953, major things were happening in the Communist world. Joseph Stalin was then pressuring the KGB chief, Beria, to get faster results in their development of a hydrogen bomb. That pressure wasn't a trifling matter, considering Stalin's tendency to eliminate people. Stalin's paranoid mind also had suggested that there was a Jewish doctors' plot to kill him. Stalin solved that problem with forced confessions, followed by executions.

Stalin had also eliminated most of his Politburo, except for Malenkov, Beria, Khrushchev, and Bulganin. None of those surviving four knew who would be eliminated next. Certainly Beria, the second-most powerful and most cruel man in the Soviet government, had to be thinking of eliminating Stalin before Stalin eliminated him.

Then, on March 5, 1953, it was reported that Joseph Stalin had died of a cerebral hemorrhage. The 1993 book *Beria: Stalin's First Lieutenant* by Amy Knight has many interesting details of the life of Beria. However, she doesn't mention the now-apparent fact from page 25 of Thomas Reed's book *At the Abyss: An Insider's History of the Cold War* that Joseph Stalin was actually poisoned by Beria. The weapon chosen was warfarin, an odorless and tasteless chemical. Beria was able to put warfarin into Stalin's favorite Madzhari wine from Georgia while the four Politburo survivors were all together visiting Stalin's dacha. Warfarin is used in rat poison, and in a large dose, it causes massive internal bleeding in any large mammal, including humans.

Three months later, on June 2, 1953, Khrushchev had General Zhukov and some of his soldiers arrest Beria, on charges of planning to overthrow the Soviet government. On December 23, 1953, Beria was executed by a Soviet three-star general. The KGB didn't get an opportunity to rescue their boss, even if they had wanted to.

Meanwhile, back in Korea, Syngman Rhea threw a wrench into the truce machinery by the release of 27,000 anti-Communist North Korean POWs on 18 June 1953. In October 1952, in an informal policy discussion session in the Medical Field Service School Advanced Officers Course, I had predicted that Syngman Rhea would release the anti-Communist North Korean POWs. The general opinion of the U.S. Army Officers in that discussion was that Syngman Rhea wouldn't dare do such a thing. But they didn't understand the mind-set of the South Korean government. It's a common American failing to not fully understand either our friends or our enemies. One must live with and listen to our friends and not just have them listen to us—if we wish to understand how they think.

The South Koreans knew how very strongly the North Koreans wanted the anti-Communist North Koreans POWs returned for reeducation or execution.

The North Koreans thought, "How dare they choose to leave our North Korean Commie-cult paradise and choose to live in South Korea?"

To the North Koreans, it was a matter of national pride to demand that their defectors return. Thus, the release of the anti-Communist North Korean POWs held by South Korea was a deliberate and predictable act, by which the South Koreans could stick their finger directly into the eye of the North Korean leadership. We shouldn't have been surprised. As it turned out, that act by the South Koreans led to a revenge renewal of the war, with many more casualties on both sides.

It should have been obvious by that time that the Chinese and North Koreans had no respect for human life. However, there were some practical limits for the Chinese. When Eisenhower ordered the movement of 280 mm cannons, capable of firing nuclear weapons onto the battlefields in Korea, he also leaked the information that atomic shells were also being sent overseas. That would have spelled disaster for the massive waves of Communist armies and it would have been deadly, night or day. That would have been a new type of war, one that the Chinese and Russians hadn't yet prepared for. Moreover, the Soviet Union, after the death of Stalin, was not yet firmly in the hands of Khrushchev. Therefore the

Chinese Communists chose to accept the reality of a divided Korea again—at least until they were ready to counter a nuclear threat on the battlefield.

Eisenhower was able to bluff them once, but once was too often for the Communists. They would want to remedy that situation—and they did. Khrushchev didn't forget. When he sent intermediate range nuclear missiles into Cuba, he also sent tactical nukes, to thwart any U.S. invasion of Cuba, with orders for field commanders to use them, if and when needed.

President Kennedy didn't know that Cuba also had tactical nukes on the ground, and he didn't know that the Russian/Cuban field commanders had the authority to use them to thwart a U.S. invasion. We would have had a real mess if we had tried to invade Cuba. I don't know if the tactical nuclear weapons are still in Cuba or not, but I wouldn't be surprised if Castro still has some in his possession.

As a part of our effort to salvage South Korea, the U.S. signed a separate treaty, giving major long-term assistance to South Korea. That separate treaty angered the North Koreans. They responded by initiating a final vicious series of assaults with artillery, aimed mainly at hilltops held by South Korean Divisions. Those assaults ceased only after the cease-fire had actually been signed with North Korea at Panmunjom on July 27, 1953. But that was only a cease-fire. It was not and still is not a peace treaty—even today.

On September 4, 1953, the screening and repatriation of POWs began at Freedom Village in Panmunjom. Over 59% of the American prisoners had died in the prison camps along the Yalu River. Some of our POWs had endured more than one thousand days of privation and torture.

But if our diplomats had been fully able to understand the Communist mind-set and their evil willingness to play a fifty-year-long nuclear chess games, it should come as no surprise to the United States today that China and Russia are both still assisting the semi-independent, but crazy, Communist cult state in North Korea, and the Muslim cult state in Iran, to develop their own independent nuclear missile programs that could bring mass destruction to the USA, directly or indirectly, by cooperating with Islamic terrorism. Fanatics apparently love the sense of power they receive by getting some NBC WMDs under their control.

Just as Russian pilots secretly flew MIG jets for China and North Korea against U.S. F-86 jets over the Yalu River in 1953, it's no less likely today that Chinese and Russian scientists are willing to secretly help Islamists with nuclear, biologic, and chemical weapons. Provided, of course, those agents are dispersed over Americans and our allies and not over Russia or China.

Thus, the next step up in the Soviet arsenals for the mass killing of armies and freedom-favoring civilian populations of the world, without destroying useful infrastructure, would be antibiotic-resistant bacteria, highly infectious viruses such as smallpox, Ebola and Marburg against which we are not vaccinated and also deadly poisons in our water systems. Ken Alibek and his associates were quite competent in their deadly work.

Soviet bio-warfare scientists were, of course, greatly aided by Kissinger's pushing Nixon to outlaw bio-weapons. We, of course, obeyed the new treaty while the KGB laughed and Gorbachev expanded their bio-warfare research efforts to have a nationcidal potential. How could Nixon have been so foolish? The Soviets only agreed to the treaty to tie our hands and to free up theirs.

At a booksigning last year for *At the Abyss*, I asked Thomas Reed if he felt that Gorbachev's massive new development of biological weapons of mass killing instead of more nuclear weapons of mass destruction and radiation pollution was a significant new strategy aimed at the United States.

Reed's answer was given in one word, "YES."

As I thought about Reed's one-word answer, I realized the reason for the Soviet's and now the Russian's reason for developing and stockpiling biological weapons for aerial dispersal would be to drastically cull population masses that they would rather replace than reeducate. The best, or should I say "worst," possible target would be North America in the wintertime, when cold air masses from Canada and from the west coast could be seeded with diseases such as anthrax, smallpox, wild strains of Ebola, or a host of other agents, and the cool weather would preserve their longevity as they floated across America from west to east. By the time the people on the west coast were becoming sick, spreading the disease and dying, the word would have leaked out that it was from germs carried in a cold air front. There would then be a panic migration to the east with abandonment of the west coast to immunized invaders from Russia and China and perhaps even from Mexico and Cuba, as well.

I listened to Ken Alibek in a TV interview last year, in which he said he thought that Russia had destroyed all of their biological weapons. That should have been good news. However, Alibek didn't suggest that in his 1999 book *Biohazard*. He said quite the opposite.

I also noted that on TV, Dan Rather visited some of the former Soviet biological warfare factory sites in the former Soviet Union, They had been turned into pharmaceutical factories. But when Dan Rather came to a nearby military base he was refused admission. Surprised? Not really! But that was where the subject was dropped by Rather, and where the investigation should begin today.

According to page 145 of *Biohazard*, Gorbachev, in 1988, signed a decree ordering the development of mobile biological warfare production equipment to keep their bio-weapons one step ahead of inspectors. That was the same Gorbachev that claimed to honor treaties. What better place to hide the mobile germ-making equipment today than on a Soviet military base with a "No Visitors Allowed" sign on the gate. Neither reporters nor bio-warfare inspectors can snoop inside Russian military bases. Neither can they visit gulags or slave factories in Siberia.

Anyone who believes that Russia isn't continuing to manufacture and stock biological warfare agents is willfully naive. It's also more than likely that the release of many tons of those agents into a cold air front in North America could eventually kill more than 200 million people.

But it takes time for people to die of diseases, and there would be very negative worldwide public relations if Russia's India-One smallpox weapons were to be released on a world that was no longer immunized because we had made the world smallpox-free. In 1958 – 1959, I was involved in combating a wild smallpox epidemic in the Usumbara Mountains of Tanzania. That was before the worldwide smallpox eradication program had gotten underway. The Usumbara wild strain of smallpox wasn't nearly as virulent as the India-One strain that the KGB rescued from destruction during the smallpox eradication program in India. Russia then made a superweapon out of that most virulent of all strains of smallpox.

On the other hand, these bio-weapons are so horrible and so hard to contain that a nuclear exchange could result if a nation was actually in the process of dying from horrible bio-warfare diseases. Some may think that no victor should win such a war or be permitted to celebrate their victory. This may be a reason for great hesitancy in using biological or chemical weapons. Their use didn't improve Saddam's reputation. Thus a *worldwide moral revulsion factor* must be considered before using bio-weapons. Even Islamic fanatics might have second thoughts. But a counterbalance to the moral revulsion might be the CSO negative propaganda factor. So, what is a CSO? Civil Society Organizations are special types of NGOs (non-governmental organizations) that may be created just for the purpose of facilitating mass popular demonstrations to influence or intimidate lawfully established governmental agencies and elected leaders to change policies or attitudes to meet the demands of worldwide restive or angry anti-USA masses of people.

The many Soviet-supported Communist front organizations that agitated students and faculty and facilitated mass demonstrations against the American involvement in the Vietnam War were types of CSOs. CSOs may be formed for good causes, like saving whales and feeding orphans, or mundane causes, like planting trees or flowers along highways. There also may be bad CSOs, established to call for the dismemberment of the USA as a greedy sovereign country. The point that should be noted is that the development and use of CSOs is no longer theory. CSOs are now being hatched worldwide and may be facilitated by provocateur foreign agents on the streets as well as on the web and in the media. The KGB and GRO, as well as the Chinese, are probably all in the international CSO influence business up to their eyeballs. It was CSO-type activity that forced America to abandon South Vietnam and smeared the U.S. military.

The reader should note that The Worldwatch Institute produces a *State of the World* report each year. Their twentieth anniversary issue, published in 2003, stressed the need to engage societies to become more sustainable and less destructive of the environment and bio-diversity. In 2004, the *State of the World* report focused on the consumer society. Since the USA is the world's biggest consumer society, we didn't do well in the world's eyes as a desired sustainable society. Indeed, thousands of agitating CSOs might make it appear that the USA is the biggest pig in the world, depriving the rest of the world of better opportunities. For the have-less and have-not citizens of the world, especially those who haven't been able to emigrate from their countries to America, hatred for America may be easy to foster. This year (2005) the *State of the World* message was on redefining global security. There was a lot in that book about the essential role of CSOs in engaging civil society to bring about change, especially whenever governments were slow to respond to the real needs of the people as demanded by CSOs.

Would you like to guess who wrote the forward to the 2005 *State of the World* book? It was none other than Mikhail S. Gorbachev, the Chairman of Green Cross International. As far as I know, Gorbachev has never apologized for ordering the development of smallpox as a weapon. Now Gorbachev wants to use CSOs around the world to bring about a new world order, in which national sovereignties and national militaries would be merged into an environmentally-friendly system of global governance. It would, of course, become a global dictatorship of the elite and powerful, in which the USA would be diminished or extinguished and world elections would be a farce. Russia and China would then, by default, become the new world superpower on behalf of the unelected U.N. membership, representing nations without either sovereignty or freedom.

Currently, Russia continues to sit on their microbiological weapon stockpiles, wondering what to do with all of the nasty stuff, while the United States continues to be occupied with lively presidential chess games every four years and neither political side wants to be accused of indulging in "conspiracy theory," because that is an insulting accusation that few would-be sophists in academia or governments wish to be tagged with today. Placing a conspiracy theory tag on someone suggests paranoid, irrational thinking, and that could ruin the reelection chances of a politician or cause a loss of faculty tenure in universities around the world. Conspiracy theory accusations usually don't disappear until a 9/11 type event happens.

However, today's reality is that Russia has probably manufactured thousands of tons of biological weapons of all types, and we don't know where they are stored or what they might do with them. Reality is that it was Gorbachev that ordered the development of the India-One smallpox weapon and other agents that have never been accounted for. Gorbachev is now an environmentalist and a holder of the Nobel Peace Prize. He had also written that "*history shows that we can keep the word we give and we honor the obligations assumed.*" [See page 21 in *Perestroika: New Thinking for our Country and the World,* by Mikhail Gorbachev.]

I have accented the Gorbachev statement above to illustrate the problem of slippery words. The overall impact of the sentence suggests that the Soviets keep their treaty obligations, such as the Biological and Toxins Weapons Convention that came into being in 1972. But let us examine Gorbachev's words more carefully.

You will note that Gorbachev wrote "w*e can keep the word we give.*" It doesn't say they always do keep the word they give. Gorbachev said "*we honor the obligations assumed.*" He didn't say how they honored their obligations. Was it honored by strictly adhering to the letter of the treaty at all times or was it honored by beguiling the world with slippery words? It sounds good, but his words don't nail down legal points with precision. The world's diplomats love slippery language wherein there is a caveat to manipulate around one way or another.

As if to demonstrate the flexibility of his slippery words, it was Gorbachev himself that ordered the 1987 billion dollar expansion of the Soviet five-year bio-weapons program after they signed the treaty banning biological weapons. [See pages 117-118 of *Biohazard.*] To top that off, Gorbachev appended a final line to a decree limiting the military future of Biopreparat. [See page 189 of *Biohazard.*] In that final line, Gorbachev instructed Biopreparat "to organize the necessary work to keep all of its (bio-warfare) facilities prepared for further manufacture and development." In case anyone noticed, that little extra sentence was a final stab into the heart of a treaty banning the manufacture of biological weapons. That extra sentence, in essence, authorized the Soviet military to keep the biological weapons programs active, in spite of the clear intent of the international treaty banning biological weapon production.

If our leaders don't read and think for themselves or don't have someone that loves America that they trust to do the essential reading for them, they simply can't be well enough informed to expand the number of free nations in the world and to avoid the slippery slope of all nations being absorbed into an unelected U.N.-led world government. The U.N. is not the best hope for the world. Rather, the God-excluding U.N. together with Russia and China are the biggest threat to the world today.

I would urge readers to read articles in newspapers that deal with human rights abuses. Over time, you'll accumulate a small stack of articles that describe many remorseless deeds of inhumanity to man. Just as the Iraqi scientist casually told Colonel Dolan that they used prisoners to test the effects of biological or chemical weapons, there was an article by Jeremy Kirk in the November 29/ December 5, 2004 *Washington Times* telling of three North Koreans "detailing chilling experiments in which prisoners were placed in glass chambers and exposed to chemicals that killed them within hours."

According to Rabbi Abraham Cooper, associate dean of the Simon Wiesenthal Center, a Jewish human rights group in Los Angeles, "The attitude of the North Korean scientists was that these were political prisoners; they were as good as dead anyway, therefore, utilizing them for experiments held really no moral implication whatsoever."

That little article was just another window into the atheist's utilitarian perspective on human life.

Another small article by David Holly of the *Los Angelus Times* and reprinted in the *San Antonio Express News* on 19 March 2005, notes that at the beginning of this decade, smugglers in Ukraine shipped ten cruise missiles to Iran and eight to China. Each Russian KH 55 missile was capable of carrying a 200-kiloton nuclear warhead for 1,860 miles at low levels to escape radar detection. It wasn't stated in the article, but each of those same cruise missiles could also carry multiple canisters of liquid or dry biological agents that would break apart on impact with the air as the missiles circled over a large city or upwind of population centers. [See pages 140 - 141 of *Biohazard*.]

The same San Antonio paper also carried an article by Jim Yardley of the *New York Times* on recent Russia-China war games held with India and Pakistan. The reader must realize that most of the military forces of the world conduct training exercises that may be in the field, on oceans, or in classrooms, with computers and large screens. Most such exercises are conducted with potential enemies in mind.

In 1996, Casper Weinberger and Peter Schweizer authored a book entitled *The Next War*, published by Regnery Press. That book contains many lessons that should be learned by our military and political leaders today. Indeed, our many left-leaning college professors would do well to imbibe a bit of reality as we move through the terrorist era into the rise of the Russian/Chinese combo superpower era that lies ahead of us.

The current North/South Korean and the China/Taiwan tensions both have the USA in the crosshair sights of any expanded war involving China in the Pacific. This is why China today continues to manufacture huge trans-Pacific nuclear missiles just as fast as they can get them off their production lines in southwest China. But U.S. leaders should also realize that the reason China seems to get so belligerent on matters related to Taiwan independence isn't just due to Chinese national pride, but because Taiwan could provide China with an excuse to go nuclear and/or biological for the conquest of the USA. Why would China want to do that? The reason would be to gain control of the American breadbasket for their needed expansion.

In 1995, the Worldwatch Institute published a small book entitled *Who Will Feed China? Wake-up Call for a Small Planet.* Other experts, writing in the *Wall Street Journal*, criticized the science and projections of the *Who Will Feed China* book. However, the scientific correctness of *Who Will Feed China* won't be decided by the *Wall Street Journal* but by the CPC (Communist Party of China), together with the leaders of the PLA (People's Liberation Army). The fact remains that the industrialization of China and the building of many huge hydroelectric dams in China is now displacing cropland as China heads into a severe drought period. It's interesting to note that in one of the potential future wars described in the book by Weinberger, the Chinese military leadership was very concerned with their shortage of water and cropland compared to the rest of the world. China has 946 square meters of land per capita while the rest of the world has 3,200 square meters. [See page seven of *The Next War.*]

In the near future, China's need for oil may be of less concern then their need for water. Oil may be found and claimed in the South China Sea between China and the Philippines. Oil may soon be piped in from Siberia. But the U.S. has never really rebuilt its military since our military drawdown after the KGB contrived collapse of the Soviet Union. The military forces of China and Russia are growing daily. Because of China's propensity to abort female babies and keep male babies, they now have at least fifty million young men of military age without female companionship. This would make a motivated invading army. A new world war would probably start in the east, over North Korea and Taiwan and over Israel in the west, perhaps all at the same time.

If China was able to displace the governments and drastically reduce the populations now resident in North America by NBC warfare, China would gain expansion land with water for a half billion of their citizens.

However we can hardly consider the potential threats from Russia since we are curretly occupied with militant Islamic terrorism, which is a religious war whether we wish to admit it or not. To gain some perspective on the religious aspect of terrorism today I would like to relate a story. In 1987 while in Cairo, I was invited to have afternoon tea at the home of an educated senior Egyptian gentleman. This was a distinct honor that I was pleased to accept. The invitation came about because the senior Egyptian's son, an Egyptian army oficer, who had been assisting us during our visit, had observed that my wife and I had Bibles that we were reading. The senior Egyptian had met many American officials inCairo but he had never met an educated American man that was a bible believing Christian. Thus he had hoped to have a discussion to compare the merits of the Glorious Qur'an with the Holy Bible.

Now it so happened that I had already obtained a copy of Muhammad Pickthall's English/Arabic bilingual translation of the Qur'an from the Saudi

Embassy in America and had looked up references to Jesus and other key items in the Qur'an. We compared texts concerning many issues such as wheather Jesus had died on the cross or not. The Bible said yes and the Qur'an said no. We also discussed whether there was sex activity in heaven, Jesus said there would be no marriage or giving in marriage in heaven, (Mark 22:30) and the Qur'an said yes. See Surah LVI 35-38 about specially created virgins to be lovers and friends for Muslim martyrs. At the end of our meeting my host stood and we shook hands as he said "when the end comes we will know which book is the true Holy Book." It had been a pleasant afternoon as we each considered each other's views. Then to my surprise he uttered with some anger a denunciation of the many Americans including our embassy officials who pretended to be Christians but did not believe their Holy Book. He also expressed the view that all such infidels should be condemned if they did not become Muslims. I could not but disagree with his assertions and pointed out that judgement was not up to man but up to God and God had said He would avenge, (Romans 12:19) and (1 Samuel 24:12). But it was also clear in 1987 from this educated defender of the Qur'an in Cairo, that the significant differences between two very different Holy Books could lead to a religious war. Indeed it seems to be happening today because jihad is prescribed in the Qur'an. We do live in interesting times.

Part Three
What is God's perspective on our world today?

It is the epitome of arrogance to presume to answer the question above. Why? Because what mortal could possibly know the mind of God—the infinite, eternal, all-knowing creator of the universe and of all the laws of nature. God's sovereign will for all of His living creatures on this small planet Earth is beyond our understanding, is it not? We can't know everything, even if our knowledge was augmented with thousands of crash-proof, virus-resistant computers. However, while we can't know everything, we can know many things about God, because God has revealed Himself in His creative works and in the 66 inspired books of the Bible.

The divine revelation that God actually talked to some people in the past is rejected by many today. Perhaps the question we should ask is: does God speak to anyone these days? Many believers today feel that God does speak to the hearts and minds of men and women through the Bible, but few believe that God still speaks to chosen individuals in their native language, as in the days of the prophets and disciples.

Today when some one says they hear a voice telling them to do something, we think of calling in a psychiatrist to determine whether the individual who claims to have heard a voice is a schizophrenic in need of medication. Insanity isn't considered a valid means of gaining spiritual insight about God. Satan may or may not be involved with insane human minds, but not God.

As noted in this book, a leading or a foreboding of the Lord seemed to come to me by a tight gripping in my abdomen. The Lord's approval came by a sense of exhilaration and freedom to do whatever I needed to do, without fear or worry. However, for me, the hearing of audible speech from God has never happened, at least not yet.

However, in our travels in Africa, Rosemary and I encountered a man of Muslim background who was very helpful to us. As we sat down to eat, I asked Abdul (not his real name) about his home and background. During our conversation, we learned that he was a Christian, a believer in Jesus Christ as his Lord and Savior. Rosemary then asked Abdul if he would mind telling us how he became a Christian. At first, he hesitated to tell us his personal story. Then finally he agreed to share his experience with us.

For the next hour, four of us sat enthralled around a table, listening to him tell of his personal verbal encounter with Jesus Christ. The enclosure marks {—} below contain Abdul's story as I recall hearing it. It's what I recall hearing, and not a composite of the recall of all four listeners.

{My father was a Muslim who had served as a soldier for many years in the army of our country. When he reached retirement age, he returned to his tribal area and did manual labor and gardening. But life was difficult and he wasn't able to supply money for my high school education because he just didn't have money to give me. I had to do all types of work to pay my school fees. My mother wasn't a practicing Muslim, but followed tribal traditions. One day, when I was in my last year in high school and while my mother had gone to visit relatives, I received an urgent message from the headmaster at school, telling me to return home immediately. I didn't know what the problem was, but when I arrived home the next day, I found that my father had been beaten to death. There wasn't much to steal in the house, so the police had no idea of why he had been killed or who might have done it.

After a Muslim burial of my father, I came to understand from others that it was my duty, for my father's honor, to find out who had killed my father and then to plot how to kill all of those who had been involved in that evil deed. So I searched around and finally found a man with a machine-gun pistol with clips of ammunition for sale. By trading other family items, I was able to buy the gun. I practiced firing the gun until I was sure I could hit a man with the bullets. After a month of investigation, I found that my father had had disagreements with four men and bad feelings had existed between them. Others also informed me that they thought those four men were guilty of beating my father to death. So I started to study each of their movements, in order to find the best place and time to kill them, since they weren't always together. Our house was in a somewhat isolated area, but it was near a path where people walked, going to and from our village. Those men would occasionally walk by our house.

The police were doing nothing, so I felt it was up to me to avenge my father's death. I became obsessed with plotting to kill each of those four men. I dug a hole through the mud wall of our house nearest the path, through which I could aim the gun. I made other holes through the wall to see out and waited for the opportunity to kill one or more of them as they walked by. One day, I saw one of the four men walking by our house. But as I jerked the gun out from under my belt, it went off and shot me through the upper part of my right leg and broke the leg bone, causing me to fall down. My mother hid the gun in the house and got friends to take me to the hospital. A pin was put through my leg, above my knee, and I was put into traction until the bone could heel. It was very painful.

I became very angry with myself and decided I would kill myself because I'd failed to avenge my father. So I saved up pain pills and sleeping pills for a week and then took them all at one time. But I only slept for 42 hours and woke up feeling worse. There was one Christian nurse that took pity on me. She brought me some things to read, including the New Testament part of the Bible in our native language. Having nothing else to do, I started to read from the first page.

I became intrigued with the story of Jesus. He seemed to be a wonderful man and He did miracles of healing. I thought that if Jesus had been there, He would have healed me, because He could even call a dead man back to life. But as I read on in the book, I learned that Jesus was killed on a cross, and I couldn't understand why anyone would want to kill such a wonderful man. I became very sad and cried because Jesus had been killed. But as I read on in the Bible, I learned that Jesus came back to life again, talked to his followers, and then went to heaven to be with God. In fact, Jesus was God.

Then I thought that since Jesus was alive and Jesus was God, then he could heal me. I just knew that Jesus could heal me, so I called out to Jesus.

Then I heard a voice, in my own language, calling to me and saying, "**Take the pin out of your leg.**"

I looked around and there was no one there, but I was convinced that Jesus had heard me and had healed me. But I couldn't get up and walk out of the hospital because I had a pin in my leg and was in traction. So I called for the nurses and doctors and told them to take the pin out of my leg, but they would not do it, because the bone wasn't yet healed. However, I kept insisting that the doctors should take the pin out of my leg, and finally they agreed to do so, but first they put me in a body wrapping (cast) so I couldn't walk.

After they had left me, a voice called to me, saying,

"Take off the wrapping."

So I called out to the staff and when they returned, I asked them to take off the wrapping, but they refused to do so and left the room.

I said nothing more as they left, but in a few minutes, they returned in an angry mood saying, "How dare you scream after us, demanding that we take off your cast?"

I told them I hadn't screamed after them, but they insisted that I had done so, and since I had insisted, they were going to take the cast off and put me out of the hospital.

The doctors and attendants were very rough as they tore off the wrapping and put me in a wheelchair. The nurse that had been kind to me understood what had happened to me, because she was a Christian. The Christian nurse wheeled me out of the hospital and helped me into an automobile that took me home, where I was carried in and put on a chair. Then when everyone was gone, I stood up to try to walk. After the first trembling step, I took another step, and I've been walking ever since that time.

But I hadn't been cured of my desire to avenge my father, and when I saw one of the men walking by, I got out the gun, set it for single shot, took careful aim, and pulled the trigger, but it just went *click*. So I ejected that cartridge to reload. I took aim again, and again the gun just went *click*. I was angry that I hadn't yet avenged my father, and in that moment of my frustration, I heard the voice again.

The voice spoke in my native tongue again, saying,

"I am Jesus and you are mine and I will avenge."

At that point, I put the gun on automatic and emptied the clip in a rapid fire burst of shooting into the ground. I then went out, sold the gun, and bought food for my mother.}

At that moment, Rosemary and I, as well as the two other Rafiki missionaries with us, were silent as we contemplated the significance of the personal testimony that we'd just heard. Silently, I thanked the Lord for His mighty work in that young man. I was aware that other missionaries had toiled for years without seeing a single Muslim convert. Yet here the sovereignty of God was manifest before us, for Jesus had reached down and called that man directly out of Islam to be one of his chosen people. It reminded me of Paul's conversion on the road to Damascus.

I then asked Abdul what had happened to the four men who had murdered his father. He responded:

{It is now several years since Jesus spoke to me. I went to the four men and spoke to them and they became Christians. We are now good friends. There are now hundreds of Christian converts from Islam that are witnessing, even in mosques, telling people that Jesus is our Lord and Savior. Please study the Bible to find out the truth. My mother became a Christian. I now have a Christian wife and a daughter. I will bring them to meet you. When I heard that you were Christians and had come to help us with orphans and street children, I came to offer my assistance to help you find your way among my people.}

That ended the testimony of Abdul. Because of the living testimony of that African, my answer to the question "Does God does still speak directly to people today?" is **yes**. He may when it serves his purposes. Indeed, God has always been able to speak to people according to His sovereign will. But for the most part, God speaks through his words in the Bible and through his leading or restraining of our minds, hearts, bodies, and circumstances. He also speaks through the witnessing of some of his modern disciples, such as Abdul.

Today there is a shifting of the focus of God from calling people to Himself from Europe and America. God's focus is now on Africa, Latin America and some parts of Asia. There is now a turning of many Muslims in Africa to Christianity. Abdul wasn't an exception. But in Europe and Canada, where hearts have grown cold to the Gospel and false teaching is being expounded instead of the truth of the Bible, where cathedrals and churches are empty and many are being turned over to Muslims—God is turning away. Where abortions are being advocated, where sexual promiscuity and homosexuality is promoted, where people declare there is no God, where the name of Jesus Christ is no longer welcome, where God's existence is no longer recognized by national and international institutions, God's judgment is sure to follow.

Think about Abdul's testimony. When he could do nothing else, he read the New Testament and believed with his whole heart that Jesus arose from the dead and that he was alive and could heal him. Then a miracle happened. Jesus spoke to him and healed him. He only had to remove the pin from his leg. What pin is holding you back from a living faith in Jesus Christ? Is it hate, pride, pleasure, lust, envy, revenge, or just ignorance? Christ can free you, but first you must humble yourself and recognize Him as your Lord and Savior. He is waiting for you to call out to Him in faith. He that believes in Jesus will be saved. You may be assured that Jesus Christ will return with all power someday. How soon, we don't know. But we should be ready when he calls us.

CONCLUSION:

This book encompasses seventy years of observations, experiences, continual reading, comparing references and collating strands of information on different subjects. As a physician I was habitually collecting biomedical data to facilitate presumptive diagnoses, even as more definitive information was sought to confirm or alter one or more possible causes of sickness. In working in Africa, it was commom to have more than one diagnosis, indeed many diagnoses could be suspected and confirmed and all would require treatment in a logical order to avoid overstressing the patient with multiple treatments at one time. An example could be a patient afflicted with acute malaria, anemia, malnutrition, worms causeing intestinal obstruction, tuberculosis and pneumonia all at the same time. Thus a doctor working in a tropical country must have background data on the country, as well as suspicions based on his/her history, physical and laboratory testing.

As I finished writing this book, I have been encouraged to write on a number of other subjects such as HIV/AIDS control, our years spent in Bumbuli in the Usumbara Mountains of Tanzania and on the founding history and the future of the Kilimanjaro Christian Medical Centre in Moshi, Tanzania. I am also inclined to expound more on the history of the cold war and the currently developing stockpiles of nuclear, biological and chemical weapons of mass destruction or mass killing by Russia and China. What is the NBC-WMD/K implication for the United States of America? What is the WMD/K relevance, if any, in biblical eschatology? What is the relevance of the past meetings of the CPSU and CPC to the build up of WMD/K? Our politicians and our worldly pundits, as well as the CIA and FBI seem to be willfully ignorant of these sources of information. Thus it is that we think we won the Cold War and we think the collapse of the Soviet Union was not engineered by the KGB. How foolish can we be?

I have already collected much of the needed background data. However, since I will be eighty on my next birthday it is reasonable to wonder whether the Lord will allow me to tarry here on earth until I have put all of the assembled data into books. However, of one thing I am sure – I shall not be bored and the Lord will be faithful to fulfill His promises, whether I am here or not. I am just a country doctor who has had a full life by God's grace. I am ready to go when He calls, but in the meantime I will keep scribbling.

Robert Travis Jensen MD, drrtj@satx.rr.com

Appendices

Appendix A: I. Army Organization and II. Ranks

I. Army Organization

Army
- I Corps
- IX Corps
- X Corps
  - o 1st Marine Division
  - o 7th Infantry Division
  - o 3rd Infantry Division
    - 15th Infantry Regiment
    - 65th Infantry Regiment
    - 7th Infantry Regiment (Cottonbaler)
      - Regimental Commander and Executive Officer
        Administration (G-1)
        Intelligence (G-2)
        Plans and Operations (G-3)
        Supply and Support (G-4)
      - Regimental Headquarters
        Tank Company
        Heavy Weapons Company
        Artillery Company
        Medical Company
        (Platoons of above Companies attached to the three Battalions as needed)
      - 1st Battalion

1st Battalion Commander and Executive Officer
Administration (S-1)
Intelligence (S-2)
Plans and Operations (S-3)
Attached 1st Medical Platoon of Medical Company
Supply and Support (S-4)
Able (A) Company
Baker (B) Company
Charlie (C) Company
Dog (D) (Heavy Weapons) Company
Headquarters (HQ) Company
(Each Company has three Platoons and each Platoon has three Squads)
- 2nd Battalion
2nd Battalion Commander and Executive Officer
Administration (S-1)
Intelligence (S-2)
Plans and Operations (S-3)
Attached 2nd Medical Platoon of Medical Company
Supply and Support (S-4)
Easy (E) Company
Fox (F) Company
George (G) Company
How (H) (Heavy Weapons) Company
Headquarters (HQ) Company
(Each Company has three Platoons and each Platoon has three Squads)
- 3rd Battalion
3rd Battalion Commander and Executive Officer
Administration (S-1)
Intelligence (S-2)
Plans and Operations (S-3)
Attached 3rd Medical Platoon of Medical Company
Supply and Support (S-4)
Item (I) Company
King (K) Company
Love (L) Company
Mike (M) (Heavy Weapons) Company
Headquarters (HQ) Company

(Each Company has three Platoons and each Platoon has three Squads)

II. Ranks

Enlisted Ranks
- Private (PVT or Pvt.)
- Private First Class (PFC or Pvt. 1st Class)
- Corporal (CPL or Cpl.)
- Sergeant (SGT or Sgt.)
- Sergeant First Class (SFC or Sgt. 1st Class)
- Master Sergeant (MS or M Sgt.)
- Command Sergeant Major (CSM or Command Sgt. Maj.)

Ranks Between Enlisted and Officers
- Warrant Officer (WO)

Officer Ranks
- Second Lieutenant (2nd Lt.)
- First Lieutenant Captain (1st Lt. Cpt.)
- Major (Maj.)
- Lieutenant Colonel (LTC or Lt. Col.)
- Colonel (Col.)
- Brigadier General {1 Star} (BG or Brig. Gen.)
- Major General {2 Stars} (MG or Maj. Gen.)
- Lieutenant General {3 Stars} (LTG or Lt. Gen.)
- General {4 Stars} (Gen.)
- General of the Armies {5 stars} (General Douglas MacArthur)

Appendix B: Medical Company Awards

NAME	RANK	DATE OF ACT	AWARD
Sarka, Rudolph A.	1st Lt.	11/28/50	BSMV
Jensen, Robert T.	Cpt.	11/29/50	SSM
Prystas, Nicholas	Sgt.	12/15/50	SSM
Cobb, Jack N	2nd Lt.	1/2/51	1st OLC to BSMV
Wilkins, T.	Pvt. 1st Class	2/6/51	BSM
Heaton, Jack H.	Cpl.	2/7/51	BSM
Wheeler, Robert C.	Sgt.	2/16/51	BSMV
Byland, Guy J.	M/Sgt.	2/18/51	SSM
Mover, Robert A	Sgt.	3/24/51	BSMV
Shoy, Charles N.	Sgt.	3/24/51	1st OLC to BSM
Stauffacher, Paul V.	Pvt.	3/24/51	BSMV
Herrick, William H.	2nd Lt.	3/29/51	SSM
Ogden, Charles H.	Sgt. 1st Class	3/31/51	BSMV
Miller, Luis A.	Cpl.	4/23/51	BSMV
Crisofulli, Tony	Cpl.	4/24/51	BSMV
Farnsworth, Norman R.	Pvt. 1st Class	4/24/51	BSMV
Finn, Joseph M.	Cpl.	4/24/51	BSMV
Heath, George P.	Cpl.	4/24/51	BSMV
Damm, Albert V.	Sgt.	4/25/51	BSMV
Dudyk, Paul P.	1st Lt.	4/25/51	SSM
Herrick, William H.	2nd Lt.	4/25/51	1st OLC to SSM
Campbell, Gilbert S.	Cpt.	5/31/51	1st OLC to SSM
Cennamo, Sebastian	1st Lt.	6/2/51	SSM
Shelton, Walter	Sgt.	6/3/51	SSM
Scalf, Jack R.	Sgt.	6/4/51	BSM
Glenn, Willie R.	Sgt.	6/6/51	BSM

Gros, Albert J., Jr.	Sgt.	6/6/51	BSM
Ogden, Charles H.	Sgt. 1st Class	6/6/51	1st OLC to BSM
Bridges, Clyde E.	Sgt.	6/7/51	1st OLC to BSMV
Hillenbrand, J.	Sgt.	6/7/51	BSM
Carpenter, Lloyd	Sgt.	6/10/51	BSM
Cornwall, Richard O.	Sgt. 1st Class	6/10/51	BSM
Fernandas, L. S.	Sgt.	6/10/51	BSM
Murphy, Harold	Cpl.	6/10/51	BSMV
Smith, Francis J.	Sgt.	6/10/51	BSM
Sweeney, John E.	Pvt. 1st Class	6/10/51	BSM
Kays, Robert C.	Sgt.	6/11/51	BSM
Fournier, Wilfred J.	Sgt. 1st Class	6/13/51	BSM
Koschak, Andrew M.	M/Sgt.	6/13/51	BSM
White, Thomas W.	Sgt.	6/13/51	BSM
Bishop, Jackie W.	Pvt. 1st Class	6/25/51	SSM
Cuticchia, Anthony	Pvt. 1st Class	6/29/51	SSM
Covert, Stanley B.	Cpt.	7/2/51	BSMV
Beach, David L.	Sgt.	7/7/51	BSM
Byland, Guy J.	M/Sgt.	7/7/51	BSM
Dishman, Lawrence	Sgt.	7/7/51	BSM
Fatalo, Angelo M.	Sgt.	7/7/51	CRW/M P
Heaton, Jack H.	Sgt.	7/7/51	CRW/M P
Preputnich, Michail	Sgt.	7/10/51	BSM
Shelton, Walter	Sgt.	7/10/51	BSM
Lowe, Ernest	Sgt.	7/25/51	1st OLC to BSM
Bell, Joseph J.	Cpl.	8/10/51	BSM
Sarka, Rudolph A.	1st Lt.	8/25/51	CRW/M P
Wilson, Howard W.	Cpt.	8/28/51	CRW/M P
Jensen, Robert T.	Maj.	11/50-10/51	1st OLC to BSM

Award Abbreviations

BSM	Bronze Star Medal
1st OLC to BSM	Bronze Star Medal with Oak Leaf Cluster
BSMV	Bronze Star Medal with V-Device
1st OLC to BSMV	Bronze Star Medal with V-Device and Oak Leaf Cluster
SSM	Silver Star Medal
1st OLC to SSM	Silver Star Medal with Oak Leaf Cluster
CR w/MP	Commendation Ribbon with Media Pendant

Appendix C: Middlemas' Letter

Dear Tova and Israel,   July 24, 2000

Last night I received an unexpected call from a member of The Clan of Warriors. Tova, I mean your father. In the hour or so of our chat, we crossed many bridges. I was honored that he called. The highlight of the recent reunion in Orlando was seeing your father after these many years. Even more was the surprise at meeting his lovely daughter and her far-from-disinterested husband. I was also amazed at the joyful way that the both of you reacted to your father, even with pride. I do remember saying that I would write you later on and give you some examples in which you would understand his membership in the Warrior Clan.

I am not a wordsmith. How do I explain feelings, fear, and the physical events surrounding an action? Can I explain the frame of mind of a person going up the side of a hill at 3:00 AM with fire from the top of the hill coming down at you, no sleep in 30 or more hours nor anything but frozen cans of rations? Is this the action of a rational person? Was the pay that great? What was the motivation to go out and seek death??

Your father, as a young medical office, joined the 1st Bn 7th Infantry Regiment as our surgeon, never knowing the impossible tasks that lay ahead. The military, prior to the Korea Affair, was at the same level which we find it today. We left Fort Devens, Mass. with just about 30 soldiers per company and not 208. In Japan, we received 200 Koreans just drafted off of the streets. They gave us three ten-day training periods before combat in Korea. This is just some background, most of the medical support he had was Korean soldiers, none of which spoke English, and none of the Americans spoke Korean. This in itself was a major challenge.

I remember up north, just before the Chinese came in, we were in a holding position. The Eighth Army was 50 miles away on our left and the 2nd Bn of the 7th was 17 miles to our right. Our Intelligence reports said the Chinese had not come in, but my short wave radio, with reports from Hong Kong, said they had. Then, of course, was our nightly gun battles and the dead Chinese soldiers we found the following morning. That was the beginning of body bags piling up outside of your father's First Aid Station. Soon the Chinese had us within their grip.

A typical day would be carrying ammo and equipment to the top of the hill some 717 meters, and it was cold, 10 to 15 below zero. Night meant no sleep; you had to be alert for the next attack, which usually started around midnight. Around 3:00 AM, the drums and bugles would start. Prior to this was heavy mortar fire onto our lines and into the small valley where our vehicles were, along with supply train and First Aid Station. Our kitchen tents and those of the First Aid Station had so many holes, they were useless.

All of us had long periods without sleep. You just did not have the time. This was real; this was playing for keeps. During these nights with wounded coming down the hill, your father, with nothing to speak of, was performing major operations, gaping chest and stomach wounds, or arms just hanging on. The only light he had was a Coleman gas lantern; no heat, equipment not made for the job at hand. Regardless of being a American, Korean, or Chinese they got the best and first-class treatment. HE HAD NO FALL BACK; HE HAD TOTAL RESPONSIBILITY.

His First Aid Station was not always in the safest place for him, it was always at the point that he would be able to care for the wounded. A good friend, Doug Barrows, would not be alive today but for your father, as so many others, for us he was the right man at the right time.

I spoke with Harley F. Mooney Jr. before writing this letter. Moon is a retired One Star General who was in our Bn. In fact, I was his Best Man. Over the years, we have often spoken of your father and his numerous accomplishments. We both agree that he was one of the finest Combat Medical Heroes we have known.

The end of April 1951, I remember arriving at the 7th Infantry Regimental Aid Station. Well, I arrived on a stretcher.

Your father, upon finding out that I was among the wounded, rushed over and exclaimed, "Well, you old son-of-a-gun [or some thing like that], they finally got you." Then he said, "Wait, I've got something for you."

"Wait," as if I was going to get up and run off.

He returned in seconds with a bottle of brandy to toast my forthcoming vacation in the hospital. I had been shot in both legs, and yes, I did spend three months in a hospital in Japan. After three months, I got rather tired of hospital life. Rather than waiting until they wanted to discharge me, I returned to Korea and my outfit. I was surprised to note the number of new faces.

Well, I have bored you enough with events almost 50 years old. Tova, you have no reason not to be proud of your father. He has the track record, as they would say, "proven and tested under fire." Perhaps we might meet again at some future reunion. I might say that Bob is lucky to have a daughter like you and certainly a son-in-law like Israel.

Your father told me of the addition to the family, a baby girl. One thing I can say, it is a lot more fun dressing little girls than little boys. No, I never played with dolls when I was young, just had a house full of daughters.

Our warmest regards, God Bless the Family,
John Middlemas

Appendix D: I. Scripture References and II. Hymns

I. Scripture References (King James Version)

Psalm 23:1-6
The Lord is my shepherd; I shall not want. He maketh me to lie down in green pastures: he leadeth me beside the still waters. He restoreth my soul: he leadeth me in the paths of righteousness for his name's sake. Yea tho I walk through the valley of the shadow of death, I will fear no evil: for thou art with me; thy rod and thy staff they comfort me. Thou preparest a table before me in the presence of mine enemies: thou anointest my head with oil; my cup runneth over. Surely goodness and mercy shall follow me all the days of my life, and I will dwell in the house of the Lord forever.

Psalm 28:1-7
Unto thee will I cry, O LORD my rock; be not silent to me: lest, if thou be silent to me, I become like them that go down into the pit. Hear the voice of my supplications, when I cry unto thee, when I lift up my hands toward thy holy oracle. Draw me not away with the wicked, and with the workers of iniquity, which speak peace to their neighbors, but mischief is in their hearts. Give them according to their deeds, and according to the wickedness of their endeavors: give them after the work of their hands; render to them their desert. Because they regard not the works of the LORD, nor the operation of his hands, he shall destroy them, and not build them up. Blessed be the LORD, because he hath heard the voice of my supplications. The LORD is my strength and my shield; my heart trusted in him, and I am helped: therefore my heart greatly rejoiceth; and with my song will I praise him.

Proverbs 17:28

Even a fool, when he holdeth his peace is counted wise: and he that shutteth his lips is esteemed a man of understanding.

Matthew 19:14

But Jesus said, Suffer little children, and forbid them not, to come unto me: for of such is the kingdom of heaven.

John 3:3-18

Jesus answered and said unto him, Verily, verily, I say unto thee, except a man be born again, he cannot see the kingdom of God. Nicodemus saith unto him, How can a man be born when he is old: can he enter the second time into his mother's womb and be born? Jesus answered, Verily, verily, I say unto thee, except a man be born of water and the Spirit, he cannot enter into the kingdom of God. That which is born of the flesh is flesh; and that which is born of the Spirit is spirit. Marvel not that I said unto thee, ye must be born again. The wind bloweth where it listeth, and thou hearest the sound thereof, but canst not tell whence it cometh and whither it goeth; so is every one that is born of the Spirit. Nicodemus answered and said unto him, How can these things be? Jesus answered and said unto him, Art thou a master of Israel and knowest not these things? Verily, verily, I say unto thee, we speak that we do know, and testify that we have seen; and ye receive not our witness. If I have told you earthly things and ye believe not, how shall ye believe if I tell you of heavenly things? And no man hath ascended up to heaven, but he that came down from heaven, even the Son of man which is in heaven. And as Moses lifted up the serpent in the wilderness, even so must the Son of man be lifted up: That whosoever believeth in him should not perish, but have eternal life. For God so loved the world, that he gave his only begotten Son, that whosoever believeth in him should not perish, but have everlasting life. For God sent not his Son into the world to condemn the world, but that the world through him might be saved. He that believeth in him is not condemned: but he that believeth not is condemned already, because he hath not believed in the name of the only begotten Son of God.

Acts 10:1-48

There was a certain man in Caesarea called Cornelius, a centurion of the band called the Italian band, a devout man, and one that feared God with all his house, which gave much alms to the people, and prayed to God always. He saw in a vision evidently about the ninth hour of the day an angel of God coming in to him, and saying unto him, Cornelius. And when he looked on him, he was afraid, and said, What is it, Lord? And he said unto him, Thy prayers and thine alms are come up for a memorial before God. And now send men to Joppa, and call for one Simon, whose surname is Peter. He lodgeth with one Simon a tanner, whose house is by the sea side: he shall tell thee what thou oughtest to do. And when the angel which spake unto Cornelius was departed, he called two of his household servants, and a devout soldier of them that waited on him continually, and when he had declared all these things unto them, he sent them to Joppa. On the morrow, as they went on their journey, and drew nigh unto the city, Peter went up upon the housetop to pray about the sixth hour. And he became very hungry, and would have eaten, but while they made ready, he fell into a trance, and saw heaven opened, and a certain vessel descending upon him, as it had been a great sheet knit at the four corners, and let down to the earth. Wherein were all manner of four-footed beasts of the earth, and wild beasts, and creeping things, and fowls of the air. And there came a voice to him, Rise, Peter; kill, and eat. But Peter said, Not so, Lord; for I have never eaten anything that is common or unclean. And the voice spake unto him again the second time, What God hath cleansed, that call not thou common. This was done thrice: and the vessel was received up again into heaven. Now while Peter doubted in himself what this vision which he had seen should mean, behold, the men which were sent from Cornelius had made enquiry for Simon's house, and stood before the gate, and called, and asked whether Simon, which was surnamed Peter, were lodged there. While Peter thought on the vision, the Spirit said unto him, Behold, three men seek thee. Arise therefore, and get thee down, and go with them, doubting nothing: for I have sent them. Then Peter went down to the men, which were sent unto him from Cornelius; and said, Behold, I am he whom ye seek: what is the cause wherefore ye are come? And they said, Cornelius the centurion, a just man, and one that feareth God, and of good report among all the nation of the Jews, was warned from God by an holy angel to send for thee into his house, and to hear words of thee. Then called he them in, and lodged them. And on the morrow Peter went away with them, and certain brethren from Joppa accompanied him. And the morrow after they entered into Caesarea. And Cornelius waited for them, and he had called together his kinsmen and near friends. And as Peter was coming in, Cornelius met him, and fell down at his feet, and worshipped him. But Peter took him up, saying, Stand up; I myself also am a man. And as he talked with him, he went in, and found many that were come together. And he said unto them, Ye know how that it is an unlawful thing for a man that is a Jew to keep company, or come unto one of another nation; but God hath shewed me that I should not call any man common or unclean. Therefore came I unto you without gainsaying, as soon as I was sent for: I ask therefore for what intent ye have sent for me? And Cornelius said, Four days ago I was fasting until this hour; and at the ninth hour I prayed in my house, and, behold, a man stood before me in bright clothing, and said, Cornelius, thy prayer is heard, and thine alms are had in remembrance in the sight of God. Send therefore to Joppa, and call hither Simon, whose surname is Peter; he is lodged in the house of one Simon a tanner by the sea side: who, when he cometh, shall speak unto thee. Immediately therefore I sent to thee; and thou hast well done that thou art come. Now therefore are we all here present before God, to hear all things that are commanded thee of God. Then Peter opened his mouth, and said, Of a truth I perceive that God is no respecter of persons: But in every nation he that feareth him, and worketh righteousness, is accepted with him. The word which God sent unto the children of Israel, preaching peace by Jesus Christ: (he is Lord of all) that word, I say, ye know, which was published throughout all Judea, and began from Galilee, after the baptism which John preached; how God anointed Jesus of Nazareth with the Holy Ghost and with power: who went about doing good, and healing all that were oppressed of the devil; for God was with him. And we are witnesses of all things which he did both in the land of the Jews, and in Jerusalem; whom they slew and hanged on a tree: Him God raised up the third day, and shewed him openly; Not to all the people, but unto witnesses chosen before God, even to us, who did eat and drink with him after he rose from the dead. And he commanded us to preach unto the people, and to testify that it is he, which was ordained of God to be the Judge of quick and dead. To him give all the prophets witness, that through his name whosoever believeth in him shall receive remission of sins. While Peter yet spake these words, the Holy Ghost fell on all them, which heard the word. And they of the circumcision which believed were astonished, as many as came with Peter, because that on the Gentiles also was poured out the gift of the Holy Ghost. For they heard them speak with tongues, and magnify God. Then answered Peter, Can any man forbid water, that these should not be baptized, which have received the Holy Ghost as well as we? And he commanded them to be baptized in the name of the Lord. Then prayed they him to tarry certain days.

Romans 4:3-24

For what saith the scripture: Abraham believed God, and it was counted unto him for righteousness. Now to him that worketh is the reward not reckoned of grace, but debt. But to him that worketh not, but believeth on him that justifieth the ungodly, his faith is counted for righteousness. Even as David also describeth the blessedness of the man, unto whom God imputeth righteousness. Even as David also describeth the blessedness of the man, unto whom God imputed righteousness without works, saying Blessed are they whose iniquities are forgiven, and whose sins are covered. Blessed is the man to whom the Lord will not impute sin. Cometh this blessedness then upon the circumcision only, or upon the uncircumcised also? For we say that faith was reckoned to Abraham for righteousness.

How was it then reckoned? When he was in circumcision, a seal of the righteousness of the faith which he had yet being uncircumcised that he might be the father of all them that believe, though they be not circumcised; that righteousness might be imputed unto them also. And the father of circumcision to them who are not of the circumcision only, but who also walk in the steps of that faith of our father Abraham, which he had being yet uncircumcised. Of the promise, that he should be the heir of the world was not to Abraham, or to his seed, through the law, but through the righteousness of faith. For if they which are of the law be heirs, faith is made void, and the promise made of none effect. Because the law worketh wrath: for where no lay is, there is no transgression. Therefore it is of faith, that it might be by grace; to the end the promise might be sure to all the seed; not to that only which is of the law, but to that also which is of the faith of Abraham; who is the father of us all, (As it is written, I have made thee a father of many nations,) before him whom he believed, even God, who quickeneth the dead, and calleth those things which be not as though they were. Who against hope believed in hope, that he might become the father of many nations, according to that which was spoken, so shall thy seed be. And being not weak in faith, he considered not his own body now dead, when he was about an hundred years old, neither yet the deadness of Sarah's womb. He staggered not at the promise of God through unbelief; but was strong in faith, giving glory to God; and being fully persuaded that, what he had promised, he was able also to perform. And therefore it was imputed to him for righteousness. Now it was not written for his sake alone, that it was imputed to him; but for us also, to whom it shall be imputed, if we believe on him that raised up Jesus our Lord from the dead.

Romans 5:1-10

Therefore being justified by faith, we have peace with God through our Lord Jesus Christ: by whom also we have access by faith into this grace wherein we stand, and rejoice in hope of the glory of God. And not only so, but we glory in tribulations also: knowing that tribulation worketh patience; and patience, experience; and experience, hope: and hope maketh not ashamed; because the love of God is shed abroad in our hearts by the Holy Ghost which is given unto us. For when we were yet without strength, in due time Christ died for the ungodly. For scarcely for a righteous man will one die: yet peradventure for a good man some would even dare to die. But God commendeth his love toward us, in that, while we were yet sinners, Christ died for us. Much more then, being now justified by his blood, we shall be saved from wrath through him. For if, when we were enemies, we were reconciled to God by the death of his Son, much more, being reconciled, we shall be saved by his life.

1 Corinthians 13:1-13

Though I speak with the tongues of men and of angels, and have not charity, I am become as sounding brass, or a tinkling cymbal. And though I have the gift of prophecy, and understand all mysteries, and all knowledge; and though I have all faith, so that I could remove mountains, and have not charity, I am nothing. And though I bestow all my goods to feed the poor, and though I give my body to be burned, and have not charity, it profiteth me nothing. Charity suffereth long, and is kind; charity envieth not; charity vaunteth not itself, is not puffed up, doth not behave itself unseemly, seeketh not her own, is not easily provoked, thinketh no evil; rejoiceth not in iniquity, but rejoiceth in the truth; beareth all things, believeth all things, hopeth all things, endureth all things. Charity never faileth: but whether there be prophecies, they shall fail; whether there be tongues, they shall cease; whether there be knowledge, it shall vanish away. For we know in part, and we prophesy in part. But when that which is perfect is come, then that which is in part shall be done away. When I was a child, I spake as a child, I understood as a child, I thought as a child: but when I became a man, I put away childish things. For now we see through a glass, darkly; but then face-to-face: now I know in part; but then shall I know even as also I am known. And now abideth faith, hope, charity, these three; but the greatest of these is charity.

I Corinthians 15:19

If in this life only we have hope in Christ, we are of all men most miserable.

Ephesians 2:1-20

And you hath he quickened, who were dead in trespasses and sins; wherein in time past ye walked according to the course of this world, according to the prince of the power of the air, the spirit that now worketh in the children of disobedience. Among whom also we all had our conversation in times past in the lusts of our flesh, fulfilling the desires of the flesh and of the mind; and were by nature the children of wrath, even as others. But God, who is rich in mercy, for his great love wherewith he loved us, even when we were dead in sins, hath quickened us together with Christ, (by grace ye are saved;) and hath raised us up together, and made us sit together in heavenly places in Christ Jesus: that in the ages to come he might shew the exceeding riches of his grace in his kindness toward us through Christ Jesus. For by grace are ye saved through faith; and that not of yourselves: it is the gift of God: Not of works, lest any man should boast. For we are his workmanship, created in Christ Jesus unto good works, which God hath before ordained that we should walk in them. Wherefore remember, that ye being in time past Gentiles in the flesh, who are called Uncircumcision by that which is called the Circumcision in the flesh made by hands; that at that time ye were without

Christ, being aliens from the commonwealth of Israel, and strangers from the covenants of promise, having no hope, and without God in the world. But now in Christ Jesus ye who sometimes were far off are made nigh by the blood of Christ. For he is our peace, who hath made both one, and hath broken down the middle wall of partition between us; having abolished in his flesh the enmity, even the law of commandments contained in ordinances; for to make in himself of twain one new man, so making peace; and that he might reconcile both unto God in one body by the cross, having slain the enmity thereby: and came and preached peace to you which were afar off, and to them that were nigh. For through him we both have access by one Spirit unto the Father. Now therefore ye are no more strangers and foreigners, but fellow citizens with the saints, and of the household of God; and are built upon the foundation of the apostles and prophets, Jesus Christ him-self being the chief corner stone.

II. Hymns

Fairest Lord Jesus
Text by Munster Gesangbuch, 1677

Fairest Lord Jesus, Ruler of all nature,
Son of God and Son of Man!
Thee will I cherish, thee will I honor,
Thou, my soul's glory, joy, and crown.

Fair are the meadows, fair are the woodlands,
Robed in the blooming garb of spring:
Jesus is fairer, Jesus is purer,
Who makes the woeful heart to sing.

Fair is the sunshine, fair is the moonlight,
And all the twinkling, starry host:
Jesus shines brighter, Jesus shines purer
than all the angels heav'n can boast.

Beautiful Savior! Lord of the nations!
Son of God and Son of Man!
Glory and honor, praise, adoration,
now and forevermore be thine.

Jesus Loves Me
Text by Anna B. Warner, 1860

Refrain
Yes, Jesus loves me!
Yes, Jesus loves me!
Yes, Jesus loves me!
The Bible tells me so.

Jesus loves me! This I know,
For the Bible tells me so.
Little ones to Him belong;
They are weak, but He is strong.

Jesus loves me! This I know,
As He loved so long ago,
Taking children on His knee,
Saying, "Let them come to Me."

Jesus loves me still today,
Walking with me on my way,
Wanting as a friend to give
Light and love to all who live.

Jesus loves me! He who died
Heaven's gate to open wide;
He will wash away my sin,
Let His little child come in.

Jesus loves me! He will stay
Close beside me all the way;
Thou hast bled and died for me,
I will henceforth live for Thee.

Jesus Lover of My Soul
Text by Charles Wesley, 1738

Jesus, lover of my soul, let me to Thy bosom fly,
While the nearer waters roll, while the tempest still is high.
Hide me, O my Savior, hide, till the storm of life is past;
Safe into the haven guide; O receive my soul at last.

Other refuge have I none, hangs my helpless soul on Thee;
Leave, ah! leave me not alone, still support and comfort me.
All my trust on Thee is stayed, all my help from Thee I bring;
Cover my defenseless head with the shadow of Thy wing.

Wilt Thou not regard my call? Wilt Thou not accept my prayer?
Lo! I sink, I faint, I fall—Lo! on Thee I cast my care;
Reach me out Thy gracious hand! While I of Thy strength receive,
Hoping against hope I stand, dying, and behold, I live.

Thou, O Christ, art all I want, more than all in Thee I find;
Raise the fallen, cheer the faint, heal the sick, and lead the blind.
Just and holy is Thy Name, I am all unrighteousness;
False and full of sin I am; Thou art full of truth and grace.

Plenteous grace with Thee is found, grace to cover all my sin;
Let the healing streams abound; make and keep me pure within.
Thou of life the fountain art, freely let me take of Thee;
Spring Thou up within my heart; rise to all eternity.

Onward Christian Soldiers
Text by Sabine Baring-Gould, 1864

Refrain
Onward, Christian soldiers, marching as to war,
With the cross of Jesus going on before.

Onward, Christian soldiers, marching as to war,
With the cross of Jesus going on before.
Christ, the royal Master, leads against the foe;
Forward into battle see His banners go!

At the sign of triumph Satan's host doth flee;
On then, Christian soldiers, on to victory!
Hell's foundations quiver at the shout of praise;
Brothers lift your voices, loud your anthems raise.

Like a mighty army moves the church of God;
Brothers, we are treading where the saints have trod.
We are not divided, all one body we,
One in hope and doctrine, one in charity.

What the saints established that I hold for true.
What the saints believĔd, that I believe too.
Long as earth endureth, men the faith will hold,
Kingdoms, nations, empires, in destruction rolled.

Crowns and thrones may perish, kingdoms rise and wane,
But the church of Jesus constant will remain.
Gates of hell can never gainst that church prevail;
We have Christ's own promise, and that cannot fail.

Onward then, ye people, join our happy throng,
Blend with ours your voices in the triumph song.
Glory, laud and honor unto Christ the King,
This through countless ages men and angels sing.

Trust and Obey
Text by John H. Sammis, 1887

Refrain
Trust and obey, for there's no other way
To be happy in Jesus, but to trust and obey.

When we walk with the Lord in the light of His Word,
What a glory He sheds on our way!
While we do His good will, He abides with us still,
And with all who will trust and obey.

Not a shadow can rise, not a cloud in the skies,
But His smile quickly drives it away;
Not a doubt or a fear, not a sigh or a tear,
Can abide while we trust and obey.

Not a burden we bear, not a sorrow we share,
But our toil He doth richly repay;
Not a grief or a loss, not a frown or a cross,
But is blessed if we trust and obey.

But we never can prove the delights of His love
Until all on the altar we lay;
For the favor He shows, for the joy He bestows,
Are for them who will trust and obey.

Then in fellowship sweet we will sit at His feet.
Or we'll walk by His side in the way.
What He says we will do, where He sends we will go;
Never fear, only trust and obey.

Appendix E: List of Reference Books

I have starred those titles I consider to be the best references. Reference books prefaced by a dash were borrowed from the personal library of Wayne R. Austerman, Ph.D., Command Historian, U.S. Army Medical Department Center and School. These books contained maps of public domain that have been used throughout this book. Maps have also been used, with permission, from *3rd Infantry Division in Korea*.

* 3rd Infantry Division Staff. *3rd Infantry Division in Korea*. Tokyo, Japan: Toppan, 1953.

Alexander, Bevin. *Korea: The First War we Lost*. New York: Hippocrene Books, 1986.

Albats, Yevgenia. *The State Within a State*. New York: Farrar, Straus and Giroux, 1994.

Alibek, Ken. *Biohazard*. New York: Random House, 1999.

Andrew, Christopher. *KGB: The Inside Story*. New York: Harper Collins, 1990.

Andrew, Christopher. *The Sword and the Shield: The Mitrokhin Archive and the Secret History of the KGB*. New York: Basic Books, 1999.

- Appleman, Roy E. *U.S. Army In The Korean War: South to the Naktong, North to the Yalu*. Washington, D.C.: Office of the Chief of Military History, United States Army, 2000.

Atkinson, Tex. *From the Cockpit*. Houston, Texas: John M. Hardy Publishing Company, 2004.

* Batson, Denzil. *We Called it War*. Leawood, Kansas: Leathers Publishing, 1999.

* Blair, Clay. *The Forgotten War: America in Korea 1950-1953*. New York: Doubleday, 1987.

Brady, James. *The Coldest War: A Memory of Korea*. New York: Orion Books, 1990.

Brzezinski, Zbigniew. *The Grand Failure: The Birth and Death of Communism in the Twentieth Century*. New York: Charles Scribner's Sons, 1989.

* Carlson, Lewis H. *Remembered Prisoners of a Forgotten War: An Oral History of Korean War POWs*. New York: St. Martin's Press, 2002.

Courtois, Stephane. *The Black Book of Communism: Crimes, Terror, Repression*. Cambridge, Massachusetts: Harvard University Press, 1999.

* Cowart, Glenn C. *Miracle in Korea: The Evacuation of X Corps from the Hungnam Beachhead*. Columbia, South Carolina: University of South Carolina Press, 1992.

Cumings, Bruce. *The Origins of the Korean War Volume II*. Princeton, New Jersey: Princeton University Press, 1990.

Dailey, Brian D. *Soviet Strategic Deception*. Lexington, Massachusetts: Lexington Books, 1987.

Douglass, Joseph D., Jr. *Betrayed*. United States: 1ˢᵗ Books Library, 2002.

Douglass, Joseph D., Jr.
Red Cocaine: The Drugging of America and the West. New York: Edward Harle, 1999.

* Fehrenbach, T.R. *This Kind of War: The Classic Korean War History*. Dulles, Virginia: Brasseys, 1998.

Goldman, Marshall I. *Gorbachev's Challenge*. New York: W. W. Norton, 1987.

Goldman, Marshall I. *USSR in Crisis: The Failure of an Economic System*. New York: W. W. Norton & Company, 1983.

Golitsyn, Anatoliy. *New Lies for Old*. New York: Dodd, Mead & Company, 1984.

Golitsyn, Anatoliy. *The Perestroika Deception*. New York: Edward Harle, 1995.

Gorbachev, Mikhail. *Perestroika: New Thinking for Our Country and the World*. New York: Harper & Row, Publishers, 1987.

Goulden, Joseph C. *Korea: The Untold Story of the War*. New York: Times Books, 1982.

Hastings, Max. *The Korean War*. New York: Simon and Schuster, 1987.

- Hermes, Walter G. *U.S. Army In The Korean War: Truce Tent and Fighting Front*. Washington, D.C.: Office of the Chief of Military History, United States Army, 1988.

* James, D. Clayton. *Refighting the Last War: Command and Crisis in Korea 1950-1953*. New York: Free Press, 1993.

Kirp, David L. *AIDS in the Industrialized Democracies: Passions, Politics, and Policies*. New Brunswick, New Jersey: Rutgers University Press, 1992.

Knight, Amy. *Beria: Stalin's First Lieutenant*. Princeton, New Jersey: Princeton University Press, 1993.

Knox, Donald. *The Korean War: An Oral History, Pusan to Chosin*. Orlando, Florida: Harcourt Brace Jovanovich, Publishers, 1985.

Knox, Donald. *The Korean War: The Concluding Volume of an Oral History, Uncertain Victory*. Orlando, Florida: Harcourt Brace Jovanovich, Publishers, 1988.

* Leckie, Robert. *Conflict*. New York: G. P. Putnam, 1962.

Lee, William T. *The ABM Charade: A Study in Elite Illusion and Delusion*. Washington, D.C.: Council for Social and Economic Studies, 1997.

* Lunev, Stanislav. *Through the Eyes of the Enemy*. Washington, D.C.: Regency Publishing, 1998.

MacDonald, Callum. *Britain and the Korean War*. Cambridge, Massachusetts: Basil Blackwell, 1990.

- Mossman, Billy C. *U.S. Army In The Korean War: Ebb and Flow November 1950 – July 1951*. Washington, DC: Office of the Chief of Military History, United States Army, 1990.

* Marshall, S. L. A. *The River and the Gauntlet*. Nashville, Tennessee: The Battery Press, 1970.

Pickthall, Muhammad M. *The Meaning of The Glorious Qur'an: Text and Explanatory Translation*. Saudi Arabia: The Muslim World League, 1977.

Reed, Thomas C. *At the Abyss*. New York: Random House, 2004.

* Ridgeway, Matthew B. *The Korean War*. New York: De Capo Press, 1967.

- Schnabel, James F. *U.S. Army In The Korean War: Policy and Direction: The First Year*. Washington, DC: Office of the Chief of Military History, United States Army, 1972.

Sejna, Jan. *We Will Bury You*. London: Sidgwick and Jackson Limited, 1982.

Shafhid, Igor V. *Inside the Red Zone*. Las Vegas, Nevada: Global Strategic Resources, 2004.

Stokes, Gale. *From Stalin to Pluralism*. New York: Oxford University Press, 1991.

* Toland, John. *In Mortal Combat: Korea, 1950-53*. New York: William Morrow and Co., 1991.

The Worldwatch Institute. *State of the World: 2004*. New York: W. W. Norton, 2004.

The Worldwatch Institute. *State of the World: 2005*. New York: W. W. Norton, 2005.

Indices

Index A: Awards Printed in Manuscript

Index B: Maps

Index C: Persons, Military Units, Places and Events

B

C

F

G

Printed in the United States
45549LVS00005BC/64-366

9 781594 085406